PSYCHODYNAMIC ORGANISATIONAL THEORY

On the surface, people go to work and come home again. They sometimes manage people while most are managed themselves. But beneath the function and structures of the work itself, a whole range of emotions affects the success of the relationship between employee and manager and ultimately the organisation they both belong to.

Psychodynamic Organisational Theory: Key Concepts and Case Studies provides a comprehensive but accessible introduction to this fascinating field of study. Featuring case vignettes which bring the various concepts to life, the book is divided into four parts. Part I looks at how the individual relates to the organisation and the unconscious energies they bring, while Part II examines group dynamics and how they affect productivity, including a chapter on meetings. Part III explores the realm of leadership and what roles a manager can play in managing their staff, while Part IV introduces the idea of personality and describes how the manager's personality influences management dynamics as well as the wider organisational culture.

Central to the book, as well as the idea that organisational phenomena are often unconscious, is the understanding that relationships are always reciprocal. Through complex psychological dynamics, manager and employee influence and change each other during the process of managing and being managed.

This text will be essential reading for students and scholars of leadership, HRM, and organisational psychology, as well as consultants and managers looking for practical insights into how human relationships affect the success of every organisation.

Jacob Alsted, PhD, has authored a number of books and articles on organisational psychology, sociology, motivation, and the history of the state. He has worked as a consultant for more than 20 years and co-owns the consultancy company Haslund & Alsted with Ditte Haslund.

Ditte Haslund has authored a number of books and articles on organisational psychology. She has worked as a psychotherapist and consultant for more than 20 years and co-owns the consultancy company Haslund & Alsted with Jacob Alsted.

PSYCHODYNAMIC ORGANISATIONAL THEORY

Key Concepts and Case Studies

Jacob Alsted and Ditte Haslund

LONDON AND NEW YORK

First published 2020
by Routledge
2 Park Square, Milton Park, Abingdon, Oxon OX14 4RN

and by Routledge
52 Vanderbilt Avenue, New York, NY 10017

Routledge is an imprint of the Taylor & Francis Group, an informa business

© 2020 Jacob Alsted and Ditte Haslund

The right of Jacob Alsted and Ditte Haslund to be identified as the authors has been asserted in accordance with sections 77 and 78 of the Copyright, Designs and Patents Act 1988.

All rights reserved. No part of this book may be reprinted or reproduced or utilised in any form or by any electronic, mechanical, or other means, now known or hereafter invented, including photocopying and recording, or in any information storage or retrieval system, without permission in writing from the publishers.

Trademark notice: Product or corporate names may be trademarks or registered trademarks, and are used only for identification and explanation without intent to infringe.

British Library Cataloguing-in-Publication Data
A catalogue record for this book is available from the British Library

Library of Congress Cataloging-in-Publication Data
A catalog record for this book has been requested

ISBN: 978-0-367-02716-2 (hbk)
ISBN: 978-0-367-02717-9 (pbk)
ISBN: 978-0-429-39823-0 (ebk)

Typeset in Bembo
by Apex CoVantage, LLC

CONTENTS

List of figures	*vii*
List of tables	*viii*
Preface	*ix*
1 Management and employees	1

PART I
The employee in the community   **13**

2 The dual relationship of individuals to groups	15
3 Cooperation and psychological defences	34
4 Acceptance of new employees into the organisation	48
5 The individual's expulsion from the community	70

PART II
Group processes   **89**

6 The group as an independent unit	91
7 Productivity of groups	106
8 Meetings	129

vi Contents

PART III
Management 147

  9 The content of management 149

10 The manager as teacher 158

11 The manager as authority 184

12 The management group 200

PART IV
The manager's personality 219

13 Personality and management 221

14 The maturity of the manager 234

15 The manager's influence on the organisation 249

16 Conclusion 269

Bibliography *272*
Index *279*

FIGURES

1.1	Theoretical premises of the book	8
1.2	The connections between the themes	10
2.1	Rationalism: the individual is seen as independent of the group	18
2.2	Functionalism: the individual is seen as dependent on the group	19
2.3	Social constructivism: individual and group are seen as mutually dependent	19
2.4	Maslow's pyramid of needs	24
3.1	The group constitutes a hierarchy of systems, which consists of three subsystems in a mutual relationship	37
3.2	The development of a greater span between the dilemmas in tandem with the psychological process of maturation	39
3.3	Example 1: projective identification	41
3.4	Example 2: projection	43
3.5	Example 3: integration	45
7.1	Linear dialogue	109
7.2	Circular dialogue	109
9.1	Model of situational leadership II: the four fundamental forms of management	151
11.1	Authority is composed of several systems	186
12.1	Management system	202
12.2	The manager is swallowed up by the community	213
12.3	Chinks in management groups	214
16.1	Subsystems dealt with in the book	270

TABLES

7.1	Overview of terminology of selected authors	112
7.2	Bion's three types of basic assumption states	113
8.1	Characteristics of pseudo-dialogue and genuine dialogue	135
8.2	Observation points	138
9.1	The four management functions	152
9.2	Interpretive frames and management tasks	152
9.3	The Greek square and management tasks	153
9.4	Overview of the four motivational needs and theories	154
13.1	The eight types	225
15.1	Overview of forms of management that can activate splitting defence mechanisms in the organisation	254
15.2	Overview of management behaviour that can promote repression	256
15.3	Overview of management forms that can activate integrative defence mechanisms in an organisation	260

PREFACE

The relationship between managers and employees is getting increasing global attention and at the same time is developing in complexity. We would like to untangle some of the complexity by showing that it is basically about human interactions and emotions and the ability to interact and flourish in such an environment. Specifically, the aim of this book is to make the sometimes abstract and "pathologizing" character of psychodynamic organisational theory more accessible.

The book is widely used in Denmark in different types of leadership training and organisational development programs. We have had an encouraging amount of positive feedback on the content, particularly on the close connection between theory and practice, which many readers have found useful in their daily work.

We are, therefore, proud and pleased to present the book in an English version with the hope that its content will be equally useful to an international audience.

We are thankful for the many inspirational sources for this book. We especially want to thank our clients and our students who have generously shared their experiences and thoughts with us.

We also want to thank editor Russell George at Routledge for his forthcoming and professional attitude towards us and Russell Dees for his thoroughness in translating the text from Danish to English.

September 2019
Jacob Alsted and Ditte Haslund

1

MANAGEMENT AND EMPLOYEES

This book is about a special relationship between people, namely, the relationship between manager and employee. This relationship is defined by a formal structure in which the roles are attributed in advance, but it is fundamentally a human relationship that plays out under particular conditions. That the relationship takes place between people means that the whole human spectrum of emotions is involved. It is consciousness of this and the ability to manoeuvre in the field between structure and human dynamics that determines whether the relationship between manager and employee is successful.

The joy of creation and cooperation, the pride at good results, and the challenge of achieving new goals are among the driving forces when people work. But just as ordinarily and unavoidably, phenomena such as power and powerlessness, discomfort, doubt, anxiety, and wounded self-respect occur when people are to coordinate with and adapt to each other. If the latter types of emotion (those often called "negative" emotions) remain unspoken and partially unconscious to the participating parties, they are not recognised as the natural premise of "positive" emotions. Instead, they are shunted off to live a hidden life in the organisation. From this murky position, they can have a lasting destructive effect on cooperation. This book is based on the conviction that an understanding of the importance of structure and the integration of the whole spectrum of human emotions is the key to productivity and job satisfaction.

Since the relationship between manager and employee is by definition asymmetrical – because the manager has power over the working conditions of the employee and, ultimately, power to take away the employee's job – the manager has a special ethical obligation to understand the processes at play in the relationship. Potentially, a manager has an enormous influence on the productivity and flourishing of his or her employees. Therefore, it is necessary for the manager to understand and recognise this influence and take responsibility for how she or he personally administers it. Managers who fail to do this far too often leave inefficient organisations and unhappy people in their wake.

2 Management and employees

But the relationship between manager and employee is at the same time a reciprocal relationship. People cannot *not* communicate, and both manager and employee influence and change each other through the way in which they interact. In this sense, both parties can be said to have a responsibility for each other and to have deserved each other. It can be provocative for employees to hear that they have the manager they deserve, but this view is to make employees aware of the reciprocity of the relationship because consciousness of this can liberate much positive energy. The reciprocity provides employees responsibility for their own part in the interplay with the manager; and in this responsibility there are many – and often unexploited – possibilities for employees to support and influence their manager.

The relationship between manager and employee includes, on the one hand, the employees who are provided security, recognition, transparency, and challenges at an appropriate level, and on the other hand, the manager, who gets emotional satisfaction, influence, and authority.

When the relationship is successful, the manager helps the individual member of the organisation to handle his or her relationship with the community and supports the individual to meet appropriate challenges. At the same time, the manager helps the group of employees to function as a coherent, productive collective. On the other hand, employees give the manager their acceptance, backing, and loyal work effort.

It is this dynamic people usually refer to as "personnel management", which is in reality a somewhat misleading name because it does not describe the two-sided dynamic in the relationship.

Personnel management is an active relationship between two parties that plays out with a particular purpose, within a defined framework, and through the development of complicated, psychological processes. These processes are described and discussed more thoroughly in later chapters.

At the same time, it is important to remember that managers are also employees. Great demands are placed on today's managers, and managers – like all other employees – have a need for support and guidance from their own manager in order to be able to carry out their job function in the best way possible. All too many managers work in a management vacuum in which they receive deficient or no support from *their* immediate supervisor. This creates a burdensome solitude in the job, and the manager is in danger of burnout. Therefore, it is important to maintain a dual gaze in a job as manager and to remember that every manager is at the same time an employee.

What is management?

> Two people who do not know each other are washed up on a deserted island. After lying on the beach for a while, they get up. "Where to?" asks one. "Over there!" replies the other. They begin to walk in the direction indicated.

Will two people placed on a deserted island quickly develop a form of community in which one leads and the other is led? "Yes", many would think, because the will and the ability to lead and to be led is a part of human nature and because leadership is necessary for human development. Some claim that the ability to lead is a special quality in special individuals, while others believe that all people are potentially leaders and that it is determined by the specific situation whether the individual acts as a leader or is led.

How might the division of roles in the preceding vignette arise? One explanation might be that the person doing the questioning is a child who, because of lack of experience, naturally lets the grown-up take the lead. This is a *biological* framework of understanding. Another might be that the person asking the question "Where to?" is an adult, but he sees the captain's stripes on the other's torn jacket and, therefore, recognises that the captain has command. That is a *structural* framework that sees management as necessary for the productivity of society. A third explanation might be that the person asking feels threatened by the other person and, therefore, submits himself to the other's leadership. This is a *political* framework that focuses on management as what regulates power relations in society. A fourth explanation might be that the person asking sees the situation as difficult and therefore enters into a dialogue with the other person who, however, responds with a ready decision that the person asking accepts. This is a *social constructivist* framework that understands management as a social phenomenon that is created in an interplay between participants. A fifth explanation might be that the person asking feels afraid and is paralysed and therefore appeals to the other person to take a leadership position and that the other accepts it because he is flattered and feels obligated by the other person's expectations. This is a *psychological* framework, which points out that management fulfils psychological needs in the individual and solves dilemmas and conflicts in human interaction. A sixth explanation might be that the person asking is a woman and that, for historical and cultural reasons, she lets the man take the lead, who for corresponding reasons takes it without reflecting more about it. This explanation emphasises that the theme of management has an additional *historical* and *cultural* dimension in which the view of what management is and who managers are changes over time and can be different from culture to culture.

The theme of management may be inscribed in many frameworks of understanding that must not be seen as mutually exclusive. To the contrary, one should try to maintain every dimension in an overall understanding of what management is. This book focuses on management understood as a social phenomenon that has psychological premises and psychological consequences for the people involved. The book will also examine problematics that are linked to the regulation of power relations.

Management is a relationship between people

Regardless of what framework or point of view one focuses on at a given moment, management always describes an interpersonal relationship between manager and employee. This relationship can play out in extremely different ways, all of which can be fruitful, but the purpose of management is fundamentally the same: to coordinate the efforts of the individual and the needs of the community (the organisation).

4 Management and employees

Thus, a manager's most important function is to be a connector. The manager connects the organisation's various components together: the manager binds employees into a unit, joins his or her own management with the rest of management, connects his or her group or department with other groups or departments, and links the efforts of his or her department to the purpose of the firm. The manager provides each individual employee the possibility of seeing him/herself as a singular individual and, at the same time, as a part of a greater whole. Since all this plays out in the relationships among the participants, the connection occurs among the participants and requires the active participation of everyone. The manager's personality and understanding of his or her linking function, however, play a decisive role.

The fact that the manager's job is to bind the organisation together does not mean, however, that management takes place in a power vacuum or a space free of conflict. In some situations, there may be objective conflicts of interest between management and employees; there may be a political power struggle in and around the organisation and between managers mutually; there may be disagreements about goals and means; there may be ethical or environmental dilemmas; there may be insoluble resource problems, and there may be crisscrossing personal conflicts. The manager must try to act in all these areas without being naive, but she/he must also avoid losing sight of the firm's goal or his/her own fundamental function as a connector.

Most people spend a lot of their time at work, and many invest a significant portion of their physical, intellectual, and emotional resources in it because working is a basic human necessity. People work to put food in their mouths and a roof over their heads, but they also work for social reasons because work gives access to and recognition from the community. They work for individual psychological reasons because work provides personal development and satisfaction.

The modern organisation is characterised by the fact that production is knowledge-heavy and, therefore, specialised. At the same time, the various processes in production are closely connected and require a high degree of cooperation. Effective cooperation requires good mutual relations among the participants, borne by mutual trust and tolerance because daily work offers countless problems that must be solved with flexibility, creativity, and an understanding of the overall perspective. But most people have found that it can be difficult to be trusting, tolerant, and nuanced when the work tempo is intensified and the performance requirements are great, and people generally do not really have the foundation for understanding the problem from other points of view. Often, it feels reasonable to be self-protective, suspicious, and categorical. One does not need to exert oneself for that – in many situations, it comes as a spontaneous defensive reaction despite the firm's core values, which typically talk about openness, confidence, and so forth. When people do not flourish in their job, it may threaten their daily bread and mean a lack of fulfilment of social and psychological needs. The individual's resources, which could have been used constructively on the job, are now used instead to try to wait out the current conditions or to fume about them. It is often fruitless and wearying for the employee to use her/his energy in this way at the same time that it robs the firm of important resources.

The alternative to this unconstructive frustration is managers with solid knowledge about the special relationship that exists between themselves and their employees, managers who are in possession of skills that make them capable of functioning in this relationship with understanding, empathy, and perseverance. In order to do this, as a manager, you must be ready to work with yourself and get to know yourself better – both your well-functioning and less flattering sides – just as you must confront conscious and less conscious aspects of yourself. The same is true of employees. The following chapters describe in more detail how it is possible to establish collaborative relationships that are robust enough to function under the pressure characteristic of most modern businesses.

New view of reciprocity

Within our cultural circle, the view of the relationship between management and employees has changed significantly through the 20th century along with other social developments. This is reflected even in the words that are used to describe the relationship: the designation *co*-worker is itself a sign of this development. The word emphasises that there are common interests between the firm and those who work for it.

From the earlier view of management, which was primarily the same as control of resources (in which the employees were seen as management's tools – along the same lines as money and materials), there has developed a more dynamic and – some believe – more equal view of the relationship between management and employees. It might be said that the two opposing groups always constitute the other's precondition: no feudal lords without peasants, no managers without employees, but over time a greater consciousness has developed about this mutual presupposition and the reciprocal dependence of both parties. This mode of thinking about relationships has altered cooperative norms in the direction of openness, respect, and trust as a precondition for mutual, equal relationships. However, there can still be quite a bit of daylight between the norms expressed and the practice in everyday life. Today, an employee often has high expectations for management, which can be hard for management to live up to. In some cases, the expectations are unrealistic and focus too much on what management is supposed to deliver and not on the reciprocity between the two parties. In other cases, management does not live up to expectations simply because it is difficult to be a good manager in today's businesses:

> Our engagement with and joy in work is not something to be taken lightly – we are quite simply passionate about our work, [...] but we want to be valued and recognized, we want peace and quiet to work, we want to have influence on our job, and we want the necessary resources!
>
> *(Annette Kahlke, district manager for home care,* Politiken *26 August 2006)*

6 Management and employees

This statement illustrates the expectation of reciprocity at the workplace very well. The expectation of reciprocity is not always fulfilled. One can still find examples of petty municipal officials, firms with terrible customer service, arrogant doctors, and managers who treat employees as they please. But such behaviour is meeting with a harder time now because of the increased individual self-consciousness of the participating parties.

This book deals with just such phenomena: for example, the individual and the individual group have greater expectations and make greater "selfish" demands at the same time that, both locally and globally, the necessity of common coordination and mutual recognition is increasing. Is it right that, when one talks about society becoming more individualised (i.e., more selfish), it is happening at the cost of and in opposition to the community? Or is it rather that the better the conditions are for the individual and the individual group to develop, the more willing they are to contribute to the community? In other words, that individuality and community are not only opposed to each other but are also the precondition for the other? We shall try to answer this question in the following chapters.

What is an organisation?

The manager/employee relationship takes place within the framework of an organisation. But what is an organisation? An example of one prevalent way of defining the concept is:

> It is characteristic of organisations that they have a division of labour and an administrative apparatus that, on the basis of rules and informal norms, tries to ensure coordination, continuity, and goal-fulfilment.
>
> *(Bakka & Fivelsdal 2014: 20)*

One could also circumscribe it in this way: an organisation is a number of individuals who cooperate on a particular task within a defined framework. But getting a number of people to cooperate on the same task is not as simple as it sounds because of the complex connection between individual psychology and the organisation's mode of functioning. On one hand, one's understanding of organisations cannot be improved without understanding the psychology of the individual, and on the other hand, one's understanding of the way organisations function must be expanded to be viewed as something more than the sum of the psychology of individuals.

In psychodynamic organisation theory, people say an organisation has a *primary task* (Heinskou 2004: 61;Visholm 2004d: 39), which is the reason the organisation exists. But what does it mean at heart when one talks about the organisation's primary task? Can one be sure that all the organisation's members view the primary task in the same way, or is it sufficient that management does? In that case, must the entire management team be in agreement, or is it enough that the CEO is in agreement with the board chairperson? If one believes that it is necessary for everyone or a majority in the organisation to be in agreement, how does one assure that, since "agreement" is a mental phenomenon found in people's consciousness? Shall one instead put efforts into coordinating and controlling the actions of members with the help of division of labour and structure, so they help with the solution of the primary task regardless of whether they are in agreement or not, and how does one implement this in practice?

It can be tempting to think of organisations as independent creatures with their own psyche and goals – for example, when it is said that "Danske Bank announced that . . ." or "Denmark has won . . .". But in both instances, it is, respectively, a spokesperson for the bank or a sports commentator who is speaking, not the organisation "itself". However, there must be a binding force in organisations since everyone agrees that Danske Bank and Denmark, like any number of other communities, exist as totalities, as real phenomena, as social communities, as organisations. One can say that organisations consist of the *common image* members have of the organisation and that this image is shared to some extent by non-members outside the organisation. Thus, an organisation exists if a sufficient number of people continuously recreate the organisation in thought and deed.

Altogether, it can be concluded that an organisation consists of individuals who, through a division of labour, rules, and norms, collaborate around the execution of a primary task with its supporting functions. How effective this collaboration is may be difficult to measure. It is decided by how well the participants succeed in creating a common, internal view of what the organisation and its tasks are and the extent to which it succeeds in continuously negotiating how the task is to be accomplished. In this process, the type and quality of members' mutual relations are decisive. But trusting, flexible, and robust relations can be difficult to create and maintain in organisational contexts because of the psychological complexity of cooperation. Management plays a decisive role here for how the process goes, especially if management understands how to work with the psychological processes that cooperation involves.

Content and structure of the book

This book presents knowledge from the social sciences (including organisation theory) and from psychology. Psychology is divided into many different sub-disciplines of which group psychology, object relations theory, and existential psychology in particular are used. The fundamental premise of the text is based in relational and psychodynamic organisation theory, both of which are presented in more detail in Chapter 2, although with the primary weight on psychodynamic theory (Visholm 2004d). The concept of "psychodynamic" indicates that the theory tries to describe conflicting unconscious psychological forces that influence both the individual and the organisation (for definitions, see Abrahamowitz 2001: 214; Gould 2001: 3).

8 Management and employees

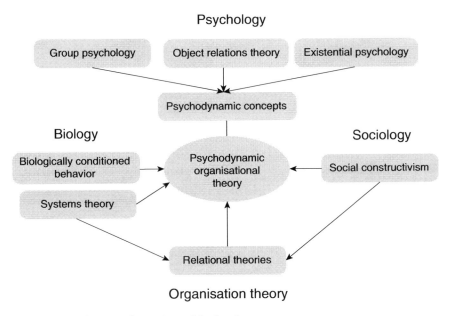

FIGURE 1.1 Theoretical premises of the book

The relationship between managers and employees may be described through the different functions in which they participate. The manager, for example, is responsible for such tasks as:

- Hiring and firing
- Conveying information to and from employees
- Strategy, goals, and framework for the job
- Follow-up and feedback on work projects
- The framework for professional and personal development
- Conflict resolution
- Support for employees with personal difficulties.

The book deals with these topics but is not directly structured around them, since that would have made it more difficult to create a coherent picture of the relationship between manager and employee. Instead, the starting point here is that the relationship between manager and employee plays out in groups. A group may be anything – an informal group, a team, an office, a department, or a division in the organisation. In this connection, the group is considered as a system, which contains subsystems that are related to each other. Subsystems in the group are constituted by individuals in the group (individual processes). The relationship between systems is constituted by the relationship among the employees (group processes) and the relationship between manager and employees (management processes). Finally, the manager, by virtue of his/her placement in the system, constitutes a special subsystem (the manager's personality).

The structure of the book follows this understanding of groups. Therefore, it is organised in such a way to describe each system – from the least complex system (the individual) to the most complex system (the group) – and the relations between them, including the special importance of management. Whether a system is viewed as a subsystem or a comprehensive system depends exclusively on how one defines the boundaries of the system being investigated. In this book, the system is defined as the group and its subsystems. Systems are seen as a hierarchy of increasing complexity in which systems refer to and constitute each other (Gould 2001: 6–8).

The book's basic viewpoint is that, if one wants to gain greater insight into the phenomenon of management, it is necessary to investigate the emotions and relations that arise between people who are creating something in common. If this is not done, it can be difficult or impossible to understand the reactions that one as a manager gets from employees and fellow managers. Therefore, if one seeks insight into what is going on in organisations at a deeper level than what is immediately visible, one must:

- Have a basic familiarity with human motivations and drives
- Have insight into the processes that are at work when individuals work together in groups
- Understand what function management has in relation to the above
- Understand what role the individual manager's personality plays in these processes.

Even though individuals, groups, management, and the manager's personality are treated in different chapters, this does not mean that one can consider them as separate phenomena. The relational approach entails that they are the preconditions for each other, they affect each other, and together, they constitute a system that is more than the sum of the individual parts of the organisation. The psychodynamic approach entails that, in the exploration of this system, weight is placed on individual as well as group psychological phenomena and that parts of these phenomena are considered to take place unconsciously for the participants.

The purpose of the book is to present knowledge and experience from these fields in order thereby to help create productive organisations that fulfil their purpose by allowing participants to thrive and gain the opportunity to develop their potential in a community.

The four parts of the book

The book is divided into four main themes:

- The employee in the community
- The community
- Management
- The manager's personality.

The connections between these themes are sketched out here:

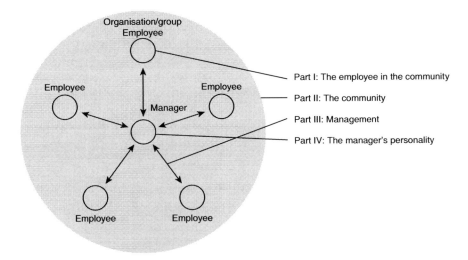

FIGURE 1.2 The connections between the themes

Part I deals with the individual, the understanding of what drives the individual, and what, respectively, promotes and inhibits the individual's self-development. Since organisations consist of individuals and since the manager's task is to create the best preconditions for the individual's productivity and collaboration with other people, it is important for the manager to have knowledge about individual psychological processes. Part I also describes the reception and dismissal of employees. Here, the issue of change in organisations and the symbolic and concrete meaning thereof is examined in more detail both for the existing organisation and for the employees who come and go, respectively.

Part II deals with the group and how individuals and groups constitute each other. Most of the work in organisations by far takes place in formal or informal groups which cooperate on a common product. This collaboration can often cause problems. As a manager, therefore, one must have knowledge about what promotes and strengthens collaboration and what mechanisms risk bringing cooperation to a halt or even set it back.

Part III describes the functions management has in an organisation. It is shown how management and employees mutually constitute each other and how relationships and communication between manager and employees are treated. Part III also discusses how the manager can help his/her employees to develop new skills. Moreover, we look closer at the authority of the manager, what it consists of, and how the manager can work with his/her own authority.

Part IV explores in more detail the significance of the manager's personality. What is personality, how does it influence the organisation, what personality traits are decisive for whether the manager functions well, and how can the manager work to develop the characteristics of his/her own personality?

Use of cases

The book tries throughout to clarify theoretical concepts and give them some nuance with the help of cases. The cases that are used in the book all come from reality but are reshaped to preserve the anonymity of the participants and may be a composite of several different cases. Therefore, if anyone were to think that they recognise themselves or their firm in a case, it is a coincidence. That all the cases are based on real events, of course, does not imply any final evidence for the validity of the theories applied to them, just as there is no guarantee that the conclusion of the analyses is "true". The cases that appear in the book are selected and adapted pieces of reality, and they could have been used with another theoretical lens to illuminate other concepts. In the real world, one would hardly make such conclusive analyses that the book uses to explain concepts. In a specific reality, on the other hand, one can use the concepts to begin an ongoing dialogue among the participants in an effort to achieve a common understanding of what is going on.

PART I
The employee in the community

As mentioned in Chapter 1, an organisation can be considered as a system that consists of a number of subsystems. In order to understand the overall organisation, one must study the different systems of which the individual – the individual employee – constitutes the smallest subsystem. The goal is to understand the individual's motivation for participating in the organisation. Part I, therefore, deals with the employee as an individual and with the employee's relationship to the community the organisation constitutes. In order to understand the individual's motives to participate in or to join the organisation, it is necessary to know something about *motivation* and *individual psychology*, which are the topics of the four chapters in Part I.

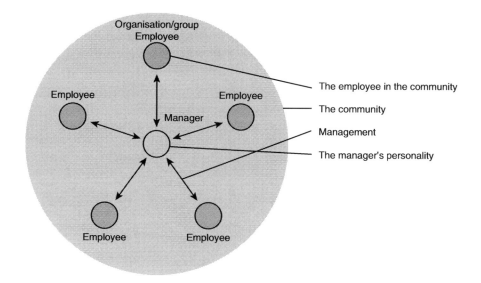

14 The employee in the community

The preceding figure illustrates that Part I focuses on the employee as an individual, on the individual's motivation and inner drives, and on the individual's relationship with the group.

Part I contains the following main points:

Chapter 2	The individual has a dual relationship with groups. The individual is both attracted to and threatened by groups.
	The individual's basic psychological motivation can be seen as contradictory.
	The individual must learn to manoeuvre within these contradictions. Emotions provide guidance here.
Chapter 3	Psychological defences help the individual to avoid paralysis.
	Some psychological defences are more effective than others.
Chapters 4 and 5	Nowhere does the individual's dual relationship to groups become so clear as in admission (employment) to and expulsion (dismissal) from the community.

2

THE DUAL RELATIONSHIP OF INDIVIDUALS TO GROUPS

In modern organisations, there is, on the one hand, a high degree of specialisation due to the complexity of production and, on the other hand, a high degree of mutual connectedness and coordination between the various functions in the firm. This is due both to the demand for an efficient exploitation of the firm's resources and the demands of stakeholders for consistent products and related services. Consumers expect that the burgers from a burger chain will all taste alike regardless of whether they are bought in London or Copenhagen, and patients expect efficient, coordinated treatment throughout their contact with a hospital's various professionals and departments.

To achieve this coordination of an organisation's activities at the same time that efficiency and quality are maintained or improved is no simple chore. It constitutes a tremendous challenge for mutually cooperative relationships because coordination requires the individual employee, who is expected to burn with commitment for his/her own project, to show interest and understanding of the organisation's other activities at the same time, and – if necessary – to put aside or modify his/her own project out of consideration for the whole. Coordination, on one hand, places great demands on employees' personal knowledge, commitment, and ability to work independently; and, on the other hand, it places just as great a demand on employees' ability to enter into, contribute to, and perhaps subordinate themselves to the bigger picture.

Thus, it is necessary for the modern organisation to maintain two phenomena side by side: decentralisation and centralisation. Decentralisation and centralisation are often viewed as opposing each other (Brunsson & Olsen 1993: 41–42; Bakka & Fivelsdal 2014: 60). We believe, to the contrary, that one should see them as preconditions for each other (Haslund & Alsted 2004). The relationship between decentralisation and centralisation is reflected in the firm's structure and its culture: how great is the individual's latitude formally and actually, how is this latitude exploited,

16 The employee in the community

and to what degree is it successful in coordinating the various activities into a productive whole through knowledge-sharing and creative collaboration?

As an employee, one is expected both to be able to work independently and purposefully on one's own tasks and, at the same time, to be able to work in the larger and smaller, formal and informal groups that, together, constitute the organisation. This two-sided demand often gives rise to problems because the individual's relationship to groups from a psychological point of view is complicated and contradictory. Human beings are born into a group context (the family), and their affiliation with groups of different sorts remain central throughout their lives (Heinskou 2004: 49). On the one hand, the individual is attracted by the group; on the other hand, the group is experienced as threatening to the individual's self-esteem and independence (Gabriel 1999: chap. 4; Alsted 2005: chap. 5). This basic opposition between individual and community plays a prominent role in many of the problems and conflicts that arise when people are to cooperate in an organisational context.

The group can threaten the individual's identity

Why might an individual experience the group as threatening? American professor of psychiatry Otto Kernberg's explanation is that individuality is broken down in the group context, so that the group winds up constituting a threat to the individual's identity. The individual will react to this threat by defending his/her individuality and identity. In particular, this phenomenon is expressed in groups in which the structure is unclear or non-existent, either because it is not defined or because, for some reason, it has dissolved. If people are placed in unstructured group contexts, there is a universal tendency toward regression, which is to say that the participants display more immature behaviour than they normally would (Kernberg 1998: 7). Anyone who has participated in "plenum democratic" discussions knows what is referred to here, and the following example provides an illustration of how a meeting can go in a group context in which there is only a loosely defined structure.

During the first parent-teacher conference for class 1.b, Jonas' father begins the meeting with a proposal that all children in the class be invited when one of them holds a birthday party. Victor's mother immediately says that she thinks this is a completely unnecessary rule. Jonas' father replies that, because Victor is so popular, he would be invited to all the parties, but she should think a little about those who are not as lucky! Victor's mother is offended and says nothing more for the rest of the evening.

Jette's mother, who is single and cannot afford to invite everyone, suggests that, instead, people agree to hold a common birthday party once a year. This is met with a chorus of wild protests from many who think this is a silly idea!

Frank's father in particular objects because he has been looking forward to celebrating a real boys' party for Frank, which the father never had when he was a child. Jette's mother is frightened by the reactions and defends her proposal aggressively, calling the others asocial and petit bourgeois.

The class teacher, who is a recent graduate, has remained passive to this point but is afraid that the meeting was getting off track. She tries, therefore, to arbitrate by saying that she could see advantages to all the proposals. This leads to a dissolution of the meeting in which people who are in agreement sit and talk to each other, while Frank's father and Jette's mother shout at each other across the table.

Suddenly, the class teacher becomes angry and hisses at the assembly: "You're all worse than the children to listen to!"

This is an example of a group that is so new that it has not yet established any kind of structure – either formally or informally – and one in which leadership is not clearly defined. Everyone is emotionally engaged in the meeting because it has to do with something very personal: the participants' children. At the same time, these children find themselves in a potentially painful process in which they are establishing the informal structure of the class in the form of children's mutual hierarchy – with the parents as anxious spectators.

The prospects, therefore, were for a stormy meeting regardless of the specific topics to be discussed; and the level of anxiety was rather high already because no one knew each other well and because there was something important at stake for everyone. A well-structured meeting with clear leadership could have dampened the level of anxiety considerably. Instead, one sees how the lack of leadership and structure led to a dissolution of the budding community and how individuals instead concentrated on defending their own (i.e., their own child, who here represents the parent's identity and individuality). The participants regressed to immature behaviour as a result of the threat they experienced to their identity and self-esteem, culminating with shouting parents and a derisive class teacher. Some of the participants were probably red-faced the next day, and it will be more difficult for classroom 1.b to achieve a well-functioning collaboration after this meeting.

According to Kernberg, it is a universal phenomenon that participation in groups or organisations can be experienced as a threat to the participants' individual identity (Kernberg 1998: 7). It can be difficult, infuriating, and at times, even painful to be or work together with other people. At the same time, people are attracted to each other and need each other. It can also be pleasurable, fun, and affirming to work together on something. The group can give the individual greater security (both physically and psychically) and a greater identity that the individual cannot establish alone. The individual is attracted by the vision of the group and by the experience of being a member of a group as in a herd. As a result of this attraction, the individual is willing under certain circumstances to be completely subordinated to the uniformity of the group and put his/her individuality aside (Hogg 1992, 2014). People who are fans of a particular football club, participate in a political demonstration, or are members of a choir will recognise the intoxicating feeling of fellowship that can arise under the right conditions but which cannot be maintained as a constant phenomenon.

The individual must constantly find a productive balance between being "yourself" and, at the same time, being a part of the group. For even though an individual's relationship to a community is contradictory, human beings have no choice, deep down: the individual can only thrive and develop in relation to others, and human societies can only exist through widespread cooperation and coordination among individuals. This is demonstrated to a marked degree at the workplace and, in order to elaborate the understanding of what seems, respectively, challenging and inhibiting to cooperation in the firm, we shall look more closely at the relationship between individual and group.

The group's influence on the individual and vice versa

A fundamental area in the study of the individual's relationship to groups has to do with how dependent one considers the individual to be on the group. In this discussion, there are a number of different positions among theorists who have been occupied with the question. One extreme claims that the individual is pretty much independent of the group; the other extreme considers the individual to be completely dependent on the group (Alsted 2001: chap. 2).

An example of a position that views the individual as independent of the group is the idea of the "rational person" with which some economic theories operate (Scheuer 1999: 20–37). When the rational person is to make a decision, he gathers all the available, relevant information and, on the basis of his needs, makes a rational decision. When a rational person is to choose a washing machine, he gets brochures on all available machines, compares the abilities and prices of the machines with his needs and budget, and then chooses the best match. In this view, the individual appears to be independent of the group (society), since the decision is made exclusively on the basis of an analysis of one's own needs and preferences. From the rational perspective, one will only join communities if it is rational to do so for oneself (Coleman 1990; Scheuer 1999: 20–37).

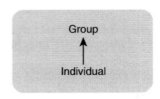

FIGURE 2.1 Rationalism: the individual is seen as independent of the group

An example of a position at the other end of the scale, which views the individual as extremely dependent on the group, is so-called functionalism (for a discussion of this, see Lee & Newby 1983: chap. 16; for an example of a more recent functionalist theory, see March & Olsen 1989). Functionalism asserts that the individual primarily strives to conform to the community of the group, also called "normative consensus". In the example of the washing machine, the individual would make his/her choice in accordance with what others choose. People choose the same washing machine as their neighbours, friends, idols, or other important figures from the community with whom they identify. For functionalists, the individual appears very dependent on the herd and to have a reduced free will.

There are also more nuanced proposals for the relationship between individual and group among which social constructivism has great influence. Within social constructivism, people talk about how the individual and the group "mutually constitute" each other. This means that the group only exists as long as the members of the group actively recreate it with their actions. In other words, groups must be maintained in order to continue to exist, and that only happens if the members agree to do it. On the other hand, the group also helps create and form the individual. The individual's identity, skills, and relationships are through his/her life connected to different groups, and one can – paradoxically – say that individuality is created in groups. Individuality is created on a running basis through contact with the community from the infant's first, intimate interactions with parents to the adult's daily contact with family, colleagues, and friends to the citizen's relationship with national and global societies.

The viewpoint described above is called social constructivism because human beings themselves construct their social reality in community with others. Social reality does not exist outside human beings but rather between them and within them. In its general form, this theoretical idea is widely accepted today among most

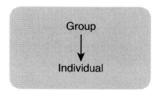

FIGURE 2.2 Functionalism: the individual is seen as dependent on the group

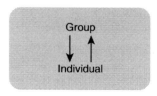

FIGURE 2.3 Social constructivism: individual and group are seen as mutually dependent

20 The employee in the community

sociologists and organisation theorists. Therefore, there is an enormous amount of literature on the topic and many interpretations of it. The idea of social constructivism has found its most famous interpretation in the so-called structure/actor theory, which describes a mutually constitutive relationship between structure (the group) and actor (the individual). The English sociologist Anthony Giddens is the originator of this theory (Giddens 1984; Alsted 2001). Among other well-known authors (with different interpretations of the idea of social constructivism) are Peter Berger, Thomas Luckmann, David Cooperrider, Suresh Srivastva, and Kenneth Gergen.

The social constructivist perspective can be especially inspiring and provide an insightful angle on constructing organisations and the relationship that plays out between employee, group, and management. But demonstrating that individual and community are mutually constitutive does not say much about the type of mutuality. Therefore, one may ask the following:

> How much influence does the individual have on the group and vice versa?

You can find a number of theoretical answers to this question, and the aforementioned representatives of social constructivism differ from one another on precisely this point. Two different positions will be pointed out here. The first is the relational position. The relational approach places primary weight on the relationships between the individuals in the group. From this perspective, the group is seen as created through and maintained by virtue of the relationships between the members of the group. Therefore, they have the following answer to the question:

> The individual has great opportunities to influence the group through the use of systemic methods such as dialogue, reflexivity, and openness, all of which are conducive to relationships. Norms, routines, and habits do not bind the group so strongly that they cannot be altered by a common effort. This can change both the group as a whole and the individual's view of him/herself and others.

A Danish representative of this perspective is Gitte Haslebo, but there are also a number of international authors with these points of view – for example, Kenneth Gergen, W.B. Pearce, David Cooperrider, and Suresh Srivastva, among others.

The other theoretical position puts weight on relationships as well as individual psychology. This perspective is called psychodynamic organisation theory and is based on a combination of individual psychological concepts (which originally derive from psychoanalysis), group and social psychology theories, and open system theory. Danish representatives of this perspective include Torben Heinskou and Steen Visholm (2004); but here, too, there are a number of international authors (see, e.g., Hirschhorn 1988; Kernberg 1998; Gabriel 1999).

The psychodynamic perspective provides the following answer to the question of the mutual influence between individual and group:

> The individual has great, albeit limited, opportunities for influencing the group. The limitations consist of deeply imbedded, partially unconscious individual and group identities and individual and collective psychological processes. In addition, the limitations may lie in specific conflicts of interest between individual and group.

According to psychodynamic theory, there is an incredibly complex connection between individual and group and, thus, between individual psychology and the way organisations function. This connection does not simply reduce organisations to mirror images of the participating individuals but emphasises that the inner lives of organisations are more and different than the sum of the individuals. But at the same time, the psychodynamic perspective says that it is necessary to be familiar with basic phenomena in individual psychology in order to create conditions for the cooperation that is a precondition for productive organisations (Heinskou & Visholm 2004; Wilke 2014).

As mentioned in Chapter 1, the present book was written on the premises of psychodynamic organisation theory. Therefore, the next section explores in more depth the psychology and motivation of the individual in relation to groups.

The psychology of the individual

There are many conceptualisations of the psychology of the individual. One branch stresses the psyche's pluralistic, composite nature, while another branch sees it as a totality that maintains consistency over time. Almost all theories accept that both aspects of the psyche – both the multiple and the unified – are present at the same time.

The fragmented psyche consists of, among other things, a number of contradictory needs and feelings. It has been said that the psyche speaks with several voices (McIntosh 1979). A fundamental condition for the psyche is, thus, ambivalence in which consideration for many different needs and feelings must be processed (Alsted 2005: chap. 4).

This task of processing falls to the self, which must be understood as a separate authority in the psyche and different from motivation and feelings (Leary & Tangney 2012: 7–8). Thus, the self is the totality-creating, acting, and analysing "superstructure" of the individual's psyche.

In the following, we shall elaborate this view of individual psychology, first by investigating the motivation of the individual, then by discussing the function of feelings, and finally by presenting a model of the self (see also Alsted & Haslund 2016).

22 The employee in the community

The individual's motivation in relation to groups

As mentioned, the relationship between individual and community has a dual nature: people are both attracted to and threatened by groups. The recognition of this duality is fundamental for the understanding of the relationship between manager and employee. The central element in all management is to find the balance between the individual employee's needs and abilities on the one hand, and the overall firm's needs and tasks on the other hand (Jørgensen 2004: 163). It can also be formulated in this way: the manager's job is to maintain both a partial and a total perspective on the organisation. In order to be able to carry out this difficult task as well as possible, the manager must have a fundamental understanding of what motivates and drives people.

Many different theories deal with human motivation (i.e., the question of what the psyche's fundamental drives are). What motivates people to act as they do? Most of these theories are formulated within the field of psychology. In the following, we shall briefly review some representatives of the different positions. The review is divided into theories that seek a single, fundamental drive in people and theories that hold that people contain many different, often conflicting drives. Historically, the theories of single, fundamental drives developed first, while theories of different, conflicting drives developed more recently.

Unambiguous and basic drives

Most well-known – even today, some 100 years after his most important works were written – are the theories of Sigmund Freud. Freud's view was that the psyche's drives were based on human biological needs, and his model of the drives, therefore, took their starting point in bodily functions. Freud believed that a chemical or mechanical reaction in the body led to a tension or "irritation" and that the energy from this process created a psychic representation in the human psyche. It is this psychic representation that Freud called the "drive". If the tension is relieved, the psyche experienced satisfaction; if the tension was not relieved, the psyche did not experience satisfaction.

Freud distinguished between two drives: the death instinct and the life instinct. The death instinct tries to eliminate the tension life itself contains, by which this drive becomes the source for aggression and hatred. The life instinct – the so-called libido – tries to sustain life. The life instinct is the psychic representation of the satisfaction of bodily tensions. Here, Freud distinguished between two forms of libido: object libido is the sexual drive, while ego libido is the individual's instinct for self-preservation (Olsen & Køppe 1985).

It is in the effort to satisfy their biological needs that human beings become social, according to Freud. He viewed group formations and other social activities, therefore, as founded in human biology. Freud stressed that it is necessary for the individual to achieve control over his/her drives if they are to enter into social communities. Since the satisfaction of biological needs takes place to a high degree unconsciously, this entails that a great deal of the individual's relationship to groups also unfolds in the unconscious.

Freud saw participation in groups as a strain on the individual: in order to satisfy their biological needs, people must enter into social contexts; but in order to do that, they must be able to control their individual needs. Otherwise, they will not be accepted in the community. The hungry child who throws himself on his little brother's meatballs and eats them with his fingers is sent away from the table until he has learned to eat properly (which is to say, according to the rules that are applicable in the relevant culture); thus he does not satisfy his immediate, physical need. In this way, the child gradually learns to subordinate himself to the community's rules and norms and to defer or repress his own needs. This is neither psychologically easy nor free of charge for the individual to learn. It costs great emotional effort. As a result, participation in the community is at one and the same time a necessity of life and a psychic cost for the individual.

Basically, Freud believed that people do not participate in groups to satisfy their social needs but to satisfy their biological needs. The effect of this is that people become socialised because socialisation is access to the fulfilment of biological needs. In other words, people are not social from desire but from necessity, according to Freud.

This point of view has spurred a great deal of criticism throughout the 20th century. Among the critics of Freud was Abraham Maslow. He developed in the 1960s and 1970s an alternative theory of motivation, which is frequently cited in a number of textbooks on organisation theory (Jacobsen & Thorsvik 2002; Bolman & Deal 2017; Bakka & Fivelsdal 2014: 197).

Maslow criticised Freud's theory that participation in social contexts required control and reduction of biological needs (Maslow 1970). To the contrary, he believed that these needs were a significant part of the attraction of being together with other people. Therefore, he formulated his famous hierarchy of needs in which physiological/biological needs constitute a basic element but only appear as one need among many (see Figure 2.4).

The needs are presented in a pyramid to illustrate that the lower needs in the pyramid are the strongest and most fundamental. The pyramid also demonstrates the hierarchical relationship between the needs, in which the higher needs in the hierarchy cannot be satisfied before the fundamental needs have been met. However, Maslow stressed that there are gradual transitions between the needs. Therefore, one can imagine a person who has 85% of her physiological needs, 70% of her need for love, and 40% of her need for self-esteem met. But the model does not allow for 70% of her need for self-actualisation to be met while only 40% of her physiological needs are satisfied (Madsen 1968: 107–109; Maslow 1987 [1954]; Bakka & Fivelsdal 2014: 199).

Maslow's hierarchy of needs contains many positive elements. First of all, it stresses the possibility for individual development through self-actualisation. It is in this way an optimistic model that emphasises potential progression in the individual's development and in the development of humanity as a whole because the

FIGURE 2.4 Maslow's pyramid of needs

model is claimed to be universally valid for all people. Second, the model points toward the importance of social relationships for this progressive development. Maslow claims that the participation of people in groups is in itself pleasurable and motivating.

But Maslow's theory also has some problematic elements. For example, it is difficult to document a clear hierarchy among the needs (Wahba & Bridwell 1976). One cannot preclude that the need for self-actualisation may arise even though the more fundamental needs are not satisfied. Just think of poor, lonely poets in a garret for whom self-actualisation is more important than daily bread and interactions with others.

But if Maslow's theory is not adequate, how can one then describe the motivational drives?

Ambiguous and conflicting drives

The research in recent years on human motivation and needs has shown that the motivational drives are unclear as well as conflicting. These contributions come from systems-oriented points of view (see, e.g., Ford 1992) and from existential psychology (see, e.g., Yalom 1999). According to this research, one cannot isolate a single need – for example, the sex drive – as the basic motivation (Mortensen 2003: 311), just as one cannot establish a hierarchy among needs.

Nevertheless, one can very well say something meaningful and usable about what drives and motivates human beings. The model presented here is a combination of a number of schools (Katzenelson 1993; Alsted 2005: chap. 4).

The great advantage and evolutionary "achievement" of humankind is its ability to mirror its surroundings in an inner, psychic representation of the world. The human being is presumably the species capable of creating the most nuanced inner picture of his/her surroundings (Engelsted 1989). This inner picture (which one can imagine as a jigsaw puzzle composed of thousands of small, interchangeable pieces) is used by the individual as a map or a guide to how the world can be understood and how one can act in it (Kernberg 1976; Kernberg 1980). This ability to create shifting inner representations of the world means that people may adapt to quite varied surroundings, which from an evolutionary point of view is an advantage. At the same time, this means that the psyche of the individual is plastic and changeable, so the psyche, or the inner map, can adapt to shifting situations and shifting relationships. Potentially, the psyche can also change over the course of the individual's lifetime along with changing life circumstances and experiences gained.

A fundamental feature about the world is its complexity and ambiguity. Nothing is permanent; destruction and change are fundamental conditions, whether you are talking about living creatures or the rest of the material world; and all phenomena in life contain good and bad sides. Correspondingly, this means that the inner representations of human beings remain complex and ambiguous, and this is the reason that human motivation and needs are conflicting. People want many things at the same time, and these things are often in conflict with each other. This external ambiguity appears as internal ambivalence in basic human motivation, and this ambivalence has decisive meaning for the individual's relationship with other people.

With inspiration from existential psychology, ambivalent human motivation may be summarised as four fundamental needs (see, e.g., Riemann 1961; Yalom 1999):

- Need to feel like an autonomous individual
- Need to feel one belongs to a community
- Need for stability and recognition
- Need for change and challenges.

It is obvious that these four needs are mutually contradictory. Therefore, one can combine them into pairs, so that two basic motivational and existential dilemmas appear:

> Individuality versus community
> Stability versus change

These two dilemmas permeate all human existence; and, in the countless specific situations of which life consists, each individual tries to the best of his/her ability to resolve them (Haslund & Alsted 2004; Alsted 2005). But it is characteristic of dilemmas that there is no real resolution to them; there is only a perpetual weighing of the two sides of the dilemma in relation to the individual's personality and the specific situation.

The first existential dilemma: individuality versus community

The balance between being an individual human with special characteristics that distinguish a person from everyone else and being a part of a community just like all the others constitutes a fundamental dilemma. This dilemma is in constant negotiation in the individual. To feel like a person with an autonomous "I" and experiencing oneself as something special is a vital need. In order to participate in a differentiated and nuanced social interplay with others, it is necessary for the individual to have a coherent experience of him/herself as something different from others. One of the consequences of this need is that the individual protects, safeguards, and is at times proud of his/her individuality, peculiarities, qualifications, and accomplishments.

But it is just as vital for human psychological and material health to be a part of the communities that surround the individual. The human experience of being an autonomous individual can only be developed through relations with others. One needs to have others to compare oneself with and distinguish oneself from, and one's inner self-representation is developed through the response and mirroring one meets in others (Kernberg 1980; Goleman 2006). Precluded from the community, the individual is nothing: neither in a material sense (the infant simply dies of starvation if it is not recognised by the community) nor in a psychological sense (prisoners put in isolation quickly lose their sense of being autonomous, coherent individuals, and their psyches are in danger of breaking down). The same phenomenon can be seen in people who have been unemployed for a long time, whose feeling of standing outside the fellowship of society many have described as the most burdensome thing about unemployment.

If one involuntarily loses one's place in the community, if one becomes too peculiar and prominent, or if one does not abide by the community's written or unwritten rules and norms, it generates an anxiety of being excluded from the community. On the other hand, if one submits to the community too much, there is the anxiety of being swallowed up and disappearing as an individual without being able to achieve one's potential threatens. It is of this that the dilemma between individual and community consists.

A person may have an ambition to become the manager of the organisation in which he is employed. He thinks: "If I become a manager, everyone will see I am something special, that I am smarter than the others. I'll never become anything if I do not become a manager". But if he achieves his goal of becoming a manager, the problem shifts focus to the other side of the dilemma. Many managers have these worries: "Do my employees like me? Am I still part of the group?" Some of the loneliness that can come with a management job is due to the individual manager's problems with finding the balance between wanting to step forward and take a leadership position and, at the same time, being afraid of stepping outside the community.

The second existential dilemma: stability versus change

Every human being strives for and needs stability and coherence to some degree in his/her life. At the same time, human beings are curious and regularly want changes and challenges in order to develop their inherent talents and abilities and to avoid boredom. But the balance between the two sides of the dilemma can be difficult to achieve.

If stability dominates too much, anxiety of constraint and stagnation threatens; but, if one makes room for change, one also makes room for the unknown, the incalculable, and the chaotic. Before a change of job, one thinks: "I must move on. I'm in a rut. My job bores me". After the job shift, the other side of the dilemma dominates. Nervousness about beginning something new appears: "Have I made the right decision? Will they accept me at my new workplace? Am I able to succeed at this new job?" A longing for one's old job arises, and grief over lost colleagues and skills can take a toll for a time. Uncertainty and anxiety often appear hand in hand with change (Visholm 2004c). This fundamental, existential dilemma between stability and change must be dealt with every time one faces a new situation or a new relationship. The ability to weigh the two sides of the dilemma against each other, therefore, is decisive for many of the choices one makes in life.

The two fundamental dilemmas – individual versus community and stability versus change – follow the human being throughout life. They do not disappear no matter how much one tries to neutralise them because they are fundamental features of human existence. But the ability to contain the dilemmas and to be able to relate to them flexibly is increased through the individual's psychological maturity. In the normally developed individual, this maturity comes naturally to a certain degree in one's development from infant to adult. But the degree of maturity also depends on factors of psychological constitution (e.g., fragility, sensitivity, robustness, temperament) and the conditions the individual encounters throughout life.

The problems with Freud's and Maslow's theories now appear more clearly. Freud assumed that being with other people is not an independent need. This is not right. Relations with other people are vital for the individual not only for biological but for psychological reasons. The socialisation of human beings is not only a consequence of the fulfilment of biological needs but a pleasurable, motivating factor in itself (McNamee 1998; Alsted 2005: chap. 4).

Maslow assumed that human needs could be placed in a hierarchy but, in reality, mixed up two different things in his model: motivation and development. There is broad agreement even today about the elements that Maslow indicated as important for motivation. But by placing them into a hierarchy with an implicit life cycle, Maslow assumed that these needs change throughout life. There is much that indicates they do not; the child and the adult, in principle, have the same psychological needs. Modern motivation research believes that human needs are to be viewed as mutually contradictory and tension-filled and that what changes throughout life and matures is the individual's ability to manoeuvre between these contradictory needs (Alsted 2005: chap. 4).

The origin and function of emotions

Instead of assuming that the individual has one clear inner motivation and will, one can view the individual's psyche as a system consisting of many parts that are

28 The employee in the community

in mutual conflict. One author, D. McIntosh, fittingly says that the psyche "speaks with many tongues" (1979). This means that the experience of inner coherence and consistency does not come of itself as an innate gift but must be constructed and maintained continuously. In this constant, internal process, emotions are the way in which the individual orients him/herself to find balance in the existential, motivational dilemmas. This sort of understanding of the function of the emotions has great significance for how the process between manager and employee can be viewed since it entails that one's emotional life is always active – also in work life. Human beings are incapable of *not* feeling because the emotions are an inseparable part of human consciousness. From this point of view, the relationship between manager and employee is borne and controlled to a high degree by emotional factors.

In opposition to this is the rational theory. According to this view, the drive in the relationship between manager and employee is rationality, i.e., that the relationship is seen as a contractual one that contains a job description and a mutual acceptance between manager and employee of the work effort expected in relation to pay and other employment conditions. If problems arise in the relationship, therefore, they will look for causes and solutions in the realm of rationality, i.e., in the terms and conditions of the employment relationship (Scheuer 1999: 20–37).

Psychodynamic theory views the relationship between manager and employee, in part, as a contractual relationship that takes place within a particular structure and, in part, as a relationship that activates deep, complicated, and often unconscious feelings that can have their origin far back in the lives of the participants (Kernberg 1998: chap. 4; Jørgensen 2004: 167). In the following is a more detailed review of various theories on the origin of emotions and their function.

The biological theory of emotions

When it comes to the origin and function of human emotions, there are a number of different views; and here, too, two extreme positions may be used as points of orientation.

One extreme position states that the primary source of the emotions is the brain's *biological/instinctive* fundament. In this understanding, emotions are automatic reactions that people experience when they find themselves in different situations. A dangerous situation triggers fear, a loss triggers sorrow, and so forth. The biology-based school views the emotional life as relatively independent of the social contexts in which the individual is involved. Instead, the emotions are considered to be determined, in part, by one's inborn personality and, in part, by experiences from early childhood. Again, Freud is the best example of an author with this view, but Jung, too, contributed to the theory by sketching out different personality types (Jung 1921; Olsen & Køppe 1985). These have become generally known through the Jungian-inspired type indicator test (the MBTI and JTI tests). The idea that each individual is a particular type whose reactions are to some degree predictable has become a widespread conception over the years, particularly through the various personality tests that are used in many workplaces (see Chapter 13).

Emotions may also be designated as "the psyche's information processes" (Mortensen 2003: 314–315). This means that emotions may have a large number of different sources – biological, psychological, and social. But there are certain biologically given "basic emotions" that could change if human beings change as a species. The basic emotions are (Tomkins 1992, cited in Mortensen 2003: 314):

- Joy
- Interest
- Surprise
- Anger
- Fear
- Anguish
- Sadness
- Disgust
- Shame.

These feelings constitute the human being's inborn, instinctive readiness to orient oneself and react to the outside world. Therefore, one can describe these feelings as thoughts without words that allow a person – for example, a small child who does not yet have language or a person who meets with an urgent situation – to react quickly and instinctively.

The biological, deterministic theory of emotions has been criticised in previous centuries as well as this one. The critique has taken two forms: relational theory and the psychodynamic theory.

The relational theory of emotions

The relational theory is the more radical and, in this overview, constitutes the other extreme position on the issue of the origin and function of emotions. The relational authors believe that emotions are formed socially in the interplay among human beings and, thus, that they are not bound to the individual but to the relations between individuals (e.g., Haslebo 2004: 163–164).

The relational critique points out that, to a high degree, emotions are culturally constructed. Thus there are a number of studies that show how the emotional life of human beings varies from organisation to organisation and from culture to culture, and also shows great variations over different historical epochs (e.g., Foucault 1976). One example of this, taken from sociology, is Norbert Elias' studies of the development of the feeling of shame in connection with manners (Elias 2000). With a series of examples from everyday life, Elias shows how emotions connected with table manners, going to the toilet, blowing one's nose, and spitting changed markedly from the Middle Ages to the Renaissance (2000: Part 2). He concludes that the boundaries for when one has violated norms for these activities were tightened over time. For example, the norms for blowing one's nose changed from something one did with one's hands to something one did with a handkerchief. Thus

30 The employee in the community

the boundaries also changed for when one felt embarrassed and ashamed (2000: 121–129). A corresponding example from current times might be the development of emotional life around smoking, which has changed markedly in recent years. Today, there are far more feelings of shame and guilt connected with smoking than there were 20 years ago, and these feelings did not exist at all 50 years ago.

Norbert Elias' study was not written from a relational perspective: Elias took his starting point in Freud's theories. However, in the relational interpretation of his work, these studies are understood as expressing the fact that emotions are not biologically or psychologically founded in the individual but socially learned. This even applies to the biological processes that are behind emotions. For example, blushing connected to embarrassment may be a culturally learned phenomenon that exists in Western culture but not in other cultures (Harré & Parrott 1996, cited in Haslebo 2004: 164–165).

Whereas the individual-oriented schools underestimate the influence that people get from their surroundings, the relational theory underestimates the importance of the individual's biological/psychological constitution. Many people who have worked with organisation development have experienced that, at times, it can be incredibly slow – or outright impossible – for a person to change his/her emotional reactions in certain contexts even though the person works diligently and purposefully to do so. Therefore, one cannot get around the fact that, in some situations, people may be subject to biologically and/or psychologically determined behaviour, which is not to be changed – at least, not within the framework of the workplace. This is illustrated in the following case.

There is an older, professionally proficient man on a work team whom the younger persons on the team view as unusually gruff in his manner and critical of their work. The older man does not himself believe that he has a problem but simply feels he is fighting to maintain the professional quality he believes is declining rapidly. The young people, however, gradually leave the team in a number that then becomes a problem for the team's work, because of the unpleasant atmosphere they feel the older employee is generating.

Therefore, the manager engages in a number of coaching sessions with the older co-worker, and it comes out that the employee had grown up with a very critical and dominating father. However, the employee does not believe this influences him in relation to his younger colleagues.

The employee then receives a week-long course in appreciative behaviour but, after the course, continues with his destructive criticisms and reacts with anger when the young people do not listen. Finally, the manager can see no other way than to dismiss the employee.

This case shows how systemic methods, such as coaching, reflexivity, and the appreciative approach (see Chapter 7) are not always able to change behaviour that, for various reasons, is deeply rooted in the emotional life of the person in question.

The manager can coach the employee, inspire self-reflection, and give the employee methods for changing behaviour. Moreover, from a systemic approach in which all participants in the system are assumed to contribute to the problem's maintenance or solution, the manager can encourage the other employees to demur constructively from behaviour they find unreasonable. But if nothing helps, the manager cannot do much more because the relationship between manager and employee is not designed to work on deep emotional changes if the employee does not want this or is not able to.

The psychodynamic theory of emotions

This book places itself between these two extreme positions (the biological and the relational), namely, in the psychodynamic theory. This position considers emotions to be individually conditioned as well as socially constructed.

Emotions provide the individual with information about inner states and serve as guidance for how to act (Mortensen 2003: 314–315). But emotions can, as mentioned before, be confusing because they are mutually contradictory. Therefore, people are inclined to sort out emotions that penetrate to consciousness, so the socially or individually acceptable feelings get free passage, while the unacceptable are sorted out. In psychodynamic terminology, it is said that the individual has different types of psychological defences whose job is to protect the psyche against the inexpedient effects of unpleasant or anxiety-inducing emotions. These different types of psychological defences and the way in which they function are described in more detail in Chapter 3.

Following is an illustration of how emotional ambivalence around the dilemmas of individual/community and stability/change (the motivational dilemmas; see above) can lead to problems in the relationship between manager and employee:

A man has strongly encouraged his female colleague to seek promotion in the firm since he thinks the colleague is competent and deserves recognition. When the colleague is named manager and, thus becomes the man's boss, he is happy on her behalf and congratulates her heartily. He looks forward to having his former colleague as manager and expects no problems to come from it since they have previously worked well together.

After some time, however, complications appear in their cooperation. The man feels that his former colleague has changed in the new management position and become more dominant and that she is not as able as he had expected. Moreover, he does not feel that she recognises his personal work effort, which disappoints him very much. He experiences greater and greater distaste for his work and finally asks to be transferred to another manager's department.

The narrative around the case is that, from the start, the man had ambivalent feelings about his own ambitions to become manager himself. He wanted it but was also afraid of it, inter alia, because he was nervous about not being as good at it as his female colleague and because he was afraid of being viewed as an unsympathetic male chauvinist. Therefore, he established unconsciously a psychological defence that dampened his anxiety by transferring his ambitions to his female colleague, whom he also liked and respected. But when the woman actually became his manager, he could no longer repress his ambivalent feelings quite so effectively. He felt envy and jealousy but, at first, drowned them out with another feeling he also had, namely, his happiness on his colleague's behalf. Gradually, however, envy and jealousy became more obtrusive and took the form of an aggressive critique of the manager and a feeling of disappointment at the lack of recognition by the manager.

The man felt ambivalence about his own ambitions; he had difficulty finding a fruitful balance between the two existential dilemmas, but he was not conscious of this ambivalence. Since he was only in contact with his positive and permitted feelings (recognition of his colleague and joy on her behalf), the negative and forbidden feelings (his ambitions and envy) appeared in the form of a repression of his own needs, a critique of the manager, and a feeling of disappointment. But they could also have appeared in many other ways. For example, the man could have become restless, irritable, or depressed (see more on ambitions in Alsted & Haslund 2016: chap. 3).

Emotions are complex signals about a person's inner state at a given point in time. Signals that tell about how the world and interaction with other people influence one and to which one can have more or less direct access, depending on one's psychological maturity. Feelings are often mutually contradictory (the man in the case is both happy on behalf of his colleague and envious of her) because they try to orient themselves in relation to the existential dilemmas, which are contradictory by definition. Or to put it in another way, feelings are not to be considered as symptoms but as information (Gjerde 2006: 76).

There are biologically conditioned basic feelings, but the importance of these basic feelings diminishes gradually as the individual gains more experience, learns more complex modes with which to understand the world, and learns more nuanced forms of reaction. It is this learning process that constitutes the cultural and social formation of emotional life and which can be administered with more or less maturity. Thus, the central thing about feelings is not the feelings themselves but the way in which they are administered individually and in interaction with others. This task falls to the self, which is the topic of the next section.

The self

Thus the psyche contains a number of contradictory needs that do not change much throughout life. At the same time, it can communicate about these needs in quite overwhelming and confusing ways through feelings.

So, if people are not running around confused, shouting and screaming, it is because, very early in life, an inner structure was formed whose job it is to try to keep these contradictory needs and the feelings they give rise to under control – namely, the self.

The self is the synthesising part of the psyche. Here, the various needs are put under surveillance. Here, feelings are processed. Here, one's life narrative is maintained and developed. In other words, the job of the self is to try to unite different impulses and demands into an overall whole that can provide a sense of a coherent person and a feeling of control over one's life (Leary & Tangney 2012).

Lichtenberg and colleagues graphically express the self's amazing ability to maintain a feeling of totality across very powerful changes of condition, for example, from a sleeping to a waking state, from happiness to grief, from being angry to being friendly, and so forth (Lichtenberg et al. 1992: 57).

Safeguarding a coherent self is demanding and draws on a number of functions (Gergely 2007: 89–91):

1. Self-surveillance. Individuals must concurrently be able to observe and recognise states of emotion in themselves.
2. Surveillance of how one's self affects other people. This is necessary in order to enter into relations with other people.
3. Self-evaluation. An appropriate self-evaluation – not too self-critical and judgmental – is decisive for a healthy internal emotional life.
4. Separation from inner emotional states from reality. This is a decisive function of the self to be able not to view inner emotional states as a part of reality.

It is characteristic of the self that these synthesising and regulating functions do not function especially well under the influence of powerful emotions. A self under a powerful emotional influence has, for example, a reduced ability to put itself in another's place – to mentalise (Fonagy & Luyten 2012: 408–409). Therefore, it is important for the robustness of the self to develop the ability to control and process feelings.

The self's ability to safeguard these functions develops throughout life. The two-year-old child screams when it may not get candy at the supermarket, but the ten-year-old does not. Most people become better at manoeuvring between their contradictory needs and better at not letting themselves be overwhelmed by their emotions (Kegan 1982). This development can be conceptualised with the help of the idea of psychological defences, which is the topic of the next chapter.

3

COOPERATION AND PSYCHOLOGICAL DEFENCES

Very few work tasks in an organisation can be done without some form of cooperation with other people. Therefore, the way in which cooperation takes place is incredibly important for efficiency and for how people feel about working in the organisation. In previous chapters, we saw that the precondition for productivity and job satisfaction is that the participants are able to administer the feelings to which cooperation occasionally gives rise in a psychologically mature way. This chapter investigates what psychological maturity means in an individual and a collective sense and what importance the various degrees of maturity have for the way cooperation takes shape. This chapter is based on concepts from motivation and individual psychology and on psychodynamic group and social psychology.

In Chapter 2, we defined four basic motivational needs that are placed within two existential dilemmas: individual/community and stability/change. As mentioned, these are dilemmas that follow the individual throughout life. But the fact that the individual is always in a negotiation around these dilemmas – on an internal level as well as in relation to other people – threatens to paralyse the individual because, in practice, no person can contain and endure such ambiguity and ambivalence. Ambivalence threatens the individual's psychological stability and drive, which is why the psyche, according to psychodynamic theory, establishes defences that protect the self from becoming overwhelmed by ambivalence.

The purpose of these psychological defences is to reduce the experience of ambivalence to an "appropriate" level for the individual. This happens by simplifying the individual's internal representation of reality. With the help of these defences, the self divides itself and the world into manageable categories and patterns of action through which a portion of the ambivalence is displaced or repressed, so that one is freed from constantly having to take a conscious position toward it. These psychological defences constitute a protection from the confusing, the ambiguous, the chaotic. People need this protection because the anxiety of choosing wrong can

Cooperation and psychological defences **35**

otherwise be paralysing (Kernberg 1976; Brenner 1982; Halton 2003: 32; Alsted 2005; Guldager 2007: 84). These psychological defences are designated by some theoreticians as "compromise formations", because they create a compromise in the individual's psyche between the two sides of the dilemmas (Brenner 1982).

Many social-constructivist writers are sceptical of the existence of these defences. This is because the idea of psychological defences is founded in an individual-oriented thought process against which constructivism turns. More precisely, many constructivists are sceptical of the concept of personality as something inherent in the individual. They believe, instead, that personality (the self) is continuously recreated in the relationships into which the individual enters (Gergen & Gergen 1998; Haslebo 2004: 238–242).

In psychodynamic theory, however, psychological defences are a fundamental reason it is important to have a model for individual motivation. The defences the individual prefers to use can be quite stable over time and can, therefore, constitute a fundamental barrier to individual change – for example, by entering into reflexive dialogues as recommended by constructivist authors (Haslebo 2004: 248–249). People who indulge in splitting or repressive defences may have difficulty reflecting upon themselves and others because their defences prevent them from receiving nuanced information about themselves and from others. This is illustrated in the following case.

After many years in the same job, Søren is about to retire in a few months. Since he works alone, there is a need for him to pass his knowledge on to colleagues before he stops working.

Søren, who has great professional pride and cares deeply about his field, produces a detailed manual that describes precisely how his job is to be done, and he also designates the person he believes should follow him in the position.

However, his colleagues have decided to use Søren's retirement as an opportunity to distribute his tasks among several people instead of hiring someone new to take his place. They also want to find new, less resource-demanding ways to do his job. Therefore, they set up a working group to study this and invite Søren to participate.

At the group's first meeting, Søren says that it is not possible to distribute his extensive duties among several people, who are already busy with other things. He also believes that it would create total chaos if the job is not done as described in his manual. When the others question this, Søren becomes very angry and leaves the meeting. Shortly thereafter, he calls in sick and remains away for the rest of the time until his retirement comes into force.

Retiring activates both existential dilemmas to a high degree. The individual is "expelled" from the community and, at the same time, faces a huge change in his/her everyday life for which work has constituted a stable centre until that point. This

36 The employee in the community

puts Søren in the case under pressure, and he is filled with ambivalence because he is also looking forward to retirement and looking forward to getting more time for his leisure interests. He both looks forward to and fears the future; and even though he is relieved at not having to work so hard anymore, he also feels sorrow at letting go of all the tasks on which he has spent so much time and energy.

Søren's preferred defence is repressive. Therefore, he is not conscious of the ambivalence and mixed feelings retirement is giving him. He only takes note of positive feelings. Søren has effectively repressed his negative feelings with the help of control (writing the manual and designating his successor), but the suggestion of his colleagues (somewhat callously introduced) – to distribute Søren's tasks among several people and do them in an easier way – threatens this control and gives him a feeling of being worthless and anxiety that the community can easily do without him. These feelings raise a question about Søren's entire lifework in a fundamental, existential way – "Has there ever been any meaning in my life?" – which for most people would be an anxiety-provoking question. Therefore, Søren unconsciously represses these feelings with the help of anger and by reporting in sick, which in this case is an act of self-protection and a hidden aggression against his colleagues.

The case shows how it is not possible for Søren and his colleagues to engage in an open, impartial discussion of Søren's duties and how they should be done, even though, rationally, it is an excellent idea to do at that point since Søren's knowledge and experience are still useful. The obstacles are due, in part, to Søren's repressive defences that make it impossible to talk about the real problems (i.e., their emotional aspects) and, in part, to his colleagues' lack of empathy with Søren's situation and his feelings. Their lack of empathy is due to the fact that, over time, in addition to respect and dependence, his colleagues have harboured an irritation at Søren's zealousness at work and envy of his unlimited expertise and latitude. They come to express these feelings through indirectly aggressive (hurtful and insensitive) conduct toward Søren. The lack of empathy is also due to the fact that Søren's retirement activates the existential dilemmas in his colleagues. They all know that, one day, they will be standing in Søren's shoes, and this creates anxiety, which can be repressed by not connecting emotionally with it. The same repressive reaction can arise in co-workers when a colleague is fired, becomes seriously ill, loses someone close, or in some other way arouses unconscious anxiety.

Differences in individual maturity

Social constructivists believe that personality is constantly shaped by the relationships into which the individual enters. However, psychodynamic theory indicates that, beyond these relationships, the individual is also shaped by internal relationships that one has, so to speak, with oneself.

The individual's inner self, therefore, constitutes an independent subsystem of which it is necessary to have a theoretical understanding.

As mentioned before, the individual and the group may be viewed as a hierarchy of systems (see Figure 3.1). The first subsystem is each individual's internal,

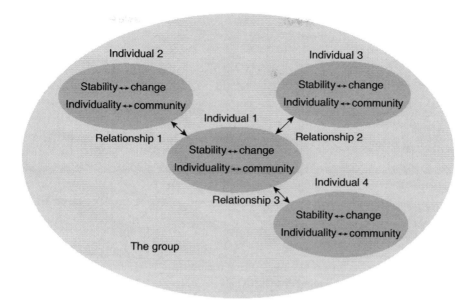

FIGURE 3.1 The group constitutes a hierarchy of systems, which consists of three subsystems in a mutual relationship

contradictory psyche. The second subsystem is each individual's distinct, contradictory relationships with other individuals. The third subsystem is the group as a whole. All three systems have independent dynamics and cannot be reduced to each other. In this hierarchy of systems, both the relationships between individuals and the relationships within individuals have significance for how cooperation in the group plays out. It is not enough to focus entirely on relationships between individuals. One must also study the individual's internal system in his/her struggle to understand the dynamic processes that take place in cooperation, since these processes provide the framework for how cooperation can develop in the long run.

In the study of the individual's internal system, the way in which the individual uses these psychological defences plays an important role with respect to how the person in question cooperates and is able to participate and contribute to the group, as the case with Søren demonstrates.

Psychological defences may be viewed as a sort of filter between the psyche and its surroundings. The effect of this filter is a simplified, internal understanding that makes one's surroundings and one's own reactions to them easier to survey and, therefore, causes less ambivalence and anxiety. The filter or the defence may assume many different forms. Not all psychological defences are equally beneficial for a given individual at a given level of development in a given situation. Some defences will seem too limiting to the individual's opportunities for developing, learning from mistakes, and conquering new territory. For example, it is difficult to learn from a mistake that one denies having committed ("It's someone else's fault"). The

38 The employee in the community

denial may be necessary to keep from crushing the individual's psyche in shame and self-contempt. But it is also conceivable that a denial was once necessary but is no longer and, to the contrary, that it seems to be inhibiting increased self-insight. In that case, the denial will lead to anxiety because the person knows deep down that he/she has made a mistake and is afraid of being discovered, and because the denial leads to an experience of a lack of authenticity and alienation in relation to the internal self. The denial can lead to an experience of being out of contact with oneself.

A certain level of defence is necessary to remain psychologically healthy and well-functioning because it serves to "keep the psyche together", but the price for avoiding anxiety, doubt, and paralysis can also be too high. If one's understanding of reality becomes too unequivocal, too narrow, and too fixed, one's grasp on reality is weakened and, thus, also one's ability to act because reality contains many different interpretations and possibilities. This constitutes a paradox: the psychological defences, whose purpose is to dampen anxiety and prevent paralysis, may in themselves (if they harden at an inappropriate level) lead to increased anxiety and a limitation of options. This situation arises if the defences do not mature in tandem with the individual becoming older and acquiring more experience and with the demands for the individual to change (Handest et al. 2003: 17–19). Moreover, the defences consume psychic energy. It is fatiguing to maintain a defence, and this fatigue may in itself be a source of anxiety. When the defence no longer works as well and when it consumes too much psychic energy to maintain it, it can be a sign that the individual is in the process of "growing out of it" and is ready to use other, more mature defence mechanisms

The immature person's defences lead to a simplified picture of the person him/herself and of the surrounding world. Such a simplified picture may exclude, for example, unpleasant feelings ("I am never jealous") or divide up the world into simplified categories ("Denmark is the world's best welfare state", "All Muslims are terrorists"). The more mature person possesses sufficient resources to create a nuanced, internal picture of him/herself and the world. In this picture, more complex feelings appear ("I am jealous of her, but I'm also happy for her"), and the world is categorised in a less simplified way ("The Danish welfare state is good in some areas but also has some weaknesses"), because ambivalence is better tolerated.

Psychological defence mechanisms develop in such a way that they increasingly allow more latitude on both sides of the dilemma. Increasing psychological maturity may be said to entail that one allows oneself both a greater degree of individuality and a greater degree of affiliation with the community. Correspondingly, the more stable one is in one's life and the more coherently one experiences it, the easier it is for one to accept change in it because it takes more to threaten one's stability. There is still a constant weighing of the two sides of the dilemmas, but the spectrum for feelings, understanding, interpretation, and action is greater in the mature person.

The more mature a defence is, the better it can contain emotional confusion and the ambiguity of reality. People who are normally considered as mature, stable people are people with effective psychological defence mechanisms.

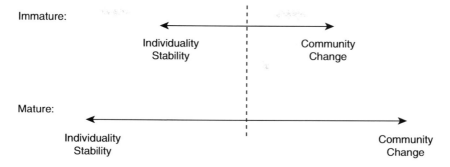

FIGURE 3.2 The development of a greater span between the dilemmas in tandem with the psychological process of maturation

The better a defence is, on the one hand to protect the psyche and on the other hand to allow the individual maximal development – that is, the greater the span between the existential dilemmas the defence allows – the more effective the defence can be said to be. "Effective" is understood to mean that the defence provides good guidance to how the world can be understand and how one can act in it. The more nuanced one's understanding of the world is, the better one can exploit the many possibilities life offers. Thus, the maturity of psychological defences is directly connected to how much each person gets out of life and how the individual is able to engage in an interaction with other people. Therefore, the concept of psychological maturity is essential to understand the dynamic of cooperation with a view toward developing a more effective and satisfactory cooperation.

Different levels of maturity

Defence mechanisms serve to control emotions and, as described in the previous chapter, it is an important part of human socialisation – that is, admission into the community – to learn to control one's emotions and impulses. On the one hand, emotions are the individual's primary source for orienting oneself in the world; and on the other hand, they influence the individual's ability to relate in a nuanced way in this encounter. A rich, faceted emotional life to which one has good but controlled access gives the individual the best preconditions for living a satisfactory life; whereas, for example, exaggerated fear can make one overlook possibilities; overwhelming sorrow can make one close oneself off from all other impressions; and in manic joy, one can lose one's sense of reality.

In principle, there are three ways to relate to one's emotions:

1. One can act impulsively on one's instinctive feelings.
2. One can control one's feeling by ignoring, denying, reshaping, or repressing them.
3. One can control one's feelings by accepting and integrating them.

40 The employee in the community

In order to be able to assess better the maturity of psychological defences and to work on maturing them in the individual and group context, a number of theoreticians have postulated a division of the defences into different levels of maturity (Klein 1977; Kernberg 1980; Halton 2003). This division corresponds in broad outline to the three ways of relating to emotions mentioned above and derives from this vision different developmental theories of how the personality develops throughout an individual's lifetime. Some of the theories have also been developed to include groups and organisations, which clearly makes them relevant when it comes to the relationship between manager and employees (Kernberg 1998; Alsted 2005; Bion 2006 [1961]).

In this book, three levels of maturity are used to describe individual and collective maturity (Alsted 2005):

1 Splitting
2 Repression
3 Integration.

The three levels are described in more detail in the following subsections.

Splitting

The fundamental mechanism in splitting is to make complex reality manageable in the simplest possible way – namely, by splitting it into the good and the bad. In modern terms, one could call this a binary defence, since "binary" refers to the system used in computers, which only contains the values 1 and 0. This mode of dividing and categorising the world is basic for all people, especially for infants. It is fundamental – and belongs developmentally to the earliest psychological skills – to be able to distinguish among experiences that are a source of satisfaction and (physical or psychological) pleasure and experiences that are a source of (physical or psychological) pain or anxiety.

The world contains both pleasure and pain in all possible combinations and nuances. The binary or splitting defence provides a way to endure the ambivalence to which reality gives occasion when the psyche responds to the world. The psyche is protected against the pressure of ambivalence by splitting the understanding of one's internal world and the surrounding world. Some phenomena are categorised as exclusively good, others as exclusively bad or evil. The self and the world are experienced in black and white, and the many nuances of colour are lost. On the other hand, the picture is sharp and clear.

What sounds like a simple defence mechanism, however, may have a complex expression in practice. This is seen, inter alia, in the defence called projective identification, which is described next on the basis of Steen Visholm's very clear account of projective identification (Visholm 2004d):

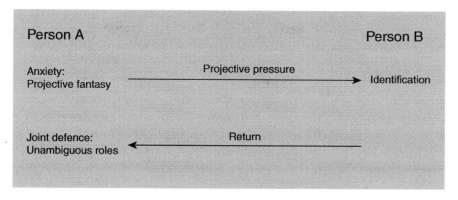

FIGURE 3.3   Example 1: projective identification

Person A has an anxiety to which he cannot relate consciously and which he, therefore, unconsciously tries to get rid of by splitting. For example, it may be a feeling of incompetence in relation to his work. Person A develops a projective fantasy that the problem is to be found in person B. This fantasy is then communicated – still unconsciously – through a projective pressure. The projective pressure may be very subtle and difficult to see through. This can happen through body language, or it may be that, through eye contact, A shows impatience (flickering or no eye contact with B) or judgment (critical, observing looks while A is listening to B). But a projective pressure can also be communicated more directly through an outburst of anger, disparagement, flirting, and so forth.

In this example, in which A has an unconscious anxiety about being incompetent, A will presumably greatly emphasise his own professional qualities and consistently overlook B's. If B has a corresponding unconscious anxiety about using his skills, the projection has a good chance of being accepted by B, who will identify with what is being projected. B will allow himself to be influenced by A's projective fantasy through the way A communicates it and view himself as incompetent. On the other hand, B will experience A as very competent, and he will communicate this back to A in a return process, which takes place through means just as discreet and indirect as A used.

B confirms A's representation of himself as very competent and stifles his own qualities in order to fulfil the role of incompetency he accepts in the projective identification. Thus A and B have established a joint psychological defence. It is easy to orient oneself toward and to understand this defence: A is competent; B is incompetent. As such, this is a clear expression of splitting: one is good; the other is bad. A has split off his anxiety about incompetence, while B has split off his competence and escaped his anxiety about the defence that follows from having to use one's skills. Both parties profit from the joint defence they have constructed, albeit it must be kept in mind that the whole process takes place unconsciously for both parties.

But this rigid role division is presumably a poor reflection of the real division of skills between A and B. The probability is that both have their competent

42 The employee in the community

and incompetent sides. At the same time, the division of roles leads to both A and B losing contact with important sides of their personality and that they are prevented from working on their respective problems because consciousness of this is projected away from the person himself. The anxiety does not disappear but is projected onto the other.

Splitting may appear in countless other ways than in the preceding example. Two widespread forms of splitting are *demonisation* and *idealisation*. Demonisation happens when a person is represented as thoroughly bad or evil. This often happens in public life – for example, politicians and criminals are commonly demonised. On the other hand, there is an exaggerated idealisation when a person is represented as a genius, flawless, totally sexy, and so forth. There are countless examples of this in the media world in which, for example, actors, rock musicians, and royalty are obvious targets for such idealisations.

However, this form of splitting frequently appears in organisational contexts as well. Managers are good targets for projection – demonisation as well as idealisation – and employees can be designated as stars or scapegoats, respectively. Therefore, we shall return to splitting and the many different forms it can take in groups and organisations in future chapters.

Repression

Repression is a more mature defence. Through repression, what is anxiety-inducing is not split off but is banished from consciousness. Repression represents a higher level of maturity in relation to splitting, because anxiety is not split off but unconsciously acknowledged as one's own anxiety and not another person's malice or genius. The protection consists in not being conscious of the anxiety.

It is both the anxiety-inducing and the repression processes that are repressed. Thus, one does not know that one is repressing. But the repressed material is constantly activated in the unconscious and appears in a distorted form, such as in (Abrahamowitz 2001: 78):

- Dreams
- Slips of the tongue
- Systematic forgetfulness in certain areas
- Symbols with unconscious content.

Repression is not the same thing as forgetting. Forgetting includes events that do not have a decisive meaning for a person, whereas repression is linked to events and feelings with great importance for the person in question (Abrahamowitz 2001: 78). There are other types of repressive defence mechanisms, all of which have in common that the person is not brought into direct contact with what is anxiety-inducing. Some examples are:

Rationalisation: Providing emotionally false but rational or generally acceptable reasons for one's actions or points of view. For example, one says:

"Unfortunately, I haven't had time to do the job" and repress that the real reason is that one is afraid of not being able to do it well enough.

Avoidance/distancing: Avoiding taking a position on internal, emotional conflicts by not confronting them. This can be done in many ways, for example, by falling asleep before a spouse wants to have sex, by forgetting meetings one fears may be unpleasant, by distancing oneself from a judgmental sweetheart, or by changing jobs every time it begins to become problematic.

Projection: Transferring internal, emotional states to persons, things, or phenomena (e.g., "management" as an abstract concept, not as specific persons). But the object of the projection is not experienced as completely dominated by what is projected as it is in projective identification because the object does not identify with the projection. By projection, one achieves a temporary relief and control of one's internal state. For example, one projects one's anxiety about saying something stupid: "The teacher probably thinks what I say is stupid", whereby the teacher becomes the temporary bearer of one's anxiety.

Let's look at the example of person A's anxiety about incompetence again but, this time, to illustrate a repressive defence mechanism. If A has some control over his anxiety (i.e., if he is so mature that he can repress it instead of splitting it off), his anxiety will be less, and the projection pressure from A onto B will, correspondingly, be less massive. One can imagine that A will project his anxiety in the form of great demands for the quality of the work being done and that he will be a perfectionist on his own and B's behalf. If B still has a corresponding anxiety about using his skills and if B can also repress his anxiety, he may experience a brief fear of not being able to live up to A's demands and try to repress this fear by suggesting that they set up some common rules for how the job is to be done. A and B have now constructed a joint psychological defence in the form of rules for doing the job that serve to repress and "store" their joint anxiety. Thus, they both avoid coming into contact with unpleasant feelings because, as long as they follow the rules, the work is by definition good enough and arouses no conscious anxiety.

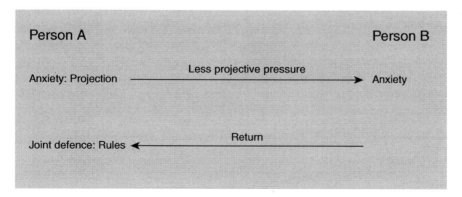

FIGURE 3.4 Example 2: projection

44 The employee in the community

The difference between the two examples of, respectively, projective identification and projection illustrates well why repression is a more mature and effective defence in the sense that it allows the individual a greater latitude and better exploitation of his abilities. The sharp division in example 1 with A as thoroughly talented and B as completely useless does not advance or develop either of the parties. A set of common rules for the execution of the work as in example 2, however, provides both A and B a better opportunity to contribute to the job – even though it remains within the framework of a set of rules. The rules lessen the risk of conflict and ensure coordination in the performance of the task, so A and B together become more productive. If B, as in the first example, is directed solely to look upon A with admiration, it bolsters the anxiety of both of them even more – A's anxiety about not doing well enough and B's about not using his skills. At the same time, it means a poorer exploitation of their resources and, thus, poorer overall productivity.

The cost of repression is that one isolates oneself from one's own emotional life and, thus, has difficulty orienting oneself in the world and understanding one's own reactions. The consequences of too much repression (which is to say, more repression than necessary), therefore, include:

- A feeling of hopelessness
- Boredom
- Fatigue
- Lack of creativity
- Lack of initiative
- Stress
- Lack of flexibility.

Integration

Integration represents a further maturation of psychological defences. Under repression's protective cape, even more sides of a conflict-filled emotional life can be integrated. One cannot say that repressions disappear, but more of them are made conscious. The result, among other things, is that the tendency to project one's internal state onto others is reduced somewhat even though it presumably never disappears entirely from human interaction. People who enter into relationships with each other are often so closely interwoven that it can be difficult to say precisely where one's feelings begin and the other's stop.

Integration can be defined as the ability to maintain contact both with the pain and the joy that life contains. Integration does not lead to fewer conflicts but, to the contrary, more conflicts – both internally and between people precisely because of the improved emotional contact. In this way, the individual and the group acquire better access to the energy located in the conflicts and the emotions linked to them.

Tolerance for ambivalence becomes greater, and one becomes less afraid of emotions (one's own and those of others). It might also be said that integration is an expression of an invigoration of the ego's ability to create compromises between

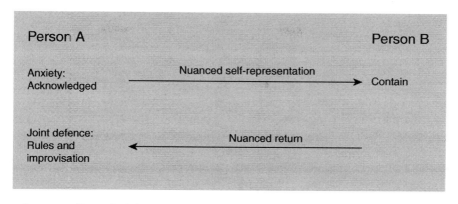

FIGURE 3.5 Example 3: integration

the self and the world. Some speak in this connection about a strengthening of the self (Kernberg 1976: 223). The individual experiences him/herself as a more coherent and less sensitive to collective norms that have a destructive impact on the individual. At the same time, one's relationship with the community becomes deeper and stronger (Lyth 1989: 43). The well-integrated person has the ability to be able to see him/herself simultaneously as a unique person and as an ordinary member of the community, which broadens the span in the dilemma between individual and community. The feeling of being more coherent and more whole makes the individual more receptive to change, which strengthens the person's ability to be in the dilemma between stability and change.

Let's look at the example of A's anxiety about incompetence for the third time, this time to illustrate an integrative defence mechanism. If A has so much contact with his anxiety that he can acknowledge and formulate it to himself instead of splitting or repressing it, his projection pressure on B will be minimal. One can imagine that he will tell B about his anxiety but without trying to have B take it over or assume it. At the same time, he will be able to be confident in the areas in which he feels competent. If, correspondingly, B can acknowledge his own anxiety, he will not feel discomfort at A's anxiety but recognition. He can express his own understanding and relate corresponding problems he himself has had. In the jargon, it is said that B mirrors and contains A's anxiety. B is neither pained by it, nor does he try to trivialise or explain away A's feelings. Instead, he accommodates them by showing his acceptance of them. A more honest and relevant communication between the parties is now open, and B can thereafter offer help to A and suggest procedures for doing their job.

In this example in which A and B are able to relate to what is unpleasant as well as what is pleasant about their job and find a common solution, integration frees even more productive powers than repression did. In example 2 with repression, A and B had to establish a common set of rules to be able to deal with the ambivalence. In terms of how much productive energy the defences liberate, however, it

46 The employee in the community

is advantageous if the persons can establish a cooperation that is based on certain rules but, at the same time, can relate flexibly to these rules and find other, creative solutions where the rules do not apply.

It happens frequently in modern organisations that the rules are not practical because the production in some areas is not suitable to governance by rules. This is due in part to the nature of the task (e.g., services that may be too individual to be governed by rules or knowledge-based contributions that may be too complex for governance by rules) and in part to the fact that requirements and conditions frequently change. The nature of the tasks and the increasing rate of change together continually give rise to unforeseen events and new problems. The requirement for the individual and for the mutual cooperation of the employees is to solve problems effectively and flexibly. But in order to do that, a high degree of mutual trust among the parties and a common understanding of what the task requires are needed. Therefore, modern organisations – if they are to be productive and, at the same time, pleasant to work in – require well-functioning relations among the participants and loyalty to the goals of the organisation. In psychodynamic terminology, one can say that modern organisations require a high degree of psychological integration.

Well-functioning relationships and loyalty

It is not accidental that words such as "trust" and "loyalty" appear in the core values of many businesses. Businesses are aware that trust and loyalty are fundamental preconditions for good cooperation. However, trust and loyalty are emotional traits or states that exist within and between people. Therefore, they are difficult to control and maintain. They are fragile states that can suddenly be jeopardised by events that, seen from the outside, seem small and insignificant. This is demonstrated in the following case.

> A business has a core values statement in which the words "trust" and "loyalty" appear several times. At a personnel seminar, where the implementation of core values is to be discussed, the mood is positive and optimistic, especially after the CEO's address in which he encourages everyone to show openness and mutual respect.
>
> Later in the day, the good atmosphere leads to an employee from a team working with the company's travel expenses to relate a bit hesitantly and shyly how the team finds that the rest of the organisation does not really respect their work.
>
> People listen attentively to the statement, but the CEO, who is leading the seminar, says that this point falls outside the agenda the planning group set. Therefore, he suggests that the team speak to their team leader about the problem.

> Suddenly, the good atmosphere evaporates. The employee abruptly sits down and says no more that day. The other seminar participants look uncomfortably down at the table. The travel expenses team members sit around the same table and exchange telling looks. An hour before the seminar is over, they leave the meeting with a remark that they are just too buried with work!
>
> Afterwards, one of the team members says that she has lost all trust in the CEO: "He's just spouting empty words".

It takes very little in some cases for trust and thereby also loyalty to be damaged. In this case, it is significant that the team is a group that already has problems with their trust of other employees and their affiliation with the organisation, which is why they are influenced by a splitting type of defence. However, they were actually on the way toward feeling a little more trust thanks to the discussion of values and because of the good atmosphere at the seminar. At that point, however, it was a vulnerable feeling susceptible to very small rebuffs. The CEO's suggestion to take the issue up with the team leader was experienced by the team (and by the rest of the seminar participants) as a rebuff, even though it was not actually meant that way by the CEO. He just did not know what he was supposed to do with the remark, and he was nervous that it would spoil the good atmosphere. The effect of the perceived rebuff was for the team to regress to the splitting defence. The team then isolates itself in the feeling they are being attacked by the rest of the organisation, and the CEO is demonised. This quite literally leads to the team "leaving" the organisation by walking out early, resulting in major cooperation difficulties between the team and the rest of the organisation in the period after the seminar.

Trust and loyalty, on the one hand, are decisive for the quality of cooperation and productivity, and on the other hand they are fragile and complicated feelings to construct and maintain. The process begins already when the individual comes into contact for the first time with the organisation, which is the subject of the next chapter: the individual's acceptance into the community.

4

ACCEPTANCE OF NEW EMPLOYEES INTO THE ORGANISATION

In Scandinavia, the individual is socialised from an early age into an institutional framework through nursery school, kindergarten, school, and so forth. Therefore, the individual acquires great experience in what it means to be in an organisation and a part of a greater whole. Nevertheless, for most people, it is a difficult transition when they first enter into a new workplace. The difference between the previous organisations with which the individual has experience and a new workplace is that, from nursery school to university, it is all about the individual's personal "project" – that is, a project within the framework of a community in which one learns consideration and cooperation but in which the goal is the individual's development and education.

Things are different in a workplace whose primary goal is not the development and education of the individual but for the employee to work for the primary goals of the organisation. Thus, the individual becomes a means for the organisation and not the goal in itself. For the employee who goes into the labour market for the first time, this will be experienced as a crucial shift in focus from the individual to a "larger" goal whereby one is drawn into the vision of the group (Hogg 1992). However, the shift may also give rise to insecurity, confusion, and performance anxiety: "What am I expected to provide to this firm, can I do what is expected, and can I do it well enough?" (Andersen & Riis 2016). Insecurity and performance anxiety are mitigated for most people as they acquire greater experience in the labour market, but almost all new employees will have a touch of it, and insecurity and performance anxiety often appear again in connection with major changes at the workplace.

That individuals are not goals in themselves, however, does not mean that the development and flourishing of the individual is without significance. As mentioned, the modern organisation is based to a high degree on the fact that its members are well-qualified and motivated, but this means that the dilemma between individual and community changes character. On one hand, there are great demands at the workplace on the individual's ability to coordinate (and, in certain cases, subordinate) his/her personal project in relation to the tasks and goals of the firm. On the other hand, there are great demands on the firm to include the individual's project (the individual employee's qualifications, ambitions, and hopes) and to be able to accommodate and use the unique personality of each employee in question (Alsted & Haslund 2016: chap. 1; Geus 1997: 190–192).

The encounter between individual and organisation

Previous chapters have described some of the phenomena – motivation, existential dilemmas, and psychological defence mechanisms – that are significant for how individual and organisation function together. Taking its starting point in these theories, this chapter will look at what happens in connection with the acceptance of new employees into a business and how the process can best be handled. One's initial period in a job can have long-term consequences for a new employee's relationships with colleagues and loyalty to the firm. As a result, it is a period that requires special attention from a manager. Since most businesses have a continuous turnover of employees, this means that there must always be a focus on the firm's ability to receive and integrate new employees.

As mentioned in Chapter 2, the individual has a dual relationship to communities, since the individual is both attracted and threatened by the community, and this becomes especially clear when the individual is to enter into a new community. On one hand, new employees will often have great expectations for their new workplace and will go out of their way to fit into the new community. On the other hand, such employees will be especially sensitive to threats against their individual identity and signs of not being accepted or respected by their new colleagues because the employees have not yet established a secure, independent identity in the workplace and have not established trusting relationships with other people. During one's initial period at a firm, the existential dilemma between individual and community, therefore, takes on a more intense significance for the new employee. The same is true for the dilemma between stability and change since changing jobs inevitably leads to a period of great change and a lack of stability. A new employee is, thus, by definition a person under pressure, which increases the probability that the person in question for some time or in some situations regresses and uses immature psychological defences in the form of splitting or repression, as described in Chapter 3.

Social constructivist theory provides that individual and group mutually constitute each other (Berger & Luckmann 1966; Cooperrider & Srivastva 1987; Gergen 1990; Gergen 1999), which in this connection means that the community in the firm will influence and change the employee just as the existing community will change to a greater or lesser extent when a new employee arrives. Changes can be experienced as constructive or destructive, depending to a high degree on how the process is approached. The process depends in part on the existing level of maturity

50 The employee in the community

in the firm and the new employee's personal maturity and in part on how consciously management works with the acceptance of new members. Over the long term, the acceptance of new elements and impulses is decisive for whether the firm is kept alive and avoids stagnating (Geus 1997).

Like relational theory, psychodynamic theory believes that, in this way, participants have many opportunities to influence the development of the community. At the same time, psychodynamic theory believes that a part of this development takes place unconsciously and, therefore, that it cannot be controlled exclusively consciously – one can try to understand and integrate unconscious phenomena rather than control them (Heinskou & Visholm 2004).

Drawing on these theories, this chapter provides a number of examples and suggestions for how employment and integration of new employees can be done in the best possible way through a combination of systematic methods and psychodynamic understanding.

Employment is based on voluntariness

In the Western world, the employment relationship is voluntary. No one forces a job-seeker to take a job at a particular firm, and the employee may leave the firm at any time. Of course, market conditions in society and the employee's qualifications play a role in the degree of voluntariness because, in times of economic downturn, one may be forced to remain in one's job for economic reasons and the choices available to an unqualified person even in times of economic upturn may be limited. But, in principle, voluntariness is always present in the relationship between employee and company.

This principled freedom is fundamental for the relationship between employee and manager because it introduces a basic equality in their relationship despite the fact that, by definition, there is an asymmetrical power relationship. The employee chooses voluntarily to enter into this power relationship and retains the right to step out of the relationship the moment he or she no longer wishes to be in it (Kirkeby 2004: chap. 13). The firm has the same right not to employ the job-seeker or to part company with him/her. However, because of this asymmetrical power relationship, legislation, collective bargaining, and so forth come into the picture, providing employees a certain protection, so the job-seeker is not discriminated against or subjected to arbitrary or unreasonable treatment.

There may be many reasons for a person to accept employment at a given firm, but people seek employment at a certain place for a combination of material, social, and psychological motives. For example, they may need an income of a certain size, may have a favourable impression of the firm and view it as an attractive, prestigious place to work, may want the social contacts that the job provides, or perhaps see a job at a particular firm as an opportunity for personal growth or career development.

New employees come on board with a variety of different motives in their baggage, but they all have one thing in common: in the given situation, they have chosen a side in the dilemma between stability and change in favour of change. This means that they find themselves in a vulnerable situation. Anxiety about the new position and not being up to the job and the anxiety about having chosen wrongly may be quite dominating feelings during their initial period, and – in combination with the threat to personal identity – this predisposes the employee to regressive behaviour affected by immature psychological defences even though the employee has entered voluntarily into the new community.

Employment is based on mutual trust

Formally, it is the employee seeking a job in the firm and the employer who hires the employee or does not. However, in today's reality, the assessment goes both ways. The employee can just as easily turn down a job. During periods in which there is a high demand for labour, the hiring procedure is turned upside down, so the firm actively seeks out potential employees and encourages them to take the job.

Because of this development, job interviews have changed from what once was an examination – or, in certain cases, an outright interrogation – of the job-seeker to a forum for mutual exchange in which both parties try to assess whether they can get their requirements and expectations fulfilled. Thus, an understanding of the mutual interdependence of the individual and the community has increased in society generally, and this is also true in the employment situation.

The most important tools for a successful job interview are experience, intuition, and knowledge about the context in which the job-seeker is to function. Basically, however, a job – like most other human relationships – must be built on mutual trust (Scheuer 1998: chaps. 2 and 11). In addition, there must be a will from both the firm and the job-seeker to provide as realistic picture of themselves as possible.

The employment situation invites both parties to present themselves at their best. This can be problematic because, in a future cooperation, it is unavoidable that less attractive sides will also come out. In order to get a more realistic impression of the job-seeker, therefore, it has become common for firms to ask what the applicant's strong and weak sides are. However, the question presumes two things that are not necessarily the case, namely, that the applicant actually recognises his/her own strengths and weaknesses and that the applicant is willing to talk about them in this special and very sensitive situation.

Much of the information that is relevant for businesses to know about an applicant cannot be checked because it is context dependent. Even though an applicant has been fired from a previous job due to disagreements with his/her boss, it is far from certain that there will also be problems in the new job with a different boss. The problems in the previous job may have been caused by specific conditions between the employee and the boss. If an applicant had low productivity in a job as a salesperson in an IT firm, this does not necessarily say anything about how the applicant will function in a government office. It may have been anything from a

52 The employee in the community

lack of sales skills to poor management or a terrible work environment that produced low productivity in the old job. Systemic theory stresses that the same person can function completely differently in new contexts (Haslebo 2004: chap. 9). So, it is a matter of getting a sense for what the new framework in one's firm may bring out in an applicant.

With respect to the applicant's ability to form a realistic impression of the firm, it, too, is limited. Only the fewest applicants have the courage to ask outright critical questions at a job interview. There is a danger one may come off as cantankerous or a potentially difficult employee if too many deep-boring questions are raised. Moreover, it can be difficult to know what the critical questions actually are when the applicant does not know the firm from the inside. Therefore, many applicants desist from asking problematic questions and try instead to give an enthusiastic and engaged impression of themselves (Scheuer 1998: chap. 6).

Both parties must reconcile themselves to the fact that many things cannot be cleared up in advance and that they must first be experienced before they can be evaluated. Instead, the participants must use their intuition to sense whether there is a basis for trust between the parties. Sometimes, the intuition is wrong, and the choice must be taken up for review again. This problem is dealt with in more detail in the section on the use of an initial period.

The emotional subtext of the job interview

In addition to focusing on the specific content of the job interview (i.e., the firm, the job, and the applicant's own qualifications), an applicant will also get a feel for the interview's emotional subtext: is the office space friendly or hostile, is the atmosphere pleasant or tense, do the members of the hiring committee seem to get along, or are there open or hidden conflicts between them, have they prepared for the interview, how is the tone between the manager and the employees, and does the applicant generally feel well-received and heard?

A large part of the applicant's emotional attention will be turned specifically toward the manager. The applicant will be focused on how he seems to the manager and how the manager seems to him. Does she seem credible and confidence-inspiring, does she seem like a boss who is loyal to her employees, does she seem competent, does she radiate authority, is she visionary, is she grounded, does she listen, does she seem positive toward the applicant? Or, to the contrary, does she hasten to talk about her own superiorities? Does she seem insecure and withdrawn? The applicant is not necessarily conscious of all these observations and their importance to him, but they give him an intuitive gut feeling about the job and the people he is to work with. Therefore, the impression of the manager plays a decisive role. This intuitive sense can be quite crucial to whether an applicant decides to take a job offer or not.

If the applicant focuses especially on the manager, it is because the manager primarily defines the emotional atmosphere of the interview and because, during the course of the conversation, the applicant must decide whether he wants to enter into a power relationship with this manager. Through her verbal and non-verbal conduct, the manager demonstrates her personal interpretation of the emotional "rules" that govern this firm – namely, *what* can be said, *how* it can be said, what can*not* be said, and what emotional states are linked to all this. The other participants in the interview (including the applicant) unconsciously orient themselves towards the manager on these points in this pre-existing distribution of roles. If the manager laughs, she creates a cheerful atmosphere; if the manager looks surly, an oppressive or nervous atmosphere prevails in the locale; if the manager is taciturn, the conversation becomes less dynamic; if the manager avoids topics of possible conflict, the other members of the hiring committee and the applicant will probably do so as well, and so forth. Since the applicant is visiting, it is the firm's communicative rules that govern, and it would be inappropriate and a display of a lack of social intelligence (Goleman 2006) if an applicant was firing off jokes while the manager kept a serious demeanour while going through the firm's core values or performance contract.

The applicant's conscious and unconscious observations help him to read and interpret the manager's emotional rule set and form the basis for the applicant's willingness or lack thereof to surrender a part of his personal sovereignty to the manager.

On its side, the company (represented by the manager and the hiring committee) tries, as long as the short interview lasts, to form an impression of the applicant "as a person". Of course, they also ask about formal, professional qualifications and skills but, since these are often known in advance through the written job application and have formed the basis for inviting the person for an interview, the primary purpose of the interview is, in reality, something else. The company wants to meet the person behind the application and assess whether this person is suitable for the job (Scheuer 1998: chap. 2). If this were not the case and only the formal qualifications meant anything, the company could be satisfied with hiring employees on the basis of a written application and school diplomas, but that happens quite rarely.

It is a common mistake in job interviews for the manager or others on the hiring committee to talk too much in relation to the applicant, which weakens the firm's opportunity to form an impression of the applicant. Moreover, there is a risk that it gives the applicant an impression that, at base, the firm does not have room for him as an individual and is not really interested in him as a person.

But even if the firm goes out of its way to listen to the applicant, the question remains of how one manages to assess the applicant's human qualities during one or two conversations. The answer is that it cannot be done. Most firms try to do it anyway by asking personal questions and, perhaps, also by giving the applicant some tasks and thereby assessing answers and solutions in accordance with a more or less structured method. The most structured method in this connection is the personality test, which many firms use. Others are satisfied with asking about formal qualifications in order to form an impression of the person in question, whereupon the committee has an unstructured discussion after the interview of whether the applicant fits the job, based on the rough impressions the participants formed.

54 The employee in the community

Often, it turns out that the hiring committee – regardless of what method it uses – is surprisingly in agreement about whom they will select out of a large number of applicants. This is thought-provoking and might indicate that, before, during, and after the interview, there is an unconscious coordination among the committee members that is based on feelings and intuition to just as high a degree as on facts and methods.

The parallel company

Anyone who has experienced it knows that it can be incredibly difficult for firms as well as applicants to assess in advance what you are getting into. The company may be inclined to oversell both the firm and the job either because the manager does not have a realistic view of how the company actually functions or how the job in question really gets done. It may also be because the manager or the committee presents the applicant with a picture that is more wishful thinking than actual conditions. The latter is illustrated in the following case.

> An experienced employee has the job of showing the firm to new applicants and telling them about the very modern principles they work with. Since the firm is expanding, there are often job interviews, and the employee has become good at doing these presentations.
>
> In the period shortly after being hired, however, it frequently happens that the new employee expresses disappointment about how it actually is to work at the firm in relation to the view they received at the presentation. They do not think things function at all in the way they were told.

The employee who was responsible for the presentations gradually realised that he had come up with a story about the company that did not exist in reality. He had not done it consciously or with ill intent, but because he wanted to do his job to management's satisfaction and because "I was myself seduced by my own story. It sounded so good!"

Many businesses are inclined to operate with such a parallel version of how their firm functions, and this parallel version is often drawn on, in particular, in a hiring situation. It makes the firm appear as more goal-oriented, better organised, more visionary, more coherent, and so forth than it is in practice. In this way, the parallel version comes to function like a repressive defence mechanism, which protects the firm as well as the applicant against the complexity of reality. This defence may be necessary to a certain degree because it serves to overcome some of the anxiety the situation contains. It diminishes the applicant's anxiety about chaos and making the wrong choice, and it diminishes the firm's anxiety about appearing incompetent and incapable of living up to its own image or attracting new employees. But the construction of a parallel version that is *too* far from reality will hit both the firm and the applicant like a boomerang. Therefore, it is a matter of finding an appropriate balance between vision and reality.

Projective pressure and wishful thinking

A new job contains great opportunities for projections from both the firm and the applicant and for the use of magical thinking. If the position is a new one, the firm may have unclear, unrealistic, and perhaps mutually contradictory expectations for what the applicant is supposed to be able to do in the job. This same is true if there have been problems with previous employees in the position, because it is tempting for the firm to use a primitive defence mechanism (splitting) in which all blame is projected onto the previous employee and all hopes are projected onto the new (unknown and therefore "unstained") hire. Correspondingly, an experiment has shown that groups with too few employees will make lower demands on applicants than groups with many employees (Cini et al. 1993). This can place both the organisation and the new employee into a difficult situation.

Likewise, the applicant may have great but unsubstantiated hopes that everything will be better in this job and in this company, more well-functioning and less problematic than in his/her earlier job (Brown 2000: 26–27). Therefore, he or she will be receptive to the firm's slightly too rosy self-presentation. The applicant collaborates in this way with the firm by constructing a parallel version of the company, so that the parties jointly create an unconscious, collective defence. As mentioned, this sort of repressive defence mechanism may be necessary in order for the applicant to mobilise the courage to take on the position, but the defence will inevitably be challenged once things have settled into an everyday routine, as the following case shows:

> Erling, who is in his mid-fifties, is hired as head of development, which is a new position in a private firm. The position was established as a result of some serious conflicts a former manager had with the board of directors and employees. After a restructuring, it was hoped that the causes for these earlier conflicts had been eliminated.
>
> At the job interview, Erling finds it difficult to understand exactly what the new position entails, but he feels a lot of enthusiasm in the firm around the position and also meets with enormous personal good will from the executive board. Therefore, he gladly accepts the offer. Moreover, he wants to get away from his present position and does not believe that a man his age will get other offers very easily.
>
> His early period on the job is marked by continued good will from both parties, but Erling is still disturbed by the many bad stories about the former manager he has to listen to from other managers and employees. He feels that the firm is giving him indirect signals about what he must *not* do at the same

56 The employee in the community

> time that it is still unclear to him what he is actually expected to do. He tries to enter into a dialogue with the executive board and his employees about this but does not feel he has gotten any response.
>
> After some time, Erling begins to show stress symptoms despite the fact that he neither works overtime nor has excessively many tasks to do. So, he wonders whether this is the right job for him.
>
> At his performance review after six months on the job, Erling learns from his boss that he is incredibly well-liked but that some are little disappointed that his work efforts have not yet brought better results.

This firm has made use of the splitting defence in connection with problems with the former manager, the establishment of the new position, and the hiring of Erling. The firm has not processed and integrated the original problems but, instead, placed them unambiguously on the person of the former manager and the old structure. As a result of this splitting, expectations for the new position and for Erling's abilities are unambiguously positive, but the expectations are unformulated and diffuse, because they have not spoken about or analysed what the real causes of the problems were. Therefore, they cannot formulate a more precise description of the new job or their expectations for Erling's efforts. They just know what they do *not* want, namely, a repetition of the problems.

Splitting is also the reason that the organisation maintains the stories about the old manager and meets Erling with such good will. This good will, however, ends up making him nervous and stressed because it is clear neither to himself nor to the organisation what he is supposed to do to meet these expectations. The disappointment to which the manager gives expression at the performance review, therefore, is unavoidable and, first and foremost, a result of the organisation's lack of maturity and its lack of clarity about Erling's position and the organisation's internal problems.

Erling represses the warning signals he gets at the job interview that the job is not clearly defined and may be difficult to do. He does this because he needs the job. At the same time, he is seduced by the positive atmosphere around his person, and he unconsciously accepts the organisation's splitting of the "bad" manager and identifies with the projective pressure on him as the "good" manager. But Erling pays for this projective identification with increased anxiety, and so does the organisation. For Erling, the anxiety leads to stress, and he considers quitting; for the organisation, the anxiety leads to nervousness about being disappointed and history repeating itself. They sense that this could happen, but they do not understand why, and no one – neither the firm nor Erling – can orient themselves in the process. Therefore, they do not know what they need to do to improve the situation.

When Erling tries to deepen his understanding by asking more systematic and concrete questions about the experiences and conflicts in connection with the former manager, he is met with such remarks as: "We're going to look forward now and move on!" The organisation thus permits people to tell stories (in the form of gossip and backstabbing) about the former manager, but it has cut itself off from any real analysis and understanding of its own history. The completely understandable desire to look forward and move on functions here as a defence against conflicts that were experienced by the organisation's members as so destructive and intolerable that they cannot even deal with them. But the consequence of this defence is a lack of learning; and, therefore, the organisation – quite the contrary to the intention – will come to repeat its mistakes.

Some of the problems that arise in this case could be remedied or, at least, discovered earlier if the job interview between Erling and the firm had been characterised by a more open and direct communication. The firm could have been more open about the problems that formerly plagued the relevant position (even though they had not completely come to terms with causes and solutions), and Erling could have formulated to a higher degree his internal sense that the job was unclearly formulated and could be difficult to do. The following section provides a more in-depth analysis of the serious consequences unclear communication during the course of the job interview can have for later employment.

Different interpretations of the same interview

A job interview is a meeting between two parties who most often are not acquainted with each other and, therefore, cannot be expected to be attuned to each other in terms of language or other symbolic conduct. In other words, it is probable that the parties interpret the events and statements that play out in the conversation differently (Scheuer 1998: chaps. 3 and 4). At the same time, as previously stressed, it is a situation that primes both parties to use repressive defences that serve to eliminate themes of possible conflict from the conversation. This is reflected, inter alia, in the language that characterises job interviews, which is often positively charged but diffuse and unspecific – "I am very social", "We put great weight on creativity" – which increases the risk that the parties see something different in what is said (or unsaid). The following case shows how even small omissions and things left unsaid can lead to misunderstandings with wide-ranging consequences:

A younger man seeks employment at a shipping firm. At the job interview, he mentions that he is continuing his education for which his current employer is paying, and he would also like this to be the case in the new job. The manager replies that the firm looks very positively on continuing education. The applicant understands this as a statement that he can continue his education under the same conditions as in his current job and accepts the job offer.

Some months later after he Is hired, it turns out that the new firm will only pay half of the expenses for his education, since there is a firm policy in this area from which they will not deviate out of consideration of the other employees.

The new employee feels that his manager has not kept his promise from the job interview, which leads to such great mistrust between the parties that the employee quits his job before the end of the initial period.

58 The employee in the community

It may be wondered in this case that the manager did not at once tell the applicant that he could have half of his education paid. The manager did not because he was eager to hire the young man and did not want a conflict on this question; instead, he wagered that this payment issue would resolve itself along the way. Thus, he underestimated or ignored the significance (concrete and symbolic) it had for the applicant that his old employer paid for his entire education.

Correspondingly, it may be wondered why the employee did not ask about whether the positive attitude toward continuing education implied that the firm would pay for his entire education. This was because he unconsciously picked up on a certain ambiguity in the manager's reply and body language. In order to avoid a conflict in the otherwise agreeable atmosphere, the employee avoided asking for a more precise answer. To request a person (and, here, a person above you in the hierarchy) to express himself more specifically and precisely may seem aggressive and seem as if you are sowing mistrust in the person speaking. Only the fewest applicants want to appear aggressive and mistrustful.

The result of the interview was that the applicant and the manager left the meeting with two different expectations for how the applicant's education was to be financed. This later gave rise to serious problems between them.

When the employee realised what the firm's policy in this area was, he felt that the manager had deceived him and broken a promise that had not been clearly formulated but which the employee nevertheless viewed as an undertaking for full payment for his education. Since, according to the employee, the manager broke this promise, the employee lost confidence in the manager and had the impression that this breach must be because the manager was not satisfied with his performance. This made the employee feel insecure, and he therefore began to avoid the manager.

The manager sensed this and became insecure because he viewed the new employee as critical of him. The manager did not notice the symbolic meaning the employee attributed to the payment issue and the subsequent interpretation the employee had of the sequence of events. Both manager and employee thus felt insecure and transferred this insecurity to each other in the form of projective pressure, which was transformed into a projective identification. Consequently, they spoke less and less together, which increasingly strengthened the projective identification and bolstered them in their view of each other. As mentioned, this ultimately resulted in the employee quitting his job, but it could just as well have led to the employee being fired.

This is a good example of how repressive defence mechanisms, as they are used in the job interview in this case, can lead to communication becoming so unclear that the participants come under serious pressure and regress to ever more immature defences. The individuals in the case are especially predisposed to do this because the employee is new with all that implies in terms of pressure and because the relationship between manager and employee is new and, therefore, fragile and unplumbed.

Furthermore, the case illustrates how unclear communication provides space for fantasies and interpretations. What people do not know about each other they are inclined to replace with speculations, fantasies, and interpretations. Thus, the employee imagines that the manager will pay for his education even though the manager has not said this. But the problem is that the manager has not said that he will *not* pay, either. The employee fills this void in the communication with his own wishful thinking. When the manager finally says that he will not pay, the employee interprets this in light of his original fantasy and, therefore, views the refusal as a breach. Then, he speculates as to what this breach could be due to and answers himself with a fantasy that has roots in his own insecurity. This fantasy – that the manager is dissatisfied with him – he projects onto the manager and, thereafter, interprets everything the manager does in the light of this projection. The manager does the same thing: speculates, fantasises, projects, and interprets based on his own feelings.

Finally, the parties are frozen in an impossible situation, which has cost them great emotional resources and which they do not think they can get out of except by parting ways. If the manager, instead, had been more conscious of the significance of communicating clearly and openly, this case might have turned out differently. Both parties bear responsibility for the way it came out since each is responsible for his own communication, but the manager bears a special responsibility because the connection between manager and employee is based on an asymmetrical power relationship and because the new employee is in a far more vulnerable position than the manager. The manager defines the "tone" and, with his conscious and unconscious behaviour, demonstrates: this is how we communicate at this firm. A new employee wants to be (and must be) especially receptive to such demonstrations and will unconsciously adjust his own behaviour accordingly but will not correspondingly be able to adjust his internal emotional life, which – as the case shows – can give rise to serious conflicts that are emotional at their core.

The case indicates some important reasons why the job interview and the initial period in a firm are so fundamental. It is here the new member learns "rules of communication in the community", and these rules can be difficult to unlearn later – even though they prove to be inexpedient or wrong – because they are mainly acquired unconsciously. But it is also here the firm gets a chance to examine and renew itself through a supple and curious acceptance of new impulses. Thus, the case contains a number of possibilities for a positive influence on the firm. On the concrete level, for example, changes in procedure might be considered, so the firm shifts towards paying the whole education as a part of an expanded care of employees. Or there might be a discussion with employees on the reasons for only paying half of the education. This might also give employees a greater insight into management's prioritisation of employee development seen in the light of the economic possibilities, the firm's strategy, and so forth.

If the manager in the case had made use of just one of these possibilities, there is a good chance that the case would have had a more positive outcome. But he did

60 The employee in the community

not do this because he wanted to avoid the problematic payment issue for as long as possible and because, partly unconsciously, he picked up on negative signals from the employee which he had difficulties understanding. Therefore, he established a repressive defence in the form of an avoidance of the entire subject.

The symbolic contract

Through an employment contract, the firm offers and the new employee accepts a number of terms and conditions that are outwardly visible. This includes an agreement on job function, and it includes an agreement on wages and other employment conditions. As shown in the preceding case, the contract will potentially be an object of different interpretations by the firm and the employee once employment has begun. Therefore, it is a matter of being as concrete and precise as possible when the contract is entered into.

However, a number of less tangible but meaningful phenomena for which mutual acceptance and recognition are the most important thing also enter into the employment relationship.

Both parties show mutual recognition by entering into an employment contract. The firm recognises that the employee is who he says he is, that they believe he possesses the qualifications he says he has, and that they have positive expectations that he will be able to carry out the job in a satisfactory way. The new employee shows recognition of the firm as an organisation and shows confidence that the firm will live up to the terms and conditions they have offered. By accepting employment, the employee implicitly acknowledges the firm's goals (the purpose of the firm) as he interprets them, and he accepts the firm's identity and core values as he understands them at the time of employment. In return, the employee expects the agreed-upon terms and conditions to be fulfilled; and, as a rule, it will give rise to problems if the employee does not believe the terms and conditions are being fulfilled.

But as a new employee, one also has another less concrete but just as important expectation of being admitted into and accepted by the firm's community just as the firm has an expectation of loyalty and acceptance from the employee for the community and its premises.

It is not possible in advance to agree upon these types of mutual expectations. Therefore, they are not described in a formal contract, but it can be said that they constitute a symbolic contract between employee and firm. The symbolic contract is entered into at the same time as the formal contract but is only visible in the form of expectations that are rarely formulated directly. As a rule, the symbolic contract only becomes visible if the expectations are *not* fulfilled.

The compliance with or breach of the symbolic contract plays an important role for the course of the employment. However, since its assessment occurs on the basis of subjective and partially hidden mechanisms, there is rarely a focus on this problem: what expectations does the community have for the new employee, what is the employee ready to contribute, and what does the employee expect to get in return?

The symbolic contract has the nature of a trade or an exchange because the employee gives up some of his/her self-determination in order to receive in return the advantages of being in the community and because the firm offers the employee acceptance and protection in order thereby to receive loyalty and work effort. But if one of the parties feels cheated in the deal, this can lead to disappointment and bitterness for many years to come.

So, even though it can be difficult to formulate these expectations, one should nevertheless be aware of the meaning of the symbolic contract. The manager should be especially attentive to whether the employee feels included and accepted in the community early in his/her employment.

The importance of the initial period

It is common for employees to feel they were never given a "proper introduction" to their job and the firm, and this complaint does not only come from new employees but also employees who have been working there for many years. As new employees, they did not feel accepted; they did not feel that the existing organisation stopped for a moment and made room for them, and they felt it to be chaotic and confusing to manoeuvre without help. The way they experienced their initial period on the job had far-reaching consequences later for their general view of the firm and their place in it.

It is just as common to encounter firms in which there is an excellent introduction programme, but it turns out that the specific introduction of the individual does not go by the book but happens randomly and unsystematically. As a rule, management explains that this is due to lack of time but that it has the decided intention to make sure the next hiring goes differently and better. It may also be that the introduction programme has degenerated into a pure formality in which everyone, regardless of job and background, is run through a standard programme, which is ultimately not relevant for anyone but more like an irritating interruption of precious, early learning time. Still other firms have had plans for years to do an introduction programme but never get it done despite the fact that the programme in itself cannot be said to be very complicated or especially time-consuming to formulate.

So, why is it that something wanted by both parties nevertheless does not work as intended in many firms?

Of course, lack of time and other resources can play a role, but the most important reason may be found in the psychodynamic factors that sharpen the dilemma between individual and community when it comes to the admission of new individuals. Missing, fossilised, or capsized introductory programmes can all be seen as an expression of the fact that the firm has problems with this dilemma, because a new employee constitutes at one and the same time an opportunity for and a threat to the community (Brown 2000: 32). It is the maturity of the existing community that determines whether it will be opportunity or threat that dominates the reception of the new employee. The new employee's personal maturity also plays a role, but every new employee has to submit to a certain degree to unwritten rules and customs in the existing firm to be accepted by colleagues and management (see Levine & Moreland 1994: 319–320 for a review of factors that influence the reception of new employees).

62 The employee in the community

As a rule, a newly hired employee who does not display sufficient tact, empathy, and respect for the existing firm will have problems, but it is different from firm to firm what "sufficient" means. The more fragile the existing community seems to its members, the more new members will be required to adapt to be accepted and the greater the risk that participants will react with immature splitting defences and vice versa. The more mature a firm is, the better it will be to absorb new impulses because it will take more for the community to feel threatened; and, therefore, the probability that immature defences will be used is less. The following case describes a firm using a repressive defence whereby the management's lack of attention causes the firm to regress into more immature behaviour:

In connection with an acquisition, Bodil was transferred from the acquired firm's personnel department to the purchaser's personnel department. When Bodil arrived on the first day, a desk and a computer were ready for her. At a brief breakfast meeting, Bodil was introduced to her new colleagues and learned that Marianne would act as her mentor. Bodil and Marianne spent the rest of the day together taking care of practical things and going over the work tasks for which Bodil would be responsible. At the day's end, Marianne said that Bodil should feel free to come to her if she was in doubt about anything.

The next day, Bodil started on her projects. In the following days, she asked advice once in a while from Marianne or one of the others, but she primarily worked alone – partly because Marianne and everyone else were very busy.

Ten days later, a departmental meeting was held – the first in which Bodil participated. Bodil took the opportunity to speak and listed various things in the department's procedures that puzzled her. In her old firm, they did things differently, and perhaps they might learn something from her? She suggested that they tighten up procedures having to do with sick leave and purchase a new IT-based HR system. Her colleagues reacted defensively, explaining the reasons behind the existing procedures and systems. After a brief discussion, the boss interrupted and promised Bodil to consider her suggestions.

But Bodil heard nothing afterwards, and she did not see much of her boss.

After another month, Bodil met with her boss. She did not feel that her colleagues in the department liked her. She had a good relationship with Ruth and Michael, but she found that the others were indifferent to her, and some were even hostile. This was especially true of Hans, a young HR consultant. She thought he spoke down to her, ignored her, and criticised her work. She had also discussed it with Ruth, who agreed with her. The boss was surprised. He had not noticed anything. But he promised to take the matter up with Hans.

Hans confirmed to the boss that he avoided Bodil but only because he thought she was brusque and unpleasant.

Acceptance of new employees **63**

The firm does a number of things here to make Bodil feel welcome: the office was made ready for her; she was introduced to the others and welcomed with breakfast; and she was given a mentor. But everyone was busy, and Bodil felt alone. At the same time, she grieved over the loss of her old job, which she did not abandon voluntarily. Bodil protected herself against the emotional pressure with the help of a splitting defence. This regression is to be expected in her situation in which her old job identity is gone and her new identity has yet to be found. At the same time, she was not the one to choose the change, which makes it more anxiety-creating and leads to greater ambivalence. Therefore, she points out how things were better at her old firm, and she splits the personnel by idealising a few of them and demonising others. Her demonisation verges on the paranoid with respect to Hans, which says something about how poorly she is doing.

The dominant level of defence in the firm is repression. They do not relate to the difficult emotional situation Bodil is in but try to structure and arrange their way out of it. At the same time, they do not follow up properly on the introduction. Certainly, Bodil received a mentor, but Marianne does not actually have time for her. Might Marianne even be avoiding Bodil because she senses that Bodil is having a hard time? The mentor programme in the case is a good example of how structure can function as a repressive defence. The structure here is used as legitimisation that it is not necessary to talk to Bodil about how she is feeling emotionally.

Another way of formulating this is to say that structure can function as a sort of "receptacle" for psychological phenomena to which one does not want to relate consciously. This does not mean that structure is bad or can be done away with – a mentor programme, for example, can be a very good thing – but it does mean that it is not structure in itself that provides or solves problems. The decisive thing is the way participants use the structure. In this repressive organisation, the structure will typically be viewed as a goal and a solution in itself. For example, one "implements" a mentor programme, which may in practice only mean that people are given a title, and the expectation is that this will solve problems for new employees.

It is characteristic of repression that the colleagues did not inquire into the proposals Bodil made and that the boss promised to consider them but never got around to it. Moreover, these repressions nourished Bodil's splitting defence. Because repression makes for unclear communication, there is room for Bodil's fantasies that, at heart, the organisation does not want her or respect her. These fantasies originate in her own anxiety but are experienced by Bodil as belonging to the others.

Bodil's use of an immature defence activates a corresponding immature defence in some of her colleagues, who react to the projective pressure Bodil puts on everyone. Some only react with more avoidance (repression) – the boss, for example. Others identify with the projection, whereupon it becomes a projective identification and, thus, a regression in relation to the dominant level of defence.

It is no accident that Bodil (unconsciously) chooses Hans as a primary target for demonisation. Hans is a young man and more of an eager beaver than Bodil.

64 The employee in the community

Therefore, he is an obvious target for negative projection, because he is "something different" from Bodil. Hans identifies with Bodil's projection, and this sharpens the conflict between Bodil and Hans to such a degree that it becomes emotionally burdensome for them both and, at the same time, more difficult to work with because their views of each other stiffen.

Ruth likewise identifies with Bodil's projection as being the "good" colleague as opposed to the "bad" Hans. This means that Bodil's splitting defence now takes a concrete shape in the form of a split in the old personnel group in which Hans and Ruth previously – before Bodil's arrival – had a fine collaboration. If the split continues, it will presumably not be long before the problems will be visible in the department's productivity. Therefore, the situation cries out for management! The boss must give up his evasive leadership style and, instead, begin to uncover what is going on in the department through conversations with his employees. Thereafter, he can try to teach his employees to talk about this by taking the first step.

Preferably, the process should have begun long before Bodil came in the form of the manager's work on the group's maturity. He should have taught the group to confront conflicts and have given them language and concepts to do it with. Through his own behaviour, he should have shown them that emotions are important indications and conditions for how the collaboration in the department takes shape. Since the group decided to introduce a mentor programme, for example, he could have encouraged discussions of what problems there might be with this kind of programme psychologically. When it was clear that Bodil was to be transferred to the department, he could have called his employees' attention to the emotionally difficult situation in which Bodil stood and asked about their considerations and feelings on this. He could have had one or more conversations with Bodil before she began, in part, to strengthen their mutual relationship and, in part, to give her an opportunity to formulate and process her feelings in connection with the transfer. By speaking openly with the employees and with Bodil about what is difficult in the situation, the manager would have made it legitimate to speak about any difficulties that might arise in the initial period of Bodil's employment, and at the same time it would have directed attention to what would have had a preventive effect.

Even though the manager did not do any of these things before Bodil's arrival, he has to do something as the situation stands if he wants to avoid a plunge in the department's productivity, and employees begin to call in sick or quit. He should try to understand what is happening on a psychological and partially unconscious level with those involved and share this understanding with his employees.

Acceptance of the community

It is always a subjective experience in an employee whether, during her initial period of employment, she feels welcomed into the community. She will, especially in the first couple of months, feel sensitive to signs of inclusion or exclusion and will, depending on personality and inclination, interpret and react to these signs. Signs of inclusion and acceptance may be small but meaningful. For most people, things such as a smile in the hallway from colleagues, respectful listening when you speak for the first time at a meeting, encouraging remarks, positive feedback on tasks, or an invitation to share a lunch table are experienced as signs that the community is interested in letting you in.

The experience of the community's acceptance can also arise through more structured measures, such as a common breakfast on the first day, a well-equipped office, IT that functions from the first day, a well-planned introduction, regular feedback meetings during the initial period, a mentor programme, and so forth. However, the firm must take note that such structured measures do not necessarily lead to positive experience for the employee. If, concurrently, other activities are taking place that are experienced as excluding – for example, the employee feels ignored by her manager or she does not feel welcome on her work team, this will typically dominate the employee's consciousness and overshadow the well-planned introduction and the flowers on the desk on the first day.

Some new employees are more sturdy and extraverted than others and, therefore, will be less sensitive to signs of exclusion or lack of inclusion than others will be. But almost everyone will react negatively to phenomena such as silence, lack of interest, critical or hostile remarks, lack of care, failure to share knowledge, or lack of follow-up by the manager or colleagues. How one tackles this and what conclusions can be drawn depend on the individual's situation and personality; but most people will consume considerable quantities of emotional energy to deal with this sort of reception on top of the other, unavoidable burdens of being new.

In contrast to what the new employee believes, a reception that feels excluding most often does not have so much to do with the new employee as a person or her qualifications but is to a higher degree a reflection of the inherent dynamics in the existing organisation and a lack of attention to the significance of the initial period of employment. In some cases, however, it may also be a combination of an immature organisation and a new employee with a poor sense of how she is supposed to handle the balance between entering into the existing order and adding something new.

The malleability of culture

Organisation theorist Mary Jo Hatch has formulated a cultural dynamics model, which shows how a firm's culture is shaped through dynamic processes around artefacts and symbols that are created in a context of assumptions and values (Hatch 1993; Hatch 1997: chap. 12). An artefact is, at base, an "object" but, in this connection, not necessarily a specific object; artefacts can also be organisational phenomena. An example of an artefact in connection with new employees might be a mentor programme, but it could also be a nameplate on the door or flowers on the table on the first work day. A mentor programme, like flowers on the desk, has the possibility of becoming a symbol for the new employee that a firm is interested in her and that wants the employee to feel at home. But they can also be symbols of the opposite: a deceitful firm that produces a series of empty artefacts that do not

66 The employee in the community

reflect its actual values. Furthermore, it can even happen that the artefacts do not become a symbol of anything at all but are simply noted with indifference, which is why they lose their importance. The fate of the artefacts is decided in the interpretation process the members of the organisation link to the artefacts.

Artefacts, thus, contain the potential for becoming powerful symbols, but Hatch stresses that this is not a process management can control; it can only try to influence it (Hatch 1997: 365). The initial period of employment is especially meaningful for an employee's acceptance into and opportunities for influencing the firm culture. Therefore, it is an obvious place for management to work with the development of culture by trying to influence the process of symbolisation. In connection with new hirings, a process of symbolisation takes place in new as well as old employees. For the new employee, the symbols will typically be linked to the symbolic contract and, thus, deal with phenomena such as acceptance, protection, wages, and so forth and together form a basic symbol of "self-in-firm". For the old employees, the symbols will be linked, inter alia, to their view of the community and its degree of permeability or self-sufficiency. But symbols that deal with solicitude and difference, knowledge and non-knowledge, and feelings to which these states are connected can also be especially active in this period.

If it is important to support new employees in their integration in the organisation, it is not only out of consideration for the employee but also the necessity of keeping the existing culture alive and receptive to new impulses (Geus 1997). Otherwise, a "strong" but stagnating culture may arise in which destructive tendencies survive generation after generation. In this type of culture, the organisation finds ways to let new members know what they are expected to do in relation to components that are viewed as fundamental in the culture. It typically turns on things such as dress, language use, work hours, distribution of work tasks, the way tasks are done, conflict resolution, solidarity with the group, and the relationship to management. The way the old culture survives unchallenged is by giving new employees unambiguous signals that only those who accept the existing culture are allowed into the community. The following case demonstrates exactly how a strong culture survives over many years by effectively excluding new impulses with stagnation and declining productivity as a consequence:

A young foreign man is hired into a work group consisting of middle-aged women who have been employed at the firm for years. Fifteen years earlier, the group underwent a traumatic period in which, in connection with a colleague's serious illness, they felt very poorly treated by management. At that time, it led to a development of the culture in the group that was particularly critical of management and which led them to stand firmly for workers' rights. There are no longer any employees left from the group at that time, but the culture is unchanged.

The young man has a number of suggestions for improvements in work methods that he proposes to the group after a short time with the firm. He also believes that it may be possible to improve the group's productivity considerably.

Thereafter, the old employees stop inviting the young man to coffee breaks. Nor is he invited to contribute to "cake days". At weekly group meetings, no one comments on what the young man says and, after some time, he stops saying anything. Gradually, group meetings stop altogether, and all communication take place informally and exclusively among the women mutually.

Gradually, the man only gets work tasks that he can handle on his own, while the women continue to do their tasks jointly.

In this case, the manager left the socialisation of the new employee to the group itself but should have been much more active in the process. The relevant subculture in the group was a big problem for the firm because the group's work constituted a bottleneck for the rest of the production. One effective way to try to change the culture in the group and thereby increase its productivity could have been to support the new worker's acceptance into the group. This would have required the manager's participation at group meetings for a period and his active assistance in resolving conflicts. Moreover, the group would have to be made more conscious of the group dynamic processes that went on in it.

When the group members spoke individually, many of them were not as critical of management and also had a desire to work differently and more productively. However, as a new employee, every one of them had found that if they did not submit to the predominant culture, they were not accepted into the community. The group's identity was to be in opposition to management and all the other departments. In the group context, therefore, everyone was subject to the immature culture, influenced by a primitive splitting defence despite the fact that no one personally really identified with this culture. Nevertheless, the employees were not able to change it themselves; they needed management's help.

Only the young man had the courage to resist the group pressure, which might be due to the fact that, even from the start, he was different by virtue of his gender and his nationality. The price he paid was solitude and isolation from the group.

Use of the initial period

With respect to hirings, the relationships between the employee and colleagues are the most decisive thing for how the employee winds up functioning in the firm. These relationships are by nature dynamic and will change when a new employee arrives. Therefore, it is not possible in advance to assess with certainty how it will go. The firm can try to assess whether the person in question "fits in", but they cannot know precisely because the system will change when the new employee becomes

68 The employee in the community

a part of it. Prior to this change, the system will be under ongoing change because of different events that arise but which are not known at the time of hiring. The firm, for example, decides to hire an older woman because they assess she will work well with another older colleague who, shortly afterwards, goes on long-term sick leave, whereupon the new hire is surrounded by very young employees. One cannot guard against this sort of thing. Therefore, it is about not taking too narrow a perspective on a future worker.

It may be necessary to test a new hire before the parties can assess how it is going, and the firm and the employee must be prepared for this. In this connection, it is more optimal if they agree to an initial period of six months since the three months that are normally agreed to do not provide sufficient time and tranquillity to test the relationship. The initial period of six months, on the other hand, is to be used actively by both parties. In this period, systematic methods, dialogue, openness, and reflexivity are used to evaluate the relationship on a continuing basis. This means that, in the initial period, there must be regular meetings in which manager and colleagues provide open feedback to new employees and in which the employees relate how they experience the job in relation to their desires and expectations and how they experience their relationships with colleagues. However, it must be stressed that it can be difficult to have an initial period of more than three months due to legal, collective bargaining, and practical reasons.

The importance of integration

This chapter has indicated the great importance of the initial period at a new job for the individual employee as well as the firm generally. It is decisive for the firm to maintain an open attitude toward the applicant over the course of employment and to look at the person's potential instead of his/her limitations. The firm must strive to give as realistic a picture of the job and the firm as possible, and the job interview should be characterised by open and direct communication, which makes it possible to get the best out of both parties and, at the same time, to talk about what might be problematic or uncertain. In addition, it is important to make it clear that not everything can be clarified or assessed in advance; and, instead, they should be prepared to use the initial period actively.

The manager has a decisive importance for how the initial period of employment plays out. Of course, this has to do with the structural part of the process (introduction programme, mentor programme, physical conditions, etc.) and, to just as high a degree, the relational part. Through close contact with the new employee and his/her colleagues, the manager must ensure that the employee actually becomes integrated and must be ready to intervene if the process does not function optimally. The manager must do this out of consideration for both the new employee and the existing organisation.

A successful integration of new members has significance on all three levels: the concrete, the psychological, and the symbolic. On the concrete level, it means an effective use of the firm's resources and a steady development of the organisation's procedures and methods. On the psychological level, it leads to a good work environment in which people thrive and new workers seek employment. On the symbolic level, a good, ongoing integration of new members can create symbols representing a firm with a great internal strength that allows it to be open and receptive, able to take care of its members.

As important as it is to be conscious of the importance of accepting new members, it is just as important to be conscious of how the firm parts company with existing members or, in other words: how dismissals are to be handled. This, too, has importance on all three levels for the person dismissed and for those who remain. The next chapter deals with this.

5

THE INDIVIDUAL'S EXPULSION FROM THE COMMUNITY

As described in Chapter 4 (on hiring), acceptance into the community is of great importance both for the individual and for the organisation as a whole. There are many degrees of incorporation into a community, and many more or less indirect ways to keep people out of the community. In all these cases, however, the degree to which it is experienced as a true expulsion from the community is a matter of the individual's subjective view. However, there is one situation in which the degree of expulsion is unambiguous and has nothing to do with subjective intuitions, namely, when an employee is fired – or, to put it in a nicer way, "dismissed", "made redundant", made an object of "organisational adjustments", and so forth. This chapter has to do with the process connected with firing and how managers can work with difficult employees to decide whether a firing is justified or not.

The simple fact that the phenomenon is an object of so many paraphrases indicates that there is something problematic and painful at stake. And nowhere is the dilemma between individual and community brought more to a head than when an employee is fired. Some fired employees claim that it is almost like a physical sensation, that the community is slamming a door in their face and saying: "You we do not need! We're better off without you". This experience can be incredibly painful and shocking and can traumatise an employee for life if the experience is not processed properly. This is especially true if the firing is unexpected or if the employee experiences it as completely unjustified.

Why is it painful to be fired?

An individual's emotional life and psychological defences are powerfully influenced by the groups in which he or she belongs. It can be said that the group's collective psychological defences become a part of the individual's defences (Lyth 1988: 73). Similarly, social constructivist authors talk about the importance of membership in a group for the individual's identity (Haslebo 2004: 34–40).

Expulsion from the community **71**

This means that being fired can be experienced as a loss of identity and internal coherence. It evokes a fear that you are worth nothing, that you will become nothing. A study of fired Welsh steelworkers described how they felt their dignity, their masculinity, and their self-esteem to be threatened (Mackenzie et al. 2006: 838–840). People who are fired can protect themselves against these threats in different ways, depending on the person's resources and maturity.

Consistent with the overview of the levels of maturity presented in Chapter 3, individual reactions to being fired can be divided into roughly three categories.

If the life, personality, and identity of the person fired have been dominated to a marked degree by the content and community of the job, it will be difficult to protect that person from a loss of identity. Here, the person fired will often regress to a splitting defence. For example, it may be that the former workplace is demonised: "The management is the worst collection of idiots" or "They never liked me". In this way, what is painful and anxiety-provoking about the firing is split off and attributed to the workplace.

On the other hand, if the person fired can compensate for the loss in some way by drawing on other parts of his/her personality, a more mature, repressive psychological defence against the loss may be observed. For example, it might happen that the person fired stresses the impersonal in the firing: "The firing was a part of a larger downsizing" or "The projects I was working on were shut down". The person fired protects him/herself by repressing the most painful part of the firing. At the same time, it is possible for the person fired to acknowledge and accept parts of the justification for the firing.

Finally, we can observe a person who is comfortable with him/herself and whose personality is well anchored in a feeling of his/her own worth. Here, the person fired will be able to acknowledge that the firing is a result of a sequence of events in which both the workplace and the person fired have responsibility for the outcome. Such a person will be able to look at the workplace in a nuanced way and accommodate the contradictory feelings to which dismissal gives rise.

Why is it painful to fire someone?

Managers, who are also employees, know that firings are painful, and almost all managers take their responsibility with respect to dismissals seriously. Many take it extremely seriously. Quite a few managers relate that, if one is not burdened by having to dismiss an employee, one is not suited to be a manager. At any rate, it is true that the position of manager provides power over the lives of other people and that the situation in which an employee is fired can be said to be the essence of this power: a person is expelled from the circle with the risk of extensive, negative psychic and material consequences for the life of the person in question.

Some managers feel the responsibility so heavily that they will do anything to avoid dismissing someone, and this illustrates the manager's dilemma very well because the manager has a responsibility for the part and for the whole. The manager's job, as described in Chapter 1, is to connect the organisation. That is, the manager is supposed to help individuals function as a collective. Therefore, the

72 The employee in the community

manager must not place the part above the whole because the manager's function is to ensure that the whole carries out its task in the best way possible. On the other hand, as discussed in Chapter 2, the whole is a construction that only exists in the consciousness of individual parts. As a consequence, the manager's job is also to maintain a good and close connection with all individuals by, inter alia, encouraging them to participate in the whole and to influence their understanding of it.

Therefore, it is important for the manager to be able to work with employees as individuals and as a group so that, on the one hand, she or he has a good sense of how the individual employee is thriving and performing and, on the other hand has a focus on employees as a productive collective. The latter entails many things, including having a constant eye on whether something disturbs or burdens the group or whether there are signs that the group cannot handle a situation itself. In the following case, there is an example of what it can cost when the manager is not close enough to the individual or the group, in the form of a lack of flourishing, poor productivity, and a dismissal.

An older employee, Jørgen, has abused alcohol for many years. This is generally known but has never been discussed openly. In connection with a customer complaint against Jørgen, however, the executive board directs Jørgen's immediate manager to dismiss him. After some consideration, the manager declares that he agrees with the decision. The official justification is that Jørgen's position is being abolished, since the executive board assesses that it will be difficult and too time-consuming to prove alcohol abuse.

Jørgen breaks down after being told. He reports in sick immediately and thereafter does not re-appear at the firm. His team colleagues react with tremendous anger and say that this treatment of Jørgen is completely inhuman and unjustified, which makes the manager seriously doubt whether the decision was correct. In the period afterwards, the team reduces its communication with the manager to a minimum, and the manager finds this to be particularly unpleasant. This becomes a contributing factor for why, six months later, the manager seeks another job, but doubt and bad conscience about the firing follow him for a long time thereafter.

After seven to eight years, the manager happens to bump into one of Jørgen's former colleagues. When, a bit into the conversation, the manager cautiously brings up Jørgen's firing, the other says spontaneously: "Oh, everyone on the team was so relieved. We were always having to cover for Jørgen's abuse – it was such a burden".

Many things go wrong in this case. The fundamental problem is that there has not been an ongoing dialogue between management and Jørgen about his abuse and about the possible consequences for his job. One of the reasons for this is that Jørgen has had countless different managers over the years, and each manager

Expulsion from the community **73**

should have spent time getting acquainted with Jørgen and assessing his efforts. The alcohol abuse has always only been mentioned through indirect hints and rumours. None of his colleagues has ever complained about him. To the contrary, it has been impossible to get anyone to say anything specific about the subject if any of the various managers asked directly about it. This is due, in part, to the powerful, normative culture around solidarity among workers – you don't "gossip" to management – and, in part, to the fact that people considered Jørgen to be fragile and could see that his whole life and identity was bound up in his job. So, even though Jørgen was a burden for the team, they protected him.

Quite often, one sees that employees wind up in a sort of dilemma with which they can only work if they get help from management. Employees will often have a clearer understanding of a colleague's lack of skills or work effort than it is possible for the manager to have, and they will more quickly discover it if a colleague has an abuse problem or something similar. The question is simply what employees will do with this knowledge. Here, it is good if the manager is clear about his dependence on employees coming to him to let him know whether there is something or someone in the group that is not functioning and makes it clear that it is also to the advantage of the group itself to have this openness in relation to the manager. In many instances, the manager does not have a chance to discover things about which employees are silent or cover up (if, for example, they always correct the mistakes a colleague consistently makes) and, therefore, the manager cannot take any action with respect to them. This places increasing pressure on the group, as was the case with Jørgen's team, because the problem is not being solved – Jørgen did not stop drinking even though his colleagues were doing his job for him – to the contrary, his colleagues involuntarily and with the best intentions helped sustain the problem.

Therefore, work has to be done on the "us-and-them" culture, so it is not seen as disloyal to tell management about one's observations, whether it involves the overall group or individual persons. It is best, of course, if the employee first takes the problem up directly with the affected colleague(s), but many feel that this is so difficult and transgressive that, in practice, they prefer to live with the problem and hope it solves itself. In other words, they display repressive behaviour. The same can be said about the revolving-door managers in the preceding case. It was known that there was a problem with Jørgen, but managers took comfort in the fact that no one said anything directly about it. Only when a customer complained did management take charge. However, because the problem had been repressed for years, the firing process was also repressive and, subsequently, splitting. Since management chose not to provide the real reason for the firing, neither Jørgen nor the team could speak openly about it, and thus the team got no help in dealing with the ambivalent feelings to which a firing gives rise. Under this pressure, the team reacted by splitting, whereupon the manager became the villain and Jørgen the victim. Only after many years was it possible for a former colleague to admit that the firing was also a relief for the group.

The manager was so strongly affected by the employees' splitting that he felt like a villain (despite the fact that he had thought much about it and was in agreement

74 The employee in the community

with the decision), and he avoided the employees because of their unsympathetic attitude, which only further deepened the employees' view of the manager as someone who spoke out of both sides of his mouth. All three parties – Jørgen, the team, and the manager – came out of this process with wounds and, with respect to Jørgen, life-changing wounds. It cannot be known whether the firing could have been avoided if, at a far earlier point, Jørgen's alcohol abuse had been brought up with him and with the team, but it is certain that the process would have been more constructive and with fewer costs for all.

Difficult employees

In the following, we have examined two different types of employees, which we have called, respectively, the rigid employee and the dramatic employee. What they have in common is that they are viewed by management (and, as a rule, also by their colleagues) as "difficult" or "troublesome". Therefore, in a number of cases, they wind up getting fired – or they find themselves regularly within the danger zone of being so. Of course, it is altogether too unnuanced to divide people who are experienced by others as being difficult to work with into just two categories because each person and situation is different, and the purpose is not to place a derogatory label on certain workers. We are using this simplified categorisation exclusively to call attention to the fact that, in our experience, these two categories have different characteristics and different causes and, therefore, may be advantageously handled differently.

The rigid employee, behaviour

The typical rigid employee has been at the firm for many years. They have had the same area of responsibility for all those years. As a rule, they are professionally talented and very responsible employees who work alone to a wide extent, as they do not feel a great need to cooperate with others. They take their area of responsibility seriously and think they have a better handle on the job if others do not interfere with it. Therefore, it is difficult to get them to document their activities (not necessary since they know how things work) and difficult to get them to share knowledge on the whole. These employees usually enjoy respect from both management and colleagues for their professional talent and are always asked for advice within their area, but they are considered to be troublesome at the same time. It is thought that they are too unyielding, that they do not want to develop, that they will not give up responsibilities or tasks they have, and that they are unnecessarily critical of others' work – particularly, management. Therefore, they wind up in conflict with other people – especially with new employees, who feel ignored or talked down to. Over time, more experienced colleagues and management have grown used to their outbursts and gruff way of speaking, just as they accept their demonstrative body language at meetings if they disagree with something or become bored.

Sometimes, the manager says about this type of employee that she "inherited" the person and would never have hired him herself. If one presses the manager on it, she might subjectively prefer to fire the person in question but does not do so because of a lack of specific justifications and, more particularly, because the firm is dependent on the person's expertise. The manager is permanently frustrated about the employee and despondent about the employee's rigidity – no development seems possible – nor does a firing seem to be possible.

Such employees feel the manager's frustration and irritation, but since they know themselves that they are really talented and dot the i's and cross the t's on their jobs, they find the manager to be deeply unjust, which only bolsters their rigidity and steadfastness. If anyone criticises them, they often use the phrase "I'm just doing my job!" as a way of dismissing criticism, since they simply do not view communication, knowledge-sharing, and so forth as part of their job.

Trust in management can be very small. The manager does not have the necessary understanding of the area and its strategic importance, the employee believes. Therefore, the manager is rarely or never asked for advice, and the employee has developed a wealth of avoidance strategies if the manager still tries to interfere. The employee is not blind to the fact that knowledge is power and their position is strengthened in the firm by keeping a tight grip on that knowledge. Correspondingly, they are nervous that they are undermining their position if, for example, they groom another employee to be able to take care of anything in their area of responsibility.

The rigid employee, causes

An employee who displays the behaviour described here is evidence, first and foremost, of one thing: a long-term lack of management of the person in question. In all probability, the employee has been allowed to run his own kingdom for many years without any support, encouragement, recognition, or criticism from management. If an employee seems to be doing his job well without problems and does not ask for attention, it is easy for a busy and burdened manager to "save" her attention for other activities. Apparently, this functions well for everyone, but in the long run it is not good either for the employee or the organisation.

First of all, the employee feels let down because he views it as a lack of interest, respect, and understanding of his field. A talented and responsible employee will most often react to this sort of let-down by taking over the full responsibility since, apparently, no one else will. Over time, the consequence of this sense of over-responsibility can become a protectionist and "I alone know" attitude in the employee, nourished by a growing mistrust of management and a feeling of isolation in relation to his colleagues.

Second, the lack of attention means that the employee does not feel seen and recognised for his efforts (which can be complex and of considerable extent, involving solutions to difficult problems, many hours of overtime, etc.). He feels he

76 The employee in the community

is being taken for granted and becomes unsure and doubtful about his own abilities because he gets no recognition at the same time that he does not count the superficial praise he does get to be meaningful because no one has an understanding of his area – except for himself. These different feelings are frequently projected onto his surroundings in the form of petulance, unconstructive criticism, and defensive emphasis on his own abilities and authority.

Third, the lack of attention also leads to a lack of *demands* from management on the employee. The rigid employee is almost always a result of an employee who, from the beginning, has not had enough guidance in what expectations the organisation has for his "soft" skills (communication, cooperation, knowledge-sharing, helpfulness, development, honouring joint agreements, etc.). If expectations have not been formulated, it is not possible, logically enough, to follow up on them or to make demands for compliance – which, in reality, is the same thing as saying that the behaviour of the person in question is OK. Many rigid employees thus indulge a form of freedom of speech in which they express themselves gruffly, condescendingly, or irritably or engage in behaviour in which they refuse to work together with certain colleagues or in which they choose to attend meetings or not as it suits them. It is confusing for the other employees – to a special degree, for new employees – that some people can be permitted such behaviour without the manager's reprimand, and the behaviour of the person in question also constitutes the most important reason that colleagues view him as difficult despite their professional respect.

The rigid employee, handling

If it is correct that the rigid employee's behaviour is primarily an expression of a long-term lack of management, the treatment would seem to consist of giving the employee in question more management. However, it is important for his current manager to be clear that a person who may have rarely or never had good experiences with management and has learned to do without it will not be interested in being managed (see Chapter 10 on the consequences of a lack of management of personnel and the development of pseudo-maturity). It is highly probable that the person in question will chafe at what seems like an unnecessary (things are fine), controlling, and bureaucratic interference.

Therefore, it is a matter of giving the employee some concrete experience with how management can be a help and a positive thing. The most fundamental thing here is for the manager to show interest in the person's area of responsibility and provide specific and continual recognition of his efforts. Perhaps, as a beginning, the manager should get a more detailed knowledge of the professional content of this area than she herself immediately feels a need for, since recognition of the rigid employee only works if it is given from quite substantial familiarity with the area. This is because, for a long time, the employee has exclusively identified with the content of his work and knows his area so well that he has no respect for shallow feedback.

Expulsion from the community **77**

One way for the manager to show her true interest can be to arrange one or more sessions in which the employee teaches the manager. It is also conceivable for the manager and the employee to go to a conference in which the manager would normally not participate (and, for example, do a joint presentation subsequently) or for the manager to go along to some meetings in which she usually does not participate. The purpose in all these cases is to build up trust between them as the manager becomes more qualified to spar with him and, at the same time, support the employee if he needs it.

At the same time, it is necessary for the manager to be honest in relation to what she considers to be problematic about the employee's behaviour and to sit down with the employee to come up with a plan for how they can work on it. The manager should accept her fundamental part of the responsibility (also on behalf of previous managers) that the employee has been able to pursue his unfortunate behaviour without intervention by management, but she cannot, of course, take responsibility for changing it. On the other hand, she can be available to help with the process. It is important not to propose a plan that is too comprehensive or too ambitious, which may seem overwhelming or patronising to the employee. If the manager believes that there are problems with both his meeting discipline and meeting behaviour as well as his documentation and cooperation with a younger colleague, then it is most constructive to select a single problem area – for example, his meeting discipline and meeting behaviour and work to improve this area first.

The key words for the process are follow-up, follow-up, follow-up. Every step forward, every improvement must be acknowledged and discussed, as should lack of progress or backsliding. Only through a concrete approach can one hope to see any gradual, positive changes, small or large. In this connection, it can be constructive to inform the other colleagues that the employee is engaged in a process of doing such and such. It may increase colleagues' tolerance for the person in question to see that he is working on his problems and provides colleagues an opportunity to help by giving him support and feedback.

From the start, it is necessary for the manager to formulate the nature of her assessment of the problems. Is it behaviour problems that disrupt a little and where any progress at all would be fine? Or are the problems so serious that the employee cannot keep his job if they continue? In the latter case, she must make the seriousness clear to the employee but without sounding like a threat, à la "One more mistake and you're out!" The employee must feel secure that the firm wants to keep him if it is at all possible and that the manager genuinely wants to help him in this. This also means that the manager must be conscious of her own frustration and despair in relation to the employee and try to change this. Otherwise, the process cannot succeed. Finally, it is central for the manager to relate openly that, if the employee continues to be as rigid as before, he will place himself in a vulnerable situation if events outside the manager's control, such as new technology or cutbacks or a merger leads to some employees being fired.

Management bears a heavy responsibility if it allows employees to sit in a corner and tend to their own affairs. Instead, managers should give them opportunities

78 The employee in the community

and incentives for development. But the individual employee has the responsibility to elect to take advantage of these opportunities and which opportunities he selects. It is clearly his right to choose not to develop himself (unless the employer makes specific, obligatory demands a part of the job), but the rigid employee will be an inevitable choice if it becomes necessary to dismiss people, and the employee should be made clear about this.

The dramatic employee, behaviour

In our experience, the dramatic employee is not nearly as frequent as the rigid one. On the other hand, the dramatic employee is a stronger presence and often gives rise to extensive organisational turmoil. It is a different sort of behaviour that characterises this type of employee, and the manager, therefore, should react differently than to the rigid employee.

In a number of cases, it may be a relatively new employee. If one looks at the person's previous jobs, a pattern of frequent, short terms of employment may appear. The person in question most often comes on strong on the new job and has many good proposals and initiatives, which makes those around the person enthusiastic and increases their expectations. But already after a short time, the new employee begins to become dissatisfied with different things, and she or he does not hold back from calling attention to this. The dissatisfaction is expressed many times in a dramatic and emotional way, which others find quite annoying, and they also find the person in question to be unstable in her moods: sometimes, she is exceedingly kind and enthusiastic; and, at other times, it is the opposite – with sudden and unpredictable alteration. However, the quick-tempered and dramatic are typically more dominant than the friendly.

The employee is inclined to feel unjustly or unreasonably treated and calls attention to it loudly. However, since her ability to reflect on her own behaviour and how she is viewed by others is often not very well-developed, she does not understand people's dismissive reactions when she complains about something. This bolsters her feeling of being poorly treated. Naturally, this can make her internal insecurity greater. However, since the insecurity is mostly expressed as testiness or a know-it-all attitude, it more often unleashes conflicts than sympathy. In a number of instances, her aggressive behaviour even seems so unpleasant (or directly terrifying) to colleagues that they try to avoid conflict by avoiding the employee, who is then isolated even more and becomes more insecure – and more frustrated and angry.

Correspondingly, the manager may be inclined to avoid measures that trigger the wrath of the employee – in part, because it is a new employee whom one would like to accept and show tolerance for and, in part, because the employee seems intelligent and committed and expected to be able to contribute positively to the firm. In addition, the person in question is often well-spoken and articulate, which can seem intimidating and make managers feel insecure about themselves and their own authority.

Expulsion from the community **79**

In the dramatic employee, there is not far from feeling to action. She is impulse-driven and does not always think her actions through because she acts on a strong emotion rather than on more thoroughly thought-out analysis. This makes her fast, enterprising, and inspiring, but her impulsive actions also bring her into a number of muddled situations in which she is tempted to act even more impulsively to get out of the situation – for example, by quitting on short notice, as happens in the following case.

An employee, Mia, was hired by a private firm and, in her first month, under-took some wide-ranging initiatives with respect to two important customers on her own. When the manager reprimanded her not to do that sort of thing without consulting the manager, Mia became furious and said: "I can't work like this!" She let it be known that she felt that, because of her expertise in the area, she should be given wider berth for self-determination. The manager dis-agreed. Not long afterwards, it turned out that she had arranged yet another meeting with one of the two customers without informing the manager.

The manager decided to let it pass without saying anything both to avoid an even worse outburst of anger from Mia and because the customer was enthusiastic about her and her many good proposals. This made the manager unsure about the right thing to do. Perhaps, he thought, Mia had a grasp on something with this customer that the manager himself had not understood.

Over the course of the first months, Mia found herself in minor and major conflicts with a number of her colleagues – conflicts, all of which had in com-mon that she did not follow the applicable rules and procedures but insisted on doing things her own way. In addition, she was critical of the way her col-leagues worked, which she called "outdated and out of step with the latest research". Two of her colleagues, one of whom she had known before, backed up her point of view, and Mia formed with these two colleagues a little group unto themselves, which produced a bad atmosphere in the department in the opinion of the others.

After a major conflict, Mia spontaneously decided to quit after five months' employment on the ground that the organisation was "far too sluggish and bureaucratic" and that she was very disappointed by the reception she had been given by colleagues and the lack of support from the manager.

The dramatic employee, causes

As opposed to the rigid employee, the reason for a dramatic employee is not a failure of management. This is seen, inter alia, already in the fact that the problems often arise shortly after the person has been hired, which indicates that it is behav-iour the person in question has brought along in her baggage, so to speak, and which, in many instances, gives her problems not only in her work life but also in

80 The employee in the community

her private life. In other words, the behaviour is linked to basic traits in her personality more than it springs from the relevant work-related situation.

In psychodynamic terms, her behaviour would be characterised as dominated by immature defence mechanisms such as projective identification and splitting (see Chapter 3). She views things in an unnuanced black/white way, and her conduct, therefore, also becomes unstable and poorly integrated, swinging between opposing emotional states. Because she succeeds in projecting her negative self-image onto others through her aggressive behaviour and eloquence, she remains immature and without much empathy for herself or others, just as she does not learn to control her impulses because she is overwhelmed by changing emotional states and is not able to reflect upon them critically.

This creates in her a chaotic internal drama; and it is in this drama that those around her may become unwilling participants as she unconsciously attributes to them (perhaps, changing) roles as, respectively, good or bad. Since she projects this, she does not perceive it as her own drama, which is important for understanding the behaviour of the dramatic employee. Quite concretely, she *experiences* other people as evil, uncomprehending, critical, unjust, and so forth, and she clings, obviously, to the few good people she identifies as such. Therefore, one often sees that there is splitting around the dramatic employee in which some are "against" and others are "for" her, as was the case with Mia. This is because her projective pressure on those around her is immense and difficult to resist.

But it is an important point that Mia is not maliciously or consciously manipulative. She just understands herself and those around her through her immature psychological defences. For, as described in Chapter 3, it is a trait of such defences that they provide an interpretation of reality that is experienced as "true". The more immature the defences are, the more unnuanced the interpretation of reality becomes – and this provides the dramatic employee both her progress and her problems.

The dramatic employee, handling

As manager, the task is not to undertake a deep analytic investigation of the employee's personality structure and the causes therefor. A manager is not trained for that, and it is not part of either the concrete or the symbolic contract between the firm and the employee (cf. Chapter 15, the section on manager as therapist). Therefore, the manager must not speculate about the underlying causes or conjecture on possible diagnoses. On the other hand, he must be attentive to employees who display some of the aforementioned signs of psychological immaturity. It is important for the manager to deal with the problem as soon as he becomes aware of it and before it has more wide-ranging consequences for the employee him/herself and for the organisation.

The manager must respond with clarity, empathy, and respect to the behaviour of the person in question and its impact on colleagues and the work effort. On this basis, the manager can function as a sort of advisor for the employee with regard to understanding the behaviour of others and a better understanding of her own reactions. This falls within the manager's domain, and it is from this position he can

Expulsion from the community **81**

meet with the employee and give her clear and constructive feedback on her efforts and especially her behaviour.

But with the dramatic employee, a manager comes under pressure in many ways, and this makes management of this type of employee into a challenging task.

The employee's enthusiastic and infectious approach can have a seductive effect on both the manager and others. From the beginning, this can lead to the manager accepting a special latitude with respect to the employee as was the case with Mia. In certain cases, it can be fine, because the idea is not to discourage a new employee or shackle her ideas and initiatives. But if the cause for this special latitude is that the manager unconsciously fears the wrath and criticism of the employee, it is a bad idea. When others signal that they are afraid of her, Mia becomes more afraid for herself since she already has problems with controlling her aggression, and her anxiety is aroused with conceptions of her own dangerousness if she feels that others cave in. This is especially true if the manager does this since the manager concretely and symbolically constitutes an important bulwark for her against the chaos of the surroundings.

Because of her relatively unintegrated personality structure, the dramatic employee has problems with boundaries because she has a hard time distinguishing between herself and others in a sufficiently nuanced way. So, if the manager begins to grant her fluid boundaries, it can make it more difficult for her to establish and maintain boundaries on her own, for example, in relation to working independently. Since Mia's manager said nothing about her arranging yet another meeting with the customer, he actually granted her a special status and demonstrated to her and to her colleagues that other rules applied to Mia. She was happy about this in a way, but she had a hard time dealing with it, and it also created problems with her colleagues.

Therefore, Mia would function better with a manager who sets clear boundaries for her behaviour and who does not avoid following up on it because he is afraid of her or becomes uncertain about himself. She will undoubtedly vigorously oppose any boundaries the manager defines, but in the long run she will probably feel better about that and, thus, have more composure in regulating herself. If the manager gradually feels she is developing her self-regulation in a better way, he can begin to give her more self-determination in order thereby to give her wealth of valuable ideas freer rein.

If one were to briefly summarise the difference between how managers should deal with the rigid and the dramatic employee, respectively, one can say that the rigid employee gets too little attention and needs more, while the dramatic employee gets too much attention and needs less. Or one can formulate it in this way: the dramatic employee needs an *appropriate amount* of boundary-setting and supervisory attention.

But it is not an easy task, and it is not certain it will succeed. The dramatic employee may face serious challenges in fitting into an organisational context, where it is expected that the members have a rather high degree of emotional stability, that they are capable of displaying empathy with others, and that they are

82 The employee in the community

able to some degree to set aside their own needs for the community (see Chapter 2 on the individual's dual relationship to groups). The manager must always be aware of whether he uses too many resources on one employee in relation to what comes out of it and in relation to the other employees. In a large, public organisation, for example, they hired an employee who came with an excellent professional reputation but was, right from the beginning, dissatisfied. First, the locale in which she was supposed to work was not good enough. Then, she could not stand the colleague who worked next to her. Then, the manager did not understand her. Over a year and a half, the employee was moved around physically or structurally five times without being satisfied. Only after the fifth attempt was the employee fired, and that was probably three to four times too many.

There are many possible reasons to show understanding for and to try to help the dramatic employee, because she often finds herself in a painful and confused state, but her difficulties cannot always be accommodated within the framework of a firm and within the conditions that are linked to being able to function in such a context.

Scapegoat?

In several places in this book, we have referred the concept of the scapegoat (see Chapter 3 on the splitting defence, Chapter 4 on the acceptance of new employees, and Chapter 7 about the splitting group), i.e., the phenomenon that a group unconsciously "designates" a particular employee as difficult and to blame for all the group's problems or attributes to the person in question particular negative traits or points of view (Obholzer & Roberts 2003). When a manager has to deal with a difficult employee, therefore, there is every reason to ask himself whether the difficult employee might rather be a target for projection for unconscious dynamics and problems in the group – that is, a scapegoat.

Høeg and Thybring have a fine case analysis of how, by shifting focus from the individual-centred to the relational perspective, one can get a different understanding of a group's negative bellyacher (Høeg & Thybring 2014). It shows that there actually are many in the group who share viewpoints and concerns with the negative employee, but they have not proffered their opinion and, instead, hide behind the bellyacher. Here, it is important to emphasise that this is not something the group has mutually agreed to do; it has happened without anyone being aware of it.

The psychodynamic perspective explains it in this way: these mechanisms take place, to a large extent, unconsciously in those involved, and the purpose is to curb anxiety and unease in the group by projecting the "dangerous" viewpoints onto a single employee. This calms the rest of the group, so they do not need to deal with them or with the person in question, who is typically isolated in the group and who, as a result of this projective pressure, will most often identify with being the burdensome and critical employee.

It is said that it is not random whom the group designates as the bearer of its projections. The person in question must be suitable, so to speak, as a target for projection. If it is a negatively charged projection, a good target for projection in many cases will be someone who separates him/herself from the group, for example, by

Expulsion from the community **83**

being a leader or a new employee, having a different nationality, or being either a rigid or a dramatic type of employee. In other words, it is possible that one is both a difficult employee in the sense described earlier and, at the same time a target of projection for unconscious things stirring in the group. The dramatic employee, for example, may be the object of the group's envy because she has gotten so much attention, and the rigid employee may be excluded because he represents an aspect of resistance to changes that can arouse discomfort in everyone.

But how does a manager find out whether an employee is functioning as a scapegoat for the group?

One of the things to which a manager can attend is whether the stories employees tell about the person in question are strikingly similar, even down to the use of the same choice of words regardless of who is talking about the person. Spontaneously, most managers might think that, if everyone from the group says the same thing, there must be something to it, but that is not necessarily the case. Identical stories may just as well indicate that the group has unconsciously reached a concurrence in their views about their colleague. This concurrence takes place primarily through the exchange of feelings in which the group learns from each other what is "right" to feel in relation to the colleague, and this is reflected in their use of language. By using the same words, they tell others that they feel the same as them, and this helps strengthen the group's cohesion but at the cost of the scapegoat (see Chapter 2 for a more detailed description of the function of emotions).

Another aspect for the manager to take note of is how nuanced the mode of consideration is in relation to the potential scapegoat and how respectful the language is. The more unnuanced or derogatory, the greater the probability there is that it is a scapegoat mechanism a play. At the same time, it can easily be that the person in question evidently does things that burden the group by, for example, not coming to meetings or keeping agreements made or not doing his/her part in work tasks. However, the hardened approach and negative language of the rest of the group and the scapegoat's identification with the projection (he becomes more and more intransigent and difficult) point to the fact that the group cannot handle the problem on its own.

It is also possible that different things entirely are burdening the group, such as a deep conflict between two other members or external pressure for greater productivity and that the group is protecting itself against a confrontation with the real problems through a displacement of the problem onto the scapegoat: "If Rita could just be moved to another group, everything would be better!"

When the solution is firing

If an employee does not function satisfactorily in relation to the whole, the leader has three fundamental but different modes of reaction available that reflect the level of maturity of the manager and the organisation:

1   The manager can split off the problem by, for example, being snide or persecutory to the employee or by moving to immediate dismissal. The manager can also split

84 The employee in the community

off the problem by idealising the employee ("Preben just has his little idiosyncrasies") or the organisation ("We make room for everyone here"). Idealisation will be more obvious for the manager who wants to avoid dismissing someone at any price, whereas another type of manager will use demonisation and seize on a quick firing or bully the employee into a corner or out of the organisation.

2   The manager can repress the problem by simply not seeing it or by not following up on the problems she sees or is told about. The manager may also choose to follow up in a repressive way, for example, by transferring the employee, which in reality does not solve the problem but simply moves or postpones it. A firing can also be repressive if the manager dismisses the employee without giving the right reason, without having investigated the matter to the bottom, without taking into consideration all the factors (including the manager's own role), or without having explored alternative options.

3   The manager can integrate the problem by using systemic methods to involve the employee and his colleagues in the solution. While listening and being supportive at the same time, the manager can be clear about her demands and expectations and call attention to the consequences if the employee does not live up to them. If the manager is honest enough and the contact between them is good enough, the employee will be prepared for a firing if the manager assesses at some point that the problems cannot be solved within the framework of the firm.

The nature of the foregoing process is decisive for how all the participants experience an eventual firing. For one must be attentive to the fact that a firing leaves traces not only in the person being fired but also on the manager and the employees who remain.

Many managers relate that they will never forget the dismissal(s) they have had a hand in because it has made such a huge impression on them. "The expression on her face when I told her she was fired is chiselled into my memory", says one. Therefore, it is very important for the manager's continued work that the manager herself feels she has done the right thing and has made peace with the decision. This feeling is hard to achieve if the process has been characterised by the use of immature defences because they cause unease and anxiety (consciously or unconsciously) in the manager. The unease and anxiety, for example, may be displayed through years of speculation about the firing ("Did I do the right thing?"), as a nagging conscience, as doubt about one's own abilities, or as anxiety about employee criticisms. On the other hand, it can also lead to a brutalisation of the manager in which he/she underrates the feelings of discomfort the firing has caused.

The employees who remain also react to a firing, but the reaction can be hidden and difficult to observe (see Hareli & Tzafrir 2006 for an overview of the feelings of those who remain). If the process up to the firing has been good (that is, integrated), there will probably be some form of acceptance of it, and the employees will be prepared for it. This does not mean that there cannot be feelings of anger, defeat, sorrow, or loss connected with the situation, but if these things are handled openly, the integration process will continue, and the organisation will be able to learn from the experience.

Expulsion from the community **85**

If, on the other hand, the process has been characterised by splitting or repression, the reaction of employees will probably be characterised by the same thing. In the case of splitting, the person fired may be proclaimed a villain, and all problems ascribed to him ("Yeah, Ole has left everything in a terrible mess!"), and everyone in the organisation agree that it was a good thing to get rid of Ole. Or the person fired is made into a helpless victim, which supports the employees' view of the manager as hard and unjust or the organisation as a firm that does not take care of its staff. Both of these forms of reaction increase the level of anxiety in the organisation.

The good dismissal

Some managers believe instinctively that there is no such thing as a good dismissal just as many employees imagine that a firing is the worst thing that can befall them, but neither of these is necessarily correct. A dismissal can be a natural process with evident causes that may be anything from cutbacks or professional incompetence to personal conflicts with the manager, all of which can be named and dealt with professionally (see Cox & Kramer 1995 for a study of the reasons for and communication in connection with firings). The goal is to ensure that the person fired does not lose his/her human dignity, that the manager is not unreasonably burdened, and that the firing does not have destructive effects on the organisation.

The means for doing this are openness, understanding, and respect. The most important thing is openness between the manager and the employee about their mutual requirements and expectations and the feelings linked to them. This openness begins, as mentioned, already at the job interview.

Openness is just as important with the employee's colleagues since, in many cases, they can be both a part of the problem and a part of the solution. Some managers are reluctant to discuss problems in connection with a particular employee with the whole group, and it is also a given that there are certain problems that are so personal that they are not to be discussed with the whole group. But, generally, problems in one place in the system affect the whole system on the concrete, psychological, and symbolic level; and, therefore, the problem cannot be hidden. Since the group needs to work on the problem in one way or another, lack of openness often leads to whispers in the corner instead, which can be especially unpleasant for the employee affected.

> Pia always comes late in the morning and, since the group has to deliver a particular product at a given time, it increasingly irritates the others.
>
> The manager gets complaints about Pia and decides to initiate a general discussion of the problem at a meeting, saying that it is important for everyone to be on time for work. This makes the other employees see red since they are always there on time, but no one says anything and Pia seems unaffected.

86 The employee in the community

> The next morning when Pia is late again, her colleagues are so furious that they refuse to work with her. Pia is very shocked by this since she had no idea about the extent of the problem.

It seems obvious that it would have been better in this case if the manager had addressed himself more directly to Pia. Most people would probably think that the manager should talk to Pia in private; but, by doing that, he prevents the group's participation in the solution to the problem. If the group learns to speak openly about the fact that it is a problem that Pia comes late, they will better be able to support her, be humorous about it, or object clearly before they become so irritated that they explode. If the whole group talks about it, it may also show that Pia has reasons for coming late that are relevant for the group. Perhaps, she feels left out of the morning coffee break or she thinks the division of tasks happens in an unfair way. Or the group gets a better understanding of Pia's reasons for coming late (which may be personal) and thereby a greater tolerance for the problem.

How to do it?

But what should a manager do if Pia continues to come late for work if she is often sick and if cooperation with the others no longer works no matter how much they talk about it? What if he has made it clear to Pia what the requirements for working in the group are and if he thinks he has listened and supported her to improve without it helping?

The first thing he should be clear about is that his assessment of whether this has helped is ultimately decisive. Pia may well think things are going fine, but if the manager does not think so, there is a problem. It is quite a burden a manager assumes to undertake this sort of assessment of an individual's contribution to the community's production. He has *not* taken on the task of assessing Pia's human value or the many other qualifications Pia possesses, and he must guard against mixing up his assessment of Pia's contribution to the organisation with an assessment of Pia's worth. If one feels robbed of one's worth as a human being, there is a risk of feeling marked for life by a firing. On the other hand, most people, once the first emotional waves are behind them, can relate to the concrete reasons that form the basis for an honest statement by their manager. They might not agree with the assessment, but they can deal with it and, gradually, also accept the consequences. In the final instance, no employee wants to work for a manager who does not think they are good at their job.

Some managers draw out making their assessment or deciding what they really believe far too long. Therefore, it is a good idea for a manager who thinks an employee's performance is problematic to take stock of himself as to whether he actually believes things will get better? And if the answer is yes, is it because he likes the employee or feels sorry for her or is it because he is afraid of firing her?

Or does he have realistic grounds to believe in improvements? If there has been progress, does he or the employee have ideas for new measures to be taken and does he believe in them? It can be difficult to undertake this assessment because sympathy, discomfort, or fear can veil or disturb the picture, but this is important to do for two reasons.

First, because the manager risks drawing out a firing longer than necessary, and this happens at the cost of his/her colleagues. Many good employees may leave in frustration about the problems while the manager chases his tail.

Second, because the manager cannot hide it from the employee if he no longer believes an improvement can be made. It is actually easier for the manager to hide it from himself than it is to hide it from the employee because the employee reads the manager's hundreds of indirect signs of lack of faith in her, which may be unconscious to himself. As usual, when it comes to communication, the signs may be small – indeed, almost invisible – but effective. It may be that the manager stops greeting her or greets her less heartily. It may be that he forgets to call the employee to an important and interesting meeting. Perhaps, he looks tired when the employee asks to speak to him, or he stops calling attention to things he usually complains about, and so forth. All these signs may be read and interpreted by the employee and lead to her feeling invisible or non-existent, which is a gruelling and undermining feeling in the long run. What seems to the manager to be a considerate approach can be experienced by the employee as rather cruel without being able to put her finger on it.

Thus, a firing is justified when:

1   There is a dysfunction in the manager's opinion that is so extensive or fundamental that it cannot be accommodated in the firm.
2   The manager has observed all the formalities with respect to legislation, agreements, oral and written notices, union representatives, clarification with his own boss, and so forth.
3   The manager can honestly confirm that he has loyally and over an extended period of time tried to create optimal conditions for the improvement of the employee.
4   The manager must – just as honestly – answer no as to whether he believes in an improvement.

It is the manager's assessment that counts (see Levine & Moreland 1994: 308 for an overview of how complex this assessment process is). It is his responsibility that he may be wrong; but, unless the manager plans on changing jobs, it is defined in advance in the division of roles that it is the employee who must leave the firm. It may hurt, but it need not be traumatic.

If, on the other hand, the manager avoids doing anything in a critical situation, he actually risks taking the organisation as well as the employee as hostages in his distaste for confronting the unpleasant. This can be significantly more costly for all parties and do much more harm than a firing that is done with ethics intact.

PART II

Group processes

Almost all organisations consist of groups. In part, these are formally defined groups that constitute a part of the organisation's structure. In part, they are informally defined groups that, for example, have arisen on the basis of sympathy, education, age, gender, or common interests and points of view. Collaboration in the organisation plays out within, between, and across these formal and informal groups. Although the manager only manages formal groups (the informal groups will typically be without management or have an informal leader), it is fundamental for a manager to be familiar both with the processes for managing formal groups and their mutual interplay and with how the dynamic of informal groups can affect the work of formal groups. Group processes in both formal and informal groups play a decisive role for the flourishing of employees and the effectiveness of the cooperation.

A group can be considered as an independent unit if its inherent dynamics function independently of its members to a certain extent. This means that management of groups is not the same as management of individuals. For a manager, then, it is important to be able to relate to employees as individuals and to employees as groups at the same time. For employees, it is beneficial to know something about how, as a member of different groups, they are influenced by conscious and unconscious group processes.

Within this area, there is an entire scientific field with a number of theoretical schools that deal with the group as an independent unit: group psychology. This field is an object of closer examination in Part II.

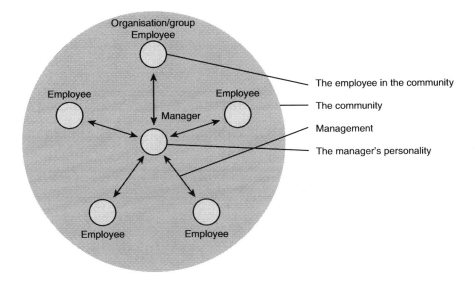

The examination is divided into three chapters. Chapter 6 describes how one can understand groups as independent units that are partially independent of the individual members of the group. Chapter 7 accounts for different theories of the productivity of groups. Chapter 8 demonstrates how meetings function as important concrete, psychological, and symbolic fora for the group and its cohesion and what positive or negative effect meetings can have on the maturity of the group.

Part II contains the following main points:

Chapter 6	Groups can be defined by the feeling of a community among their members.
	Groups have a tendency to create "uniformity" among their members.
Chapter 7	How this uniformity occurs has a great influence on the effectiveness of groups.
	The effectiveness of groups can be described by analysing their psychological maturity.
Chapter 8	Meetings constitute an important part of the inner life of groups.
	The conduct of meetings has a great influence on the development of the group's psychological maturity.

6

THE GROUP AS AN INDEPENDENT UNIT

When the concept "group" is used, it is most often to designate a collection of people who, in one sense or another, coordinate their actions. It might be a family, a volunteer group, a government office, a military unit, a self-help group, a women's group, a study group, and so forth. The group concept implies that it is the group's collective expression that is important, while the individual group member has less significance. The concept of the group focuses on the community and the collaboration between the participating persons (Bion 2006 [1961]: 131). If people want to describe a more individual-oriented collection of people, the concept "network" is most often used today, in which the community has a slightly more restrained role, while the individual relations between each member of the network has greater significance (Uzzi & Dunlop 2005). If one uses the concept "group" about a collection of people, one has also made a choice: the group's common expression is considered in context as more important than the personal expression of the individual members.

But how is a group defined more precisely? In group psychology, there are a number of different definitions of the concept "group", of which some are listed next.

A group exists when:

- Two or more individuals view themselves as members of the same social category (Turner 1982: 15);
- Two or more individuals define themselves as members of the group, and its existence is recognised by at least one other person (Brown 2000: 3);
- A small number of people have a certain relationship with each other – this relationship is not very organised but is, at the same time, not completely unstructured (Foulkes 1964: 48).

92 Group processes

A more comprehensive definition was suggested by Alderfer (Alderfer 1987: 204): a group of people is a collection of individuals:

1 Who have significant mutual relationships of dependence;
2 Who view themselves as a group and distinguish between members and non-members of the group;
3 Whose group identity is understood by non-members;
4 Who, when group members act alone or together, have significant mutual relationships of dependence with other groups;
5 Whose roles in the group, therefore, are a function of expectations for them from the other group members and from non-group members.

Even though it becomes clear in Alderfer's definition that a group also depends on its relation to the surrounding world, the most important characteristic of all the preceding definitions is the mutual relationship among the group members. The relationship between the members, their understanding of what the group is and what it is to be a member of it, constitutes the core of the group concept. This means that it is possible for a group to exist formally but without anyone experiencing themselves as a member because no one feels an affiliation with the group. Groups cannot exist independent of the consciousness of the members, claim these definitions. This phenomenon can be seen, for example, in connection with changes in an organisation in which management has defined a new organisational structure that introduces new departments, teams, projects, and so forth. If there is no work on employees' subjective experience of being members of the new group, the group only exists in the organisation's diagram for a while, whereupon it quietly dissolves itself.

The formal and informal structure of groups

There are at least three different views of how to understand the structure of groups. These views are designated, respectively (Alsted 2005: 51–58):

- Formal structure
- Informal (cultural) structure
- Motivational structure.

The formal view of group structure focuses on a description of the division of functions and labour in a group or organisation. Here, the structure of the group or organisation is equated with the agreed-upon or described division of labour or procedures for collaboration. This classic way of viewing the structure of groups or organisations is reproduced in almost all textbooks on organisational theory (see, e.g., Borum 1995; Jacobsen & Thorsvik 2002; Bolman & Deal 2017). Important viewpoints in this perspective are that:

- Structures are to be shaped, so they adapt to the environment of the organisation
- Effectiveness comes from division of labour

- Coordination and control through hierarchy are necessary to achieve goals
- Problems can be fixed through restructuring.

This view of group structures is expressed in organisational diagrams in which the organisation is presented as being divided up into a series of mutually – most often, hierarchically – connected "boxes" (divisions, departments, offices, groups, and projects). But, as many have experienced, this presentation rarely corresponds completely to the actual structure of the organisation. All organisations contain a number of transactions that go across and against the formal structure (see, e.g., Schein 1990: 21).

As an extension of the formal view of group structure, therefore, a number of perspectives have been developed that focus on the informal structure in groups and organisations. The informal perspectives on group structure all emphasise that there are a number of relationships in organisations that evade the regulation of formal systems. A good example of this sort of perspective is the new institutionalist perspective. The core of the new institutionalist perspective is that organisations are not guided by a rational division of labour but by the "logic of appropriateness", which is based on norms, values, habits, rules of thumb, and so forth (March & Olsen 1989: 23). This logic is divided into three different types (DiMaggio & Powell 1991: 57):

- The coercive, which is made up of laws and rules
- The normative, which is made of culture
- The mimetic, which is made of the desire to resemble other groups.

For new institutionalists, these three types of logic constitute the most important structure in organisations and groups. The three types can be viewed as the social rules that, together, control the behaviour in the group. This view of the structure of groups and organisations is more dynamic and, presumably, more precise than the view of the formal perspective. However, it is a problem that the new institutionalists do not justify or explain precisely why these three structures should be the most important. Moreover, the concept of management is absent from the contributions of the new institutionalists, from whom one can get the impression that the logic of appropriateness functions automatically and almost autonomously.

So, how does management come to be a part of group structure? To get an answer to this question, one must turn to an understanding of group structure as being based on the motivation of the members.

The motivational structure of groups

If it is correct, as claimed in Chapter 2, that the relationship between individual and group has the nature of a trade, then an important part of the raison d'être of groups – from the perspective of the individual member – is to help people to fulfil their needs. The individual member must find there is an advantage to belonging to a group. One must expect to see this quality reflected in the group's structure.

94 Group processes

According to motivational theory, the most fundamental structure of groups will be neither the formal structure nor the informal (cultural) structure but the motivational structure, which does not mean, however, that the formal and informal structures do not exist or play no role. But it does mean that the motivational structure is the most significant and decisive for how the group's collaboration takes shape.

In Chapter 2, the two existential dilemmas, individual versus community and stability versus change, are defined as fundamental conditions for the life of the individual person. In an earlier work, Alsted (Alsted 2005) has suggested that the connection between individual motivation and group structure can be described this way:

- Individual vs. community: cooperation
- Stability vs. change: task resolution
- Compromise creator and integrator: management.

The theory is that all groups have a tripartite structure whose basis is the members' motivational needs. These needs permeate all the group's activities and, consequently, also its structure.

The first structure is constituted by the dilemma between individual and community, which has to do with cooperation in the group – the social content. A group's cooperation consists of one long exchange between the contributions of the individual and the community's acceptance or rejection of the individual's contributions. Over the course of this exchange, formal and informal rules and norms are created that apply to this dance between individual and community. This could also be called the "ideology" of the group.

The second structure is constituted by the dilemma between stability and change, which has to do with the goal of the group's work – the professional content. In an exchange between what exists (stability) and what does not exist (change), the products of the group are created, whether it is knowledge, claims handling, services, or goods. This could also be called the group's "economy".

In practice, of course, cooperation and production cannot be separated since, in the group's concrete life, they are interwoven. This happens through the constant negotiation of motivation dilemmas in the group. Think, for example, of the discussion about change that almost all groups and organisations have on an ongoing basis. Here, the negotiation is often about finding a spot between two extreme positions: preferably, new, exciting challenges (promoting change), but not too extensive or too quick (promoting stability). Another example is discussion around wages: there may well be pay differences (promoting individuality), but they must be objectively justified so they are experienced as fair and, therefore, do not split the group (promoting community).

Groups constantly face the prospect of making new compromises between the motivational dilemmas. Some of the compromises are established completely unconsciously to the participants; others are clarified through discussions over lunch. Still others have a more formal and permanent character and become rules and agreements in the organisation whose defensive character, however, can be unconscious to the participants even though the rules are established consciously. For example, a very common organisational phenomenon such as education plans can be interpreted as a collective defence against conflicts that would otherwise arise due to insecurity and envy if there were not "rules" (in the form of plans) for the area. Education plans thus regulate (i.e., are compromise-creating for) both motivational dilemmas because they:

1 Create compromise between change (they ensure a certain level of education) and stability (they link education with daily work and existing skills);
2 Create compromise between individuality (education takes into account the individual's needs) and community (education must have relevance for the firm and is to be distributed in relation to the needs of everyone).

However, in remarkably many places, one encounters education and competency plans that are implemented only partially or not at all and remain purely paper plans. The employee agrees to an ambitious education plan at the annual performance review, but nothing ever comes of the plan. There may be many reasons that plans are not implemented as they were conceived. However, often beneath the immediately visible causes, a decisive reason such plans capsize often proves to be inadequate or unclear compromises between the motivational dilemmas.

The third central part of group structure is management. The manager's role is to be the compromise-creator or the connector of the many interests in the group as well as in the surrounding world. It is this compromise-creating function that makes it possible to keep the group together and ensure its productivity. Several authors talk about management "on the edge" of a system/group (Ashbach & Schermer 1987: 117; Roberts 2003: 65). This must be understood in the way that the manager has an important role as maintainer and administrator of the boundary between the group's internal world and its surroundings.

Freud believed that the ego's role in the individual is to create compromises between the individual's own, inner needs and the requirements of those around him/her. In Freud's terminology, the ego creates compromises between the id and the superego. In accordance with this, some authors describe the management of a group as the system's "ego" (Kernberg 1998: 15) because management (the group's ego) monitors the internal world (the group's "id") and the external world (the group's "superego") and creates compromises between the motivational dilemmas. In this way, the manager becomes a central bearer of the system's collective, psychological defence just as the ego is in the individual.

That is to say that, whereas the ego's role in the individual is to establish a defence that protects the individual's psyche, the manager's role in the group context is to establish a defence that protects the group's cohesion. Of course, the manager does not do this alone. The process takes place unconsciously and in a close interplay between the manager and the group. But the manager has the dominant role in the development of the group's maturity. From this comes the close

96 Group processes

connection between the manager's personality and the development of the group or the organisation.

The motivational structure in practice

The following case demonstrates how the three structural levels – cooperation, task resolution, and management – concurrently interact and influence the work ability of a group.

A work group at a public institution has functioned for an extended period of time without a manager. Things have gone fine in terms of getting the job done at a satisfactory level, but at one point the executive management becomes aware that most of the employees have accumulated a huge amount of overtime. In addition, the travel budget has been exceeded by 100%.

Therefore, the executive board names a group manager whose primary task is to ensure that a reasonable relationship between work assignments and time spent is maintained and that the travel budget is observed. A time registration system is introduced, which leads to a number of changes in the daily routines of the employees. Moreover, the group manager determines that all trips are to be approved in advance by her, and she works up a set of rules that describes what types of trip have the highest priority.

At first, the group reacts with great anger at having a leader "fobbed off" on them since they felt no need for one. They believe that the quality of their work will fall drastically because of the altered time resources, and they feel that the registration system is an expression of unnecessary bureaucratisation and control.

By contrast, most of the employees do not react to the new travel rules. It turns out that it is one employee who used approximately 80% of the budget. This single employee is terribly frustrated at the new working conditions, which he views as an immense decline from before; and, as a consequence, he ends up leaving the group.

The other members are eventually pleased with the new manager and, after a while, think it is nice that the social norm, whereby people always worked overtime, has been changed.

The registration system, however, never really works. After six months, it is scrapped, and they go back to the individual "private accounts" for the small quantity of overtime that arises now and then.

There are no complaints about poor quality from the interested parties.

When it had a period without a leader, the group in the case unconsciously established an ideology for cooperation that was based on a conviction that many work hours were the same as a job well done. The group found in this structure for

The group as an independent unit   **97**

collaboration a compromise between individual and community, which consisted of everyone putting in more and more hours to the community. The many hours became the symbol of the individual's loyalty to and membership in the group, but it was not a very good compromise because it did not take individual differences into consideration. Not all tasks required an equally large work effort, and not all employees had a need or possibility for working so much overtime. The group's ideology, however, made it difficult to assess the necessity individually in relation to each task and to draw the line on overtime if it was not appropriate. The underlying anxiety was that, if you did not have many hours of overtime, you would be left in the dust (without influence on the group) and that you would lose standing. Thus, overtime became a container for the mutual competition that always exists in a group.

As far as the travel budget is concerned, the group entered into a compromise between individual and community that overstressed the individual. There was a long tradition in the firm that the employees themselves decided their travel activity to conferences and so forth, and that it was not something others should interfere with. Consequently, the majority of employees accepted without discussion that a single employee used 80% of the budget at the same time that they took no position on the fact that the group as a whole went over budget by 100%. By contrast, they talked often about the positive significance they attributed to the independent orchestration of their work, including travel activities.

The group did not experience any need for management because it was not conscious of the fact that the structure for cooperation (the group's ideology) affected the group's other structure for task resolution (the group's "economy") in an unproductive way. The cooperative structure did not allow people to relate openly and inquisitively to task resolution either with respect to quantity or quality. It was not possible to discuss whether a task could be resolved with fewer hours or what the quality level should be or to compare the solutions of different employees. As long as one could show that he or she had spent x number of hours on a project, any solution was accepted. Similarly, it was not possible under the predominant ideology to discuss which trips were more important in relation to the task because people were afraid that sort of discussion would split the group. Therefore, everyone decided for themselves.

But the many overtime hours as well as the travel expenses had consequences for task resolution about which the group was not aware. The many hours could have been used for something else either in employees' private life or on other tasks the group did not solve, and the exceeded travel budget led to cutbacks in other activities of the group. During the period in which there was no manager, the group undertook an indirect prioritisation of its resources (time, work effort, and money) but was not aware of the choices it was taking. In other words, the group's ability to create compromises between stability and change (task resolution) was not optimal because the way they solved the tasks (the ideology) was primarily a result of norms that, respectively, over-emphasised the community (overtime) and over-emphasised individuality (trips).

98 Group processes

Therefore, the group needed a manager who could help them shape more flexible and motivating compromises between the existential dilemmas. Even though the employees did not themselves feel this need, the need was clear when the problems that existed with the group's production were considered from the outside. In the initial period, the new manager became bearer of the group's preferred, collective defence – repression – but, since the manager's job was to get control over the overtime and the travel budget, she (unconsciously) "moved" the repression from overtime and unlimited trips to a time registration system and rules for trips. As the manager came to know the employees and the group saw that its tasks could be done to the customers' satisfaction without overtime and that it was a relief to have a normal workday, confidence increased between manager and employees. Concurrently, the cooperative structure was marked by less mutual competition and greater security. The group's cooperation matured, so it became possible to talk more about common solutions and about individual contributions and needs. Therefore, it was agreed to get rid of the registration system, which was always viewed as an unpleasant control measure out of step with the fundamental values of the organisation.

The group manager introduced in this case came to function as an integrator of the two other structures, cooperation and task resolution, because the manager seized and developed her role as a creator of compromise. The group's productivity and work satisfaction increased significantly as their ability, with the manager's help, to enter into flexible compromises around the dilemmas increased.

The tendency of groups to make members uniform

A central characteristic about groups is their tendency to standardise the conduct of their members, something that has preoccupied many theoreticians of group psychology. A number of authors have written how groups de-individualise and stereotype their members (Collins 1990; Canetti 1996; Kernberg 1998; Brown 2000; Bion 2006 [1961]). Uniformity at first sounds negative but, actually, a certain homogenisation of the group's members is considered to be a fundamental presupposition for the group's existence. A group can only exist if there is something that holds the people in the group together, and the group's collective drive – its productivity – is directly based on its coherence. As a result, all groups in one way or another and to one extent or another must work to homogenise its members.

But how does this homogenisation occur? In Chapter 2, it was claimed that groups, organisations, and society do not exist independently of the individuals who create them. But for people who are members of groups, organisations, and societies, they seem to have a very real and, to them, independent existence. How can this apparent contradiction be explained? There are a number of different explanations among theoreticians.

The new institutionalist model of explanation

A frequently used explanation for why the group is felt to have an existence independent of its members is the new institutionalist theory, which is often cited in textbooks on organisation theory (see, e.g., Bolman & Deal 2017: 282–285). The new institutionalist writers indicate how relations and cooperation in groups quickly take the form of norms, habits, and routines. Once these things have been re-created over several months or years, group members experience them as coming from the outside as given realities. But the group members themselves have created them (Berger & Luckmann 1966). Norms, habits, and routines are called institutions, to use a catch-all concept. Institutions – used in this context – may be organisations (e.g., Local Government Denmark), traditions (e.g., marriage), or norms (e.g., the way people greet each other).

The new institutionalists, thus, provide a convincing explanation of how groups and society are at once created by the members themselves and, at the same time, seem to the members to be independent of them. The new institutionalists believe that groups, organisations, and societies are permeated by institutions. Therefore, new institutionalist writers are focused on how institutions affect human choices and actions in everyday life. They believe that these choices are determined by "the logic of appropriateness", which was mentioned earlier in the chapter. What is appropriate is determined, first and foremost, by the norms and culture of the organisation in question (March & Olsen 1989: 22–23; Brunsson & Olsen 1993: 21). The homogenisation of the organisation's members occurs imperceptibly and develops gradually through compliance with procedures, conventions, strategies, and roles. In this way, the institutions shape their members. The institutions help their members to create meaning (March & Olsen 1989: chap. 3).

In this way, the new institutionalists convincingly explain the great influence institutions have on our conduct. On the other hand, however, they are not as interested in how the participants can help change these institutions through their actions. Nor do they write much about why people are so quickly inclined to establish norms, habits, and routines when they are together in groups. In order to answer these questions, which have to do with unconscious relations between people, one must turn to group psychology.

The group psychology model of explanation

For group psychology, the examination of the unconscious coordination that takes place among members of a group is also a central issue. One of the founders of group psychology, Siegmund H. Foulkes, described the group's unconscious relations as a "matrix, a communicative network" (Foulkes 1964: 70). Foulkes believed that the matrix bound group members together in an overall system, like the neurons in the nervous system.

A central conception in group psychology is that the members establish common psychological defences to keep the group together (Ashbach & Schermer 1987: chap. 5; Kernberg 1998: chap. 1; Heinskou 2004). Just as the individual uses psychological defences to hold together his/her own psyche, individuals in relationships, families, work groups, and organisations must establish *common* psychological defences against life's ambivalence in order to keep the community together. The defences are said to be common because they are activated by the participants'

100 Group processes

mutual interplay. They help create images and views of reality which the participants share and bolster the participant's experience of being in a group.

The rapport of the group members on an unconscious level happens through projection and projective identification (see Chapter 3). Projection is when individuals or groups transfer (project) inner conflicts to outside relationships or persons. What actually originates as an inner feeling is experienced by the person(s) projecting as something others are doing against him/her or as feelings others have or as qualities others possess. Since everyone has inner conflicts, this means that the quantity of projections even in small groups can be large. A projection becomes a projective identification, if the person on whom there is a projection "receives" or identifies with the projection. The receiver of the projection may also be a group. A group, for example, identifies with a projective pressure to be super-effective, while another group identifies with a projective pressure to be difficult. This projective pressure may come from both the group members themselves and from people outside the group.

The construction of common defences is an ongoing process in all groups. One can view it as an always in process "negotiation" among the members of the group. This negotiation occurs unconsciously and may be more or less successful, but the purpose is always to create a common picture of reality that helps the members make the reality manageable. At the same time, the collective defences have the effect that the group members become less threatening to each other because they confirm each other in a particular interpretation of events and phenomena in and outside the group.

The manager's task is to try to nudge the creation of these common defences toward an ever-increasing maturity. That is to say to encourage and help the group to move from immature defences such as splitting or repression to integrating defences. In order for the manager to be able to do this, it is necessary to have an understanding not only of why but also how common defences are established.

The importance of feelings in group rapport

Feelings play an important but often overlooked role in establishing psychological defences. In the mutual communication between manager and employees and between the employees themselves, the emotional life is often repressed into the unconscious. From this position, it can have great influence on the mutual rapport in the group and the behaviour consequent thereof. For the manager, it is about having an oversight of the many layers in the group's communication: the immediately apparent – for example in which the group members disagree about the office furnishing – and the less apparent – for example, in which the discussion about the furnishing activates a wealth of different emotions among the participants. The manager must be able to relate to and work with all these layers at the same time.

An important part of the group's communication, thus, takes place unconsciously through emotions, and the rapport occurs, inter alia, through the group members trying to "feel the same" in particular situations. Many scholars have indicated that

The group as an independent unit **101**

groups frequently develop rules for what one "should" feel in different situations. For example, it may be that one should feel benevolence toward a client, empathy for a colleague's illness, or joy at the firm's profits (Poder 2004: 41–51).

Hochschild has explored how members of groups and organisations try to control their emotions in accordance with these unconscious rules. She believes that emotions can be controlled in two ways (Hochschild 1979, cited in Poder 2004: 44):

1 One can try to arouse an emotion in oneself
2 One can try to suppress/repress an emotion one has.

Moreover, she describes three fundamental techniques for controlling one's emotions:

- *The cognitive technique*: One tries to change images, ideas, or thoughts that are linked to a feeling in order thereby to change the feeling;
- *The bodily technique*: One tries to change one's bodily expression of the feeling – for example, through breathing or hand movements;
- *The expressive technique*: One changes one's external expression in order to change one's internal state – for example, by smiling in order to divert anger.

Similarly, Ashforth, Humphrey, and Kreiner work with how feelings are controlled in organisations (Ashforth & Humphrey 1995; Ashforth & Kreiner 2002; Poder 2004: 49–50). They believe that there are four general ways to regulate feelings in social contexts:

1 Neutralisation: actions that can arouse certain feelings are forbidden.
2 Compartmentalisation/postponement: expression of feeling is moved to innocuous occasions.
3 Prescription: rules for what feelings are acceptable.
4 Normalisation: feelings are rationalised or limited. Here, there are several techniques:

   - Amelioration of feelings: for example, through humour.
   - Rationalisation: strong feelings are explained with more muted grounds.
   - Adaptation: strong feelings are routinised, and sensitivity is reduced – for example, at hospitals.
   - Ritualisation: strong feelings are placed within a fixed framework with standardised procedures, such as funerals or farewells.

These different contributions show how group members can communicate and coordinate mutually without being conscious of it. This apparently "mystical" coordination and homogenisation of group members may be convincingly explained by the involvement of unconscious forms of communication.

On the concrete level, projection pressure is communicated through all the forms of communication available to people. This is to say that it happens via body

102 Group processes

language, movements, mimicry, eye movements, and via language through ironic remarks, silences, slips of the tongue, lapses of memory, tone, and pitch (Johansen & Toft 2001: 58). People are good at reading each other – particularly in the non-verbal area – but a large part of this mutual observation takes place unconsciously. This means that people are not always conscious of what they are reading in other people, which does not preclude, however, that they react to what is read even though they may not be able to account for how and why. The employee who cuts off her presentation because the manager begins to drum his fingers is not necessarily aware why she suddenly does not want to say any more.

Working with the maturation of collective defences

Just as psychologically immature individuals may be inclined to create pictures of themselves and the world around them that are far too simplified, this holds true for groups as well. For example, it may appear in claims such as "the teamwork in our group is uniquely good" or "management *always* ignores our group". Somewhat disparagingly, one can say that collectives fool themselves. Sometimes it is necessary for the group not to fall apart, but often the simplified view of things can be an obstacle that keeps the group from relating in a nuanced way to its surroundings and affects the group's collective drive.

These common images must be continuously maintained, or – one might say – groups must always be actively held together in order to keep them from falling apart. This "integration work" takes up a large part of any group's resources. Thus, it is a challenge for all groups to get the work of keeping together as a group to go in the same direction as the work involved in solving the group's tasks. It is in this connection that the manager plays a decisive role for the productivity of the group. The manager must help the group keep a focus on work, and this is done by teaching the group to realise when its interpretations are so "primitive" and unnuanced that they prevent or hinder the job. In order for these conceptions to be dissolved and replaced by more mature ideas, the manager must encourage the group to reveal the emotional conflicts that are behind the activation of these primitive defences. If the group does not succeed in establishing more mature, effective defences, the social community – like the individual psyche – may well be hampered or dissolved in doubt, self-destruction, failure to thrive, and paralysis.

There may be many reasons for a group to adopt immature defences, but it is always a sign that the group is experiencing pressure on its identity and existence – either from external or internal causes. For example, it may be:

- That the group is an autonomous group that has not existed long and has not received sufficient help in its establishment;
- That there has been an organisational change (perhaps, far back in the history of the firm) in which the group felt that it lost face and influence in relation to other groups;

The group as an independent unit **103**

- That the group has experienced a lack of attention from their manager and has interpreted this to mean that the group is not important in management's eyes;
- That the group has become insecure because it has interpreted the manager's lack of attention as a sign of a weak manager who cannot protect the group;
- That the members feel incompetent and insecure in relation to the new tasks the group is to take on;
- That there are destructive forces at work in the group internally (for example, in the form of power struggles or manipulation) that the group itself does not feel it can deal with and threaten the group's cohesion.

Regardless of what made the group feel threatened, it is characteristic that the group is not conscious of establishing a defence against the threat. It occurred unconsciously.

The establishment of immature defences is far from an unknown phenomenon in an organisational context in which one or more groups or, in some cases, the overall organisation can function so poorly in periods that it has a serious impact on the ability to work on the primary task. That the group or the organisation functions poorly may be a sign that the establishment of the common defence was not successful and, therefore, that the defences are ineffective. The greater the span the defences have in relation to the existential dilemmas between the individual and the community and stability and change, the more effective and mature the defences are said to be. This is also true for collective defences that are established in groups.

In order to be able to work effectively on a common product, the group members must on concurrently attune their views of what the group's job is, how they can do it together, and what the group's function and relationship is to the rest of the organisation and to external stakeholders. This takes place on the conscious level in which members agree on a framework, tasks, ground rules, and so forth for the group's work and through an unconscious process in the group in which the participants establish common, unconscious images, symbols, and views of reality. In some cases, they may stand in direct contradiction to the members' conscious views and agreements. This is true in the following case.

A work team is having problems getting their tasks finished on time because of a lack of coordination, and therefore they agree to hold a group meeting every Wednesday. They decide that attendance is mandatory and that everyone is to be prepared and active at the meetings.

But at the same time, an unconscious view has been built up among the members that the group's work is not important. This view is due, among other things, to the fact that the members who had a poor relationship with their earlier manager interpret their new manager's frequent absence from the group as a sign that the group is not important to the organisation.

> This is not formulated directly by anyone in the group but is imparted indirectly through the members' mutual communication. They use irony about the absent manager; they make derogatory remarks about the group's work area ("It's not used for anything anyway!"); they sit in the far back of the room when there is a personnel meeting for the overall organisation, and no one ever says anything positive about the group's work tasks.
>
> In the subsequent period, there is a huge drop in attendance at group meetings – most often without any notice, and those who come to the meetings remain passive except for a few people who always talk.
>
> The problems with the lack of coordination of tasks continue.

This group has unconsciously built up a common defence against the anxiety that comes from the group being afraid of being superfluous to the organisation. The defence works well insofar as it keeps the anxiety away from the consciousness of the group members, but it is ineffective because it does not allow members to relate in a sufficiently nuanced and open way to reality. The group does not know whether, purely factually, it is *actually* superfluous because it is not capable of investigating the issue and testing it against reality since the repressive defence has the effect that the group is not conscious of what it is afraid of. Under these circumstances, the group gradually becomes less and less productive because the individual employee has difficulty keeping focus on and engagement with work that is experienced as meaningless. In addition, coordination and development of the group's activities are hindered by the fact that the group is rarely assembled and that there is no real dialogue taking place at the group meetings. Thus, the group is rapidly and unconsciously realising its worst fear: it is making itself superfluous in practice by not creating value for the organisation. The group members, however, find this to be a *confirmation* of their original fear and not the *result* of a process that has its source in the group itself.

Since the group's fear is not expressed directly but only communicated indirectly, the manager feels left high and dry. He is not able to interpret the group's unconscious signals, in part, because he himself has a distant relationship to his own emotional life and, in part, because he does not know the group's history with the former manager. He experiences the group as sluggish and resistant, and he views this resistance as directed toward him as a manager and a person. He lacks the experience and knowledge to dig deeper into this resistance and, together with the group, to investigate what its components are; in other words, he is incapable of accommodating and reflecting the group's resistance. Therefore, he is unable to function as a compromise creator between the splitting defence the group has established, which gives them an unnuanced view of reality, and a more mature defence that would allow a more nuanced view, anchored in reality. This is because the manager himself becomes captured by – or becomes the bearer of – the group's splitting defence and begins to experience the group as his enemy. Thus, he places projective pressure on the group, which corresponds to the pressure the group is placing on him. As a consequence of this, he develops a pattern of behaviour in which he prioritises other groups more highly – namely, the groups in which he feels welcome and respected – and stays away from meetings with the "difficult" group. This further cements the group's view of not being important to the organisation, and its productivity falls even more.

In summary, it can be said that the group psychology theories point convincingly toward the close connection between the defence level of groups and their productivity, which the preceding case also illustrates. The next chapter deals more extensively with the question of group productivity and how to increase it.

7

PRODUCTIVITY OF GROUPS

Most people find that some groups are more productive than others; the question is how to conceptualise this difference. In Chapter 6, we found a close correlation between a group's maturity and its productivity, and that it is the job of the group leader to integrate the needs of the group with the demands from the outside. But how can the group leader and the group maintain and increase the productivity of the group? To answer this question, we draw on a number of theories about group development to describe the differences between more or less productive groups. Only when we have the theory in place to describe how to determine which groups are productive, and which are not, can we take deliberate steps to increase productivity.

Many have attempted to analyse and understand this, and in the following, we shall present some of the important contributions. We divide the different theories into three broad categories: stage theories, relational theories, and psychodynamic theories. The relational theories excel at producing outstanding methods to enhance the productivity of groups, and the psychodynamic theories put these methods into context and provide an explanation of why these methods sometimes fail to produce the desired results. The stage theories, however, are widely used, and consequently have had a major impact on the development of groups, and therefore we shall present them first.

The stage theory about groups' productivity

In 1965, Bruce Tuckman published a paper in which he presented an overview of the existing knowledge about team development (Tuckman 1965). He reviewed 55 papers on the subject, and found that the studies behind the papers could be

Productivity of groups 107

summed up in a model of team development that comprises the following four stages:

1 Forming
2 Storming
3 Norming
4 Performing.

Forming (creation/establishing the group) refers to the stage where the members learn to navigate the new context they find themselves in, and to negotiate what constitutes acceptable behaviour in the team. They look for leadership, and may develop a level of dependency on the person who assumes a leading role. At the *Storming* stage, the relations in the group are stormy, and each member gradually carves out a space to act out their own individual personality. This engenders conflict, and subgroups may form in the team. At the *Norming* stage, the team resolve their conflicts and begin to define their own norms and rules in the fellowship. At this stage, there is more room for individual differences and a strong emphasis on team harmony.

At the *Performing* stage, the members are sufficiently at ease with each other and the team to actually address complex problems systematically (Tuckman 1965).

Tuckman's model is quite popular and is widely used, not least because most people can relate to his four stages. The stages have even served as inspiration for studies of individual development in group therapy (Stone & Spielberg 2009). The model is, however not without flaws; first, it is assumed that all groups eventually pass through all four stages (i.e., that all groups develop from a low level of productivity to a higher level). This assumption fails to capture the complexity in groups' development. Anyone who has any experience with teamwork knows that groups go through highs and lows in productivity. What Tuckman's model fails to take into account is that teams sometimes experience setbacks and that progress slows down.

Secondly, Tuckman's model assumes that groups are best understood in terms of a life course perspective, which implies that the group is similar to a living organism that goes through youth, adulthood and old age (cf. Adizes 1979). The idea that organisations can be described in terms of life cycles is based on the assumption that organisations to some degree resemble living beings (see Hatch 1997: 53 for an explanation of this view). However, organisations are not living creatures; they are made up of living creatures (i.e., people), who try to coordinate their efforts. As such, we cannot say that an organisation has life phases corresponding to the biologically determined childhood, adolescence, and old age that people go through. Unlike people, organisations constantly renew themselves. New people join, others leave, and the organisation continuously evolves and adapts in response to inner or outer pressure. Not only does this mean that organisations can outlive people,

108 Group processes

it also means that an organisation, or a group within the organisation, can change from one level of productivity to another many times in the course of its existence.

Third and finally, Tuckman's model assumes that collaboration in the team will improve continuously for as long as the group remains intact. This is, however, an assumption that may not be true. It is by no means a given that a team will eventually become effective and productive. To achieve that calls for a steady and active effort from team members and leader alike. Only very rarely does a group become productive without a conscious effort to make it so.

Relational theories of groups' productivity

As described earlier, systemic organisational theory emphasises that the key element of any organisation is the relation between the individual members and the organisation. This implies that organisations are bound together by relations. Thus, one key tenet of systems theory is that an organisation is formed by its members. That way, systems theory continues the legacy from new institutionalism, but while new institutionalism and various stage models, such as Tuckman's, consider the development of collaboration an inevitable and automatic process, systems theory is more concerned with how the participants can actively and constructively develop this collaboration towards better productivity and work satisfaction. Systemic, or relational, theorists distinguish between linear forms of dialogue on the one hand and circular, acknowledging forms on the other. This differentiation implies an implicit dichotomy between less productive (linearly thinking) organisations, and more productive (circularly thinking) organisations (Gergen & Gergen 1998; McNamee 1998; Haslebo 2004; Helth 2006).

Traditional linear thinking is based on a linear conception of the temporal relation of causes and their effects. One classic example of this is the project plan; first we will do A, then B, and the result will be C, because that is how it was planned. However, if things fail to go as planned, which of course has been known to happen, linear thinking will make you look for the cause of the disruption in one particular place in the organisation, very often connected to a specific event or individual, which again engenders a linear form of communication. The net result is that all events are evaluated as either beneficial or detrimental in relation to the desired result, which means that everything individual members do is constantly up for evaluation. This makes every individual's behaviour and responsibilities the focal point in the life of the organisation, and means that whenever a problem occurs, a "guilty party" is soon identified. Furthermore, this type of organisation is less concerned with the relation between actions and with how the interaction between different events and people's communication influences both.

The reason this type of dialogue is a hindrance to productivity is, according to the experts in relational theories, that it leads to suspicion, withdrawal and loneliness among the members of the organisation, because everyone and everything is constantly under evaluation and at risk of being singled out as the root cause of some problem (Haslebo 2004: 57).

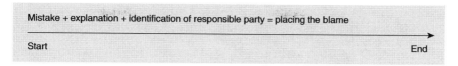

FIGURE 7.1 Linear dialogue

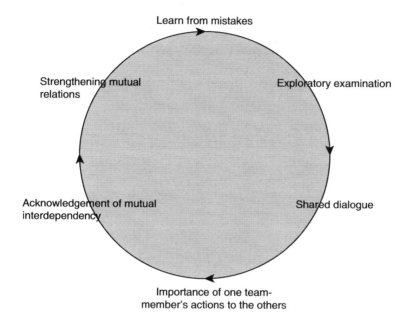

FIGURE 7.2 Circular dialogue

Circular forms of dialogue, on the other hand, concern the relations between individuals in the organisation. Thus, the causes behind events take second place to patterns in the collaboration and the intentions behind people's actions. It is assumed that all individuals have valid reasons to act the way they do seen from their specific position in the organisation. The circular form of dialogue is based on a systemic interpretation of the group, and it is assumed that everybody has an impact on everybody else. In this view, responsibility for any given result cannot be placed on one single individual, but is considered a shared product that the entire group has contributed to, and bears (at least partial) responsibility for. The circular form of dialogue provides a better opportunity to examine and discuss how individual members of the team contribute in terms of actions and their emotions, because assessment and blame are set aside in favour of connections and mutual influences. Thus, the circular form of dialogue allows for a more efficient group, which is much better suited to address challenges and problems as a team (Haslebo 2004: 58).

110 Group processes

One key message from the authors of relational theories is, therefore, that circular dialogue can help members of groups and organisations to improve their collaboration. In order to actually be circular, the dialogue must fulfil certain criteria, which can be boiled down to the requirement that is has to be acknowledging. To that end, the relational approach has developed a very useful method called "appreciative inquiry".

Appreciative inquiry (AI) has become widely popular in organisational development. Originally developed in the 1980s by Cooperrider and Srivastva, AI is based on the simple notion that if you look for something specific, that is what you will find (Cooperrider & Srivastva 1987).

This means that if you go looking for problems and things that do not work in an organisation, you will find just that. If, however, you look for things that work, and focus on people's resources and for the reasons they have to stay in the organisation, you will find the things that matter and that are worth building on. This method finds qualities instead of problems, and things that work rather than things that do not.

Thus, the question "What makes this valuable?" is a key question in AI, just like the basic notion behind AI is that any organisation is a miracle!

However, relational theories are incapable of explaining why the circular dialogue works as well as it often does in practice. This is because relational theories focus more on the conscious relations between people than on the subconscious relations. This makes it difficult for relational theories to explain why a circular appreciative inquiry has such huge potential to transform an organisation.

We have to be mindful, however, of the linguistic trap inherent in the distinction between the conscious and subconscious aspects of individuals and of relations, because this distinction may well lead us to the wrong conclusions. The word "conscious" has a positive connotation, and is often associated with positive qualities, such as reason and rationality, tolerance and so forth, whereas "subconscious" tends to connote a lack of reflection and haphazard behaviour. In a psychodynamic context, both terms are free from any connotations. In this context, we cannot say that it is better to be conscious about something than to act on subconscious impulses. The terms are used in a strictly descriptive sense, i.e., to describe whether phenomena (emotions, thoughts and actions) are readily available for analysis.

When relational theory talks about transitioning from a linear to a circular mode of thought, there is a certain similarity with the development of the defensive levels described by psychodynamic theory. One problem of relational theory, however, is that a distinction between linear and circular dialogue is hardly an accurate description of the difference between productive and less productive forms of collaboration. One reason for this lack of precision is that the relational theories are less inclined to investigate why the two different modes of communication emerge. Why, when it is obviously more enjoyable and productive to use the circular mode, do all dialogues not play out this way? Is it just a bad habit, or is there something else at play?

Psychodynamic theories about groups' productivity

This is the "something else" that the psychodynamic theories attempt to explain when they describe the differences between productive and non-productive groups, and draw heavily on the concept "psychological maturity of groups". A number of analyses and theories show how psychological maturity is a key determinant for an organisation's ability to produce results. Most famous in this respect is Wilfred Bion and his work on the psychological states of groups, which we will return to again later (Bion 2006 [1961]). Kernberg, in particular, has explored the importance of the leader's personality and maturity for the group's productivity (Kernberg 1998). Menzies-Lyth has, among other things, analysed immature defence mechanisms in the health sector (Lyth 1988). Jaques studied bureaucracy as a bulwark against regression (Jaques 1976). Armstrong and Rustin (2014) have revisited the latter two in their recent anthology. Finally, Alsted has established a set of concepts for interpretation of the interplay between productivity and the maturity of individuals, organisations, and societies (Alsted 2005).

The aforementioned authors all agree that the more psychologically mature a group is, the more productive it will be. In this context, productivity is a broad concept that denotes not only the quality and quantity of products, but also the context for the production, such as the proficiency of the team members, their ability to make good decisions, to solve conflicts, and so forth.

How, then, do we define psychological maturity? The obvious choice would be to introduce some sort of grading for different levels of maturity. In the 1940s, Melanie Klein developed a theory to describe the psychological development from infancy to adulthood, and introduced two levels of maturity, or "positions", that the child progresses through as part of its natural psychological development: the depressive and the paranoid-schizoid position (Klein 1977). Several of the aforementioned authors used Klein's work when they transferred the two positions to the analysis of group psychology. For groups, however, there is no "natural" progression through stages. Rather, groups swing back and forth between the depressive and the paranoid-schizoid position. In this book, the paranoid-schizoid position corresponds to the splitting defensive level, and the depressive position to the repressive and parts of the integrating defensive level. The pathologising terminology in Klein's and Kernberg's models now appears dated and offensive, and since the aim with the present book is not to pathologise quite normal psychological responses, neither for individuals nor groups, we strive to adopt more descriptive and normalising terms.

Wilfred Bion, who also counts as one of the founding fathers of group psychology, also distinguished between two states (levels of productivity) for groups to be in, and he called them the basic assumptions group and the work group, respectively (Bion 2006 [1961]). The basic assumptions group corresponds to the splitting defensive level in this book, and the work group corresponds to the repressive and parts of the integrating defensive level (Alsted 2005).

Table 7.1 shows how the different authors' terms correspond.

112 Group processes

TABLE 7.1 Overview of terminology of selected authors

Klein	*Kernberg et al.*	*Bion*	*Alsted*
Paranoid–schizoid phase individual	Paranoid–schizoid phase individual/ group	Basic assumptions group	Splitting individual/ group
Depressive phase individual	Depressive phase individual/group	Work group	Repressive and integrative individual/group

Bion's theory, in particular, is widely known in group psychology, and is used in a number of Danish and English texts on leadership and collaboration (Lyth 1989; Kernberg 1998; Heinskou & Visholm 2004; Hasselager 2006). Since Bion touches on important elements for understanding the productivity of groups, we shall take a closer look at his theory in the following section.

Bion's theory on the maturity of groups

Bion's two group states are, as mentioned, comparable to the splitting and repressive defensive levels that were introduced in Chapter 3, and which will be explained in more detail in relation to the maturity of groups later in this chapter (Alsted 2005). Thus, the work group state can be interpreted as a type of repressive and sometimes integrative state, while the basic assumptions group can be interpreted as splitting (Kernberg 1998: 7)

In the work group state, the group is keen and able to work in a focused way towards fulfilling the group's task, according to Bion. The members are able to collaborate rationally while also maintaining their individual identity. The collaboration in such a group is characterised by mutual trust, and the group will strive to develop (Bion 2006 [1961]: 98–99). In short, the group can strike a productive balance between individual and group, and between stability and change.

In the basic assumption state, however, the group is unable to focus on the task, and is instead completely distracted by seemingly irrational subconscious needs. The individuality of group members suffers, but on the other hand, the team spirit is valued highly. While it remains in this state, the group does not develop, according to Bion (Bion 2006 [1961]: 141–165). People in this state are both happy and unhappy at the same time; happy because the roles are simple, responsibility is limited and feelings such as anger or fear are disassociated, but also unhappy because individuality and competences are reduced – people feel disempowered. Bion assumed that the basic assumption state is a defensive mechanism to ward off psychotic fear (Bion 2006 [1961]: 163, 189). He assumed that basic assumptions are adopted as a subconscious defensive mechanism if and when there is a high level of fear in the group (e.g., if the group is newly formed, or if the group suddenly finds itself under pressure).

Productivity of groups **113**

Bion believes that the basic assumption state occurs in three different types:

1   Dependency
2   Fight/flight
3   Pairing.

The characteristics of each type are outlined in Table 7.2.

Bion's description of the three basic assumption states holds a number of examples of the various states from his work with groups. Furthermore, anyone with experience from an organisation can intuitively grasp the division into basic assumption state and work group state, because most people will have experienced a group that never was, or has ceased to be, productive. However, the notion of the basic assumption state comprises a certain ambiguity, which can make it difficult to apply in practice.

What if, for instance, there are more basic assumption states than the three in Bion's model? Why are these three particularly fundamental? Actually, a number of

TABLE 7.2 Bion's three types of basic assumption states

Dependency	Fight/flight	Pairing
• The leader is considered omnipotent.	• The group stands united against a vague external opposition (be it "terrorists" or "the competition").	• Group members focus on a pair in the group (not necessarily an actual couple and not necessarily of opposite genders).
• Group members consider themselves inadequate and incompetent.		
• Group members strive for knowledge, power, and goodness from the leader.	• The group expects that the leader directs the battle against the enemy and prevents intra-group conflicts.	• The pair symbolises the group's hope for survival and reproduction.
• Therefore, group members are always greedy and unsatisfied.	• In case of differences of opinion, the group splits into subgroups that fight among each other.	• The pair becomes a sort of saviour figure for the group, and is expected to lead the group into a glorious future.
• When the leader fails to live up to these expectations, he/she loses status and the search for a replacement commences.	• Subgroups often evolve into "defenders" or "opponents" of the group leader.	• The pair becomes the centre of the group and the other members become their audience.
	• Group members attempt to control the leader, or believe they are being controlled by the leader.	• Intimacy in general and sexual attraction in particular serve as a defence against dependency and aggression.
	• Aggression is projected onto the external enemy.	
	• Group unity is preserved by denial of any intra-group conflicts.	

114 Group processes

authors have added further basic assumption states to the model, states just as fundamental as Bion's (cf. Heinskou 2004: 54–57). All these authors seem, however, to agree with Bion's basic premise, which is that a group can lose its focus on the task out of fear, but also emphasise that a group's defensive mechanisms against this fear can assume other expressions than Bion's three basic assumptions.

Two of Bion's basic assumptions have gained particular popularity, and are often quoted by others, namely, "Dependency" and "Fight/Flight". Weak groups, which depend on strong leaders, or groups that define themselves in terms of external foes, are both very frequent and very diverse. Most people have personal experiences with these types of groups. Bion can help us identify these groups and to explain how and why they are unproductive, and he also explains how they emerge. Bion's third basic assumption, the "Pairing", is a somewhat different story, because this condition can be much more difficult to identify.

Bion's theory of the pairing condition

This condition can be difficult to identify in the form that Bion described. However, since subconscious processes in groups are closely related to the initial experiences people have with groups (i.e., with their family), it is important to be able to recognise and to consciously work with this condition. Group work can be very similar to the relations in a family, and, according to several authors, group members tend to project their own early experiences from their own family onto the group (see, e.g., Kernberg 1998; Heinskou & Visholm 2004). Obviously, the pair is essential for a child's early experiences in the family, where the parents are the utterly dominant force, and serve as both "judges" and "saviours". According to Bion, a pair in a group can become so engrossed in an exchange of opinion or in some collaboration between them that they form a special bond. If the rest of the group then remains passive, this pair will gain a special status in the group and become a sort of messianic figures that represent the group's hope for salvation, help and "fertility" (Bion 2006 [1961]: 62, 150–151).

While it is beyond discussion that a pair can become very important for a group's collective defence, Bion's description fails to depict the immense diversity between the actual expressions of this mechanism in practice. Bion's description shows how one pair can be idolised by the group, but pairs can also be demonised by the group, and be the subjects of envy and anger from the other members, in line with the child's perception of its parents as both saviours and judges. Thus, it seems likely that there is some correspondence between the individual group members inner image of "parents" and their predilection for, subconsciously, using the pairing condition as defensive mechanism.

The driving force behind the basic assumption "pairing" condition might then be that the physical or emotional intimacy of the pair threatens the group, and that other group members subsequently envy, and feel kept out by, the pair. Thus, every member of the group is forced to come to grips with the pair in order to not be left out in the cold. This makes the group attempt to "take over" and control the pair in order to use it for its own purposes (i.e., to reduce the level of anxiety). The

Productivity of groups **115**

overtaking manoeuvre can play out both in a positive way, through idealisation, and negatively, through demonisation, but the overall aim is the same: to reduce the threat against the group's existence that the pair is perceived to represent.

Examples from public life can serve to illustrate this point. A well-known public couple can force the public (i.e., the group) into a pairing condition. Bill and Hillary Clinton in the United States, and Danish Crown Prince Frederik and his wife, Princess Mary, are examples of this. Couples who live in the spotlight often spark textbook examples of societies in the pairing condition. Particularly effective are royal weddings, which can make entire societies respond with collective and simultaneous splitting, where all negative feelings have been disassociated in favour of pure idolisation, although everyone knows that the couple may later run into trouble, get divorced, and so forth.

When a divorce happens in a royal family, and the couple obviously is no longer a pair that people can project their pairing ideals onto, the condition ends. This leaves room for more nuanced narratives about the involved, as amply illustrated by Prince Charles and Lady Diana, and similarly by Danish Prince Joachim and Countess Alexandra, who were also discussed in markedly different terms after their divorce.

This is relevant for group work in organisations because pairs occur in organisations as well as in public life. Everyday work life engenders a range of emotions, and sometimes these emotions lead to more or less legitimate, and sometimes even imaginary, pairings, the existence of which can have a profound impact on the other members of the group. In Bion's work, a pair can be either an actual couple, or a symbolic set of parents for the group, as illustrated by the following case.

After completing her studies, Inge finds a job with a small advertising agency. After six months and following a recommendation by Inge, Lotte is also taken on board. The two women became acquainted during their education and are friends outside of work. Both are extraverted, and after a while they acquire a position as informal leaders, not least because the formal leader at the time appears weak and indecisive.

The rest of the group looks up to Inge and Lotte. Inge in particular, but Lotte is also recognised by all as being highly skilled. People often come to the pair with professional questions, and eventually all major decisions are run past the two.

But at the same time, many feel uncertain about the two. Private conversations reveal that the rest of the group have countless ideas about the nature of Inge's and Lotte's partnership outside of work, and people believe it is much deeper and important than the two think themselves. Many find that the two are a negative influence on the rest of the group who are "left out of the loop" and "don't have a say in things". Inge and Lotte are referred to as "the besties", and there are those who indicate that Inge and Lotte are perhaps "more than just friends".

116 Group processes

This case serves to illustrate how the group establishes a subconscious defence against the anxiety that is caused by a weak and indecisive leader. The pair is "elected" to stand in for the absent leader, but at the same time, the pair is perceived to represent a threat against the coherence of the group, because the mere existence of a pair represents the threat of exclusion for everyone else. The alliance between Inge and Lotte is perceived as so strong that the others are powerless against it. The group defends itself against this threat, which is perceived as very real, and which consumes a large amount of the group's attention. Many members are of the opinion that all problems in the group are caused by this "group in a group" that Inge and Lotte represent.

At this stage, the group is transitioning from a work group state towards a basic assumption state, specifically to the pairing condition. The group's focus gradually shifts from the tasks at hand towards the pair, the perception of the pair solidifies, and Inge and Lotte are no longer perceived as two distinct individuals; problems are explained away with simplified explanations, and the conditions for collaboration deteriorate quickly. An increasing amount of the group's emotional resources is spent on the situation within the group rather than on the group's tasks.

The group defends itself against this emotionally unpleasant and stressful condition by erecting immature defences of a splitting nature. The group alternates between idolising (e.g., by exaggerating their professional skills and diminishing the rest of the group's skills) and demonising the pair, and tries to cause a division in the pair by presenting Inge as slightly more competent than Lotte. Note also how the emotional instability in the group makes people imagine things. In an attempt to explain and control the situation, people invent a narrative that exaggerates the nature of the pair's relationship and hint at or even suggest a sexual element to the union.

Alsted's theories about the maturity of groups

As explained earlier, Alsted applies three levels of maturity for groups, because this allows for a more nuanced characterisation of group maturity than two levels (Alsted 2005). The three levels of maturity were introduced in Chapter 3, in relation to the maturity of individuals. In the present chapter, this model is expanded to include groups as well.

1   In the *splitting*, or binary, group, there is very little room for individuality, and any sense of community exists only within the group or organisation. The worldview is black and white. The world around the group or organisation is seen as foes or all-powerful heroes, and there are limits to the trust internally in the group.
2   In the *repressive* group, the scope for individuality and community is expanded. The call of duty is often referred to, and denotes the duty each member has towards other members and the community. There are many rules for how to

do things, but on the other hand, the individual also has certain rights, such as a limit to the number of work hours, limited responsibility, and so forth.

3   In the *integrating* group, the differences between individual and community are expanded even further. The individual is not only obliged to deliver a certain minimum effort but is also expected to be committed to the cause and to be proactive. In return, the individual expects the community to demonstrate genuine interest, care, and attention.

In conclusion, we can say that the allowed level of individuality and sense of community goes up for each step on this ladder. In the following, we shall explore each level in further detail.

The splitting or binary group

As mentioned in Chapter 3, the terms "splitting" and "binary" denote that group members subscribe to a worldview where things are black and white, pleasant or unpleasant, good or bad.

When splitting is used as a defence mechanism in a group, it means that the group's internal and external reality is divided ('split') into just two categories. Groups and organisations tend to fall back to this defensive strategy when the group or organisation's identity is perceived to be under threat and in danger of collapse. The threat can be real (e.g., a school facing shutdown), but it can also be imaginary and a result of emotionally founded fantasies among the group members (e.g., that the leadership does not respect the group members). When the danger of losing the group's identity is perceived to be imminent, a large part of the group's resources is devoted to preserving or reinforcing the group's or organisation's unity by defining the group or organisation in opposition to other groups or organisations.

The splitting group tends to perceive the surrounding world, such as partners or competitors, as either all-powerful and enviable, or as incompetent and hostile. For instance, it is not rare to see distrust between the sales team and the development team in a private company, or between two public agencies that work with the same group of citizens. This predisposition for mistrust is usually an expression of splitting, at least when it is not based on specific experiences and knowledge about the other part. However, even specific experiences can be interpreted as splitting, so that no matter what the other part says or does, it is interpreted as either incompetent or as proof of either fundamental ignorance or of the other part's hostile intentions.

The binary organisation is quite complex and can be very confusing, because it appears to have a strong sense of community while at the same time the competition inside the organisation is quite fierce. To understand this dichotomy, it is important to remember that splitting is a very basic defence, which can be activated when the identity is in danger. If a group suddenly is in danger of disintegrating, most members will respond with anxiety, and start to question their own identity:

118 Group processes

Who am I? Where do I belong? If the danger to the group is perceived as critical, some members can give up their individuality and identify completely with the group instead. In those cases, we say that the self fuses with the group and becomes one with the group or the organisation (Kernberg 1998: 5–6). In a frantic search for something firm to hold on to, individuals can identify completely with the group in order to prop up a self that is in danger of dissolution. In this case, any threat to the group is a threat to the individual, who is afraid that if the group fails, so will he. This makes people see the world in binaries: those who support the group and those who do not support the group, which is the root of the apparent strong sense of community within the group.

However, when one's personal identity is that closely tied to the group, it becomes even more important to do well within the group. If you have no value in the group, you have no value whatsoever. If all the members of the group feel this way, a fierce competition for status will erupt, along with a strong fear of not making it. This means that a binary organisation or group is also characterised by inner division, conformity, and a lot of mutual surveillance.

The strong emphasis on the community in binary groups and organisations leaves very little room for individuality and very little tolerance for diversity. Any unique skills are viewed with suspicion because they implicitly threaten the unity of the group. This is true both inside the group, but also in meetings with people from outside the group. In its extreme state, this type of organisation can be considered totalitarian.

Excessively splitting organisations are often engaged in some big cause (e.g., a (civil) war or a revolution). Many of the more radical political and religious groups are binary in nature. However, the binary type is also found in more everyday contexts. One typical example is an organisation under existential threat due to bankruptcy or heavy cutbacks. A serious threat can often turn an organisation binary. Consider for instance a school closing down, major staff reductions in public organisations, or other types of major reorganisations in public or private organisations.

The sense of community does have its limits, however; often the group fails to maintain the close relation between individual and group, because the foundation is somehow lacking. This often leads to the development of a series of "sham rituals", such as joint meetings where everyone seemingly agrees to use a certain method, or seminars where everyone loudly expresses their support for the group. However, outside of these rituals, individuality rears its head. The method may not be seen as meaningful at all, or the reward for support to the group is seen as insufficient. The individual strays from the demand for uniformity and loyalty to the group, and the strict demands can lead some members to assume a secret individuality within the group. This life is at odds with the stated norms of the group, and is experienced as shameful and as a tacit undermining of the group. And yet, it may seem preferable to adhering to the empty rituals that reinforce uniformity (Kernberg 1998: 279). Sham rituals show how inner division limit the group's ability to act in unison despite a seemingly strong sense of community.

One characteristic of the relations in the splitting group is an intense struggle for dominance within the group and with the surrounding world. Any type of praise or criticism is met with immediate response, because criticism is seen as a threat to the group's identity and praise as a confirmation, and both lead to strong emotional responses. The actual causes of the praise or criticism are less important. Thus emotions run high and ruin any attempt at open, nuanced dialogue, and individual members' personal feelings are loudly expressed as anger or joy. Furthermore, information is only shared sparingly, because knowledge is power in the splitting organisation.

Other characteristics of the splitting group

Splitting groups or organisations can be recognised by certain characteristics, although not all of them have to be present all at once.

The leader is demonised or idolised

In the splitting group, the leader is often idolised and enjoys an exalted status. This group derives its identity and purpose from the leader. This leader can, in principle, not be wrong or argued with; group members will project every positive quality they want onto the leader. Should the leader, however, fail to satisfy the group's expectations, the situation may reverse itself and the leader is suddenly demonised, is unable to do anything right, and is considered the root cause of all the bad things that happen.

The leader manipulates instead of leading

Another potential problem is if the leader employs a splitting strategy him/herself and plays the game of "divide and conquer" with the group members. This draws members' attention away from the leader, for example by linguistic ploys such as these: "I want you, Peter, to do this task, because you are much better qualified than Paul", or "I fought against this cutback all I could, but you know how boneheaded the board can be".

The organisation has a simplistic view of itself

Splitting groups waver between over- and underestimating themselves. When they overestimate themselves, there are no limits to its power and potential: "We have a great spirit of collaboration here", or "We are among the best in our field". The overestimation, however, often include its own opposite, self-deprecation: "We are bumbling amateurs compared to the others", or "We don't collaborate very well". Public organisations, for instance, often have wildly inaccurate ideas about how effective the private sector is as well as other similarly self-deprecating views about efficiency in public organisations.

120 Group processes

Threat of elimination from the community

Failure to immediately accept and adhere to the group's norms and ideology can result in newcomers being kept out of the good graces of the group, as described in Chapter 4. Binary organisations often employ scapegoats – individuals who are, or are perceived to be, different from the majority, and who therefore threaten the uniformity of the group (Obholzer & Roberts 2003; Alsted 2007).

The group is referred to as an organism with its own needs

This happens through phrases such as "The group requires . . ." or "The group thinks that . . .". Typically, phrases like these are used by a select few, while the majority of the group keeps silent out of fear of rejection from the group. The validity of the statements is rarely obvious, and there are no balancing follow-up statements from individual members.

Members' private lives are subject to control

This includes things like sexual behaviour, romantic affiliations, implicit dress codes, and other types of "accepted behaviour". Mild versions of this can be found in any kind of organisation (e.g., the use of uniforms), but when they become systemic and involve a large part of the members' private lives, it is a sign of a splitting organisation.

Fierce competition for professional standing

Competition exists in all groups and organisations, but in a binary organisation competition can be particularly fierce, because it seems to be so dangerous to be expelled from the group. This makes it difficult to talk about the competition; it is a sensitive subject, and threatens the fragile structure and identity of the group. Thus, competition takes place in the shadows, which makes it difficult to address and deal with.

Widespread loneliness at work

A perceived lack of a shared sense of community leads to widespread loneliness and a basic uncertainty about one's position in the group, which again leads to depression and of lacking a sense of purpose. People speak *about* themselves rather than *with* each other.

Basic structures and systems are untrustworthy

In this situation, internal meetings, budgets, accounts, quality assurance, and so forth do not offer any immediate rewards to those people who maintain these systems, and so they are often left to fester in a binary group or organisation. The collaboration within the group lacks sufficient force to maintain these activities, and the overall sense of purpose is insufficient for these tasks to seem meaningful.

The repressive group

Repression is what happens when we store away the feelings of anxiety that follow from certain relations and situations deep in our subconscious. Thus, these feelings are more integrated than under splitting conditions, yet not completely, because repression hinders a conscious processing of the causes of the anxiety. And yet, repression is a boon, in that it spares the members of a group from the rampant mood swings that are associated with the splitting condition.

This means that every member of a repressive group has a vested interest in maintaining the repression, since it protects them from the unpredictable conflicts that play out in a binary organisation. The various means of repression, some of which were outlined in Chapter 3, represent ways to address the aggression that will occur between members of a group. However, repression comes at a price: it places a constraint upon a key factor of behaviour; our emotions. Thus, one characteristic of relations within a repressive group is that they become "boring". When causes for anxiety and aggression are stripped away from the interaction between members, some of the authenticity of relations disappears as well, and all that is left are pleasantries and polite behaviour. Many workplaces with a cheerful atmosphere may in fact be much less happy places than they first appear. The cheerfulness may be a defence against, and a way to avoid, conflicts. The cost of this approach is that conflicts are left unaddressed, and are therefore not used as the drivers of improvements that they could have been.

To face one's repressed thoughts and feelings, and to engage openly in a discussion about conflicts may be so intimidating that most people will go far to avoid them. We should never underestimate people's desire to avoid conflict and confrontations at work; they may even go so far as to lie to co-workers, managers – or themselves. Avoidance of conflict can also take many other forms, however. Some of the typical include routines, systems, and rituals as means to maintain repression. In the repressive group, just like in the binary, there are limits to individuality, because the conflicts arise in the negotiation between individuals' different needs and wants. In the repressive organisation, this negotiation is ritualised, and can only be expressed in strictly controlled ways (through hierarchy, promotions, workplace agreements, etc.). Thus, the repressive organisation allows for a greater difference between individual and group, because the group and the organisation have better guards against dissolution.

The classical hierarchical bureaucracy is the quintessential repressive organisation. Each task is dealt with according to fixed rules, and decisions are made at the appointed level of the hierarchy. A modern organisation is less strictly hierarchical but does borrow a lot from that mode of organisation. The aim to design an organisation devoid of conflict, where the production runs like clockwork, has many contemporary expressions with one thing in common: they attempt to map out and plan each step of a given process. Quality assurance, project plans, competence

122 Group processes

development courses, and resource management systems are all examples of measures to reach that goal.

It is characteristic for the way relations develop in the repressive group that communication is generally informative and distant, and that it is kept in abstract terms. Comments seem to demonstrate harmony: "great", "very good", and "exciting" are often used, regardless of what the speaker actually means. Responses are generic, while less emotionally laden than in the binary group, and personal opinions are left unsaid. Praise and criticism are both scarce and vague: "I think you are doing a great job", or "Not to criticise or anything, but I think this could be done better".

Discussions in this group are not genuine dialogue, but rather parallel monologues, where no one is really listening to what the other person says, where communication is often disconfirmed, and where no one expands on what the other person has said. As a result, discussions lead nowhere, are repetitive, and have very little potential to generate change.

Other characteristics of the repressive group

Compared to the splitting group, the repressive group represents a step in the right direction in terms of efficiency and coherence. The repression of the conflicts enables a reinforcement of the bonds that tie together the group or the organisation. However, since emotions and conflicts do not disappear but are merely repressed, they will find other and less direct means of expression. This effect is evident in a number of ways.

These reactions all allow the individual or the group to express emotions or conflicts in ways that do not challenge the group's preferred repressive defence.

Loss of initiative and creativity among the employees

One of the most serious consequences of repression is that initiative and creativity are stifled or lost. When access to emotions is obstructed, new ideas are blocked as well. The routines that help a repressive group avoid conflicts generate a conservative atmosphere with little room for innovation, and the shallow communication leaves no room to explore complex issues such as improvements or innovation.

Incessant re-organisation

Repeated reorganisations may be a sign that problems and conflicts are dealt with in a roundabout way by "reshuffling the deck" and "keeping people on their toes". However, the lack of attention to the actual issues mean that they go unresolved and are carried along into the new structure.

No follow-up on past decisions

Plans are made, but are never carried out. In the repressive group, there is usually no lack of unrealistic sales projections, overly optimistic growth strategies, budgets

Productivity of groups **123**

and project plans that are ignored, meeting schedules that people fail to follow, and so forth. When these plans are not followed, it is often because they were made without allowing for conflicts and problems that get in the way of these plans. In the repressive organisation, however, people cannot talk openly about this and learn from their mistakes, and so the cycle of unrealistic planning is repeated over and over.

Missed deadlines

Deadlines can be hard to follow but are only rarely actually impossible. One common characteristic of repressive groups and organisations is that deadlines are frequently missed, and that it often takes a long time before anyone bats an eye at the delay. Missing a deadline is one way to express frustration, uncertainty, disagreement, or aggression in a way that refers to facts (e.g., lack of resources) rather than to emotions and personal feelings.

Missed meetings and agreements

If it is commonplace that people show up late or unprepared for meetings, or fail to hold up their end of a deal, there is usually more to it than merely personality or happenstance. It will more often than not be due to some unresolved conflict that ties to the specific situation or to the group in general.

Too many long meetings that lead nowhere

Repressive groups are also characterised by too many and too long meetings. Usually, these meetings lead nowhere in particular, and this will often be due to a lack of "relational competence", because the conflicts that get in the way of firm decisions and results cannot be brought out into the light at the meetings. Instead, people talk endlessly in circles around the actual problems.

Complaints about stress

Stress predominantly occurs in repressive organisations. Complaints about stress can be a way to cope with phenomena such as feelings of inferiority, professional incompetence, lack of recognition from management, lack of influence, and so forth. Stress has become recognised as a way to objectify a condition brought on by the individual's feelings and by the group's and the leaders' ways to address these feelings.

Abundance of sick leave

In some groups, sick leave is generally accepted as a means to vent one's dissatisfaction or anger. By calling in sick, people can express unpleasant feelings in a way that does not cause further conflict, and can thus excuse themselves from unpleasant or

124 Group processes

problematic situations at work. Many groups accept sick leave as a matter of course and only rarely take it up with the person in question ("Everyone can fall sick, no one can be blamed for that"), despite the fact that company policy calls for sick leave meetings; and if these meetings are held, they are usually devoid of meaningful content.

Lack of loyalty towards management

If the desire to avoid conflict keeps people from criticising the management openly, one can always vent one's frustration by speaking about management behind its back. This type of disloyalty is very widespread and generally accepted by employees (and in fact also by the management) in a repressive organisation.

Gossip and slander

When emotions are repressed, they take on a shadow existence in the form of, among other things, slander and gossip. Gossip allows people to talk about things that are left out of the superficial relations, and slander takes the edge off unresolved conflicts. There is no way to get rid of slander and gossip in a repressed group (even if company policy and values talk about "trust" and "freedom of expression"), because they are quite necessary safety valves. Their impact, however, can be devastating, and may hinder maturation of the group or even cause a regression to the splitting condition.

The integrating group

Even if it is an explicit aim, far too many organisations fail to combine people's efforts towards a common goal. The integrating group, however, has better chances of success than the splitting or the repressive group.

People in the integrating group are characterised by the fact that they manage to relate to one another without resorting to power struggles or repression of any conflicts that might occur. This allows people to focus on the common goal, to the benefit of both employees and the organisation. The intra-group dynamics consume fewer emotional resources, which are thus available for productive work instead.

There are not fewer conflicts in an integrating group. In fact, there are typically more, because they are allowed to come out into the open, and because working on resolving old conflicts sometimes leads to new ones. In conflicts, however, lies a lot of energy and information, which can be used to solve the tasks at hand. Conflicts can be a powerful driver towards improvements in the way tasks are dealt with. This is probably the most important fact about integrating groups and organisations; that managers and staff are able to tap into the emotive and actionable energy from conflicts without losing sight of the overall objective, and without threatening the participants' selves or mental well-being.

Productivity of groups **125**

No one group can address every conflict in a mature way. All individuals are at risk of regression under emotional pressure. What distinguishes integrating groups from the other types is how many of the conflicts the group is able to address openly. It has been said that a good marriage is characterised by the spouses being able to argue without holding a grudge for too long afterwards. Something like that could be said about the integrating group: disagreement is allowed without it turning into animosity, and without the individual having to disassociate, suppress, or even repress significant parts of one's emotional responses.

In an integrating group, people truly feel that they have a common goal. The sense of community is stronger than in the splitting or the repressive organisation. This leaves room for more individuality and more nuances within the community. Therefore, an integrating group is more open to new views and ways of doing things than other types of groups. Furthermore, both internal and external communication is typically much more specific and focused on the common cause.

The range of responses is also more varied. It is possible to recognise good and bad elements about a given thing, and people can disagree in a respectful manner. Praise and criticism are given freely, but specifically and in relation to the common goal. Personal opinions are openly shared, but in a nuanced way.

In this group, creativity is high, because making mistakes neither means automatic rejection from the community nor does it lead to snide remarks. Mistakes are not ignored, but criticism is given openly and with respect for the individual and the individual's place in the group. Intentions and actions are considered separately, and the basic assumption is that people's intentions are good.

In conclusion, we can say that the integrating group is capable of addressing the fundamental dilemmas between individual and community and stability and change better than the other types of groups, while also leaving room for more individuality and a strong sense of community. Furthermore, there is sufficient stability and sense of meaning for changes to be developed and incorporated without undue problems.

Other characteristics of the integrating group

It is characteristic of the integrating group that its members display a pattern of behaviour, which shows that they have access to, and control over, their emotional responses. Thus, they are better able to deal with their own weaknesses, which makes it easier for everyone to navigate through each other's responses.

Loyalty to the organisation

In organisations of a certain size, maintaining a sense of shared purpose can be difficult, as larger organisations are typically subdivided into several disparate units with each their separate purpose, and may even be situated in different locales. The experience of a shared purpose, however, is vital for the individual's loyalty to the organisation. Integrating groups successfully preserve the sense of community, both

126 Group processes

locally and towards the organisation as a whole, regardless of how big the organisation is. Preserving the sense of community is very much the task of management, and is based on a strong mutual loyalty both between the individual and the community but also between management and staff.

Extensive collaboration

In integrating groups, you will often find a high level of collaboration between employees. In binary and repressive groups, work is delegated more than shared. In integrating groups, whatever work delegation is required is resolved through close collaboration. For example, it may be discussed what to put down on paper before it is written, or people take turns adding to a text. This high level of collaboration will, in most cases, lead to a number of disagreements or conflicts between the collaborators on issues such as style, key points, length, time consumption, and so forth. This is only natural. In the integrating group, the collaborators deal with these conflicts as they occur, which leads to an even better collaboration and a better end product.

Systematic evaluations

The ability to recognise one's own mistakes and to learn from them is a key competence of the integrating group, and is only possible when each member feels certain that they are accepted members of the group, and that they all share the same overall goal. This certainty helps people bear the pain of having one's own and others' flaws and mistakes discussed in public. Systematic evaluations help incorporate regular discussions of new measures and allows the group to discuss daily practice on a regular basis.

Meetings are brief and efficient, and genuine dialogue takes place

Facilitating efficient meetings is one of the most difficult things to do in an organisation, both for management and staff. In the integrating group, meetings comprise a balance between open discussions and more focused control over proceedings and decisions. To get this balance right calls for a high level of tolerance and mutual trust among the participants, as well as a shared understanding of, and focus on, the common goals.

More conflicts are discussed in public and without mutual condemnation

Integrating groups are better equipped than other types of groups to discuss conflicts publicly and systematically. "Publicly" means that the parties at odds know that they are (or are informed that they are) parts in a conflict, and "systematically" means that management addresses conflicts in accordance to the policy on arbitration (impartially, empathic and in an attempt to find win–win solutions).

Plans are followed

Revisions of a plan are not necessarily a setback, but recognised as responsible behaviour and as necessary to achieve the shared goals. When plans are not followed, it is usually because those who were supposed to implement them did not actually support the plan, or that the plan was unrealistic. Integrating groups can address such issues and act on them before a given plan is derailed.

Five reservations against the defensive levels

Before we begin to apply the three defensive levels to describe actual groups or organisations, we must recognise five reservations related to these levels.

Firstly, groups and organisations are fully capable of "forgetting" more mature defence mechanisms, for instance if a new and less mature leader takes over, or in case of increased outer pressure, such as increased demand or a change in government. It can also happen through major reorganisations or during mergers with other groups or organisations. Rather than stages in a life cycle, each level should be understood as indicative of the collaboration within a group or organisation at any given moment. The levels tell us something about the current maturity of the collaboration and indicate how we can help it develop and mature into a more effective version of itself.

Secondly, we are dealing with an open-ended scale. There is no upper limit to maturity, even if integration is presently the top tier. We might see new and even more mature forms of organisation in the future.

Thirdly, the scale is devoid of moral judgment of immature groups or organisations. Immaturity is not a conscious choice but a subconscious defensive mechanism against something that is seen as frightening or threatening. Thus, everyone has valid reasons for doing what they do, despite the relative immaturity of their actions. Our aim is therefore that this scale should help others identify and understand sub-standard working relations, and to use that knowledge towards more mature and productive relations.

Fourthly, we have to question the relation between individuals' and groups' maturity. A binary group does not necessarily comprise immature individuals. If the leader, or just a few key people, resort to immature defensive mechanisms, they may cause the entire group to adopt the same tactics. The leader's use of immature defences can therefore be crucial for the level of maturity of the entire group or organisation, because the members "learn" how to deal with ambivalence from their leader.

Fifthly, actual groups and organisations will typically comprise a mixture of the various defensive levels. At any given time, all the different defensive mechanisms can be seen at play simultaneously, and subgroups within the larger group can form their own sub-culture, which operates on a different level than the organisation at large. The predominant defensive mechanism determines how we identify the maturity level of the specific group or organisation. If, for instance, we refer to a group as repressive, this is merely an overall assessment. The actual social and psychological situation in the group is far more complex than a mere distinction between three levels can ever hope to capture. Thus, the levels are more like landmarks than complete and coherent descriptions of an actual situation.

On the other hand, we would like to add that we, through our consultancy work for organisations, have found the three levels and their defining characteristics extremely helpful in determining an organisation's dominant defensive level. Likewise, they help a lot in interpreting the change in level that can occur when an organisation is undergoing a major change (e.g., a change in leadership).

8

MEETINGS

The two preceding chapters describe the group as a collective, and it was shown how there is a direct connection between the maturity of a group and its productivity. One of the places in which the maturity of the group is on display is at meetings. Meetings are a mirror of the group's maturity: one can glean a lot of information about the group's level of maturity by observing its meetings. And it is one of the most important opportunities the group has to develop its maturity. The point of a meeting is to arrange a proper *meeting* between the participants, but it is far from always that it succeeds. This chapter will investigate how a manager and employees can develop their maturity through the way the group conducts meetings.

In the modern organisation, as the firm grows more complex and specialised, the need for coordination becomes greater. There is a need for the services or products of the firm to be consistent and coherent, and there is also an increasing demand for an effective exploitation of resources. In order to accommodate these requirements (which do not always converge in and of themselves), a "cooperation on cooperation" is required. Work groups need internal coordination as well as a coordination of their activities with other collaborative partners in and outside the firm. Most firms, therefore, often hold meetings, which turns meetings into an activity that uses many resources. Of course, it is not without significance what comes out of these efforts.

The rational, formulated goal of the meeting is to coordinate the work efforts of the participants in order to accomplish the firm's tasks. The precondition for an effective coordination, however, is a certain level of trust between the persons who are to do the coordinating. So, if one views organisations as being held together by members' mutual relations and by their common view of what the organisation is and what its tasks are, then meetings are absolutely necessary. Thus an important but often unformulated purpose for meetings is to confirm and develop the mutual relations and commitment of the participants. This sort of confirmation happens

130 Group processes

through many channels, both conscious and unconscious. Meeting face-to-face can have great value for generating mutual trust in the participants and for their ability to coordinate, but it can also have the opposite effect. Personal contact can promote a nuanced illumination of what is to be coordinated and support the mutual understanding of the participants, but the opposite can also occur. It depends on the group's maturity and the way meetings are conducted.

The three dimensions of meetings

Daily life in a firm provides countless informal opportunities for participants to meet: at the coffee machine, at the lunch table, on a smoke break, on trips, in the hallway, through informal office talk, and so forth, but what is special about a "meeting" is that it takes place in a structure defined in advance.

It may be expedient to analyse the structure of meetings from these three dimensions: framework, content, and process:

- *Framework* has to do with the surroundings of the meeting (Bay & Blicher-Hansen 2006: chaps. 7–10). The framework of a meeting includes the calling of the meeting (time and place), the meeting room, technical equipment, furnishing and lighting of the meeting room, agenda, minutes, meeting memos, and food and drink. In short, everything that is needed to hold the meeting the way you want it. It is not necessarily very complicated to arrange a meeting, but it does not happen by itself. The meeting framework, therefore, can tell a lot about the firm's ability to coordinate and prioritise on the practical level. Perhaps one prioritises it highly and, therefore, earmarks resources to make meeting rooms ready, make coffee, and so forth; or, perhaps, it has a very low priority (or status), which is why meetings take place randomly or ad hoc as far as the framework is concerned.
- *Content* has to do with the subject matter of the meeting: what are you meeting to coordinate? (Bay & Blicher-Hansen 2006: chaps. 5–6). A meeting has a purpose, one or more topics, and often some goals that are to be achieved during the course of the meeting. If the content of the meeting is only implicitly defined, there will often be murkiness or divided opinions about why the meeting was held, and this may hinder the dynamic of the meeting.
- *Process* concerns how the meeting is held: meeting management, the engagement of the participants and their mutual relations, methods of decision-making, verbal and non-verbal communication, conflict resolution, positive and negative symbol creation, and so forth (Schwarz 2002; Weidner 2005). The concept of process in meetings actually has to do with particularly complicated exchanges between participants that encompass a number of different elements. The following section, therefore, describes the meeting process in more detail.

Many people only focus on the content dimension when they prepare for a meeting. A need for coordination is found and a meeting is called, but no one considers the importance of the framework or whether a meeting is even the right means. Nor are the explicit purpose and eventual goal of the meeting formulated or the most expedient procedures for the meeting thought through. The lack of these considerations will almost always affect the meeting negatively in the form of a lack of propulsion, a lack of engagement, or a lack of ability to make decisions.

The meeting process

None of the three dimensions of a meeting – framework, content, and process – itself decides how a meeting will play out, but it is the process that ties together the other two dimensions. Therefore, the course of a meeting depends a great deal on the ability of the group and the manager to relate consciously to the process. A meeting can take place at a luxurious spa with an important and interesting topic on the agenda and nevertheless be experienced as unpleasant or a direct waste of time. Another meeting can be held in a dark cellar without an agenda but nevertheless be experienced as intense and relevant. If the meeting process for some reason does not function well, things such as a good meeting room, delicious food, or engaging content do not make up for it as a rule. By contrast, a good process can compensate for many deficiencies with respect to both framework and content.

In order to understand what happens in the meeting process and in order to be able to work on it in a way that matures cooperation, the process must be examined in the light of the group psychology concepts that were summarised in Chapters 6 and 7. In addition, it can be a help if one is familiar with different methods for facilitating a meeting. Within this field, there is a large quantity of application-oriented literature. It is characteristic of the best of these books that they do not only present a series of methods but link the use of different methods with an understanding of the fundamental importance of the process (see, e.g., Schwarz 2002; Ghais 2005; Weidner 2005).

In other words, the focus of a meeting must be what is going on with and between participants because that is what is crucial for the outcome of the meeting. The procedural components are often overlooked but have a decisive impact on the participants' ability to act with respect to the specific content of the meeting. The procedural components can be divided into:

* The emotional component
* The communicative component
* The symbol-creating component.

In practice, of course, the components cannot be separated but, for the sake of understanding, they are each described separately in the following sections.

The emotional component

Meetings give participants a snapshot of the group's relations or of its "emotional climate". In this way, a meeting gives occasion to the formation of inner

132 Group processes

perceptions in the participants of how the group members feel about each other. If these inner perceptions are uniformly negative in everyone, this causes problems with the meeting's productivity, just as it is also a problem if the participants have very different perceptions of the emotional climate. If some think it is a very nice meeting while others think it is an extremely unpleasant meeting, this mirrors a lack of coherence in the group on a more fundamental level. By contrast, uniformly positive perceptions of the emotional climate are not in itself a guarantee of a productive meeting. The perceptions of the group's relations must always be seen in the light of the group's psychological maturity. Both positive and negative perceptions can be an expression of splitting and repression as well as integration. It depends on a specific evaluation on the basis of the different characteristics that were described in Chapter 7.

The meeting participants read and interpret the group's emotional state in countless ways (a large part of which takes place unconsciously) and, subsequently, adapt their behaviour to their interpretation. Thus, there need not be many meetings with an indefinably unpleasant atmosphere before this can be read outside of the meetings in the form of, for example, lack of initiative, increased levels of conflict, more frequent sick leave, or some other form of deteriorating productivity.

In order to analyse and understand meetings, one must include all dimensions of the meeting – framework, content, and process – and illuminate them with the help of the emotional component. Since the emotional component can vary colossally from situation to situation, this means in practice that the same content in the same framework with the same process can have a widely different effect in different meetings. At one meeting, a strict meeting management that provides security may function fine and help the group to coordinate better; at another meeting, a strict meeting management may be experienced as oppressive and disempowering and, thus, impair the benefits from the meeting. The participants' subjective, emotional experience is crucial.

The communicative component

It is an important part of personnel management to keep staff informed, and many managers choose to do it at information meetings, which may be fine. But as manager, one should be aware that the value of information meetings may be relatively limited. One often sees meetings in which the process consists of the manager informing while the staff listens passively. It is difficult for employees to become engaged when they are not expected to participate actively in the meeting; and, thus, it becomes difficult to understand and remember the information that is given. In a psychological sense, it can be said that passive reception may give the individual anxiety about being "swallowed up" by the community because it is not possible to distinguish one's individuality actively. In this situation, one way of maintaining or protecting one's individuality may be simply not to listen.

This can result in a frequently seen situation in which the manager thinks that he is constantly providing information, but the employees find that "we are never told anything". So, while information from the manager may not be conceived as solicitation to debate, it may be reasonable to invite a dialogue in connection with it anyway. Otherwise, things may go as in the following case.

A director holds a monthly information meeting for all employees (approximately 60 people). No minutes are taken at these meetings. The manager is enthusiastic and articulate and has a lot of information to provide; and since only half an hour is set aside for the meeting, he feels under some time pressure and does not invite dialogue along the way. At the end of a meeting for which the time allotted has already been exceeded by five minutes, he asks whether there are any questions. There are none.

The manager is satisfied with the meeting because he has been able to pass on some important information despite the short time frame. It was especially important that people be informed that the new filing system would come into effect in a month and that they understood how and why they should use it.

An internal consultant from the HR department has taken notes, and she reckons that, in the course of the 35 minutes the meeting lasted, the manager has given the staff 27 different pieces of information – both large and small.

Subsequently, the consultant takes an informal poll of the employees, and it shows that:

- People can remember between five and eight of the pieces of information.
- Which pieces of information people remember are very different.
- There are many misunderstandings of the information people remember.
- Just under half have grasped that the filing system is going into effect in a month. Of them, only a quarter have understood how the system functions, and no one can explain why management has decided to introduce it!

The important message in this case is that what on the surface looks like effective, goal-oriented communication may, in reality, prove to be a waste of time because it has been forgotten that communication requires both a sender and a receiver. The word "communication" means "to make common". So, if it does not succeed in making the information common, communication has simply not taken place (Engquist 2000: 41).

Furthermore, it is probable that a meeting like the one in this case may give rise to negative symbol-creation, such as "this is a firm where only the director has a voice" or "this is a firm where it doesn't matter whether you listen or not because nobody notices". Such negatively charged symbols may unconsciously impair the receptivity of employees in subsequent meetings.

The premise for a successful meeting in which real communication takes place is the ability of the participants to enter into a dialogue with each other. Dialogue creates a direct precondition for the development and improvement of an

134 Group processes

organisation. But what is dialogue? In Chapter 7, the difference between linear and circular forms of dialogue was described. This chapter introduces the concepts of pseudo-dialogue and genuine dialogue, which have many points of similarity with, respectively, linear and circular, acknowledging dialogue but which describes the differences in a slightly different way. Put in terms of levels of maturity, pseudo-dialogue corresponds to the splitting and repressive level, while genuine dialogue corresponds to the integrating level.

When one is present at or participates in meetings, one hears many conversations that, prima facie, sound like dialogues, since the parties take turns speaking. But if one analyses the conversation more closely, one discovers that it is a pseudo-dialogue or what one could also call parallel monologues. Table 8.1 shows the different characteristics for pseudo-dialogue and genuine dialogue, respectively, and how the two modes of speaking together are different from each other on decisive points.

Here are two examples of a pseudo-dialogue and a genuine dialogue, respectively. The scene in both examples is a meeting that, for sake of clarity, has only two participants: manager A and employee B. The agenda is the same for both meetings: feedback from A on statistics B has just compiled.

Pseudo-dialogue:
A: I think you did a really good job with the statistics, but I wish it could have been a bit clearer.
B: Yes, you can always do things better.
A: It's so important for statistics to be clear.
B: I went to a lot of trouble on this job.
A: Then, in the future, could you work a little on this?
B: Absolutely – if I have time.

Genuine dialogue:
A: I think you did a really good job with the statistics. You were finished on time, and it gave us some really usable information about sales. The only remark I have is that I wasn't entirely satisfied with its clarity.
B: No, I wasn't satisfied, either, but I still think it ended up quite well. Where did you think it seemed unclear?
A: I didn't think it was exactly unclear, but on the last two pages, I thought you should have merged the data from the first six months with the second six months. That would have made it easier to read.
B: I don't think that is a good idea because there are several departments where people need to be able to distinguish the first six months from the second.
A: I can see that, now you mention it, but what about adding an extra page on which the two periods are merged?
B: Yes, that's actually a good idea, but I'll start from next year. I don't think it's so important that I should spend time on changing it now.
A: I agree with that prioritisation.

Meetings **135**

TABLE 8.1 Characteristics of pseudo-dialogue and genuine dialogue

	Pseudo-dialogue	Genuine dialogue
Level of conversation	General, no examples	Specific, use of examples
Listening	Passive, sympathetic	Active, empathetic
Exchange	Parallel monologues	Builds on the other's statements
Response	Idealising, repressive	Complex, nuanced
Assessment	Unexpressed, implicit	Formulated, explicit
Character of conversation	Orienting, static	Transforming, dynamic

Because pseudo-dialogue appears to cause fewer problems and conflicts, the parties may leave a meeting in a friendly atmosphere. On the other hand, they are not much wiser than when they came. B does not know what A means by "clarity", and A does not know whether B will actually introduce any changes or what they might be in the given case. It is also conceivable that B leaves the meeting with a feeling that his manager has criticised him or B may have the idea that A thinks the document as a whole is crap or that the manager thinks that B is generally bad at his job.

B can get this perception (which creates anxiety and, therefore, makes B defensive) because A neither praises nor criticises anything specifically, and B can get this feeling despite the fact that A says he did "a really good job". Praise sounds hollow when it is not supported specifically, and non-specific criticism has a big risk of being over-interpreted or ignored.

Presumably, B does not agree with A's proposal for change (even though he says he does) because he makes an indeterminate reservation by referring to a lack of time (one of the top scores when it comes to repressive behaviour), which can make A feel that B is sluggish and unwilling even though A has nothing specific to hang that feeling on.

As it appears from the two examples, the genuine dialogue tends to take a longer time than the pseudo-dialogue. On the other hand, the parties reach a nuanced and specific understanding of each other's point of view and they find a common solution that they would not have reached otherwise by themselves. In the real world, it does not always go as easily as in the example of the genuine dialogue, which is one of the reasons that the pseudo-dialogue is tempting. The genuine dialogue can reveal disagreements and lead to conflicts that may not always be able to be solved on the spot. On the other hand, the parties can reach a common view of the disagreement, which provides a far better starting point for working on it.

Seen in relation to the levels of defences, the pseudo-dialogue, as mentioned, is a splitting or repressive function, while the genuine dialogue has an integrating and transforming function. Therefore, there is important information about the firm's level of maturity hidden in what type of dialogue dominates at meetings. If pseudo-dialogue is predominant, it will place serious limitations on the group's ability to develop and to work with the problems and conflicts that naturally arise in an everyday workplace.

136 Group processes

The symbol-creating component

Symbols can be described as the individual's inner pictures or perceptions of certain phenomena. They are internal representations of phenomena, such as "management", and are formed unconsciously. Even though the person is not conscious of the symbol, it can have a significant influence on his or her interpretation of the world. Thus it is obvious that a negatively charged symbol for management will influence the way the person in question views his or her manager. The formation of symbols cannot be controlled directly, neither by the individuals themselves nor by others, but one can sharpen one's awareness that all human behaviour and interaction can give rise to the formation of symbols and that these are always affective (i.e., emotional) (Hatch 1997: 365). To every symbol, there are one or more emotions attached.

Meetings are important spaces for the formation of symbols that represent phenomena having to do with the life of the group or organisation. It may have to do with symbols for the group, the individual's relation to the group, the group's options, cooperation, solicitude, community, the firm, the purpose of the firm, management, and the personality of the manager. Symbols are formed on the basis of experiences with life in the group and the organisation, and they subsequently affect the individual's view of the events and the individual's view of his or her own options in relation to the events.

When it is said that organisations are held together by the participants' common internal images, it is referring to this unconscious coordination of symbols representing different aspects of the organisation. Since group meetings provide much of the "raw material" for the symbol formation within the organisation, it is also for this reason that it is of great importance how meetings unfold. A boring meeting is a waste of time on a concrete level. But its greatest damage may be that it creates space for negative symbol formation, such as "This is a group that cannot allow change" or "This is a group where it is OK to waste time". Such symbolic perceptions may be difficult to change because they set up camp in the unconscious, where they are not directly accessible to consciousness even as they influence the participants' patterns of thinking and acting. Who wants to contribute energetic and focused work efforts in a group where change is not possible and where it is OK to waste time?

Therefore, one should always – particularly, if one is a manager – try to assess what symbolic effect a specific meeting may have. Might the meeting give rise to common, positively charged symbols or be a source for general, negatively charged symbols, or is it more likely that it will lead to the formation of individual, fragmented symbols? There is no guarantee that one's assessment is correct, but as a manager one may reflect on the potential symbol formation and observe attentively the imprints the symbols leave in people's behaviour. Afterwards, the manager can discuss his observations with employees, as the manager does in the following case.

In a meeting, a manager tells her employees that there will be cutbacks in the firm and that, for their group, this means, unfortunately, that Eva must be let go (the manager has oriented Eva before the meeting).

The manager then sits quietly with a facial expression that is difficult to interpret, but the employees notice that she has moist eyes.

Everyone waits expectantly and says nothing, but suddenly the manager gets up and spontaneously walks over to embrace Eva. People relax and begin, bit by bit, to talk about their feelings in connection with Eva's dismissal, and Eva says that she is sorry to have been fired.

After the meeting, a number of employees say that the manager's embrace of Eva has made a big impression on them.

Shortly after the meeting, the manager notices a change in the way the group interacts and their relationship with her. It is not something the employees themselves are conscious of, but the manager tells the group after some time about the changes she has observed: she is experiencing greater responsiveness from employees and an altered, more open and honest tone at meetings. It appears from employee feedback to the manager's observations that the manager's hug changed employees' view of her as unfeeling and also affected their view of what a manager's role can be. This has given them a new view of the place caring can have in the firm and a different perception of what feelings it is possible to express in the group.

The case shows how the manager's unconscious behaviour (the moist eyes) and spontaneous action (the embrace) were observed and interpreted and thereby had a profound symbolic influence on the employees. This does not mean that managers should "stage" their behaviour to have a positive symbolic effect, because this is something they cannot control. But it does mean that managers must be especially conscious of the possible symbolic effect of their behaviour. This is something of which managers must be aware in all contexts, but it especially applies to meetings in which the manager's conscious and unconscious behaviour is observed closely by employees and can potentially be transformed into powerful – positively or negatively charged – symbols.

Observation in meetings

As mentioned, meetings are laden with information, and an important part of relating consciously to the meeting process consists in being good at observing meetings and reading the information the meeting contains. It can be said that one trains one's ability to be a process observer. This is an ability people naturally possess, since people try to orient themselves on the basis of all accessible information in their

138 Group processes

interactions with each other – not merely on the verbal. But most people are not conscious of most of these observations. Being a good process observer primarily entails becoming more conscious of the observations one makes. It is not possible to capture and describe everything that happens between meeting participants, but one can train one's ability to capture those (sometimes rather subtle) phenomena that can be decisive for how a meeting plays out or that provide vital information about the group's conflicts and maturity.

To be observant in meetings includes, first and foremost, being observant about the process but is also about the framework and content of the meeting and the way the three dimensions affect each other. If, as the leader or participant in a meeting, one is observant about what is going on, it will provide a good sense of what happens with and between the participants and a basis for intervening and altering an inexpedient turn of events.

Table 8.2 provides a proposal for useful and informative observation points:

TABLE 8.2 Observation points

Before the meeting: silence, chitchat, who talks to whom, when do people arrive, how do they arrange themselves in relation to each other, are people prepared?

Purpose of meeting: is it clear to everyone, is it kept in mind throughout, is it evaluated on a running basis and/or at the end? Is there an agenda?

General level of activity at the meeting: how many participate in the debate, in what sequence, how long do they talk, are some people entirely passive, etc.?

Atmosphere: is it relaxed, fervent, playful, tense, aggressive, sluggish, engaged, or something else? Does it change along the way, and when?

Dialogue: do people listen to each other, do they build on each other's statements, do they ask questions, do they hold monologues? Genuine or pseudo-dialogue?

Language use: is it defensive, aggressive, consensus-seeking, soothing, confrontational, inquiring, open, or something else?

Division of labour: how are the tasks divided up, is there agreement about the division, is it clear what the tasks are?

Disagreements and conflicts: are they open, hidden, constructive, destructive, are they resolved?

Decisions: are decisions made, are they clear, is there any follow up on previous decisions?

Background noise: is there turmoil, chitchat, runs to the toilet, telephone calls, doodling, reading documents, etc.?

Level of vitality: in the individual or in the group as a whole, is the level even, increasing, or falling, what makes it shift?

Body language: are the participants sitting up straight, leaning back, slouching, distracted, uneasy, defensive, aggressive, or something else?

Eye contact: is there eye contact between all the participants, only between a few, only with the manager, or none at all?

Meeting structure: is it maintained, developed, dissolved, productive, inhibiting? Does it follow the agenda?

Conclusion of meeting: confusion, dissolution, summarising, focusing, energetic, evaluation?

Analysis of a meeting

As a conclusion to this chapter on the function and importance of meetings, we provide a detailed examination of a meeting because it is in the details that many of the relational and symbolic dramas play out. In order to make the examination more comprehensible, we shall comment on the case on a running basis. The commentary relates to the basic emotional mood and the three dimensions – framework, content, and process – as they unfold during the meeting.

The case has to do with a work team that recently acquired a new team leader. The group's identity has come under pressure because it has not had a leader before and because the team leader is inexperienced. Because of this pressure, one would expect to see regression with the use of more immature defences in employees as well as in the leader.

> There is a meeting of a development team at a major IT firm. The team consists of nine persons including the team leader, Kaj, who was appointed a month ago by management. Previously, the team had no leader. As something new, Kaj has instituted a team meeting every Friday morning between 8:30 and 9:30 a.m. This is the third team meeting.
>
> There is a fixed agenda for the meetings. Therefore, no notice of the meeting is sent out in advance. Kaj has an expectation that everyone will be prepared in relation to the fixed agenda and that they will consider in advance whether they have anything to contribute with respect to any of its points.

Fixed agendas may act as work-saving devices and, psychologically, provide a good sense of familiarity, control, and overview, but the content must be considered thoroughly and adjusted on an ongoing basis. Otherwise, fixed agendas can be deadening and come to symbolise "Nothing new happens here" or "You don't need to be prepared here".

The fact that no notice of the meeting is sent out can create doubt about whether there is actually a meeting and whether it is necessary to attend. It can also create doubt about whether Kaj takes the meeting seriously. Since Kaj is so new as a leader, his behaviour is especially open to the creation of negative or positive symbols among employees. An action that is interpreted by employees as Kaj not taking the meeting seriously can form the basis for more negatively coloured symbols, which has to do with Kaj's respect for the group and the group's respect for Kaj and his authority. In this initial period of his leadership, therefore, it would be a good idea to have clear formalities from Kaj about the meetings because, on the symbolic level, it stresses the importance of the meeting and Kaj's respect for the group's time. This can be done, for example, with a notice of each meeting being sent out even though there is a fixed agenda.

140 Group processes

Has Kaj communicated his expectation that employees will be prepared for the meeting? And does he bring it up if people come unprepared to the meetings (e.g., without having the necessary papers along)? As a new leader, Kaj will probably be reticent about pointing out lack of preparedness, but it is precisely at this time that it is important to do it. Once the employees have grown accustomed to the fact that there are no consequences to coming unprepared, it will be difficult to change it later. The employees' view of Kaj's "leadership profile" is fixed quickly because, among other things, it creates security for employees to label Kaj as a certain kind of leader. Therefore, Kaj must be especially conscious of his behaviour in the initial period.

Bente comes to the third team meeting at 8:25. The lights are off, and there are remnants on the table from a meeting the previous afternoon. Bente leaves again, making an irritated remark. At 8:30, Carl arrives and begins to prepare the room for the meeting. Between 8:35 and 8:40, four participants arrive, including Bente again. Kaj has not turned up yet.

A room that is messy and uninviting may have a destructive effect in certain contexts. If the team is functioning well and eager for a meeting, the framework does not mean that much. But in this case, one may imagine that the messy room is a symbol for the employees that they are not important enough to have a proper meeting room. Hence, Bente's irritated exclamation. But why didn't Bente clean up a little since she came early? The mess may also symbolise that it is not worth expending energy in this group. This may be the reason Bente leaves again.

The basic emotional mood is already set here, and the appearance of the room helps define it. A group that knows each other well and works well together may think that mess is nice and cosy; but, in this case, mess has the effect of irritating Bente. This irritation (which could cover up a feeling of disappointment or a feeling of not being taken seriously) Bente brings along to the meeting, and it affects the mood of the others.

Carl apparently has a different view, and he is the only one to come on time, but it later proves that he is so isolated in the group that he is not able to affect the dominant underlying mood.

In this case, the framework for the meeting does not promote an atmosphere of confidence and engagement. Messy surroundings do not need to be a problem if other aspects of the meeting function well. It cannot be concluded that coffee in plastic cups makes for a bad meeting. It depends on the procedural context. In this specific context, it would without doubt have been a good investment for the meeting if Kaj himself had cleared the room the previous afternoon or if he had made sure someone else did it.

Meetings **141**

> Since Kaj has not yet arrived, there is uncertainty about whether there is a meeting today. One person believes that Kaj is at a course. Two of the participants leave after getting this information.

It may have an extraordinarily destructive effect on the formation of a new and uncertain group that the leader comes late. It creates uncertainty about the group's coherence for which, at this point, the leader is an important guarantee and symbol. And it creates uncertainty about Kaj's respect for and interest in his employees.

The internal flow of information is not functioning properly, since no one knows with certainty whether Kaj is at a course. Employees should always know where Kaj is. This is especially important in the initial period because the group – which, according to Bion's definition, can be said to be in a state of dependency – otherwise risks falling apart. This happens specifically at the meeting when two of the participants leave, presumably to take care of their own individual work chores. The dilemma between individual and group is under pressure because of the insecure group formation, and it easily falls to the advantage of individuality if the group does not offer a solid and attractive alternative.

> At 8:42, Kaj arrives with the excuse that he has arrived late because he was supposed to buy danishes for the group. Carl goes out to get the two who left and to see whether the other team members who have not turned up at all are in their offices.

Kaj should, at the very least, have called and warned of the delay. As it is now, he has involuntarily provided support for the already established atmosphere of irritation and lack of engagement. By his conduct, he has also legitimated the practice of coming late. This conduct will quickly spread to employees and can take a long time to get rid of again. The leader's behaviour is especially crucial at the beginning of the group formation for establishing the group's norms and habits.

At the symbolic level, Kaj's behaviour risks being interpreted as "This is not an important meeting" or "Kaj is a leader who does not respect employees". Both perceptions may be difficult to change later.

Is the primary purpose of the meeting breakfast since Kaj prioritises this instead of coming on time? If it is the most important purpose of the meeting, that is entirely OK, but it must be communicated and made clear to the employees. Often, breakfast and work meetings do not function well together – they each pull in different directions. The leader must be clear with himself and the employees whether the social aspect is the most important or it is more important to coordinate work activities.

142 Group processes

Carl is still working to keep the team together – primarily because Kaj does not do so. His leadership is leaving a vacuum that Carl tries to fill, which confuses distribution of roles between Kaj and Carl in which the rest of the team becomes uncertain whether Carl is a sort of informal leader or just a "class monitor"? But Carl's habit of fetching participants for the meeting is a bad habit since they are expected to have an interest in participating themselves. If they do not, it is a problem the leader has to deal with or, alternatively, a common norm must be established that says that precision is not so important. If everyone agrees on this norm, it is not necessarily a problem that the meeting begins 15 minutes late. It depends on the symbolic significance the participants attribute to it.

> At 8:45, the meeting begins with seven participants; the two missing participants have not sent regrets. Their absence is not commented on.

Kaj must make it clear that all members are expected to participate in common meetings. If, in special cases, they are unable to attend, they must let the leader know why and they can then discuss whether the prioritisation is correct. It is also important for the leader to let the rest of the team know the reason for the absence, since those present might otherwise get the feeling that those absent are not interested in them. It can give rise to a negative symbol formation which says "What is interesting is happening somewhere elsewhere than in this meeting" and lead to even more absences at the next meeting. Thus, this irritated, unengaged underlying mood is not created only by the delayed beginning but also by the absence of two people.

If everyone already knows why some people might have to be absent, then the absence can strengthen the feeling of being a coherent group in that everyone knows and approves the reasons some people cannot attend. However, many meetings suffer because it seems clear that what is supposed to be a coherent group is, in reality, many different groups due to the varying attendance from meeting to meeting. This leads to a lack of continuity in information shared and decisions made and to an orgy of repetitions from meeting to meeting. If the leader does not comment on the absence and make his expectations for attendance clear, this discontinuity may go on for a long time and create major coordination problems.

> The conference table is long and broad with room for 16 persons. The participants are spread over all sides of the table, so that there are many places with empty chairs between them. Kaj sits down in a corner of one of the long sides. Kaj is the only one with papers laid out in front of him.

The spontaneous placement of the participants in the meeting room often functions as a sort of physical impression of the current state of the group. The scattered placement of the employees in this case tells about the lack of coherence in the team, and Kaj's placement in the corner (instead of in the centre or at the end of the table) tells of a leader who does not feel comfortable in the role. If the meeting had been better prepared, they might have removed an extension to the table, so that the participants would sit closer together and have better contact with each other. This could potentially have affected the internal picture in the direction of "We are a close team with good contact" and changed the underlying mood to something a little better. Closer placement might also have provided better eye contact among the participants, and this could have positively affected the underlying mood.

That Kaj is the only one with papers in front of him indicates that he is the only person who has prepared and shows that the employees do not feel that they need to prepare because "Kaj will take care of that". Here, the group is demonstrating an immature splitting defence between Kaj and the group.

At this point in the meeting, it is clear that neither Kaj nor the other participants relate consciously to the meeting process. Kaj's delay may be an expression of a conflict within him of which he is not conscious. He may be nervous about the meeting. He may think it is an unimportant meeting, or he may have wanted to demonstrate his new power as leader. Kaj utilises a repressive type of defence to handle his internal conflict. One cannot immediately deduce from his behaviour what the conflict is about, but it is under no circumstance a coincidence that he arrives late. He can allow himself that because he knows that he meeting won't start until he has arrived. At the same time, he is not conscious of the negative procedural consequences of his conduct.

> Kaj introduces the meeting by asking whether there are any remarks on the minutes from the last meeting?

It is not very dynamic and an unfocused way to begin a meeting with a point that, most often, has no or very few remarks, and it exacerbates in this case the unengaged atmosphere, so it becomes decidedly indifferent. Minutes in many cases are good to have, but it is better to send them out before the meeting and asking for written comments. Only if there are very problematic objections should one use precious meeting time on this point.

Instead, the leader should begin the meeting on a "high note" – focus in an energetic way on what the meeting is about at the same time he convinces the employees about the importance of this meeting with his body and verbal language. If he senses that the employees do not think the meeting is important or that they are unsure what the purpose is, he must address this issue at once. It is far better to deal with resistance or confusion at an early point in the meeting than to ignore it and hope it goes away by itself.

144 Group processes

> Nobody reacts. "Well, then, we'll move on", says Kaj.

The little phrase "well, then" is not an energetic expression of faith and confidence in the impetus of the meeting. Rather, it seems hesitant or reluctant as if Kaj does not entirely know where the meeting should go or why. This is read by employees and can lead to insecurity or distaste about the meeting and lack of confidence in Kaj's management of it. This reading takes place unconsciously, quickly, and almost invisibly because it only has to do with a small phrase, but it nevertheless becomes significant for how employees experience the rest of the meeting.

> The next point on the agenda is announcements. Kaj has prepared a list of things about which he is to orient the employees. The topics are a mixture of minutes from various meetings Kaj has attended, announcements from management, and various pieces of administrative information. This point takes 40 minutes.
>
> Bente and Therese whisper together; Jørgen looks out the window most of the time; Benjamin is taking peeks at a longer document. When 20 minutes have been spent on this point, Frank gets up and goes out with a telephone in his hand. Only Carl, who is sitting closest to Kaj, is apparently following, interested, and the only one who asks questions.

As mentioned in the previous case, the value of presenting a huge amount of information at once is doubtful when the receiver is expected to receive it passively. Most people stop listening after a few minutes if the speaker is not fascinating and engaging; and at the same time, the receiver must preferably already have an interest in the subject. A long list of various pieces of information may end up falling through all the cracks where no one can really see the relevance for themselves personally and, therefore, quickly stop listening.

The indifferent basic emotional mood becomes significantly worse during this long point and approaches hopelessness and desperation. The employees (except Carl) feel "used" by Kaj and only think about escaping the meeting – mentally or literally.

The division of roles in the team with Carl as "the good employee" is cemented even more as a result of a splitting between Carl and the rest of the group. At the same time, the group is also split and dissolved into subgroups (Bente and Therese) or individual activities.

It is not OK for Frank to leave without saying why or when he is coming back. This may give the rest of the participants (including Kaj) a feeling that Frank does not feel like wasting time on them. But it is characteristic that no one from the team asks Frank why he is leaving and that Kaj does not have the authority to do it.

> When Kaj is finished with his announcements, there are only five minutes left before the meeting is supposed to be over. A number of people have begun to fidget and say that they are busy and have to go to other meetings. Kaj asks whether anyone else has any announcements. Therese begins a long account about how her project lacks resources, but while she is speaking, several participants get up and leave. The meeting ends 10 minutes late without anyone commenting on Therese's contribution.

As the leader of the meeting, it is Kaj's responsibility to ensure that there is a reasonable flow at the meeting with a reasonable temporal division among the various points. That Kaj fills almost the entire meeting with his own announcements may be experienced by the employees as an aggressive act against the employees. It seems to them as if Kaj is more interested in talking than listening and as if he keeps employee problems out of the meeting by using all the time himself. At any rate, it is not reasonable to ask whether the employees have any points when there are only a few minutes left for the meeting. It goes without saying that you cannot undertake a serious discussion of anything in such a short time, and the fact that no one comments on what Therese says bolsters even more the group's tendency toward fragmentation. It does not seem encouraging to bring something up in this forum when you cannot expect a reaction from anyone – not even from the leader.

During the final minutes, the mood shifted from hopelessness to anger and aggression. The employees react to what they are experiencing as an "attack" from Kaj. They are angry at being forced to listen passively for so long and not being invited to participate, and they are angry that the meeting goes late. They do not show the aggression directly but indirectly by being fidgety, non-responsive, and finally (for some) by leaving. Therese tries in despair to call attention to her problems and likewise experiences frustration and anger that it did not succeed. For everyone but Kaj and Carl, then, the meeting ends in an angry and hopeless mood about which the participants are not fully conscious but which will affect cooperation negatively in the future and at future meetings.

The way this meeting ends is characteristic of many meetings: it fizzles out as people get up and leave and others stop listening. This is the worst possible way to end a meeting because this diffuse impression may easily get stuck in the consciousness of the participants. Instead, it is essential – just like at the introduction of the meeting – for the leader to end the meeting on a "high note": that is to say, that he emphasises with conviction and energy what they achieved with the meeting – perhaps, even provide a short summary of what was agreed to; he can also confirm when the next meeting will take place; and finally, it is good to thank the participants for their active input during the meeting. Under no circumstances should the leader allow the participants to trickle away. On the other hand, people have a right to expect the meeting to end on time.

146 Group processes

This case has to do with a group that, because of their new leader, is in the process of transforming itself into a new group. This is a group with an uncertain identity that needs to find its collective legs. In this phase, the group's meetings play an especially decisive role, because it is here leader and employee meet face-to-face and here many of the group's mutual relations are strengthened or weakened. The meeting process itself is of decisive importance, and its symbolic importance is high because everyone is in the process of orienting to the new group identity. The group will examine the leader's conduct right down into the very tiny details and, from this, try to understand and interpret the group's identity. Likewise, each individual will strive to find his or her own place in relation to the leader and the others in the group. Along the way, the participants, in order to protect themselves from this burdensome state, will be inclined to use splitting defences but also some repressive defences, such as staying away, coming late, or leaving the meeting early.

In the initial phase, the group cannot avoid immature defences, but it is important that the immature defences do not take on an all too negative colour. It is far better for a period if the group feels itself to be something special, like the world champions in their field. These feelings may gradually become more nuanced as the group matures. In other words, it is crucial for the group not to get stuck at an immature level because, if it does, it will have a hard time in the long run functioning as the productive collective it is conceived to be. It is the leader's job to help the group with the maturation process, and this chapter has tried to show why meetings are one of the manager's most important fora for this work.

The manager must be conscious of the three dimensions – framework, content, and process – and their significance for meeting dynamics, and he must have a good understanding of the connective function of the process. He must train his ability to sense and read the underlying emotional mood and to work on this, among other things, by formulating his observations. At the same time, he must be conscious of the importance of his own conduct and realise that only when he himself is able to be engaged – an active listener, acknowledging, specific, and focused on the matter at hand – can he teach his employees to be the same.

PART III
Management

The relationship between manager and employee is central for teamwork in a firm. Part III describes why and how. In this area, too, there are many different approaches. Some of the most important are described here, such as Kernberg's ideas of projection pressure on the manager (Kernberg 1998), the manager's role in connection with employee learning, and the manager as an authority.

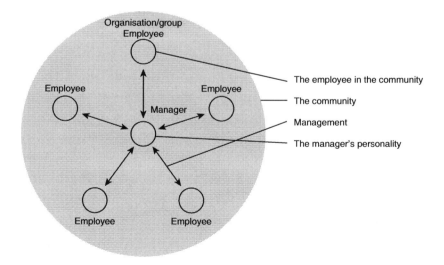

Management is a widespread phenomenon. Not only is it found at all levels of society, it is also found at all times in history. Management seems to be a fundamental part of human social life. But why do people need management? It might

148 Management

be expected that this question and its answer would be at the heart of the abundant management literature that exists; but, strangely enough, this is not the case.

In order to answer the question, one must first understand what management is. Generally speaking, the question of management can be divided into two themes. The first theme has to do with the content of management. Content in management means what functions the manager carries out for the employees and the organisation – the manager's job description. This may be to define rules, to make decisions, to provide care, to create a framework for development, and so forth. These topics are dealt with in Chapter 9.

The second theme has to do with the interaction between manager and employee. This means the distribution of responsibility and the division of power between the two parties. These topics are dealt with in Chapters 10 and 11. In Chapter 12, the management group and its significance for management in organisations is discussed.

Part III contains the following main points:

Chapter 9	The content in the relationship between manager and employee has a direct connection to individual motivation. The individual needs management because management helps to fulfil motivational needs. Everyone needs management: anyone who faces something immense and difficult needs management to overcome it.
Chapter 10	The manager has a role as "teacher" for employees. In this role, the appreciative approach may be useful and constructive.
Chapter 11	The manager has a role as authority for employees. In order for the manager's authority to function well, it must come from a number of sources at the same time.
Chapter 12	It can be difficult to create good teamwork in management groups. Therefore, management groups need management.

9

THE CONTENT OF MANAGEMENT

The concept of management has been described over time in myriad ways, and there are countless models that provide various versions of the content of management. Common to them all is an attempt to define and understand what management is. For a new manager, it can be difficult to get an overview of the function of management, but even an experienced manager may be in doubt about what the job consists of. This may be due, among other things, to the fact that, even among people who have worked intimately with the topic, there is no agreement about what management entails.

The many contributions to management literature seem to encompass three different types of strategy for understanding and describing the subject matter of management. The first strategy is an *implicit strategy*, in which the subject matter of management is not described explicitly but emerges indirectly. The second strategy is a *simplifying strategy*, in which models are used that contain two fundamental management functions. The third strategy is a more *complex strategy*, in which the models established contain four management functions.

Implicit management model

One strategy for understanding management is not to concern oneself with the subject matter of management itself but, instead, to focus on other elements in management so that the subject matter emerges implicitly. This strategy is seen in relation-oriented writers from whom one looks in vain for accounts of management functions. Neither in Haslebo nor Gergen does one find a description of the most important tasks a manager has in an organisation (Gergen & Gergen 1998; Haslebo 2004). Instead, the authors mentioned focus on the manager's procedural and relational abilities.

150 Management

One of the reasons that relational authors avoid the issue of management's subject matter is presumably that the subject matter of management is linked to the personality of the manager. The relational authors criticise individual or ability-focused organisation theory and, instead, focus on relations (Gergen 1999: 117–137). Some relational authors thereby cut themselves off from investigating an important area in the life of organisations – namely, the issue of what management is.

The simplifying model of management

Another more traditional approach is to understand the subject matter of management as being divided into two parts. This strategy is widespread. As a rule, the two parts are defined by variants of the following two functions: instruction and support. A well-known model that uses this division is situational management. Situational management was originally developed by Paul Hersey and Kenneth Blanchard (Hersey & Blanchard 1969), and it was later developed into Situational Leadership II (SLII) by Kenneth Blanchard et al. SLII has gained wide acceptance in many firms and education programmes (Blanchard et al. 1985). Among other authors who use or discuss a similar division, Bales, Blake and Mouton, and Brown (Bales 1950; Blake & Mouton 1985; Brown 2000: 94 ff.) can be mentioned.

Instruction is understood to be one-way communication from manager to employee with respect to structure, control, and supervision. Here, emphasis is placed on the manager as representative of the community. Instruction means that the manager tells the employee how a task is to be done or a situation is to be handled. The employee receives knowledge and information that, seen from management's point of view, supports the solution of the assignment at hand. In practice, this entails instructions for action ("Do such and such") and good advice ("It is my experience that the best thing to do is …").

Support is understood as two-way communication between manager and employee in which the manager listens, supports, encourages, and praises the employee. Support means that the manager provides the employee emotional backing to find solutions to problems or to handle various situations. As a part of emotional backing, then, a manager will help the employee to deal with feelings of incompetence and confusion.

In SLII and similar models developed or discussed by the other authors mentioned, it is the manager's ability to combine the two management functions, instruction and support, in an expedient way that determines how well employees function.

The model has gained broad acceptance because it categorises management into two areas with which everyone has experience in work life: the rational handling of the assignment at hand and feelings in connection with it. It is common and widely accepted to distinguish these two spheres as the conceptual pair of rational versus irrational. Furthermore, the model apparently provides a solution to the dilemma of the autocratic manager (instructing) versus the democratic manager (supportive). It is not a question of choosing between two forms of management but of being able to shift between them in a constructive way.

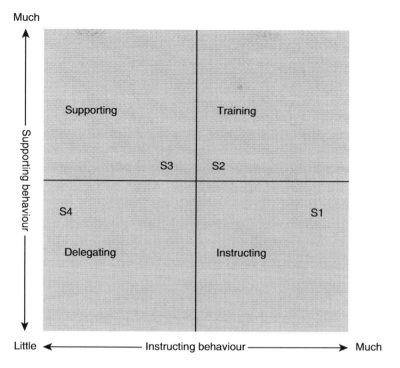

FIGURE 9.1 Model of situational leadership II: the four fundamental forms of management

Source: Blanchard et al. (1985).

However, the model provides no explanation of why precisely instruction and support are the most important management functions. Nor does the model encompass other important aspects of the job of management, such as the manager as a common symbol (the charismatic manager) and the manager as politician (the powerful manager). Therefore, it can be concluded that the simplifying model only provides a partial answer to what management is.

The more complex models of management

The third strategy for understanding the subject matter of management is to create more comprehensive models that work with more dimensions of management. This strategy is also used by a number of authors. Here are three selected contributions that all work with four dimensions of management.

The first theory was developed by the authors Liebermann, Yalom, and Miles. In a study of groups of university students, they investigated what form of management made for the best functioning groups. They subsequently defined four management functions – emotional stimulation, caring, meaning attribution, and

152 Management

executive function – all of which proved to be important for the functioning of the groups.

The study showed that the group leaders with the right balance among these four functions created the best functioning groups. The right balance was emotional stimulation and executive function in limited quantities, while caring and meaning attribution could, in principle, be provided in unlimited quantities (Lieberman et al. 1973).

The second theory is from a 1984 book by Bolman and Deal, in which the authors carried out a comprehensive study of existing organisation theories. This study resulted in a definition by Bolman and Deal of four frames for organisation theories – the political, the structural, the human resource, and the symbolic frames – into which all the various organisation theories were placed (Bolman & Deal 1984). In their later book from 2017, Bolman and Deal include the concept of management and argue that the subject matter of management is that the manager must be capable of working with all four frameworks at the same time. The manager must be able to work with the organisation from all four angles because they are equally important, each in their own way. If the manager is unable to do this, he or she misses important insights into the organisation's mode of functioning and thereby weakens his or her ability to influence the development of the organisation (Bolman & Deal 2017: chap. 15).

The third theory appears in Ole Fogh Kirkeby's book *Det nye lederskab* [*The New Leadership*]. Kirkeby also works with four different angles on the subject matter of management: the good, the just, the true, and the beautiful. In Kirkeby's

TABLE 9.1 The four management functions

Emotional stimulation	Express feelings, personal values, and attitudes, and encourage employees to do the same
Caring	Offer friendship, protection, acceptance, warmth
Meaning attribution	Provide concepts for understanding and explaining relations and events in the group
Executive function	Provide structures, framework, decisions, and goals

TABLE 9.2 Interpretive frames and management tasks

Interpretive frame	Management tasks
Political frame	Struggle for the right to feel special
	Provide space for different points of view and construct coalitions
Structural frame	Control, create framework for community
Human resource frame	Offer caring, stability
Symbolic frame	Create meaning, interpret the world

The content of management   153

TABLE 9.3 The Greek square and management tasks

The four corners of the Greek square	*Management tasks*
The good	The leader's responsibility and empathy to his or her employees
The just	Recognition as the equilibrium between the organisation's support for the employee and the employee's support for the organisation
The true	The leader's ability to assess and use knowledge
The beautiful	The leader's artistic authenticity to the employees and what is produced

terminology, these angles constitute four corners of the "Greek square", which is the "new stage of leadership". The four corners are elaborated later in the book to constitute 12 leadership virtues (Kirkeby 2004: chaps. 3 and 17).

In the middle of the Greek square is "freedom", which means that the leader achieves freedom to integrate aspects from all four corners of the square. The leader has the freedom to choose to do this or not (Kirkeby 2004: 31–32, 42–43).

The more complex models mentioned here all represent improvements in relation to the simplifying models of management because they include more aspects of the complicated relationship between manager and employee. At the same time, the models are still relatively clear and thereby offer a good, accessible "index" of the subject matter of management. They provide a nuanced version of what management is and, in this way, can be a help to the manager in understanding and defining his or her tasks.

It is worth noticing that there is a certain coincidence of categories in the three theories. At the same time, they all have the same message: the manager must be able to consider, analyse, and evaluate all four angles (or frames or corners) at the same time. This is what makes management into a complex competence that requires the manager to possess many different skills.

This sort of coincidence between the theories may have many explanations:

1   It may have arisen by chance.
2   It may be due to the influence of the authors on each other.
3   It may be due to the authors describing the same phenomenon: management. This would be the realistic or essentialist (that things have an essence) explanation.

If one chooses explanation 1 or 2, there is no reason to investigate the coincidence in the concepts between the three theories more closely.

If one chooses explanation 3, one must investigate why the theories resemble each other. Here, it is clear that the three theories overlook an important aspect

154 Management

of the issue of the subject matter of management: namely, why are precisely these four categories designated as important? None of the theories has an explanation of this. The next section, therefore, attempts to illuminate this question in more detail.

The relationship between management and individual motivation

In order to understand what management is, one must relate management to individual motivation. One must look at the reasons management appeals to employees. What need does management fulfil for employees?

In Chapter 2, we presented a model for individual motivation that contains four motivational needs in two fundamental, existential dilemmas (i.e., individual versus community, and stability versus change). With a starting point in these two dilemmas, it is clear that there is a striking accordance between the four motivational needs and the four management functions that the three theories describe.

This similarity may be briefly expressed in this way: management helps employees by creating motivational compromises between the existential dilemmas. The connection between the four motivational needs and the theories described in the previous section are outlined in Table 9.4.

There is not complete overlap between the four sets of concepts in the table, but the concordance is convincing enough that it is probable that the motivational model from Chapter 2 and the three theories from previous sections fundamentally describe the same four management functions.

This means that the authors in their theories of management have described how management relates to the individual motivation of employees: the good manager serves the needs of the community by helping his or her employees to develop by stimulating their various, conflicting needs.

The description of the connection between the subject matter of the concept of management and individual motivation indicates that the relationship that exists between the four motivational needs – individuality, community, stability, and change – and management must be quite complicated. This relationship is the topic of the next section.

TABLE 9.4 Overview of the four motivational needs and theories

Motivational model in Chapter 2	Lieberman et al.	Bolman and Deal	Fogh Kirkeby
Stability	Caring	Human resources frame	The good
Change	Meaning attribution	Symbolic frame	The true
Individuality	Emotional stimulation	Political frame	The beautiful
Community	Executive function	Structural frame	The just

The relationship between management and motivational needs

There are a number of different perspectives on the process between the leader and the led. Two important points of view are the functionalist and the social constructivist points of view, respectively.

According to the functionalist point of view, the manager is a powerful person who exploits or uses employees for the purposes of the organisation. Here it is assumed that the manager has more power than the employees.

The power of such a leader is often based on a collective agreement that the leader represents something greater than him/herself. It is said that power is not bound to the person but to the position. Thus, the presidential airplane Air Force One does not belong to the president personally but to the US president as an institution. Power in this perspective is connected to institutions. In a private firm, the manager's institutional power is granted by the owners through property law or other legislation. In a public enterprise, a leader has power because he/she acts as representative of a greater community that is constituted by a municipality or a state. This provides the leader with the opportunity to exercise power that reaches beyond their individual, personal traits.

A manager's formal, institutional position as representative of a greater community gives access to the means of power such as hiring and firing, salary setting, and so forth. These are the means of power that are not found in ordinary relationships between two people, whether in a friendship or as a couple.

In the traditional picture of the relationship between manager and employee, this asymmetry is described as being so strong that the employee has no other option than to obey his/her manager. This asymmetrical power relationship between manager and employee is a completely integrated part of the social structure and cannot be escaped (Lee & Newby 1983: 118–121, 278).

With the acknowledgement in recent years that agents and structure mutually constitute each other (as described in Chapter 2), the traditional view of management has changed. An organisation's management can be understood as a structure in the organisation that defines the manager as a position with affiliated authority. Since, with insight from social constructivism, it is known that structures are only found because the stakeholders continuously re-create them, the result is that the manager only remains manager if the employees treat the person in question as manager. Thus, the employees re-create their manager every day with their acceptance and their actions, and the manager's function as manager is dependent on this. This introduces an entirely different reciprocity into the relationship between manager and employee than what one operates with in the functionalist theory or ordinarily connects with the concept of management.

From the social constructivist perspective, one can see management as a reciprocal bargain between manager and employee (Kaufmann & Kaufmann 2003: 313–314). Both parties assess on a running basis whether the effort one puts in

156 Management

corresponds to the return. Effort and return are not measured only in money and time but also in feelings and skills (Levine & Moreland 1994; Whitener et al. 1998; Christensen 2007: 76–77). It is complicated to describe which components enter into this transaction, but a simple way might be to say: the manager is attributed influence in return for the employees getting reduced responsibility and increased security.

This opens up a different way of viewing the manager's function. Through this lens, one can view the manager as an instrument of the employees rather than the reverse. Employees use the manager to protect themselves from the outside world, or to make it more manageable. This point was already formulated by Bion in the 1940s (Bion 2006 [1961]: 39, 55–56). But, as a sociological insight, it achieved widespread acceptance only in the 1980s and later.

There may be reason to look more closely at Bion's description of the relationship between manager and ordinary group members (employees). According to Bion, the central processes that are involved in this relationship are projection and projective identification. Managers are almost always a target of projection for their employees. Bion speaks directly about the manager being "designated" by the group to satisfy their needs (Bion 2006 [1961]: 38–39). Employees unconsciously use the manager to make the world more manageable and understandable.

For the person who procures a leader, there are a number of psychological advantages to be gained:

- The number of decisions one must take is reduced
- The responsibility for mistakes becomes less
- The responsibility for colleagues becomes less
- One can blame the leader if something does not work.

An illustration of this may be the observation that many people complain that they have an incompetent manager. It can be imagined that, in many cases, the complainant separates out his/her own conflicts by transferring them onto the manager through the use of projective identification. In certain situations, the manager can be transformed into a scapegoat if he/she does not meet the group's expectations.

The reciprocity between manager and employee is quite wide-ranging. Kernberg speaks directly about the fact that it requires precise studies to ascertain whether regression in a group or in an entire firm is due to the manager's personality or regression in a group of employees (Kernberg 1998: 53).

Since management, seen from this perspective, involves a bargain between managers and employees, both parties can always withdraw their offer if they do not think the other party is fulfilling the terms and conditions. This means that the manager who does not fulfil his part of the bargain will have difficulty mobilising the acceptance of the employees. If the employees feel poorly treated, they simply withdraw their backing. They work more slowly; they are more obstinate and less cooperative. It will become difficult to get holiday plans to work, they will get sick easier, they will not want to take on new assignments, and so forth.

The content of management **157**

It should now be easier to understand the bargain between community and individual, as was discussed in Chapter 6. Management can be described as an unconscious bargain between the community, the individual, and the manager as a person. The bargain consists of the individual getting security, recognition, clarity, and challenges at an appropriate level by joining the community. The community, in return, receives the individual's backing and loyalty. The manager as a person gets emotional satisfaction, influence, and authority.

If the bargain succeeds, the manager helps the employee to handle his/her relationship to the community and supports the individual in finding a conducive balance between stability and change. At the same time, the manager helps the employees as a group to function as a coherent, creative collective. This process in an organisational context is normally called personnel management. The process is elaborated in the next chapter.

In its immediate form, it is not obvious that the manager is the instrument of the employees, as claimed by the social constructivists, when the employees, for example, are ordered to do certain tasks or are fired from their jobs. So, there is a need to make clear how one can understand the concepts of power and authority when the relationship between manager and employees is seen at the same time as mutually constitutive. Therefore, this process is analysed in more detail in Chapter 11 on management and authority.

10

THE MANAGER AS TEACHER

Continuing learning and skill development have become a necessary part of the job at today's workplaces. Therefore, it has become an important part of the manager's area of responsibility to create a framework for this to happen. This chapter describes the fundamental conditions and methods for management's work on this and how the manager can expand his/her understanding of the organisational learning and development process. Organisations today must constantly be under development with regard to both the production itself and the organisational framework. Organisations that cannot do so risk being unable to adapt to changing conditions or being unable to preserve their position within their field. The fact that organisations must develop means, de facto, that its members must also develop. They must develop as individuals in that the individual employee must be able to adapt to new knowledge and acquire new skills and as a collective in that employees together must be good at sharing their knowledge and experience to build up new knowledge on the basis thereof.

There is a comprehensive field of literature that deals with learning in organisations (see, e.g., Senge 1990; Christensen 1997; Illeris 2012a; Lave & Wenger 2003; Andersen et al. 2004). These contributions operate with very different roles for the manager in connection with the learning and skill development of employees (Clematide 2006; Sørensen 2008; Helth 2011b).

One of the most fundamental conceptions of the manager's role in employee learning is found in Weber's theory of bureaucracy from the beginning of the 1900s. In this theory, Weber stresses hierarchy and meritocracy as important characteristics of the bureaucracy (Weber 1947: 650–678; Lee & Newby 1983: 192–196; Bakka & Fivelsdal 2002: 31–51). Meritocracy encompasses the idea that it is the civil servant's professional qualifications that entitle him to employment (as opposed to personal connections or bribes). Managers in a bureaucracy, therefore, are also recruited in accordance with meritocratic principles. The working procedures in a bureaucracy are typically of a nature that everything the civil servant produces is checked by the manager in order to ensure that it has the right professional quality. These work procedures are widespread in many of today's organisations but can have a special expression in public bureaucracies. Thus, it can still happen that the management to which civil servants in government ministries are subject consists primarily of their drafts of memos coming back from the manager filled with red notations.

When managers are recruited according to meritocratic principles, the conception of the manager as the foremost professional person in the group appears. The manager is superior to the employees by virtue of his/her greater professional ability and insight. This conception is deeply anchored in the prevalent mode of thinking about organisations, and good professional qualifications are frequently the basis for recruiting managers. Nor is there any doubt that professionally talented managers can have an important function as teachers or mediators of the professionalism that is a necessary precondition of work performance, just as the professionally talented manager can achieve immediate respect among employees.

However, people who are professionally talented are not necessarily good managers. They can have a far too narrow view of the function of a manager, which may have the effect that they focus exclusively on professionalism and not on "the whole person" and the collaboration between people. The purpose of recruiting managers on the basis of their professionalism is to ensure that, professionally speaking, the best problem-solving skills are available. But emphasis is not always put on the manager's other leadership abilities, such as being good at relating to people and having an understanding of what motivates employees. Moreover, the manager must be clear about the decisive role she or he plays in the creation of a positive learning space as a framework for the individual and organisational learning process (Bottrup & Hagedorn-Rasmussen 2011). In the following two sections, managerial conflicts about the exercise of personnel management are described as well as the consequences it has for organisational learning when the manager neglects this area.

The manager's conflict between professionalism and personnel management

Personnel management is of fundamental importance for whether the organisation is capable of learning from experience, adapting to new requirements, and proactively innovating itself. If the manager sees it as his/her task exclusively to ensure a professionally responsible execution of the job, there is a great risk that the organisation's members will stagnate and that the organisation will not develop sufficiently. This is because, inter alia, a lack of goals, lack of meaning, lack of follow-up, and lack of conflict resolution block the desire and ability to learn something new.

As mentioned in Chapter 1, personnel management can be described as encompassing the following tasks:

- Hiring and firing
- Information to and from employees

160 Management

- Goals and framework for the job
- Follow-up and feedback on work tasks
- Framework for professional and personal development
- Conflict management
- Support for employees with personal difficulties.

These functions can be delegated to some degree, for example, to group coordinators or to the employees themselves, depending on how the firm is organised and how management is distributed. Hirings can be delegated to a hiring committee; the definition of specific goals and frameworks can be given to employees; follow-up and feedback on assignments can be done by colleagues in the group; conflict management can be done with the help of an external consultant; and support for personal difficulties can come from an affiliated psychologist.

But in the final instance, it is the manager's responsibility to ensure that all the above-named tasks are taken care of and to determine how they are taken care of.

If employees find that the manager does not take responsibility for personnel management, that he does not have time to talk to people but, time and again, cancels meetings, that he avoids conversations and does not provide information, and so forth, it may be relevant to ask whether the manager actually wants and is able to handle the position of personnel manager. If the answer is no, it is often because the manager was named because of his professional ability and not because of his general management skills. This happens because the view that management is an independent profession with its own theoretical frame of reference, methods, and skills has far from broken through in all firms.

In particular, in relation to middle managers, there is a tendency to believe that the manager must have the same professional background as his/her employees. This view of management, which as mentioned derives from the bureaucratic form of organisation, is an underlying premise for many people's view of what a good middle manager is. It is also correct that it can provide the manager a direct advantage vis-à-vis employee acceptance and respect if they have common professional training. It may also make certain types of decisions easier if the manager has professional familiarity with the field. However, as this book has shown, modern management is a complex task that makes great personal and professional demands. A newly appointed manager is in a difficult situation if he/she is not prepared for this complexity but has conceived of being a manager in terms of his/her original professional training.

Thus, it can come as a surprise to the manager how much time goes into personnel management and how many skills one must possess to do it well. As a result, the manager may feel split between his/her original field and the field of management. After some time, the manager may feel pressured to choose between keeping up to date in his/her professional field or being a manager. It is a difficult decision whose long-term consequences may seem incalculable. One way to "solve" this schism is to avoid taking a position and, instead, try to do it all at once. In practice, this means that certain things (consciously or unconsciously) are rejected.

There may also be other reasons for rejecting or de-emphasising daily, informal personnel management. It can be time-consuming; the manager is rarely measured directly by it, and the many other professional and administrative tasks are experienced as more pressing because, in practice, they have a higher profile and priority. The consequences of this lack of personnel management are more obscure and difficult to put one's finger on than if the manager has failed to take a position on acquiring new materials or getting the statistics done on time. Moreover, this close, everyday contact with employees may be the area in which the manager feels least comfortable because he/she has received little or no training in it and because insufficient support is offered from his own manager in this area.

However, since the most important part of personnel management takes place through ongoing, unstructured contact (and not primarily, as many managers believe, through formal contact at information meetings and employee development conferences), this means that employees do not find that the manager fulfils his/her role and his/her part of the bargain. Employees react to this by withdrawing their "authorisation" from the manager.

The consequences of a lack of personnel management

Employees pick up on a de-emphasis of personnel management and may react to it in various ways. For a period, employees may reach out more to the manager in an attempt to change this prioritisation. Therefore, frequent inquiries to the manager (often about trivial things) may be a sign of a managerial deficiency in the firm. The manager comes under increased pressure and does not understand what the employees are asking for. The manager may react by withdrawing even more from employee problems and conflicts and, instead, entrenching himself behind his professionalism. In this vicious circle, employees gradually become resigned, and those who appreciate the manager's professionalism will be satisfied with that. The other employees fall into frustrated passivity, talk about the manager as being "averse to conflict", "indifferent", or "incompetent", or seek employment elsewhere because of "bad management". It is obvious that the employees who are the most enterprising will choose the latter solution, which in itself has the effect of draining the firm of assets.

The employees who choose to remain at the firm may develop a sort of pseudo-maturity in which the individual employee apparently makes do on his/her own and does not seem to have a great need for management. This supports the manager's view of having the priorities of his/her own work effort right because "these people are grown-ups and can take care of themselves". In reality, however, the organisation is atomised and everyone is left to his/her own devices. The result is a firm in which the conditions for cooperation and organisational learning are drastically worsened and most of the employees feel lonely and exasperated. However, some individuals thrive thanks to the many opportunities for uncontrolled and independent development, which allow them to cultivate their own projects and to pursue their own personal interests.

The lack of personnel management is costly for the individual as well as the overall firm. It leads to a poor work environment and poor contact between the members of the firm and many hidden, unprocessed conflicts that lead to impaired productivity, lack of development, stress, and staff exodus. But these phenomena appear only as indirect costs. Their connection with the lack of personnel management is not directly visible and cannot be read from the annual accounts even though they leave quite a toll both in human and economic terms.

On one hand, the manager has a central role when it comes to creating a beneficial framework for employee learning and development (i.e., the creation of a so-called positive learning space in which "space" is understood as both a physical and a psychological space). On the other hand, learning and the development of knowledge, ideas, and experience are not something the manager can control or order. Learning cannot be controlled through linear tools, such as development plans and personnel policy, or by having the manager send employees to courses in connection with change projects (Helth 2011a). Learning is about processes that play out in every employee and play out between the individual and the rest of the organisation and the surrounding society. Learning processes can activate both conscious resistance (e.g., to new technology or loss of jobs) and unconscious defences (e.g., loss of identity or increased insecurity) (Illeris 2012b). The manager must try to understand these mechanisms and, through his behaviour, create opportunities to work on resistance as well as defences while, at the same time, being aware that he cannot control the process.

The manager as teacher

As mentioned in Chapter 9, management can be attractive to the individual if management helps the individual to meet his/her motivational needs. One aspect of these needs is the dilemma between stability and change: the balance between, on one hand, wanting things to be as they usually are and, on the other, the desire for new challenges and the development of the individual's skills.

The individual needs people who can help him/her to find the balance in this dilemma. Individuals try to find good role models to help to overcome personal challenges. The individual can seek and find this help many different places – typically in the family with parents and grandparents and outside the family with friends and teachers. But when one leaves the education system for a workplace, many will also seek help for this dilemma from their manager.

This means that, in almost all relations between manager and employee, there is an expectation that the manager, in some form or other, is to function as a guide, teacher, coach, and "parent" (Alsted & Haslund 2016: chap. 4). This type of expectation is also found in many theories of management (see, e.g., Whitmore 1996; Rasmussen 1997; Clematide 2006; Gjerde 2006).

The relation between manager and employee, thus, includes an educational component that may resemble the relationship between teacher and student or the relationship between parent and child. The relational perspective on management here shows its strength because it especially stresses the manager's role as process consultant and coach. From this perspective, the manager's primary task is to help the employee to learn and develop through an appreciative approach. This proves to be especially useful in the many cases in which the employee has greater professional expertise in his/her field than the manager has. The manager, therefore, cannot base his/her management on greater professional knowledge. Instead, the manager can encourage and support employee development and sharing of knowledge.

The appreciative approach and learning

In a now well-known article from 1987, "Appreciative Inquiry in Organizational Life", Cooperrider and Srivastva examine the fundamental principles in appreciative inquiry (AI) (Cooperrider & Srivastva 1987). The first and most important principle is that any examination of an organisation and its potential begins with appreciation. Appreciation is shown for successes and skills, and people are regarded as having positive intentions behind their actions. The method emphasises positive feelings, and the focus is on solutions instead of problems. One enquires into dreams of and wishes for the future rather than failures in the past, and one looks at the opportunities and potential of the organisation instead of its limitations.

The conviction behind the method is that people flourish and develop by being appreciated for what they are and what they can do instead of being confronted with what they *cannot* do. Therefore, if one wants to innovate and improve an organisation, it can only be done by taking one's starting point in what is best and build on that. The appreciative approach will promote creativity and encourage participants to throw themselves into new things. By contrast, an approach that is only interested in problems and deficiencies has the long-run effect of exhausting and de-motivating people because it overlooks existing resources. This makes it difficult to see where change should come from and to believe that something can be changed. The mind-set that focuses on deficiency robs people of hope.

The second principle in AI is that the goal is not just to make people feel appreciated. The method is to lead to concrete innovation and changes in everyday practice, which makes the organisation function better. In other words, the proposals for change must be concrete and realisable.

The second principle is to be balanced with the third principle, which is that AI is to be inspiring and visionary, so the participants have the opportunity to see their organisation with new eyes and thereby discover new possibilities. Through the appreciative approach, participants have the opportunity – in a non-threatening atmosphere – to explore their common reality and to relate to whether there are things in it they want to change. The method, then, suggests that life in organisations is in a constant process of development and learning.

The fourth principle is that the method builds on collective cooperation in an equal dialogue and that all participants are obligated by the insights and decisions that have been reached by the community. Thus, the method is characterised by the consensus method in which one strives for a flow consisting of dialogue-consensus-obligation-implementation.

164 Management

The four principles are often described as the 4-D model – discovery, dream, design, and destiny. *Discovery* stands for exploring, appreciative examination; *dream* stands for the visionary and the desired future; *design* stands for realisable goals; and *destiny* stands for their implementation (Dall & Hansen 2001: chap. 2).

The appreciative permeates the language one uses when talking about events or phenomena in the firm. Whereas in the traditional, problem-oriented approach, one would say "we are very bad at keeping to the time schedule for our meetings", one would say in the appreciative approach, "it's good we have so much to say. Let's figure out what is important for us to talk about and whether there might be other ways to achieve the same thing".

Open, curious questions are a fundamental part of the method, and they are based upon the individual's positive experiences, such as:

- What is the best experience you have had with your team?
- What made this experience special?
- What did you do to make it work well?
- What did your colleagues and your manager do?
- What did you appreciate about yourself on that occasion?
- What did you appreciate about your colleagues and your manager?
- How can these experiences be transferred to other situations?

If everyone in the group or in the entire organisation contributes their positive experiences, good stories gradually accumulate, which allows one to ascertain what people would like more of and how they can achieve it. From there, one may continue with more concrete formulation and implementation.

In the book *The Thin Book of AI*, author Sue A. Hammond summarises AI in the following eight points (Hammond 1998):

- In any society and any organisation, there is something that works well.
- What we focus on becomes our reality.
- Reality is created in the moment, and there are a number of different realities.
- The way inquiries are made in a group or organisation affects the group.
- People are more secure going into the future if they bring something from the past.
- If people bring something from the past, it must be the best.
- It is important to appreciate difference.
- The language we use creates our reality.

The appreciative approach and the maturity of the organisation

AI can be an inspiring approach to organisational development, and the method contains great potential for change. It can be an enormous relief to shift one's attention from problems and conflicts to what actually functions well. The method can give hope for change, and the presence of this hope is a crucial precondition for people to invest their energy in the process of change. Moreover, the method can increase the understanding of the mutual dependence that exists in the workplace. The appreciative approach demonstrates how everyone helps create the reality the workplace constitutes. But the method requires an organisation or group of a certain maturity to give returns.

In a binary organisation, the experience is that AI is difficult to use because the tendency to black-and-white thinking and the designation of enemies makes it extremely difficult for people consistently to build upon in positive resources. On the other hand, it is conceivable that the use of AI can help nudge the organisation in the direction of more mature defences.

In a repressive organisation, the use of AI can have an idealising and problem-denying function. It fits very well with a repressive defence mechanism only to "think positively". If anyone says something negative or points toward something that is problematic, one can easily shut them up by saying, "This is not an appreciative approach!" However, this is a misunderstanding. It is certainly possible to discuss problems and conflicts with the help of AI as long as it happens in an appreciative way. One could also point out that, if it were not possible to deal with something problematic with the help of AI, it must mean that everything was perfect, and then there would be no reason to invent AI, the purpose of which is to improve the organisation.

In order to give an impression of how it is possible in an integrated organisation to discuss a problem in an appreciative way, the following example is given here.

A: I'm glad that the IT system has been updated. This helps everybody. It must have been a huge job and difficult to do with that short time frame.

B: Yes, it was, but we did it because we work well together in our group and because your department worked overtime since the system had to be tested. So, thanks for that.

A: After the update, some of the functions I used to have disappeared. Do you know whether there was a reason for that?

B: Yes, it was because they are special functions that were only available for your department. Is it a problem for you?

A: Not an immediate problem, but we would like to have them again by Wednesday next week, when we have to do the invoices. Can you do that?

B: Unfortunately, we won't be able to do that. Is it OK if it's not until Thursday? Otherwise, I'll try and do it Wednesday evening after my course.

A: No, don't do that. Thursday is fine.

166 Management

Take note of how the appreciative approach permeates the whole conversation. A begins by appreciating something that is good, namely, that the IT system has been updated and expresses appreciation of the work done by B's group. B recognises that the update was successful because the cooperation in his group was good and appreciates at the same time the extra input of A's department.

At this point in the conversation in which both parties have taken their starting point in what works well and have expressed their mutual appreciation, it is possible to point out something problematic (the functions that have disappeared) without anyone feeling accused or labelled as difficult or blameworthy. A first describes the problem and asks an open, curious question about whether B knows the reason for it. Since B does not feel accused by the question because he knows that A recognises his work effort in relation to the update, he is capable of answering with a focus on the problem instead of defending himself.

For his part, A feels recognised in that B asks whether it is a problem for A that the functions disappeared. Because B's question intimates that it might be problematic for A, A does not need to expend energy convincing B about this. Instead, A can provide a nuanced and specific description of what the problem is. At the same time, he remembers to appreciate that B has other things to do than help A by asking whether B can reinstall the functions by Wednesday.

Because B does not feel that he needs to react defensively, he can answer that he cannot get it done by Wednesday. But, with his offer to work overtime, he creates a possibility for a common discussion of whether that solution should be chosen. Since A feels his problem has been recognised and feels accommodated by B's offer, he can undertake this evaluation calmly and discern whether he can wait until Thursday. But it would also have been OK to accept B's offer as long as A remembered to explain why it was necessary and expressed appreciation of B's overtime and accommodation.

One may wonder why not all conversations at the workplace take place this way when mutual recognition is so conducive to the result. It is because, in reality, it requires a rather mature organisation with good, trusting relations to discuss a problem with the help of AI (Engquist 2000: chap. 8). If A had felt that B's group did not understand the problems of A's department and was otherwise indifferent to them, he would probably have leaped directly into aggressively pointing out the problems that arose because of the functions that had disappeared. And if B had correspondingly felt that A's department did not understand and respect the work of B's group, he would have defended himself or counterattacked A.

In some cases, it can happen that the use of AI in an immature organisation may help to mature the organisation because the genuinely appreciative approach breaks down unnuanced and simplifying views of the world. This is illustrated in the following case.

In an outpatient clinic, the nurses are very frustrated that patients often have a long waiting time; at a meeting, they agree that this cannot continue. Something drastic has to happen! The manager asks how many patients are treated on average during the day and when it last happened that they sent someone home without treatment.

It turns out that the number of patients has risen by 20% without any additional personnel and that it never happens that patients are sent home without treatment. In addition, a questionnaire shows that the patients are quite satisfied with the outpatient clinic because of the friendly atmosphere.

The manager says that, on this basis, she thinks the personnel are doing a fantastic job and asks how it is possible under these difficult circumstances. What are they doing that works so well?

After this, the mood changes. People congratulate themselves and each other with everything they are achieving despite the increasing number of patients, and they begin to investigate how they have done it and how they can use this knowledge from the present to bring down the waiting time in the future.

This case illustrates some of the dilemmas in AI. One can, as mentioned, read it as an illustration of how the manager's appreciation has the effect of maturing the organisation and making it capable of building on the results achieved instead of panicking about the problems. But one can also read it as an example of how a manager uses AI to manipulate employees away from their frustration at the lack of resources to becoming interested in how they can provide even more work to the organisation! The manager does not take a position on the conflict the employees are raising – that they are frustrated and stressed because the number of patients has risen by 20% – but diverts their attention instead.

In an extension of this last point of view, a contribution written by the Danish psychologist Claus Elmholdt for the periodical *Erhvervspsykologi* [*Business Psychology*] may be mentioned. The article provides a sharp critique of AI:

> AI literature, like humanist interview studies, is strikingly silent about power relationships. In the article by Cooperrider and Srivastva (1987), the organisation is consistently discussed as a homogeneous whole. There is no differentiation between employer and employee interests or conflicts of interest and differences linked to different employee groups, gender, or individual identity projects. It is assumed to be unproblematic that appreciative recognition and equal dialogue creates a background for consensus around realisable visions for the common good. *Contra* AI, the literature on organisations widely documents that organisations are not harmonious but characterised by differences, contradictions, and conflicts
>
> *(Elmholdt 2006; our translation)*

In her book *Anerkendelse i ledelse* [*Appreciation in Management*], Inge Schützsack Holm also has a critique of AI. She believes that the search for appreciation is a struggle for identity and that organisations play an increasing role in the creation

168 Management

of identity. In return, the individual provides involvement and motivation. But, according to Holm, organisations are poor contexts for recognition/appreciation because hierarchy and asymmetry of power hinder equality, intentionlessness, reciprocity, and voluntariness (Holm 2010: chap. 10).

It is correct that organisations are arenas for conflicts and opposing interests that cannot be eliminated either with the help of AI or other methods. Thus, it is not about denying or getting rid of all conflicts or opposing interests in organisations because that cannot be done. But despite conflicts and varying interests, cooperation is necessary on both organisational and social planes. Therefore, it is a question of investigating which conflicts and conflicts of interest are real and which are merely imagined because of distorted inner perceptions. It is also a question of being able to deal with, contain, and integrate these real conflicts into the life of the organisation. The appreciative approach has proven to be a usable and constructive method to separate out imagined conflicts and integrate real conflicts.

One of the absolutely essential components of AI – and of all communication – is listening. The following section, therefore, provides a more detailed description of the phenomenon of listening in order to strengthen the organisation's capacity for learning and for more precise communication.

Listening

The fundamental thing in any conversation is listening because, without reciprocal listening, the parties are incapable of building on each other's statements, which effectively precludes any genuine *con*versation. But listening is not a simple activity. The way one listens is decisive for how one positions oneself in relation to the other person (Haslebo 2004: 320–322). One must also be attentive to the fact that the ability to listen can be disrupted due to conscious or unconscious emotional conflicts in the person listening (Gjerde 2006: chap. 6). For example, it may be that the listener is bored, irritated, or impatient with the person speaking; or the listener may have a relationship dominated by conflict or competition with the person speaking. It may also be that what is being said arouses distaste or a feeling of inferiority or helplessness in the listener.

An employee who begins to cry during a performance appraisal may make a manager feel uncomfortable because the manager does not know what he is to do with the employee. This makes the manager stop listening and end the conversation, either literally or mentally. And the employee who feels the manager is angry with him may become so afraid that he does not hear a word the manager is saying (Engquist 2000: chap. 6).

It may also be that the listener has a deeper view of life marked by mistrust and pessimism that disturbs his/her ability to listen, or it may be that the listener projects inner feelings of insecurity and self-contempt upon the person speaking, which, of course, also impairs the ability to listen. But even without the presence of such internal conflicts, the act of listening can arouse an existential anxiety in the person listening. One can be afraid of losing oneself and being "swallowed" by

The manager as teacher **169**

the other person if one surrenders oneself and listens to the other person on his/her premises. This anxiety is at the core of many communication problems and has its roots in the feeling that one is insufficiently anchored in oneself. The person listening feels a lack of self-definition, a lack of an ability to feel and express one's own needs, and a lack of ability to distinguish oneself emotionally from others. This disturbs the ability to listen (Engquist 2000: chap. 6).

The more developed one's self-esteem is, the less the anxiety of being swallowed up will be, and the better the conditions for empathy and listening will be.

One often distinguishes between passive and active listening, but passive listening is not necessarily the same as not listening. It is absolutely possible to sit quietly and listen intensely since listening is partially a question of personal style and a question of how one prefers to acquire new knowledge. Listening also depends on the circumstances; passive listening, for example, is more natural in a larger gathering.

Since inner processes are always happening in every person regardless of how passive they seem to be, it can be claimed that the concept of passive listening does not exist. When one speaks of passive listening, therefore, it means passive as seen in relation to the person speaking. If the listener does not relate actively, the person speaking may wonder: "How can I see you are listening?" If the listener stays passive — that is, sits still, has a neutral facial expression, and is silent, it increases the risk that the person speaking will be in doubt about whether the other person is actually listening. Passivity also means that the person listening cannot clear up any misunderstandings of what is said. Therefore, there is a greater risk for disruption of communication by passive listening.

The person speaking in any conversation is in a vulnerable position by definition because the person in question cannot know in advance how well he or she will succeed in formulating and communicating what they want to express. The greatest vulnerability, however, is in the fact that the person speaking — regardless of how articulate the person may be — has no control over how what is said is interpreted and received by the listener. The primary benefit of active listening, therefore, is that it reduces the conversation's inherent vulnerability and allows the conversation to flow more freely and be less disturbed by unconscious, emotional subtexts. At the same time, active listening improves the opportunity for the person listening to understand what the person speaking means, which increases the precision of the communication (Gjerde 2006: chap. 6).

That is why active listening is the cornerstone of the appreciative approach and, thus, the organisation's ability to learn from its experiences and continue to develop.

The means one uses for active listening are:

- Various verbal tools
- Attention to body language and process.

The two following sections provide a more detailed examination of, respectively, verbal tools and the importance of body language.

170 Management

The use of verbal tools in active listening

The most important verbal tool in active listening is to say something, but it is not a matter of indifference what one says and how. It may seem to be contradictory for the listener to speak, but the exclusive purpose of the listener saying something is to elaborate the listener's own understanding of what is being said and to help the person speaking to achieve greater clarity in what he wants to say. The listener must constantly be aware of these purposes in order not to take over the conversation and turn it into something about the listener's own views and needs (Gjerde 2006: chap. 6).

Some conversations are defined with a fixed division of roles throughout the entire conversation in which there is one person listening and one person talking (e.g., a coaching session); but, in many conversations and meetings, people change roles between being listener and speaker. It may be difficult to assess when it is time for a role change, but the most important thing is to be conscious of the difference between the two roles. As a rule of thumb, it may be said that one can shift from listener position to speaker position when one feels certain that one has understood what was said precisely enough and when the person speaking gives an indication of being understood.

It is important to distinguish between listening actively on the premises of the person speaking and agreeing with the person speaking. If one mixes these two things up, one may unnecessarily activate the previously mentioned anxiety of losing oneself. Listening actively and empathetically is not the same as agreeing with the person speaking. By inquiring into and elaborating on one's understanding, the listener has not thereby declared himself in agreement with what was said; he has only acquired better premises for assessing the content. At the same time, with the help of active listening, there occurs a processing of emotional barriers between the parties to which disagreements may otherwise lead because the speaker has space to express himself before the listener formulates any disagreement. This will be viewed by the speaker as a sign of respect and thereby remove anxiety that the other person does not respect the viewpoint of the speaker.

The various verbal tools that the active listener uses serve three goals:

1 To make the listener's understanding more precise and nuanced
2 To support the clarification of the speaker's meaning
3 To show understanding and respect to the speaker.

The most important verbal tools for active listening are:

- Repetition
- Clarification
- Formulation
- Reformulation
- Positive reformulation

The manager as teacher **171**

- Summation
- Conclusion (Gjerde 2006: 133–142).

Repeating what is said is a simple but effective tool. Sometimes, it can be enough to repeat a single key word.

S(PEAKER):	I feel almost invisible when I'm with these people.
L(ISTENER):	Invisible?
S:	Yes, I think it's because no one talks to me. It's very unpleasant and makes me insecure.

In this case, repetition gets the person speaking to reflect on why he uses the word "invisible". He realises what is happening in the situation and how it makes him feel.

In other cases, the listener can repeat a whole sentence or an entire point of view in an inquisitive tone in order to get the speaker to reflect deeper on what he has said and, at the same time, provide the listener with more information. By using repetition, the listener functions as a mirror for the speaker, which can have an extremely good effect. On the other hand, it is a tool that must not be misused, because no one wants to speak to a mirror all the time.

Clarification means that the listener makes enquiries in order to elaborate his own understanding. The questions "have I understood you correctly that you're say-ing . . .?", "does this mean you're in favour of . . .?" are good for this purpose because they mirror what is said and, at the same time, invite the speaker to confirm, correct, or elaborate on the listener's and his own understanding. The tone in and the inten-tion behind the question, however, are decisive. The question must be genuinely open and curious and must be without aggressive, mocking, or accusatory under-tones because the latter are, in reality, just an attack disguised as a question.

Formulation means that the listener tentatively formulates something on behalf of the speaker, which the speaker is having a hard time formulating himself. This formulation, however, must always take place with an implicit question mark.

S:	So, I marched out of the room!
L:	Because you were really angry!?
S:	Yes, I was!
L:	But you also felt wounded and insecure?
S:	No, not so much that, just angry!

172 Management

Reformulation can make the listener more certain that he/she has understood something correctly. If a word can be changed or added without altering the meaning, it makes it more probable that one has understood the essence of what was said. At the same time, the reformulation mirrors what was said for the speaker and, perhaps, adds new nuances to the speaker's understanding.

> S: I have put up a tall bookshelf between me and the others.
> L: You've put up a tall bookshelf because you would like your own area to be in peace?
> S: Yes, you're right about that.

To undertake a *positive reformulation* is not just to add new nuances to what was said but to impart to the speaker an entirely different, positive perspective on what was said. Therefore, it is an especially effective tool that is often used in the appreciative approach, coaching, and conflict resolution.

> S: I've taken far too long writing this report!
> L: It could also be said that you've been thorough and careful with it.
> S: It shows that I'm a pathological perfectionist!
> L: It shows you take your responsibility seriously.
> S: Yes, that's right. I do. The report has influence on many people.

One can *sum up* several times during the course of a conversation and also at the conclusion of a conversation or a meeting. Summation has the effect of clarifying to both parties what was said and, perhaps, agreed to. The listener checks to make sure she has understood everything correctly, and the speaker can correct things he does not agree with. At the same time, the speaker receives help in ascertaining what is important. Especially in longer conversations or meetings, a short summary can be useful along the way in order to maintain focus.

> L: Before we continue talking about your new assignment, I'd like to sum up that you have decided to finish up the old assignment this week. Is that right?
> S: Yes, that's right. I said that. But now that I think about it, it's probably not realistic.
> L: When do you think it would be realistic?
> S: I need another week.
> L: So, that would mean it's finished just before Christmas vacation?
> S: Yes.

Conclusion means that one briefly outlines (typically, at the end of a conversation or meeting) what the speaker emphasised or decided or what the parties jointly agreed to, and so forth. People often neglect to spend time on conclusions – perhaps, because, in the situation, it seems obvious what the conclusion is. However, people forget that it may not be so obvious the next day. Often, people say they omit concluding remarks because there is no time for it, but the real reason in many cases is that people are nervous about opening things up for new discussions or conflicts. However, it is far better to conclude that people do not agree than to leave a conversation with a false agreement that will not hold longer than until people are out of the room.

> L: So, can we conclude that you'll take over the clean-up of the copy room?
> S: What? No, you should continue with that. I have enough of that sort of thing.
> L: Then, I must have misunderstood you.
> S: Yes, we'll need to have another meeting where we can look at the overall number of jobs.
> L: OK, that's a good idea. Until then, I'll continue to have responsibility for the copy room.

The importance of body language in active listening

What the person listening strives to communicate to the speaker is focused attention, respect, and understanding. In this connection, it is important for there to be accord between the listener's body language and the verbal activity. There are countless indirect and discreet ways to undermine a speaker with the help of non-verbal tools. This is rarely due to a conscious desire by the listener to annoy the speaker. It is rather due to a lack of consciousness and a lack of knowledge of the importance of non-verbal communication.

It may be due to previously mentioned emotional conflicts in connection with communication that can be expressed through the body. Since the body's reactions to inner conflicts most often take place unconsciously, one can hardly control them directly, but one can increase one's attention to their importance (Guldager 2007: 66–69).

The primary points of attention are:

- Eye contact
- Facial gestures
- Breathing
- Spontaneous exclamations
- Voice
- Gestures
- Posture
- Body stance
- Body activity.

174 Management

Deficient or poor *eye contact* can be inhibiting or directly disturbing to communication. The listener does not look at the speaker but looks away or at another in the group that may have higher status, for example. This pattern of eye contact is often seen in meetings. One must take special note of it if, generally speaking, the meeting participants do not look at the person speaking. This may be a sign of reduced or complete lack of listening either because of internal problems in the participants or because of relational problems between them. For the speaker, the lack of eye contact from the listener almost always becomes subject to interpretation and may be a reason the speaker feels uneasy or uncomfortable. In connection with meetings, therefore, it can have a beneficial effect on communication to make the participants aware of the lack of visual connection between them. A conscious change of this behaviour can have a powerful influence on their relations.

The alternative to a lack of eye contact is not maintaining constant eye contact, since that can seem intimidating and dominating. The listener needs to sense his way forward as to when and how often it is appropriate to establish contact because it depends on the participants, the circumstances, and the sort of conversation.

If the listener's *facial expression* is viewed by the speaker as indifferent, low energy, suspicious, or dismissive in some other way, it will distract the speaker and get him to shorten his presentation or to keep the chair longer than necessary in the hope of changing the listener's expression. The listener must be conscious of how his expression may be interpreted. He must use his empathy and try to radiate what he himself would like to encounter if he were speaking.

In most situations, people are not conscious of their *breathing* and, therefore, cannot control it consciously. Nevertheless, the breathing of participants in a conversation can have influence on the communication and on the basic emotional atmosphere. Rapid breathing may be an expression of anxiety or tension and may affect the other participants with stress or other discomfort. Deep sighs, for example, may be an expression of concern or boredom in the listener and can make the speaker nervous. In order to strengthen the awareness of participants of these unconscious influences, it may be an advantage in some instances to make them aware of it and try to uncover the reason for them.

If the listener utters a *spontaneous exclamation* in the form of, for example, affirmations or denials, shaking the head, nodding, yawning, giggling with a neighbour, or drumming his fingers on the table, it is incredibly effective communication! The speaker will quickly (but, perhaps, unconsciously) register it, interpret it, and react to it: "Henrik is nodding. He agrees with me, that's good. So, I'll keep going". Or "this is the third time Peter has yawned. I'm probably boring him. I'd better finish up".

To the extent the listener's *posture* is slumped or relaxed or the listener sits aggressively on the edge of the chair, it will also influence the speaker and have significance for what happens in the communication. If the listener sits with his side turned to the speaker or cannot keep his eyes from his computer screen, it may be viewed as indifference or lack of interest, and so forth. The list could go on forever.

The point is not that the listener − for example, a manager at a staff performance meeting − must constantly keep an eye on his/her body language and bodily reactions and consciously try to change them. That would affect spontaneity and authenticity in the conversation. The point is to be attentive to the fact that the body is inclined to live its own life and to be willing to investigate what it is that is expressed through it. One's body language is an object of comprehensive, primarily unconscious interpretations in others, and these interpretations are not necessarily in accordance with what one wanted to express. Therefore, consciousness and knowledge of these phenomena are important in strengthening the ability of the organisation's members to engage in reciprocal communication.

The importance of non-verbal behaviour for communication

Particularly for managers, attention to and knowledge about the importance of non-verbal behaviour is vital because the behaviour of the manager is a special target of employee observation and interpretation. At the same time, it is also important for managers to be good at reading the non-verbal behaviour of employees because, in this way, the manager gets a lot of information that employees may not be capable of formulating themselves. The following case provides a good illustration of the problems that arise in communication if the manager is not attentive to his/her own and employees' non-verbal behaviour.

A management group of four people holds a meeting. The director is at the head of the table, running the meeting. The director introduces the meeting by saying that he needs to leave a half hour before its scheduled end but does not say why. In the meantime, he taps his foot vigorously.

The head of personnel begins to go through the new agreements. The director looks through some brochures, while he drums his fingers on his knee. The breathing of the head of personnel becomes faster and shallower. When the director clears his throat, she blushes and quickly finishes up her review.

The CFO reviews the quarterly financial statement. He shares out a copy to everyone but forgets to give one to the head of personnel, who has to ask for one. Throughout the presentation, the director furrows his brow and holds his hand over his mouth, while he leafs through the statement. He does not comment on the quarterly statement, and his head is clearly somewhere else than on what the CFO is talking about. As he leafs through the statement, the director emits small, almost inaudible sighs. The CFO begins to talk faster with a more powerful voice, and the sweat stains grow under his arms.

When it is the head of administration's turn to speak, he says he has nothing to add to the meeting.

There is less and less eye contact between the participants as the meeting gradually moves forward. The director alternates from looking at his papers to looking out the window. The head of personnel mostly looks down at the table. The CFO looks around at the others but is unable to make eye contact.

> The head of administration has shifted so he is sitting turned away from the others. When the director speaks, however, everyone looks at him.
>
> The director says that he has some important information, which he thereupon reads aloud quickly in a monotone voice. His foot again begins to tap intensely. No one comments on the information.
>
> Thereupon, the director gets up and says he has to go. The head of administration quickly leaves the room on the heels of the director. The other two get up hesitantly and leave.

This case illustrates how listening and attention to what is being said is guided and mediated through what is not being said. The director's non-verbal behaviour influences the meeting to such a degree that it is almost a non-meeting. No one is listening to what the others say or signals that they are. The department heads interpret the director's behaviour as impatience and dissatisfaction with them and react according to their personality to this interpretation in various non-verbal behaviours. The head of personnel blushes and quickly finishes her presentation; the CFO reacts with aggression and tries to keep the director's attention (apparently, without luck), and the head of administration decides to withdraw completely, emphasising this by turning to the side.

But, actually, none of them can know whether their interpretation of the director's actions as impatient or dissatisfied is correct. It may be that the director is feeling tremendous time and financial pressure about the job and, therefore, expresses his unease through his body. He may react to pressure by withdrawing into his own thoughts, which impairs his ability to pay attention to his staff and dulls his sense of how he is affecting them.

The only way the department heads could have checked whether their interpretation of the director's behaviour was correct was by asking him. Supplementing the understanding of non-verbal behaviour with verbal behaviour is often very effective, but many people sidestep that because it is experienced as a mixture of two spheres: the said and the unsaid. The premise for verbalisation is also that one is conscious of what impact non-verbal behaviour has on the situation, and this is far from always the case.

The director is not necessarily dissatisfied with the department heads but, perhaps, with himself. He may not necessarily be having a bad time at the meeting, but the department heads definitely are, even though they may not be conscious of why. Just as it is certain that this meeting will have a negative effect on future meetings, to the confusion of both the director and the department heads, who will have a difficult time figuring out the causes for the bad mood since nothing negative was *said* at the meeting.

The reason that emotional conflicts and anxiety appear particularly in body language is that people have less control over the body than over the spoken word.

The quality and robustness of relationships play a decisive role for the productivity and creativity of an organisation because it is through these reciprocal relationships that the organisation is re-created and developed continuously (Haslund & Alsted 2004). Through imitation and adaptation, the employees "learn" from their manager's behaviour how one communicates and acts in this organisation; and to a wide extent this learning takes place unconsciously. If what the manager says and what the manager does are experienced by the employees as being in opposition to each other, the learning effect of the manager's conduct (as interpreted by the employees) will take precedence over the manager's verbal expressions. At times, verbal expressions may even seem directly to undermine the manager's credibility if the contradiction between what is said and what is done is experienced as too great. Therefore, it is of fundamental importance for the manager to be a person who likes having direct, close contact with others and who is as conscious as possible about the importance of his own behaviour – verbal as well as non-verbal.

The manager's place in the power structure means that his behaviour sets a standard for the employees and that he is heard. But this is no guarantee that the manager's intentions will be understood or followed. Managers have the potential to become powerful symbols for the meaning employees attribute to the organisation, but the manager's influence on the organisation depends on the employees' interpretation of his behaviour. Successful leadership requires the manager to take the existing "climate of interpretation" (psychological maturity) into his/her consideration. Thus, the manager is not only the one who influences the organisation but is also influenced by it (Hatch 1997: 235). The message to managers must be that they have greater symbolic power than they realise but less control (over interpretations) than they would presumably want (Hatch 1997: 365).

The manager in cross-pressure between personnel management and production

Some parts of management may take place in a structured and planned way – for example, meetings and performance appraisals. But an important part of management happens in an unplanned way because the need for employees to have contact with the manager arises spontaneously over the course of the day. This spontaneity may be experienced by the manager as a distracting interruption of his real work, and he can be frustrated and get the feeling that he does not really know what he has accomplished once the workday is done. He only knows that he has been busy and engaged the whole time and has not done the tasks he had originally planned. Over the long run, this can be exhausting and lead to the manager taking work home, going to work earlier in the morning, or staying on the job in the evening in the hope of getting everything done. In the study "Det Danske Ledelsesbarometer" ["The Barometer of Danish Management"] from 2011, 78% of managers stated that, to some or to a high degree, they "were available to [their] workplace around the clock" (Jensen et al. 2011).

178 Management

Middle managers with 10–20 employees, in particular, are liable to wind up in this untenable situation because they typically spend a lot of time on unplanned, unrecorded, and thereby invisible work with employees. At the same time, many administrative and professional duties are imposed upon them which they are assumed to have time to do. This places the manager in a serious cross-pressure in which important duties are neglected, thereby putting pressure on his relationship to his own manager and to the employees, and in which the manager rebuffs the employees. This frustrates them and makes them view the manager as absent and unapproachable. The cries for "visible management" often heard from employees can be seen as an expression of this problem.

Depending on personal style and maturity, the manager may find various ways to solve this cross-pressure. One common way is for the manager to avoid the pressure from employees by simply not being physically present. Of course, there may be rational or necessary reasons for the manager to be somewhere else than with employees, but the absence can also have a psychological dimension. Thus, it is characteristic for managers to say that they are often worried about having too little time with their employees while, at the same time, feeling incapable of doing anything about it. This may be because absence serves as a repressive defence that the manager unconsciously has an interest in maintaining.

Another way for managers to protect themselves is to give up any system or overview and let themselves be totally guided by what the day brings. As a result, undone tasks mount up, and long-term or complicated activities are deprioritised. Many people describe this way of working as "putting out fires". It is experienced as extremely frustrating for both managers and employees. But the fact that, despite the frustration, organisations continue to put out fires year in and year out tells us that there may be some advantages to this method. Such advantages may be that putting out fires acts as a splitting defence since the complicated and strategic work is split off. In this way, life in the organisation becomes more predictable. What is split off is made idyllic, into something somewhat mystical but incredibly important that one must absolutely deal with at some unspecified point in the future. Many managers frequently assert that, as soon as the work pressure slackens, they will begin to outline a strategy, implement an analysis, or bring the new, complicated system into use. But it does not happen because the reality is that the work pressure never diminishes.

At the same time, the splitting increases the level of anxiety because what arouses anxiety is simply placed somewhere else (namely, in the future). And as it gradually becomes clear that the future is always moving and, therefore, that one will never get to work on these fundamental areas, the sense of being on a ship without a rudder will increase. For managers in particular, the use of this splitting defence over the long run is anxiety-provoking because the number of undone tasks provides stress and because, in the final instance, it is the manager's responsibility if work sails off without any direction.

How managers work with cross-pressure

In order to avoid this situation and to avoid reaching the breaking point and burning out as a manager, it is crucial for the manager to understand that his function is complex: he must at one and the same time have a clear understanding of the direction to move in, and he must allow himself to be guided by where the day brings him. If he is able to maintain this dual vision of his function, two things happen: his sense of direction guides him to manoeuvre the events of the day, and the day's events guide him to adjust his direction (see Helth 2006: 55–56 for a similar point).

Working from his basic sense of direction, the manager must allow himself to be "disturbed" – that is, he must allow himself to be interrupted and to be accessible when the need arises. This is important because an organisation consists of living human beings for whom only very few things can be fit within a schema. Valuable information and development potential may be lost if the manager always puts off contact until "another day" or if he is only rarely present. In the following case, the manager understood this completely.

Every morning, an experienced, male manager of an office of around 25 employees makes his rounds, saying good morning to each employee and chatting briefly about work-related or personal things when there is a need for it. Afterwards, he goes back to his office, where, according to employees, he "just sits and reads the newspaper" with the door open, always available.

Many of the employees say he is the best boss they have ever had.

Even though the employees' view that the manager just sat and read the paper was not necessarily correct, it is still an important point in this case. It is possible that the manager was actually busy, but he was successful in giving the impression that he always had time for the employees. The other tasks he presumably also had were not prioritised at the cost of personnel's need for him, and he weighed physical presence in the office highly. Many days, he was not sought out by employees because the most acute things had been dealt with during his morning round. The fact that the employees knew that they could always reach him and that he would make time to listen to them and support them if they needed it, paradoxically enough, meant that the employees did not need to seek him out so much.

On a practical level, there are different points of view and methods for working with cross-pressure between personnel management and the manager's other tasks. One method is for the manager to enter into a dialogue with his own management in order to make his invisible personnel management more visible and to ensure himself the time – and respect – for this work.

180 Management

If the pressure from personnel management is ordinarily felt as greater by middle managers than CEOs, it is, in part, because CEOs often do not have as many employees who refer directly to them and, in part, because middle managers are closer to the operational components of the organisation. It is precisely when things are put into practice that many of the problems and conflicts arise that require a manager's resources. If top management has delegated large parts of personnel management to middle managers, it is the responsibility of the middle managers to report back to the top executives how this work can and should be done. Top management often does not have a sufficient feel for this and cannot get it without nuanced and constructive feedback from their middle managers.

Securing more time for personnel management may also entail a cutback of the manager's other duties or having the tasks done by someone other than the manager. Here, it is a good idea to undertake an examination of the manager's duties – that is, what the manager in practice (and not on paper) spends his time on – and no one is more obvious for undertaking this examination than the manager himself. Managers often complain that they do not have time to reflect on their practice, but this can become a pretext for inaction and veil a hidden notion and hope that someone will come and fix their problems for them. But managers have to make the time for this because it is about defining their own work conditions and their opportunities for doing good work.

A simple method for undertaking the analysis is to record one's work meticulously for a period of time (e.g., a month). This may be done by starting with the calendar one already keeps and merely adding unplanned conversations and other events and how much time was spent on them. After the period has run its course, the data may be analysed thoroughly, and many people are amazed at how they spend the bulk of their time. Data may be analysed with respect to certain categories (e.g., personnel management, administrative tasks, representative assignments, professional activities) and, perhaps, a visual representation can be created. This can form a good starting point for the manager's own reflections and for negotiations with his/her immediate supervisor.

For example, administrative tasks can be done by adding more administrative personnel or by simplifying administration, and some of the professional tasks that the manager did previously may advantageously be distributed to employees. It may also be that there are tasks that can be dropped entirely. They simply are not done anymore. In practice, there are many managers who end up taking the latter solution, but it places unreasonable pressure on the manager if there is an expectation that, at some point, the tasks will or should be done. It is far better and more transparent for everyone if a conscious prioritisation is made in which certain tasks are dropped. Astoundingly, many tasks are actually left undone without any great consequences in practice.

Another method is to investigate the frequency and type of unplanned interruptions to which the manager is subject. The desire of employees for contact with the manager can be necessary and useful, but they can also be a sign of an organisation in which employees have learned helplessness and do not believe they can do things

The manager as teacher **181**

themselves. It may also be a part of firm culture that makes employees nervous about taking independent decisions. In many ways, it can be easier and less risky in such a culture to ask the manager or to let the manager decide rather than to figure it out for oneself. It can also be convenient for employees to leave unpleasant or difficult decisions to the manager with the remark, "It's management's job to prioritise".

From the point of view of the individual employee, it is not necessarily very often one uses the manager in this way; but for a manager with a certain number of employees, it can mean many (ultimately unnecessary) interruptions during the day that disturb and burden her. It can end with giving her a feeling of being (mis)used and, at the same time, a feeling of being inadequate, as is the case here.

> A young, female manager takes over the management of a department of around 40 employees just as the department is moving to new offices. The move leads to a number of frustrations in the personnel, since many things do not function properly from the start, and the frustrations lead to a stream of complaints to the new manager.
>
> The manager, who is eager to make a good impression, willingly takes on the burden of trying to solve the many practical problems, but this does not diminish the dissatisfaction among the personnel.
>
> One day, a very angry employee comes to her office and rebukes her because there are no coffee cups in the new kitchen. The manager gets up from her chair and hurries out to the kitchen to unpack a case of cups she knows is on the table. Not until the last moment does she stop herself and say to the employee that he can just as easily figure out how to unpack the cups!

This manager was about to fall into the "service trap", in which the manager – for fear of not being good enough or in an attempt to buy the good will of the employees or, perhaps, out of convention – habituates employees to being serviced by doing things that are unreasonable and irrational for a manager to spend time on. In this case, the manager should have used her resources to investigate what was really behind the dissatisfaction of the employees instead of turning up the service level in an attempt to please them. Since the real problems (anxiety and insecurity in connection with the move) had not been excavated and, therefore, not dealt with, employee frustration only rose in direct proportion to the manager's service level.

In principle, with every request from an employee, the manager should ask herself whether this request is relevant and remember that relevance may be concrete, psychological, or symbolic – or all three at the same time. If the manager assesses that the request does not provide meaningful interaction with the employee, it is important to react to it. Otherwise, there is a risk the manager (on a symbolic level) will maintain a role as the omniscient and omnipotent leader and, likewise, keep the employees in a dependent and supplicant role.

Instead, the manager should refer the employee to another forum or tell the employee to take a decision him/herself but do it in a way that the employee does not feel rejected or swept aside. The manager should do this (a) to protect him/herself from being overburdened, (b) to use his or her limited time in as relevant a way as possible in relation to the overall whole, and (c) to give the employees the opportunity to take more independent decisions and to solve problems and conflicts themselves, where that is possible.

However, it may not always be easy to determine the relevance of a request quickly. Something that resembles a trivial issue to which the employee might readily find the solution may turn out to be veiling a need to talk about personal problems. What begins as a piece of information that the employee could have sent in an email may develop into a conversation about serious conflicts in the group with which the employee needs help. Or the complaint may simply be an expression of a need for attention. Therefore, the manager must listen with both ears to try to decode what the employee really wants.

The fact that people do not necessarily know or come out with what they really need to talk to the manager about is a good argument for managers with personnel responsibility to have their own office. Because even though it can be argued that the manager gets useful insight into the job and the interplay by sitting with the employees in an open office or with other managers, the risk is great that the manager will miss vital information and contact if there is no opportunity for an employee request to develop spontaneously into something else in the private space (in both the physical and metaphorical sense) between manager and employee.

The manager's role in organisational learning

This chapter has described the role of the manager in the learning process. In the organisations of bygone days, the role of the manager was to be the professional teacher who trained employees about how things were to be done. In the modern organisation, the manager is not necessarily more professionally capable or knowledgeable than his/her employees. This is due to the complexity of production, which demands in-depth specialist knowledge, and the quick pace of change, the practical effect of which is that the professional knowledge the manager may once have had quickly becomes out of date. Instead, the manager's role is to be a coach or supervisor whose function is primarily to create the preconditions for the employees themselves to develop individual and collective learning.

Creating a positive learning space implies that the manager is capable of helping employees to overcome the resistance and unconscious defences to which learning and the changes that derive therefrom may occasion. The manager does this by using an appreciative approach and by being conscious of the way he/she and the employees communicate – verbally as well as non-verbally. Through his/her own conduct, the manager shows employees more advantageous and more precise ways of communicating. The manager here uses his/her function as role model for learning and his/her knowledge of psychodynamic factors to observe and discuss what is happening in relationships that may be inhibiting or disruptive to organisational learning. This may involve conflicts that have root in real disagreements or opposing interests or which derive from imaginary or unconscious emotional conflicts. The manager's role is to help employees uncover and integrate such conflicts since they subsume so much emotional energy, which thereby does not benefit the learning process.

11

THE MANAGER AS AUTHORITY

After examining the manager as teacher, we shall describe the other side of a manager's function: the manager as authority. Since a manager is placed in a power relationship with other people, it is essential for him/her to have a good understanding of the concept of authority and to work to clarify his/her own personal authority in relation to the employees. This chapter, therefore, examines what various theoreticians have said about the concept of authority and, then, looks at different ways in which the manager may administer his/her authority.

The study of the expression of authority and power in everyday life has created a very comprehensive field of literature (see Christensen & Jensen 2001; Laustsen & Myrup 2006 for oversights on the topic). There are, at least, three general understandings of what authority and power are:

1   *The pluralist understanding*: Agent A has power over agent B if agent A can make agent B do something agent B otherwise would not do (Dahl 1957). Here, power is defined by the concrete relationship between A and B. Power shifts from relationship to relationship and from case to case and is dependent on the construction of coalitions between agents.
2   *The genealogical understanding*: Power is not linked to a particular actor or position but is found everywhere people interact (Foucault 1976; Flyvbjerg 1993). Power has an imperceptible and disciplinary effect on our view of reality and patterns of thought.
3   *The psychodynamic understanding*: The exercise of authority and power is a precondition for cooperation between human beings. This exercise takes place under the strong influence of unconscious, collective psychological processes (Visholm 2004a; Andersen 2006).

In accord with this book's focus on the psychological processes in organisations, the discussions in this chapter are limited to the psychodynamic perspective. Within

The manager as authority **185**

this perspective are many different interpretations of the concept of authority. By way of introduction, the chapter looks in detail at Steen Visholm's understanding of authority (Visholm 2004a).

Visholm distinguishes between person-based and role-based authority. Person-based authority has its source in the personality traits of the manager. Here, the manager achieves acceptance of his/her authority by being professionally competent, having a strong personality, or by having experience. One can say that it is the manager's personal traits that represent the community. Person-based authority, therefore, is based on a personal relationship between manager and employee.

Role-based authority is a structural, bureaucratic form of authority. Here, the manager acquires his/her authority by being ascribed a role by an even higher authority (e.g., the state, top management, or shareholders). Typically, the role will enter into a hierarchical, bureaucratic organisation in which each layer in the hierarchy gives authority to the underlying layer. This means that role-based authority is more independent of the person who has the role. Correspondingly, it is less dependent on the personal bond between manager and employee. This form of authority one typically sees in larger organisations and societies, Visholm believes.

A number of objections can be raised against this understanding of authority. First of all, Visholm distinguishes between authority in close relationships and authority in more distant relationships (between individuals in larger organisations and societies). Visholm describes role-based authority as being necessary in larger, complex organisations and societies in which many different attitudes and interests are represented. Therefore, role-based authority is "not, in principle, a community of interests and convictions" (Visholm 2004a: 88; our translation), whereas the community is present in person-based authority. The objection here is that all relations of authority involve a community of interests. In larger organisations, this community of interest becomes more abstract and difficult to maintain, and the means for creating authority, therefore, become different. In larger organisations and societies, one must create other systems and forms of being together in order to keep the community together than in smaller groups and organisations.

Second, Visholm makes role-based authority into a necessary evil with the following formulation: "role-based authority [is] a more or less common and more or less enthusiastic will to get the system to function" (Visholm 2004a: 88; our translation). But authority is not exclusively something to which people are forced to submit. People also want authority. Chapter 2 recounted that it is a central part of the individual's motivation to belong to a community. Chapter 9 emphasised the connection between management and individual motivation even more. In an extension of these two points, it can be said that the employee does not only accept authority as a necessary evil; they also want authority.

A model of authority

Instead of distinguishing between person-based and role-based authority, one can distinguish by the size of the communities the authority concerns. Authority uses different means in a group of 10 and a group of 10,000, but both groups must be borne by some form of community of interests and attitudes in order to be maintained.

A corresponding conception is found in Anton Obholzer, who believes that the manager's authority has three sources:

1. Authority "from above": The traditional view of authority that it is given via the position in the hierarchy. This is what Visholm calls role-based authority.
2. Authority "from below": The democratic view of authority in which nothing can be implemented unless everyone in the group is in agreement to one extent or another. In Visholm, this is called person-based authority.
3. Authority "from within": The personal view of authority in which management is connected with self-esteem (Obholzer 2003).

If the authority and, thereby, the group is to function well, authority must come from all three sources at the same time. Obholzer's model is comprehensible, makes immediate sense, and is found in a number of articles in the field (see, e.g., Jørgensen 2004; Andersen 2006). Among other things, it becomes clear in this model that role-based authority is a natural part of the manager's authority along with personal authority. The following builds on this understanding but with a moderate adjustment. One must understand Obholzer's use of the designations "from above", "from below", and "from within" as designations of three systems that must work together if authority is to function: the large system (the organisation); the medium-sized system (the group); and the manager's system (the manager's own person) (Lorentzen 2007: 41).

In order to lead the group (the medium-sized system), the manager must acquire authority from the group itself, from his/her superior, and from his/her own person. Thus, there is a negotiation around authority. This approach to authority as

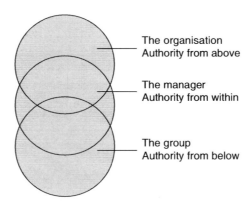

FIGURE 11.1 Authority is composed of several systems

an ongoing negotiation is not seen in many theories of management, nor in the psychodynamic ones. This is probably because, with this model, the concept of authority becomes a rather complex one that encompasses many aspects of daily life in the organisation.

Authority as an aid for the employee

In Chapter 10, it was described how the motivational need for stability and change play out as a learning process between manager and employee. This chapter looks at the two other motivational needs: individuality and community.

The concept of authority is central here since authority is closely connected to community. Accepting authority is the way one participates in the community in practice. Just as individuals need people who can help them learn, individuals need people who can help in relation to the community. For the individual, the manager's authority represents the community. By accepting this, one adapts to the community.

It can be difficult for the individual to orient himself to the requirements of the community; correspondingly, it can be difficult to create one's own position in the community. Here, the manager's exercise of authority is a guiding principle. The manager tells the individual what to do to be a part of the community, what rules are to be obeyed, and how to behave in relation to others in the group.

At the same time, the manager helps the individual define his/her position in relation to the others in the group. Michael Hogg calls this process "self-categorisation" (Hogg 1992, 2014). Self-categorisation means the individual's continual monitoring of his/her status in relation to his/her colleagues. Hogg believes that this monitoring constitutes a large part of the group's overall activities. In fact, it is the precondition for individuals' ability to cooperate. If the group members do not have a clear idea of their place in the group's hierarchy, it can be difficult for them to cooperate. One example may be the young, ambitious, over-confident employee who provokes an older, more experienced one. Here, the manager has the important task of negotiating the place of the two people in the group. It is important to create room for the young person's ambitions and, at the same time, to help the person in question to assume a more moderate form of self-expression, so there is also room for the older employee, who is just as necessary for the community.

Asymmetrical authority between manager and employee

Chapter 9 described how, to an increasing degree, the relationship between manager and employee is understood as reciprocal. At the same time, this reciprocity was described as asymmetrical.

With the model of authority as a composite of several systems, it becomes possible to understand this phenomenon better: the relationship between manager and employee is both symmetrical and asymmetrical. In the manager's work to attain authority from the medium-sized system – the group – the symmetry between

188 Management

manager and employee is great. But in the manager's work to attain authority in the large system – the organisation – the symmetry becomes less. The manager here is subject to priorities and considerations that may deviate from those that dominate the group. By virtue of this, managers attain tools of power that go beyond what their personal characteristics would be able to achieve. With the organisation's authority, he can hire and fire, negotiate wages, prioritise assignments, and so forth. It is this power that makes the relationship between manager and employee asymmetrical.

The manager constitutes the link between the group and the larger organisation, and the manager makes clear the organisation's demands upon the individual by formulating and embodying the organisation to the group. In this way, the manager becomes an important symbolic representative of the organisation.

Moreover, submitting to the authority of a large organisation gives the individual an identity. Chapter 2 described how the individual is drawn to the vision of the community (Hogg 1992, 2014). By belonging to a large organisation or a large community, one confirms one's own importance and one's conception of oneself (Kirkeby 2002: 78; Poder 2004: 107–108; Alsted 2005: 148–149). It can be said that, by being a part of something greater, one becomes greater oneself.

But this does not mean that it is unproblematic to administer this relationship. Just as learning can have conflicts, acceptance of authority may as well. Even though, on one hand, the employee wants authority, authority, on the other hand, can threaten the employee's personal identity and self-esteem. Therefore, the individual employee's relationship to the manager has great importance for how the position of authority is negotiated. Because the individual's relationship to the manager can be viewed as the relationship to the entire organisation, the specific relationship between the two becomes important for whether the employee chooses to submit to the authority of the large system, the organisation.

Authority from above

The most important way a manager receives authority "from above" is through the organisation's formal structure. Structure in this connection must be understood as a broad, umbrella term that includes phenomena such as:

*   The organisation of the division of labour (hierarchy, job functions, distribution of responsibility, job descriptions, etc.)
*   Coordination of work (meetings, channels of information, structured knowledge sharing, etc.)
*   Control of the work process (decisions, procedures, instructions, etc.).

Structure is the way organisations distribute authority "from above" to their managers. A firm with good structural authority thus has a well-defined and well-described structure that is known and recognised by the participants and basically functions as intended; that is, it supports the firm's productivity (Roberts 2003:

63–65). Jaques called this sort of well-functioning structure "requisite" (Jaques 1976: 6, 373).

Young organisations that have not existed very long may take some time to find their form, which can be frustrating for both employees and managers as long as this is the case. Anyone who has tried to work in a new structure is familiar with this frustration, and it is often heard that this is because the structure has not been properly thought through and described in advance. But the question is whether this view is insufficiently dynamic and fails to take into account the way organisations develop.

When it comes to new organisations, it is especially important to be aware of the dilemma between individuality and community which, as mentioned, is the foundation for the creation of authority. This dilemma is especially acute in a young organisation; and the participants, therefore, will establish psychological defences against this.

A repressive defence might be the notion that the insecurity and unease about everything that is new and untried can be remedied (or entirely eliminated) if the new organisation is thought through completely in advance and the structure is established in all its details. This defence, for example, has been seen in connection with the structural reform of municipalities and counties in Denmark in 2007. In this especially complicated process, many resources were used in some instances to plan the new structure in advance down to the minutest detail. However, at this early point in the process when one lacks experience with the new organisation, this is not appropriate. Clearly, one needs to establish certain fundamental things in advance, but otherwise in a preliminary phase it is far more important for the future partners to get to know each other. In this way, their ability to solve the problems that will certainly arise will be bolstered once the organisation gets going.

The period of unknowing and uncertainty in the start-up phase is not only unavoidable but may actually be useful. In certain cases, it stimulates, inspires, and forces the organisation to invent and test out different solutions and only gradually lock in on a more detailed structure. The participants must necessarily work with, experience, make mistakes, discuss, and negotiate their way to the details. In the opposite case, people build a structure that does not reflect the way the participants actually work. A structure that is not in harmony with the actual way the organisation functions will undermine the organisation's ability to ascribe authority to its managers from above. Employees do not have respect for a manager whose position is viewed as invented for the occasion and without real content. A manager who must ask his/her employees to do tasks for which no one can see the purpose loses respect and, thus, authority (Lorentzen 2007: 43–46).

However, there is reason to pay attention to an organisation that has existed for an extended period of time and still shows signs of being structurally immature. The organisation has lots of experience that has not been incorporated into the structure. There is a structural "mess" in the organisation that typically appears in haziness about areas of responsibility, hierarchical relations, interfaces, and work processes. The result is dysfunctional authority relations.

190 Management

The organisation uses unnecessary energy to do tasks because the structure, so to speak, must be continually invented anew. The participants renegotiate the structure on an ongoing basis (perhaps daily): who is to do this task, who has responsibility, when is it done satisfactorily, who is to be informed, who decides, and so forth? This sort of constant negotiation wastes energy and makes the individual uncertain of his/her place and competence. The continuing structural haziness may also nourish speculations about hidden motives and conspiracy theories about shady power struggles, because people try to explain why there is no control of even relatively simple things (Kernberg 1998: 128–129). This speculation (which most often has nothing to it because no such sinister mafia with an evil master plan exists) further saps the organisation of productive powers, and a downward spiral has begun.

Structural immaturity can appear in other forms than mess and confusion. An all-too-rigid structure in which everyone desperately holds onto their area of responsibility and in which people stubbornly implement work procedures that long ago became superfluous is also structural immaturity. The organisation has not been able to undertake the necessary, ongoing adaptation of the structure, and the result is again that resources are used for something that adds no value (e.g., holding meetings) and which may even be said to steal value because they are a waste of time (Kernberg 1998: 134).

However, structural immaturity may also assume the complete opposite form in which the organisation changes structure all too often. This type of immaturity is mostly seen in larger, expanding organisations in which the structure, by definition, is more complicated and requires more adaptations solely due to the increasing number of employees, the expanded range of products, increased globalisation, and so forth. Expansion increases the dilemma between stability and change, and the psychological defence against this is often repressive. The organisation or management shows an exaggerated faith in the structure's ability to solve problems that the rapid pace of change creates among the participants. Every year, comprehensive changes in the structure of the organisation are introduced, such as departments that are established and abolished, directors who are replaced after a brief period of employment, managers who get new areas of responsibility, the introduction of complicated IT and quality-control systems, and so forth. After the changes, everything is chaos for a time, whereupon the organisation goes into hibernation because major new changes are announced and so forth.

If a firm, even after several years of existence, has not organised its work areas, its interfaces, its hierarchical relations, its communication routes, and its procedures or, vice versa, constantly changes its structure too comprehensively, the real problem is not structure. The real problem lies in the relations between participants, since these relations are not sufficiently developed to enable them to negotiate a suitable structure known and accepted by everyone.

In other words, structural problems arise from the fact that there is a need to work with the relationships of authority between the organisation's managers and between manager and employees.

Authority from below

Authority from below is about how group members cooperate and how the cooperation between manager and employees functions. How precisely and honestly does one communicate, how are conflicts resolved, how are praise and criticism given, to what degree do people trust each other, how well do people build on each other's resources, to what extent do people learn from their mistakes, how well are feelings and intellect integrated, and – particularly – how do participants feel about working in the firm? Do people generally feel understood and recognised, and do they experience an accord between their desires and abilities and their specific job? Does the individual member of the organisation feel that he or she belongs and makes a difference – regardless of job function?

We have defined maturity as the ability to use mature, psychological defences to life's dilemmas, so that one relates in a nuanced and flexible way to one's own and others' ambivalence and the plurality of the world. Psychological defences are established in the individual and collectively between many people who are to work together on a common task.

Authority relations in a firm show what types of psychological defences the participants tend to use. They will reflect the way the participants think, fantasise, talk, interpret, relate to, speak to, and deal with each other. The authority relations will also be reflected in the way the individual views him/herself in relation to others. It is utterly decisive how this dynamic between the participants plays out because it is what sets the boundaries for how far the firm can develop.

If the relationships between the participants in an organisation – whether the employee group or the management group – do not have a certain maturity, which is demonstrated by reciprocal relationships that are characterised by an appropriate sensitivity, tolerance, honesty, persistence, optimism, and energy, it is difficult for the individual to thrive and live up to the demands the modern firm places on its staff. It simply becomes too burdensome to work efficiently, creatively, independently, and responsibly if one does not feel "in good hands" in the organisation, and the consequence is that the individual withdraws his/her authority from the organisation (Obholzer 2003: 70).

Contemporary work life teems with demanding jobs and unforeseen problems that should be resolved quickly and flexibly. In this process, many conflicts naturally arise between the participants' different interests – both concretely and psychologically. The goal is not to avoid conflicts but to teach the organisation to use the conflicts constructively. This requires the participants to use their empathy and to nourish mutual respect for each other. The fundament of conflict resolution must at the same time be borne by a somewhat common view of what the primary task of the organisation is.

However, a collaboration with such qualities rarely arises spontaneously and often does not survive on its own. This requires managers who are capable of putting the various tasks into perspective and to work with the collaboration problems

192 Management

that arise along the way – managers who are not afraid to get involved in conflicts that might otherwise threaten the participants' self-esteem and motivation and, thus, paralyse the organisation by undermining the authority relations between the individual and the organisation.

Psychologically immature use of authority

However, many managers feel unsure about this task, which has to do with developing their own relational abilities and working with the reciprocal relationships among employees. Such uncertainty is understandable because the task involves the manager's own personality to a high degree and because it touches the emotional lives of other people, as mentioned in Chapter 10.

But uncertainty must not result in the manager standing aside and declining to "get mixed up in" these problems in the hope that people can figure it out for themselves (see Kets de Vries & Miller 1986: 270–272 for a description of the consequences of this). It is the manager's responsibility to keep an eye on whether conflicts in the organisation are handled constructively. The manager must be responsive to the many direct and indirect signals that are sent from the organisation about this and use them to investigate the maturity of these authority relations and assess where it is especially important to intervene.

The direct signals (when employees tell the manager about a conflict they would like help with or when the manager himself is present at a conflict) are not difficult to find, but it can nevertheless be difficult for a manager to intervene if he does not feel comfortable or competent to do so.

Indirect signals can be far more difficult to discover and interpret correctly because the regression of authority relations can appear in so many different disguises. For example, it may be that employees frequently report in sick, that the quality of the work being done is falling, or that there are a lot of rumours and bad-mouthing.

All these phenomena, of course, may also be signals of concrete problems – of a large work load in relation to the resources – but even if this is the case, it is almost always worthwhile to investigate whether the phenomena might not also be an expression of relational problems. It often turns out to be the case as, for example, in the following case.

A work group that was recently formed by merging two existing groups is placed in a new, common open-plan office space. The office is newly decorated, and the employees wanted to be able to sit together as a group.

However, practical problems quickly arise in the new locale. There are complaints about noise, and the temperature is too high. At the employees' request, the manager initiates several measures to alleviate the problems. She has noise-reduction panels installed in the ceiling and half-partitions placed in the locale. The air-conditioning system is replaced with a new, more advanced one.

The manager as authority **193**

> However, now, the employees complain that they feel isolated since they can no longer see each other and that they are too cold! New, practical measures are tried, and each time they lead to new complaints about the physical facilities.
>
> Finally, the manager gives up and says that the employees must live with the locale as it is.
>
> This leads to great dissatisfaction among the employees and increasing absences due to illness, blamed on the drafty locale and the poor indoor climate.

In this case, the manager let herself be "seduced" by the specific complaints of the employees into believing that the problems were of a practical nature. But when problems prove insoluble in this way and simply seem to move to new areas, there is probably something else at play. By talking to the employees about it, the manager can investigate whether the complaints may be the employees' indirect signal that something else is wrong. The complaints may also function as an expression of something the employees cannot or do not wish to formulate directly, having to do with the fact that there are psychological conflicts involved in merging the two groups. With the merger, the group members must revise their self-categorisation. Some miss the security of the old group; some do not really trust the people from the other group; and some feel incompetent and afraid with respect to the group's new tasks. Moreover, the group is in the process of forming new constellations and alliances, which makes some people feel even more insecure and alienated.

The group needs the manager's help to understand the processes they are in the middle of. The employees need to know that it is natural that a merger may not go well automatically or only feel nice, and they need help to process the feelings that arise along the way. Instead, the group gets partitions and air conditioning, which may, at best, have the positive symbolic effect of demonstrating that the manager takes the employees seriously.

But the solution leaves the employees in the lurch in relation to what is taking place emotionally among them, which is something they cannot themselves elucidate. In the long run, this will erode the manager's authority because it is experienced as a let-down from her side (see Hirschhorn 1988: 175–176 for a similar example of avoidance). The let-down the employees experienced will make them withdraw their authorisation of the manager from below. The result is that the employees as well as the manager end up feeling frustrated and let down despite the fact that both parties are eagerly trying to improve the state of things. They have just not intervened in the relevant area.

If, in situations such as these, the manager overlooks or misinterprets the signals, if she hesitates too long, or if she does not act at all because she feels uncertain about what is going on, it has consequences for her authority. If she does not intervene, it can have a quite undermining and destructive effect on specific relationships in the group and on the psychological work environment. Therefore, it has a negative

194 Management

influence on the confidence of the manager and, thus, the manager's authority, which leads to a destructive impact on the firm's productivity. Therefore, there are good reasons for managers to practice and become better at exercising authority. In this way, they teach their employees how one can work to mature oneself and one's cooperation with others.

But the manager must be conscious that the exercise of authority is not a process that automatically moves toward ever greater maturity, as the following case demonstrates.

> A work group of 12 members is having big problems with one of its staff. The others in the group agree that she does not do her work properly and that she has created a poor atmosphere in the group.
>
> After complaints had been made for a year, the department manager decides to solve the problem by giving the problematic employee a new work area she would handle alone.
>
> A new employee was hired to replace the one that moved. At first, the group experiences a great, almost euphoric relief, but it does not take long before problems that resemble the earlier problems arise with the new employee.
>
> Now the other employees believe that it was because the new employee's areas of responsibility and competence were described unclearly; and the manager, therefore, asks the group to provide descriptions for all the job functions in the group. However, this work – to the manager's astonishment – goes slowly and does not help the problems.
>
> After some months, the new employee quits.

This group needs the manager to help them understand that they are collectively using the immature psychological defence of "find a scapegoat" (Obholzer & Roberts 2003). If the group does not ultimately become aware of this, the phenomenon will repeat itself endlessly, only clad in different disguises. The problem will never be solved with structural solutions alone unless the manager dissolves the group; and, even in that case, it is possible the group members will transfer this mode of reaction to other groups into which they are placed. In this case, the manager's authority is eroded because he accepts the description of the employee as difficult. He overlooks the signal the group members are sending by designating a scapegoat. Thus, he does not help the group members recognise and process what is experienced as a threat to the group; and, in the long term, he himself risks being designated as the group's scapegoat. As mentioned earlier, immature collective defences are triggered when a group feels its existence is threatened. One cannot immediately see from this case what made the group feel threatened. That is something only open conversations between the manager and the group members (individually and/or in group) can show.

Here is another case demonstrating the consequences of a lack of authority in the manager.

> A group consisting of eight employees has had many different department managers over time, all of whom have left the group to work independently without much attention from the management since the group appears to be functioning well.
>
> However, over the past year, problems have appeared with the group's productivity; and, since the group's product creates a bottleneck for the rest of the organisation, it has garnered increased management focus. The group has also developed cooperation problems with other groups in the department.
>
> The department manager is now aware that there are major, internal problems in the group and tries to solve them by appointing one of the members to be group manager. The group reacts with massive resistance. The group manager is frozen out of the group and, after a short time, requests a transfer to another job, and the group's anger at the department manager is enormous.
>
> At the same time, there is a major shift in personnel: new employees quickly leave the group, while the old employees remain.

This group is, first and foremost, a group that has been without management for far too long; and, therefore, group dynamics have been allowed to develop in a destructive way. It is characteristic for a group that has increasingly felt its existence threatened due to a lack of management authority to use an immature collective splitting defence. This splitting appears on several fronts: between the group and the department manager, between the group and the other departments, between the group and the group manager, and between the old and the new employees in the group.

The interesting thing in this case was that, when the group's members found themselves one-on-one with a consultant, almost everyone had noticed this. They described the group as "a kindergarten", as "primitive", and as "a childish tussle for power"; and, as individuals, a few had a rather nuanced view of the situation and its causes. They also had a significantly more nuanced view of management than the group expressed when they were together.

But the individual person did not view him/herself as a part of the group. The considerations of the group and its mode of functioning had to do with others, not oneself. And that was how the whole group felt: the group was the others, and they were not behaving very maturely!

On one hand, this shows that the group members as individuals were able to establish more mature interpretations of the situation; but, on the other hand, they were influenced by the group's preferred collective defence, splitting, when it came to assessing themselves (see Lyth 1988: 54 for a similar description of this phenomenon). They saw themselves as outside the group (as the "good" one) and the group as the others (as the "bad" ones).

The whole process was a colossal burden for all the members of the group with great personal cost to many of the participants. At the same time, there was a massive withdrawal of the group's authorisation of the department manager and the organisation, which meant that the problems with productivity constantly worsened.

Psychologically mature use of authority

Central in the maturity of the relationship of authority between manager and employee is the consciousness of the balance between individual and community. However, a complete "exposure" of all the psychological mechanisms in a group is not necessary in order to change destructive dynamics. Most often, a brief period in which the participants speak freely about what is happening between them is enough to loosen up the problems. This can also happen through regular recurrent short conversations, for example, in connection with meeting evaluations in which employees are provided with experience of talking about emotional aspects of work life.

If the employees and the manager have occasion to exchange openly and without bias some of the feelings and thoughts they have in connection with the collaboration, this in itself provides an increased consciousness of the collaboration, which allow more mature defences to take over or to be maintained. This is because open, constructive verbalisation has many beneficial effects:

- It provides immediate relief from situations that are unpleasant, burdensome, incomprehensible, or perhaps directly painful;
- It provides awareness of psychological factors that have previously been unconscious and makes them accessible to processing;
- It provides a new perspective on the situation and how it arose;
- It provides, through the above, tools to change the situation.

All this activates more mature defences, especially if the manager consciously encourages it and, at the same time, calls attention to signs of the use of immature defences. And, finally, talking about problems – handled in the right way – quite simply provides *hope* that a problematic situation can be changed. The presence of a certain hope is crucial for what effort the group members will put into the process.

It requires motivation, courage, practice, and loyal feedback from the manager and his/her colleagues for people to embark on the daring project of changing themselves (Poder 2004: chap. 8). This is where the struggle is. The following case shows how a new manager with simple means motivates his employees to change.

A new department manager is at his first meeting with a group in the department. One of the members, Jørgen, gives vent to anger at the manager over some recent restructurings of work procedures the manager has introduced.

But Jørgen is considered by his colleagues to be a bellyacher whom they usually ignore. Moreover, they think it is embarrassing for him to lay into the new manager at the first meeting. So, the conversation quickly turns to something else without anyone commenting on what Jørgen said.

> The manager sits for a moment and then says: "I think it is important to take people's feeling seriously, and I can see that Jørgen is angry. So could you tell me a bit more about why you are angry? I would like to be sure I understand it".
>
> Jørgen is at first amazed and looks suspicious, but the manager asks interested questions and clearly listens to his answers. Gradually, Jørgen opens up. He explains what he means without frustration and anger in his statements.
>
> Several people in the group appear now to have similar points of view, and the meeting ends with the manager saying that he understands the criticism now and will consider it and that he will discuss the problem with the group at the next meeting.

The new manager engages in several important actions here that will prove to have positive, long-term effects for the employees' authorisation of the manager and for employees' mutual cooperation (see Lorentzen 2007: 48–50 for another example of successful management).

First, the manager articulates that he believes that emotions should be taken seriously. Thus, he both signals specific respect in relation to Jørgen and, at the same time, says that he believes that feelings have a legitimate place at work along with rational arguments. He also demonstrates that emotions are something that can be articulated and should be investigated.

Second, he demonstrates to the other employees that ignoring what someone says and feels is not a feasible way of solving problems.

Third, he convinces the employees that negative feelings are not dangerous but that they can be examined by inquiring into them and digging deeper into them instead of avoiding them.

Fourth, Jørgen's reaction to the manager's question shows that, beneath an apparently unpleasant feeling (anger), there may be something constructive that can be beneficial for the group as a whole if the visible, disturbing feeling is deconstructed. This would not have happened if the manager had not encouraged Jørgen to share more.

Fifth, the manager demonstrates by his behaviour that, in practice, he is willing and able to enter into a dialogue with employees instead of, for example, just introducing the meeting by proclaiming that he "wanted an open dialogue".

Sixth, the manager demonstrates authority and avoids opportunism (which can be a temptation for a new manager who wants to be popular) by not necessarily agreeing with the employees in their criticism but reserving his right to think about it.

Seventh, it was viewed as a sign of respect for the existing organisation that the manager did not just say that the changes were to remain in force but that he would think about them.

198 Management

Finally, it seemed credible and reassuring to the employees that the manager stated how and when the problem would be brought up again next time. This liberated the employees from expending even more energy discussing the problem until the next meeting.

The manager's actions gather the three levels of authority in Obholzer's model: authority from above, from below, and from within. The manager demonstrates his authority "from above" by making a decision on the problem at once. The manager builds up his authority "from below" by showing respect for the feelings and opinions of the employees. Finally, the manager demonstrates authority "from within" by not being afraid of Jørgen's anger and by daring to discuss a difficult topic.

Thus, in this case, it can be seen how an apparently insignificant and brief intermezzo is, in reality, charged with meaning in the situation here and now as well as in the long term. The new manager's authority is in play from the moment he steps through the door, and the manager in this case understands how to seize the moment.

For a manager – and, particularly, for a new manager – it is decisive to be aware that, right from the get-go, employees are reading and decoding "the relationship rules in this organisation" from the manager's behaviour and the way he relates to employees. Employees typically spend a lot of energy reflecting on and talking together about their manager even as they unconsciously imitate to some degree the manager's behaviour.

Simultaneously, the manager's conduct is interpreted in an individual and mainly unconscious process, and from this interpretation, the employees' internal conviction about what the organisation is and how one can or should act to be a member is formed.

Thus, three different, concurrent processes are going on between manager and employees:

1   The employees relate to the manager's conduct on a conscious level
2   The employees unconsciously imitate (parts of) the manager's behaviour
3   The employees interpret the manager's behaviour.

In the case, we see examples of all three types of processes. The employees relate consciously to the fact that the manager says he will think about the criticism and that they will discuss it at the next meeting. This is viewed as respectful and well-structured; people are aware of it and speak about it together after the meeting.

When the manager begins to ask interested questions of Jørgen, the group unconsciously imitates the manager by reconsidering Jørgen's status in the group and beginning to listen to him, just as they imitate the manager's open attitude by stepping up and relating their own viewpoints.

Through the process of interpretation, the manager's behaviour – the countless verbal and non-verbal, conscious and unconscious actions the manager undertook – is transformed into the employees' inner conceptions about and symbols of themes such as management, community, hierarchy, and credibility, which are of significance for the authority the employees ascribe to the manager.

In the case, with simple means, the manager lays the groundwork for a positive symbolic process around the themes of emotions, conflicts, community, and authority. The manager cannot control the individual process because interpretation and symbolisation are internal processes that take place differently from person to person. But the manager can guide the process through his conduct and by inviting people in the community to try to create positively charged, usable symbols.

Ideally, there should be many situations that can be handled directly by those involved and in which the manager does not need to be active. In reality, it may be contended that it is a measure of the group's maturity how high a degree problems and conflicts may be handled on the spot directly between the parties. The manager's goal in this area is for conflicts between employees to be handled without the manager's assistance. That is, in a well-functioning, mature relationship of authority, the manager only needs to be directly involved when the problem or conflict includes the manager himself.

It is the manager's task to be aware of whether the organisation is actually functioning in this way, which only very few organisations do on their own.

12

THE MANAGEMENT GROUP

In Chapter 6 on the group as an independent unit, a series of definitions was provided of what a group is, and an introduction to the formal, informal, and motivational structure of the group was given. The present chapter builds on these insights and describes how, on the one hand, a management group has the same characteristics as all other groups and, on the other hand, has some special conditions and a special function. This makes it relevant to deal with the management group as a specific kind of group.

The goal of all management is to coordinate the individual contributions of a number of people in a common effort that results in a number of related products. Management is carried out by managers as individuals with responsibility for a given area and by managers as a group with common responsibility for the whole. In other words, management is performed both individually and collectively, and the interaction between these two forms of management has great influence on the firm's ability to do its tasks effectively, flexibly, and innovatively.

A management group may consist of many different constellations. For example, it may be a group consisting of managers on the same hierarchical level with or without their immediate superior, or it may be a management group that simply consists of a single manager and his/her immediate superior. In principle (albeit not always in practice), all the managers in a firm constitute a management group; and, finally, the executive manager and the managers who refer directly to him/her constitute a special management group because they have a special strategic influence.

It is characteristic of the definitions of a group in Chapter 6 that (a) emphasis is placed on the members' own view of constituting a group, (b) the group identity is also understood by people outside the group, and (c) the roles in the group are a function of expectations of both members and non-members of the group. Thus, it is not sufficient that a formal management structure exists that defines a number of manager fora. Individual managers must also *experience* themselves as members of a given management group and have expectations for this membership, and non-members (employees, other managers, and external partners) must understand the group as a management group and have expectations for it in this sense.

Therefore, this chapter describes, first, the function and significance of the management group seen "from within" (i.e., from the manager's position), illuminating the motivational structure in particular and including the importance of the management of the management group. Then, the management group is described as it is experienced "from without" (i.e., seen from the employee's position), describing which role the management group plays for the employees' authorisation process and the symbolic importance the management group has for the employees. Both, of course, have great significance for the firm's coherence and productivity (for more detailed discussions of management groups, see Holm 2012; Trillingsgaard 2015).

The management group as a system and formal structure

If one considers the overall organisation as an open system in constant interaction with the world, management can be said to constitute a subsystem within the organisational system. But if one focuses on management, it constitutes in itself an open system (in constant interaction with the organisation) in which the various management groups constitute subsystems in the management system, and the individual managers constitute subsystems in the management groups. In order for management to execute its collective job optimally, it is a precondition that the management system (which includes all managers in the organisation from top management to group managers and project managers) consists of closely linked subsystems.

The management system can be defined and described with the help of a formal structure, which shows:

1   The place of individual managers in the organisation, their area of responsibility, and to whom they report;
2   What management fora exist and how they are structurally connected;
3   The structure of the individual management fora: members, area of responsibility, frequency of meetings;
4   The fora that exist for interaction between management and employees.

An organisation's structure may be illustrated as consisting of a number of overlapping circles in which the highest management constitutes the innermost circle, the various management fora constitute the surrounding circles, and the overall organisation constitutes the outermost circle. This mode of illustration corresponds to looking at the organisation from above (in which the differences in height disappear), as opposed to the traditional organisation diagram, which considers the organisation from the side and, therefore, sees it as a pyramid.

202 Management

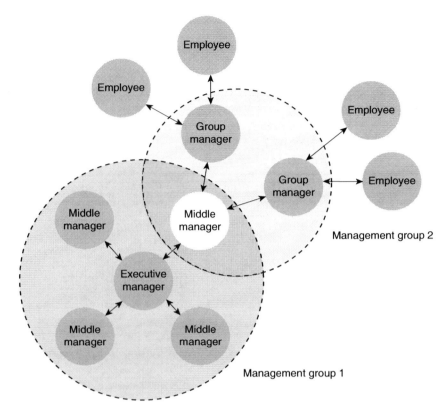

FIGURE 12.1   Management system

A circular representation has the advantage of reflecting the complex relationships of authority between the management levels and between management and employees in a more dynamic way than is possible with the pyramid, in which the relationships of authority appear as unambiguously hierarchical. When the organisation is viewed from above as overlapping circles, it becomes clear that the primary function of managers and management groups is to constitute communication points or links between different parts of the organisation. The intention is for influence and information to flow freely both ways in a reciprocal and ongoing process of authorisation. But with top management located at the core or the "inner circle" (which is an expression that is often used about the most influential part of an organisation), the circular presentation also shows that the organisation has a centre, whose task is to define, maintain, and develop the organisation's primary task on a strategic level.

The management system is defined and made visible with the help of the formal structure and, with the help of this structure, may assume a symbolic function in the consciousness of the managers as well as the employees. The structure can become a symbol of the intention or the existence of a coherent management system, but this positively charged symbol creation only happens if the members of the organisation interpret management practice as being somewhat in accordance with the formal structure.

If, on the other hand, employees find that their immediate superior seems uninformed about or without influence on the decisions of the other managers, it weakens the structure's function as a symbol of a coherent management system. The same thing can happen if a middle manager feels undermined by his/her immediate superior when the superior goes around the middle manager directly to the employees. In this case, the symbolic function of the formal structure can become an "empty" symbol, for which there is no connection between the description of the organisation and the way it functions in reality. The empty symbol may give rise to feelings of meaninglessness and powerlessness or to suspicions of hidden, manipulative intentions from upper management.

In certain cases, the structure may assume a decidedly destructive and splitting symbolic character, which occurs in the following case.

In order to have closer management contact with employees, the executive management in a medium-sized firm has named a number of group managers. The group managers are designated from among the employees; therefore, management makes much ado about stressing that the group managers are no longer ordinary employees but a part of the overall management group.

A new organisation diagram is prepared in which it is clear that the group managers constitute a part of management as the lower rung in the management pyramid. Furthermore, fixed monthly meetings are introduced at which the group managers meet with the immediate superiors and the firm's CEO.

After about six months with the new structure, upper management and department managers decide to implement a reorganisation of some employee groups. Employees and group managers are called to an information meeting and told about the changes to the organisation.

After the meeting, widespread frustration and anger spreads among the group managers who believe that they should have been involved in the decision-making process in advance and feel that they are unable to function as managers in this situation since they were not involved in the process. Many express suspicion about the true purpose of upper management in naming the group managers – "We're just supposed to be errand boys" – and the organisation diagram, which represents the group managers as a part of management, is ridiculed by many and devalued in other ways.

Lars Qvortrup writes in his book *Det lærende samfund* [*The Learning Society*] that "society can be observed as a social system for which the fundamental condition is communication, the primary challenge is complexity, and the goal is handling complexity" (Qvortrup 2001: 25; our translation). Communication is also the fundamental condition for organisations in the learning society. The goal for the members is to deal with the organisation's internal and external complexity, which plays out in a dilemma-filled relationship between part and whole and between individual and collective management. The formal structure can function as a framework around the complexity, which can make it easier to predict the actions of others and make it possible to manoeuvre in the organisation's complex social world in a less conflict-ridden way (Haslund & Alsted 2014: 103–107).

But since "the fundamental condition is communication", a structural definition of an organisation – regardless of whether it is represented as a pyramid, a circle, a matrix, or a network – is not sufficient for a formal management group to become an actually existing and functioning group. This requires the managers to see it as meaningful to be a member of the group, which is to say that they must find that their mutual communication leads to satisfactory relationships and concrete, constructive results.

The management group has this condition in common with other groups. Where a management group differs from other groups is in relation to power and the mutual competition in the group and in the fact that the management group is under particularly great pressure from the outside world, which has an impact upon and, at times, burdens the group's inner life.

The management group as political arena

In his book *Strategisk ledelse – De mange arenaer* [*Strategic Management – The Many Arenas*], Kurt Klaudi Klausen introduces the concept of the political arena (Klausen 2004). The political arena is where the organisation's members struggle for power and influence. It is also here they can form alliances with others to influence decision-making processes in and outside of the organisation (Bolman & Deal 2017: Part 4). The negotiation for power and influence takes place continually in the entire organisation, but it plays out distinctively in management groups because a management group by definition consists of people who have a formal responsibility for an area of the organisation and, to a greater or lesser degree, also real power to make decisions in this area. In all management groups, therefore, negotiations or struggles take place around strategy, on getting resources for one's own area, on getting access to making decisions, on getting influence in the organisation, and on achieving prestige in and outside of the organisation.

All forms of cooperation potentially provide an occasion for mutual competition, but the competition becomes more predominant in a management group because of the formal and real power its members possess (Trillingsgaard & Albæk 2011). A manager can be said to have more at stake and more to fight for than an employee has because the manager has more opportunities to influence the decision-making processes in the organisation. But this also means that the manager has more to lose in the form of influence, power, and prestige. A manager is more visible and subject to a greater projective pressure, which often takes the form of (unrealistic) expectation pressures. If the manager loses influence or loses a power struggle, the consequence may also be a loss of prestige in the organisation and, frequently, also in the manager's own self-esteem. In many cases, therefore, one sees that the competition in a management group assumes a more irreconcilable character than in an employee group because the members have more to gain and more to lose in the form of concrete influence, prestige, and – particularly – self-respect.

In a management group, a sharpening of the oppositional relationship between individual and community is seen that may be difficult for the group itself to relate to and control. It makes it difficult to perform the management group's function of being the link between the organisation's separate parts and creating coherence in the organisation if the competition between managers is too great. A number of management groups try to master the element of competition by downplaying it, denying it, or straight out making it taboo; but if the repression is too strong, the competition will simply appear in other ways – for example, by staying away from management meetings and, thus, avoiding having to cooperate. If the element of competition is denied or split off to a high degree, therefore, it impairs the management group's ability to work constructively with it and exploit the energy and drive that is also a part of mutual competition.

In some cases, the political arena for a management group can become an actual battleground in which individuals or groups with opposing interests openly struggle against each other. This occurs in the following case.

> A small public agency shifts from one ministry's area of responsibility and merges in the same process with another, larger agency from another ministerial area. The new management group is a mixture of managers from both establishments.
>
> The managers from the smaller agency are particularly uneasy about the merger because, before the merger, the two agencies were in competition with each other in that there was a certain overlap of their services. They are afraid that the managers from the larger establishment will exploit the fact that "their" ministerial area has won to promote their own interests and will favour their own employees and collaborative partners.
>
> The managers from the larger agency are not enthusiastic about the merger, either. They think things were fine before and cannot see that the merger adds any value for them – only a lot of trouble and more bureaucracy.
>
> Over a year and a half, management meetings are characterised by a mutual clandestineness between the two groups of managers and a very poor ability to coordinate assignments. Managers from the smaller agency see many signs that the other managers are not acting in good faith and that they are trying to take power, which leads the managers from the smaller agency to ensconce themselves in a group that only consists of themselves. They begin

> to hold preparatory meetings and work together in advance on tactics to use at management meetings.
>
> This split in the management group proves to have consequences for the entire organisation in which there are many conflicts and great mistrust between the two employee groups, which leads to serious problems with the quality of their work product.
>
> Thus, the CEO decides to work purposively to improve the work climate in the management group. He focuses especially on improving his relationship with the managers from the smaller agency with individual conversations as well as management meetings. This bears fruit after a while in the form of a more relaxed and trusting atmosphere at management meetings, and they become capable of defining new projects that, inter alia, have the goal of improving the quality of their work.

If the management group exclusively becomes a political battleground, it affects its ability to work constructively on the relationship between part and whole and, thus, get results; and it becomes more burdensome to be a manager – despite the fact that one may have success in preserving one's own narrow interests.

The motivational structure of the management group

Just like employees, managers need a safe forum in which they can exchange experiences, discuss problems, create networks, and get mutual support. If a manager does not find this in his/her management group, she or he will be inclined to compensate for this need by either forming strong alliances with his/her employees or by placing the main part of his/her energy in other formal or informal management groups inside or outside the organisation. In order to avoid this, the management group's motivational structure must be worked on – for example, as the manager in the preceding case did. That is, the manager must help the group to establish a more productive collaboration that leads to better problem-solving.

In Chapter 6, it was described how in order to *function in practice* as groups, groups must to some degree or other meet the needs of its members. It is this need fulfilment that motivates members to participate in and re-create the group. In a process that takes place in part unconsciously, the group continually negotiates "rules" for cooperation (the group's *ideology*), in which the dilemma between individual and community is dealt with. At the same time, the group deals with task resolution (the group's *economy*), in which the dilemma between stability and change is negotiated. In the preceding case, it can be said that the group's *ideology* was "don't trust the people from the other agency; fight for your own interests", and the group's *economy* was "solve problems in the same way as before the merger; do not introduce anything new". However, over the long run, this proved to be detrimental to the productivity of the new enterprise – in part because the management meetings became especially unpleasant to participate in, and in part because management and employees were not up to handling the complexity of the new organisation and, thus, were not capable of using and developing its potential. In other words, the group was not able to establish workable compromises between the motivational dilemmas. This is difficult for all groups, but it can be more difficult for management groups because the organisation as a political arena appears especially clearly in management groups. The group needs management to help create compromises between individual and community and between stability and change.

But precisely in connection with management groups, one often sees that they have deficient management or none at all. How can this be?

Management of management groups

To be managed entails that one give up some self-determination. Within the psychodynamic tradition, it is said that management may be experienced as a forced infantilisation (Visholm 2005: 36). If one agrees to being managed (by joining an organisation), it can to some degree feel like being treated as a child who cannot figure out what is right and wrong. The individual's concrete experience, of course, depends on the manager's mode of managing and by the relationship with the manager; but, in principle, it can be said that there is an ambivalence connected to being managed because management as a phenomenon includes both coercion and security.

For people who are themselves managers, one can imagine that this ambivalence is more pronounced. As a manager, one may consciously or unconsciously have a self-understanding or identity that entails that one does not feel one needs management or that one does not care to be managed. This means that groups consisting of managers do not demand management to the same degree that other groups do because their self-understanding is one of self-sufficiency with respect to management. This phenomenon is seen most distinctly in groups that consist of managers on the same hierarchical level without a formal leader. In such groups, a certain vigilance may be observed against someone in the group trying to arrogate management to themselves. The need for management in this type of management group is often solved by creating a "democratic" structure, such as taking turns being meeting chair or representing the group externally. Such structural solutions calm the group but rarely meet the group's real need for management since the rotating positions have neither a formal mandate nor de facto authorisation to assume management.

In reality, the unexpressed expectation in many management groups (both from the members themselves and from management outside the group) is that they function as self-managing groups. But the presupposition for a group to be self-managing is that the group is mature enough to establish effective psychological defences at an appropriate level of maturity. In other words, the group's internal and external communication must be capacious and precise enough to maintain a productive collaboration with an appropriate balance between the motivational

208 Management

dilemmas. Only very few groups are able to do this by themselves – most need management to help with the process regardless of whether the group is a management group or another type of group. Yet, one may consider whether management groups generally have even more need for management than other groups precisely because of the increased mutual competition and because of great pressure from without. But if the group's self-understanding and the outside world's expectation is that "managers do not need management", it is difficult for members to acknowledge a need for it just as it can be difficult for a potential manager to attain authorisation from the group.

In the cases in which the management group actually has a formal manager, it can nevertheless happen that the manager hesitates to engage in management. The manager often justifies this by saying that the members themselves are managers and, therefore, can figure out how to manage themselves. But psychologically, this justification rather veils the fact that the manager senses the ambivalence of the group to management and seeks to resolve this by overemphasising the level of equality among them and underemphasising his/her own leadership. Thus, the manager avoids the unpleasantness of having to fight for his/her authority but fails to meet the expectations that exist at the same time in the group that he or she will step into a leadership role. This expectation for management may well exist side by side with the idea that management is not needed.

Such a dynamic – in which the members both want and do not want management and in which the manager avoids assuming such a role – can lead to a vague and frustrating situation for the group, which typically leads to collective regression. That is what happened in the case with the two merging agencies in which the regression was only turned around when the CEO started assuming and fulfilling his leadership role. It took a relatively long time for the manager to do so because it is not that easy to be "a manager of managers". It requires a well-developed maturity on the manager's side and a good understanding of how one can work with the management group's more pronounced ambivalence in relation to management.

Another unexpressed assumption that occurs in many firms is that the higher in the hierarchy one is placed, the less management one needs. For example, a boss at a major firm said, "We who refer directly to the executive board are lucky if we get a performance review once a year!" The assumption that highly placed managers need less management goes well with the family analogy that is often applied to an organisation: the employees are the children, the group managers are the teenagers, the middle managers are the adults, and the top executives are the grandparents.

But this assumption risks short-circuiting the management system because an organisation is not a family but a much more fragile community, which usually demands more from members' ability to coordinate things together than a family does. If the management system is not sufficiently managed, therefore, the risk increases that the individual managers and management groups will not serve as effective links to the organisation, which means that the management system is not well connected. This will inevitably appear in the outermost layers of the organisation, as seen in the following case.

Over the years, a firm has had a number of different CEOs. As a result, the middle managers have learned to do things for themselves. At first, it was out of necessity, but gradually an ideology grew up among the middle managers that top management was only a disruptive element in the organisation from whom it was a matter of protecting oneself – preferably by ignoring them "because they're going to disappear soon anyway".

Since the middle managers had never been managed as a group because the changing CEOs had not focused on it, only a very limited community existed among them. Each member took care of his/her own shop, and there was a powerful affiliation and a great loyalty between the individual manager and his/her employees. On the other hand, there were many conflicts between the various departments; there was a lack of coordination in problem-solving; they had a hard time resolving problems that demanded an interdepartmental effort; and there was a general suspicion and lack of respect between the departments. In particular, two departments, whose jobs required a high degree of coordination, had many clashes.

After many CEOs had come and gone, a new more stable one arrived who placed emphasis on interdepartmental cooperation among the members. As one of his first acts, the manager formed a management group together with the two department managers whose employees especially had difficulty cooperating. The two managers themselves never had a problem with each other. They simply did not have a forum in which to cooperate and did not miss one.

However, it quickly proves that the establishment of a management group for the two departments has a measurable effect on the cooperation between the departments. There is better coordination, better problem-solving, and fewer conflicts; and the employees begin to speak to and about each other with greater understanding and respect.

The relationship between strategic and tactical management

A final possible reason that management groups often lack management can be that there is an embedded "temptation" in the very concept of management. Management, as a rule, entails that the manager leaves the practical execution of the work to others. Thus, it can be a temptation not to occupy oneself with the problems the execution of the task leads to in practice. Until the task returns in the form of a finished result, it is, so to speak, out of the manager's mind, which can function as a psychological defence for the manager. But the closer a manager is to the employees on a daily basis, the harder it is to maintain this defence, since the manager will typically be involved if problems arise that the employees cannot solve themselves.

210 Management

As a rule, this does not apply to managers higher up in the hierarchy on the strategic level of management since they are better protected from the employees' feelings (e.g., frustration or anger) through the so-called status shield, which is discussed in more detail in Chapter 14. Therefore, in some firms, it may be that managers on the strategic level unconsciously protect themselves against organisational complexity by avoiding close management at the tactical level, that is, management of the practical work. This phenomenon appears in the form of a distanced management characterised by one-way communication in which contact is restricted to information or instructions. Thus, it is signalled that they do not want ongoing feedback and that they only want to hear about finished results that are in accordance with instructions. Thus, it is not unusual to encounter a situation like the following.

After a comprehensive restructuring, a department manager has begun to doubt how she is to handle her employees. The employees have received new assignments, and some have been moved there from other departments. The manager ascertains that more mistakes have been made than before and that they are far behind the production plans. She is rather confused and despondent and therefore goes to her boss, who is physically located in another part of the country. The boss listens to her for a bit and then says: "I don't really understand. At the meeting in the spring, I explained to you what your assignment was and what my expectations for the department were".

If top management demonstrates in this way that they do not want to hear about concrete problems that arise in the implementation of work assignments, they risk isolating the strategic and tactical levels from each other in the organisation – a so-called Rockwool layer is developed between the two levels. When strategic management is isolated from practical work, they may come to think that any deficient results are due to the lack of talent and possible disloyalty of the middle managers or that the employees are sluggish and unenthusiastic. Strategic management can see from the firm's results or lack thereof that the intentions and decisions of management do not penetrate all the way out into the organisation, but often strategic management does not have sufficient knowledge about why this is the case. They probably have various key performance numbers that indicate that something is not working as it should, but they do not know what specific problems are at the bottom of it or what feelings these give rise to among the employees and their immediate superior.

Often, strategic management is not aware that the absence of close management in the management system is the most important reason for the lack of knowledge and impact. Seen from the viewpoint of middle managers and employees, on the other hand, the Rockwool layer between themselves and top management may be experienced as a sign that top management is politicised or unrealistic and removed and is indifferent to or has no respect for the work middle managers and employees do. The reaction can be that they each defend their own way of doing things and, as far as possible, ignore "orders" from top management. That people feel it is necessary to protect the firm from ignorant or destructive top management, however, can be a sign of great loyalty towards the firm.

The Rockwool layer may also arise in or get nourishment from the tactical level of management. Managers at the tactical level may be uncoupled from the highest level of management in that they are uninterested in and remain uninformed about topics of strategic significance, such as the firm's overall finances or the long-term consequences of any new legislation. Just as in the case with strategic management, this is a matter of the group protecting itself against organisational complexity. The Rockwool layer of tactical management consists of a lack of strategic interest and lack of investment in and understanding of the entire operation, which legitimates conduct in the short run and protects members from taking a position on long-term effects. This is the case in the following example.

For a number of years, a somatic hospital department has had increasing expenses for medicine without anyone intervening. However, when the hospital's total budget is cut by 10%, the executive committee summons department managers and stresses the necessity of saving 10% in all departments. The department managers must prepare new budgets within a month outlining the savings.

The department managers for the somatic department pass on this information to their chief consultants, who have the responsibility for medical expenditures. The chief consultants are asked for input for a new medicine budget and new guidelines for the use of especially expensive medicine. The chief consultants make no comment but never deliver the desired input.

Therefore, the department managers prepare on their own new medicine budget incorporating the department's budget cuts, which is sent to the executive committee. When, after some time, the chief consultants are made aware of the new medicine budget, they call the department managers to a meeting at which the chief consultants object vehemently to the new budget and claim it will "cost lives". The department managers maintain that the new budget is binding, and they must keep to it since, if it is not, it will affect the department's other activities and other departments of the hospital.

Six months later, the department's accounts show that the consumption of medicine had increased at the same rate as the previous year.

The case shows that the strategic and the tactical levels of management have been decoupled. The executive committee simply tells the department managers to prepare new budgets but do not go into more detailed sparring with them about

212 Management

how to do so, just as the executive committee avoids the conflict-ridden discussion about how to distribute the cuts by simply deciding that all departments must save 10%. The chief consultants do not use their opportunity for influence and, thereafter, actively oppose the decision of the department managers without taking a position on the long-term consequences of their actions in the department or the rest of the hospital. The department managers are in a "tight" situation, so characteristic of middle managers, in which they do not get sufficient support from their own superiors and, therefore, are not able in a meaningful way to couple the executive committee's decision to the conditions, values, and feelings of the chief consultants.

Whether the decoupling has its source in strategic or tactical management or both, this is a form of splitting defence, which defines the two levels of management as opposing each other and, thereby, creates a false opposition between managing and executing the work. Close, stable management throughout the entire system is supposed to dissolve such defences in favour of a more mature defence that makes possible a strategic understanding of the organisational reality on the basis of nuanced knowledge close to practice.

The importance of the management group for employees

For many reasons, employees are focused on their immediate superior and his/her position in the management group and have desires and expectations for their manager's actions in the management group and for the capabilities of the management group generally. This means that employees observe and interpret events in the management group with great attention. However, their desires and expectations for the manager are not unequivocal but contain two opposing "movements" that reflect the ambivalence to which the concept of management gives rise – tethered between security and coercion. One movement seeks to make harmless or neutralise the manager by "making the manager into an employee". The other movement seeks to secure the place of the individual and the group in the organisation.

In order to make the manager less "threatening" to the employee group, the group tries unconsciously to minimise or eradicate the difference between the employee group and the manager. From a psychological point of view, it can be said that the group tries to assimilate or swallow up the manager through projective pressure in order to achieve more control over him/her. If there is a group manager, the pressure on the manager may appear as a lack of recognition of his/her right to manage and by imposing a binding mandate on the manager when he/she is to represent the group externally. If the manager is placed outside the group, the pressure is most often more indirect and can consist of an attempt to seduce or threaten the manager to view him/herself solely as the representative of the group to the rest of the organisation and to fight exclusively for the group's interests.

A manager who does not have a solid anchoring in his/her management group will be especially receptive to such pressure, since the manager may find the employee group to be his/her only affiliation in the organisation. In the event the manager loses the group's acceptance, therefore, she can look forward to an onerous

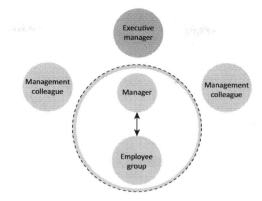

FIGURE 12.2 The manager is swallowed up by the community

organisational isolation if she does not have a management group that offers an alternative and attractive affiliation.

If the manager identifies with the projective pressure to be the same as the group, however, the manager will come into opposition with the other movement that is active in the group at the same time: the movement in which the group is focused on its own placement in, recognition by, and influence on the organisation and in which the manager is the group's concrete and symbolic representative and possible guarantor. As a result, the group consciously or unconsciously observes the management group and tries to assess their own manager's placement and importance in it, trying to ascertain how the decision-making processes generally function in management. In practice, this means that the entire management system, especially the executive management and the management group of which the group's manager is a member, enjoys much greater attention among employees than most managers realise. A manager relates the following.

> Over many months, I had some major disagreements with my department manager. However, we were very conscious about not allowing these disagreements to seep out into the organisation but kept them within the management group and were convinced that the employees had not noticed anything. When, at one point, we had resolved the disagreements, however, I was sought out by an employee who said, "It's really nice that you've resolved your conflict in the management group; it was almost unbearable to watch!"

The two opposing movements have influence on how employees view the management group and on how the management group functions internally. One movement tries to make harmless or to neutralise the manager by "making the manager into an employee". To the extent the group succeeds, it weakens the manager's opportunities in the management group because the manager with his/her binding mandate must always put his part (his own group) above the whole and will have a hard time entering into mutually binding agreements with other managers. The employees will at first experience this as positive and feel that it strengthens the bonds with and confidence in their manager. If the manager's position in the management group is "strong" enough, the employees can exploit the chinks in the management group's collaboration to their own advantage. For example, it may be that the employee group can transfer a particularly difficult assignment to another group, that the group attains special privileges, or that it gets resources at the cost of other groups.

On the other hand, the other movement that tries to ensure the place of the individual and the group in the organisation has the result that the chinks in the management group make the employees insecure – including the employees who immediately benefit from them. Since being managed entails entrusting a part of one's self-determination to "management" (understood as a collective), it is alarming and concerning if this management is not in agreement. The employees are placed in a vulnerable situation in which they risk being squeezed between rival managers, which can have great, personal costs for the employees and, for example, can mean that one gets more difficult work conditions, is moved somewhere else, or as the most extreme consequence, loses one's job.

Therefore, employees observe the management system very closely. They look for consistency, credibility, decision-making abilities, and the ability to translate decisions into organisational actions. On the one hand, they try to put pressure on the management group through their own immediate superior, and they take advantage of hard-won special rights; on the other hand, they are uneasy and insecure if they view the management system as split and lacking coherence. It is fundamental for the employees' confidence in the organisation, their pride in working

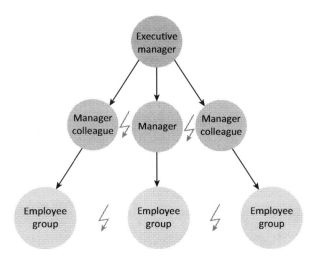

FIGURE 12.3 Chinks in management groups

at it, and their faith in its future that the management is viewed as a unit. A firm whose management is pulling in many different directions – or which does not know what direction to go – can get into serious difficulties, and they may be difficulties that ultimately cost employees dearly.

However, the employees' view of how things are going with the management group is not always correct. The employees' view can be distorted by their ambivalence toward management, which can have the effect that some events are over-interpreted. For example, people may attribute an exaggerated significance to the fact that one manager speaks more than another at a personnel meeting or that two managers do not greet each other. As in other cases, the less employees know about the details, the more room there is for misinterpretations. This constitutes an important argument for striving for the maximum transparency and openness around the work of management groups. It is fine but rarely sufficient to place meeting minutes on a common server, to hold information meetings, or to send out newsletters because the result of one-way communication is often that employees do not actively absorb information. Therefore, the individual manager is the most important source for the employees' knowledge about the work of the management group because personal communication provides the possibility for dialogue. However, if the manager is to be able to give the employees a vital, nuanced, and sense-making insight into the work of the management group – instead of simply being the messenger bearing tidings of information and decisions – it places some demands on the group's internal cooperation.

There must be a mutual understanding in the management group that openness is the rule and secrecy is the exception. That is, people must actively take a position as to whether a decision, an event, or an internal disagreement is to be kept secret from the employees; if not, the rule is openness. However, many management groups function in the opposite way – particularly in relation to internal disagreements in which the norm often dictates that it is disloyal to tell the employees about mutual disagreements. They may also be nervous about making employees insecure. But, as the earlier case showed, it is difficult to hide disagreements from employees, and one only risks making the insecurity even greater. The employees sense the conflict but do not know its true causes and extent and, therefore, are left to their own explanations, which are often worse than the reality.

Loyalty within the management group, consequently, must not be based on the ability to keep one's cards close to the chest but on the ability of managers loyally to present the conflicting points of view or disagreements that may exist in the management group to the employees. This requires a high degree of mutual confidence in the management group – or, in other words, it requires a rather mature management group. This great interest and vigilance that the employees show in the management group may have the result that the employees view inconsistency or threats to the organisation or the management group about which the management group itself is not conscious. Therefore, a greater and freer exchange between the employees and the management group can also help mature the management group because it receives more informative feedback about how the employees view the dynamics of the group and the organisation.

Reactions of the management group to projective pressure from without

As described in the foregoing, the management group is under observation by employees because cooperation or the lack thereof has tremendous impact on the work conditions and flourishing of the employees. But the management group is also subject to pressure of a more projective nature. The management group may be subject to projective pressure from employees as well as other managers in the organisation or even interested parties outside the organisation, which either has a devaluing nature ("we ignore them", "they don't matter", "they never do anything", "they can't figure anything out", or the like) or an idealistic nature ("management has taken on the case, so the problem is solved now", "thanks to the incredibly talented management we have, we've had a fantastic year", "we've got new management now, to this will never happen again", and the like).

Management groups display a broad spectrum of reactions to, respectively, devaluing and idealising pressure. If the management group identifies with devaluing pressure, one may experience that the management group falls apart and is dissolved into a battle of all against all. If the pressure comes in particular from employees, the identification may also take this form: the management group will protect itself against employees by spending a long time on management meetings to justify itself and explain to each other how they have done *everything* right; but, in reality, this is an expression of management identifying with the devaluing pressure.

If, on the other hand, the management group creates a counter-projection, the "bad" stories about the employees will dominate management meeting more and more, and the use of language will become rougher and less respectful. They tacitly or explicitly agree that the employees are hopeless and impossible, and they may openly laugh at some of the most impossible employees about whom there are particularly bad stories. In the event of this kind of counter-pressure, it is characteristic that the assessment of employees will become stereotypical and unnuanced and that none of the managers will oppose or challenge this view of the employees. A counter-projection may also be expressed in this way: the management group consciously or unconsciously tries to manipulate or guide the employees to do particular things for which the employees do not know the real justification. The group may well be conscious of the manipulative process itself but are not conscious of its nature as a psychological defence.

An ordinary counter-projection of a more repressive nature is that the management group simply does not talk about the management of employees. The management meetings deal with an exchange of information and decision-making, but they do not discuss what the management implications are, why they decide from a management perspective to do what they are doing, what dilemmas this will lead to, what consequences the decisions will have for the employees, and how this might possibly affect employee motivation. Since it is management's task to coordinate the organisation's activities, it can seem strange that the participants in these activities disappear from the communication, but it is nevertheless a rather widespread phenomenon. It can best be understood as an unconscious defence by the management group against projective pressure that comes from being in a management group. Correspondingly, a high degree of secretiveness around the management group's internal work is also understood as a repressive defence, the purpose of which is to shield the group from criticism and to protect its cohesion.

It is obviously more pleasant for a management group to be subject to idealising pressure; but in the longer term, as a rule, it leads to anxiety-ridden reactions in the group. A management group that is given the task of cleaning up quickly an area that has been skating along for years or is told to get a new project up and running in record time with far too few resources will fear in its heart of hearts that the task cannot be done even though it is wrapped in superlatives from employees or the executive manager. It is not difficult to identify with an idealising pressure, in part, because it is immediately flattering and, in part, because it is difficult to turn down, make reservations about, or point out problems when the others are sure that you will be able to do the task in no time. If the group identifies with the pressure, the anxiety of failing becomes great, and if their mutual relationships do not make it possible to talk about this anxiety, the group will have a hard time keeping itself together. Consequently, the individual members will seek individual solutions, such as getting out of the group while there is time. Another type of identification may be that the group paints a rosy picture of itself and its own efforts far beyond what there is a basis for. This also leads to anxiety because the group unconsciously fears being confronted by a lack of results. However, it is seen relatively often that a management group – particularly, at the strategic level – can maintain this state for a long time because the lack of actual results is hidden behind many promising words and constantly shifting plans for the future.

As mentioned, secrecy around the group may be interpreted as a repressive counter-projection, which can also be a reaction to an idealising pressure. A management group that is proclaimed in advance to be the best management group "of all time", whose members say that it will be "a fantastically exciting and positive challenge", will not feel that they can afford to display uncertainty or disagreement. Instead, the group will close in around itself and, probably, also be internally affected by a repressive pseudo-dialogue.

To what should the manager of a management group pay attention?

In sum, it can be said that, if a management group is to fulfil its function as collective management, it is important that there is no implicit expectation that the management group is, without assistance, capable of self-management. If the group shows signs of not being able to forge an expedient cooperation, the group needs management. The manager of a management group must help the group create fruitful compromises between the motivational needs. Moreover, the manager constitutes the most important link to the organisation's other managers.

In order for the manager to do his/her job in the best way possible, it can help to define the structural relationship around the relevant management group: who is a member, what is the group's area of responsibility, what is its organisational placement, and what authority does the manager have in relation to the group? On the basis of this structure, the manager can initiate a continuous process to get group members to view themselves and behave as a group with a common task and to get the surrounding world to recognise the group as such. In principle, this work is no different from other group management, but the manager must be aware of the special conditions that govern a management group. Consideration must be paid to the self-understanding of individual managers with respect to the need for management, to the sharpened mutual competition between managers, and to the temptation to protect oneself against organisational complexity by using the concept of management to uncouple work performance from other levels of management.

The manager must be conscious of the fact that a management group is subject to a higher degree than other groups to projective pressure from the outside world. This pressure affects the group's internal relations, and the manager's task is to encourage the group to use integrating defences instead of projective identification or counter-projections. The manager does this, inter alia, by paying attention to the group's use of language about employees and other managers, its ability to articulate disagreements and handle conflicts, its degree of mutual openness and trust, its degree of receptivity to the input of the surrounding world, and its ability to reflect on the organisation, the role of the manager, and the group itself.

At the same time, the manager must realise that the management group and its way of functioning are especially important to the employees for concrete as well as psychological and symbolic reasons. Work must be done on an ongoing basis to make sure the exchange between the overall management system, the individual management group, and the employees takes place as much as possible though unhindered dialogue. The management group is for the employees an ideal type for concepts such as cooperation, affiliation, conflict resolution, integrity, influence, and results. When this reciprocal process between the management group and the employees is successful, the employees' immediate superior plays an essential role in it. An important task for the management group, therefore, is to gird the individual manager for this function, so that the manager can discuss loyally and openly the management group's intentions, plans, dilemmas, and disagreements with the employees and to bring the employees' invaluable input back to the management group.

The manager of a management group must be especially ready to work on attaining the group's authorisation and making clear his/her management role. The group's authorisation increases when the members gradually experience advantages to being in the group. The advantages are shown by the improvement of the basic emotional atmosphere, which is clearly seen at management meetings and by the fact that the group experiences better mutual coordination and a greater, positive influence in the rest of the organisation. In this way, the individual manager learns that the management group becomes the primary anchoring point for his/her individual leadership, which correspondingly increases the management group's coherence and its ability to contribute as a close-knit subsystem in the overall management system.

PART IV
The manager's personality

It is not only the relationship between the manager and the employees that is important for cooperation within the group. The manager's personal qualities also play an important role in how cooperation is shaped because the manager's personality traits and patterns of behaviour cannot help but affect the group. At the same time, the manager's personality is in an element in setting the boundaries for how mature cooperation can come about. Part IV looks more closely at what a personality is, whether there is a special manager personality, and what requirements there should be for a manager's personality. In addition, how the manager's personality affects cooperation and how the manager can best administer his/her job are discussed.

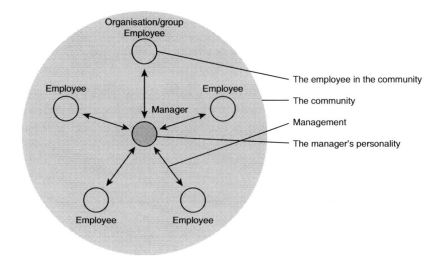

220 The manager's personality

The following topics are touched on:

- What is a personality?
- The manager's personality.
- Manager types and how they affect the organisation.
- Why does someone become a manager: influence, power, control, affirmation, admiration?
- What does the manager get out of being a manager?
- The manager as employee.
- How can the manager best administer the job?

Part IV contains the following main points:

Chapter 13	The concept of personality is a vague concept
	Instead of talking about a special manager personality, one should talk about the requirements for a manager's maturity
Chapter 14	Managers often repress their significance for employees
	Managers may benefit from in-depth coaching or therapy
Chapter 15	If the manager is immature, there is a great risk that the group will also construct immature collective defences
	Managers cannot function as therapists for their employees, but their management may well have therapeutic qualities

13

PERSONALITY AND MANAGEMENT

To a great extent, modern management is a question of being good at motivating employees through the construction of a close relationship between the manager and the employee. Moreover, the manager must be capable of helping employees to build and mature their mutual relationships. At the same time, the manager must be able to make decisions and cut through where there is a danger that the organisation will be paralysed. Mastering this combination of skills requires a good deal of personal maturity in the manager. On one hand, the manager must step back and let the employees develop and flourish. On the other hand, in certain situations, the manager must be ready to take control and decide matters about which employees may disagree. The manager must find joy in providing employees opportunities and, at the same time, possess the will to power when considerations for the whole require it. The manager must not be afraid of conflict-ridden situations or shrink from emotional expression, but neither is there much use in losing one's overview and letting oneself be controlled by emotions.

That is why the manager's personality and maturity are so decisive. But to be able to undertake an examination of how the manager's personality and maturity affect the organisation (as described in Chapters 14 and 15), it is first necessary to deal with different views of the concept of personality itself. There is a brief account of this in Chapter 2, but the topic is discussed in more detail in the present chapter. Then, the chapter will examine the extent to which a manager's personality contains any special "leadership qualities".

The concept of personality is not an unequivocal concept; there are many understandings of this theoretical concept. In the following quote, Allis Helleland, former director of the National Gallery of Denmark, expresses a quite ordinary view of what personality is:

> You are formed in childhood, and you take everything with you. For better or for worse. Like the tail Villy Sørensen writes about so beautifully. I don't

222 The manager's personality

believe you can turn over a new leaf, as they say. It is an illusion. You are what you are.

(Allis Helleland, former director of the National Gallery of Denmark, Djøfbladet, *no. 18, 2006; our translation)*

It is a widespread viewpoint to consider personality to be a fixed thing, something either inborn or established early, that cannot later be changed decisively. On the other hand, many people have found that they themselves or people they know have gone through great personality changes over the course of their lives. The father, who was always surly and strict, becomes a good and gentle grandfather; and the playboy, who lived a superficial life at the town's discotheques, changes completely when he becomes seriously ill. It is thus possible to change personality under certain circumstances, but does that mean personality is a fluid concept and that people have no fixed personality?

In his book on personality disorders, the Danish psychologist Carsten René Jørgensen outlines four different ways to use the concept "personality":

1 The individual's central, inner characteristics, a form of substance/essence or inner structure that determines the individual's behaviour.
2 A recurring pattern of psychological characteristics that are manifested across different contexts.
3 A tale about the individual that is found in several versions and revised on a running basis; a social construction without a clear-cut connection to an objectively existing "personality".
4 Stable patterns in the individual's interactions with others in which personality is primarily connected to the person's social behaviour and interplay with others (Jørgensen 2006: chap. 1).

These four different definitions of the concept "personality" hide a discussion of the extent to which people can be said to have an internal core or not. Some researchers, who believe that people have an inner core, claim that it is formed from a combination of innate traits and early experiences. These early experiences are generalised into inner, emotionally charged conceptions of oneself, one's relations to others, and the condition of the world. Thus they constitute one's "core self" (Kernberg 1976; Kernberg 1980; Stern 2000).

But there is no agreement among theoreticians about this. Some believe that human beings have no core personality whatsoever but that personality is fluid and shaped and changed continuously in the interplay with others. As a result of these interactions, one shapes the tales about oneself and others, and these changing tales constitute one's personality. This understanding sees personality as something that only exists in relationships and is exclusively manifested in social conduct (McAdams 1996; Gergen 1997; both referenced in Jørgensen 2006). Haslebo espouses a similar view of personality, which she describes as socially constructed and created in specific contexts (Haslebo 2004).

As mentioned in Chapter 2, this book's view of personality is based on an understanding that tries to unite the aforementioned views. In this merger, the healthy individual has a core personality that is established through a combination of innate personality traits (for example, temperament, introvertedness/extravertedness, optimism/pessimism, energy level) and early experiences. Personality can also be said to be an expression of the personal way each individual handles existential dilemmas (Alsted 2005: 131). The core of the personality appears as repeated patterns of feeling, thought, and action that are relatively stable over time and partially independent on social context.

At the same time, the human personality shows great plasticity, both in time and space. Over time, it is possible to change fundamental personality traits if the individual acquires new, meaningful experiences: for example, becoming a grandfather or developing a serious illness. Moreover, in different social spaces, it is possible for the same person to display very different behaviour, depending on what interaction with others activates and creates. The secretary who is a bit timid at the workplace may be an enterprising and energetic mother at home. It is this phenomenon the American psychologist and author Daniel Goleman calls "social intelligence" (Goleman 2006).

The following sections show how the concept of personality can be determined more exactly with the help of different theories and test methods.

Personality traits

There are a number of models that describe the central elements in a personality. These models share the designation "trait theory" because they describe particular traits in personality. Personality traits are defined in these models as stable patterns of behaviour that only vary a little over time and in different situations (Mortensen 2003: 386).

One of the more widespread of these models is called the "five factor" model (Kaufmann & Kaufmann 2003: 104–106; McCrae & Costa 2016; Mortensen 2003: 386–391) because it utilises five dimensions that are thought to be central in the description of a personality:

- The degree of neuroticism
- The degree of extraversion/introversion
- The degree of openness
- The degree of agreeableness
- The degree of conscientiousness.

The degree of neuroticism looks at the person's inner, emotional balance. The emotionally unstable person is worried, insecure, and uneasy, while the emotionally stable person is calm, relaxed, and basically satisfied with him/herself.

The degree of extraversion/introversion designates the extent and intensity of the person's social relations. The extraverted person is characterised by sociability,

224 The manager's personality

talkativeness, and being people-oriented, while the introverted person is reserved, quiet, and task-oriented.

The degree of openness investigates the person's willingness to explore the unknown. The open person is curious, has broad interests, and is creative. The less open person is conventional, has narrow interests, and is down to earth.

The degree of agreeableness shows the person's conception of other people. Here as well, there are two extreme points: the sympathetic person versus the competitive person. The sympathetic person is soft-hearted, trusting, and straightforward. The competitive person is cynical, shameless, and ruthless.

The degree of conscientiousness has to do with how directed the person is. The very conscientious person is well-organised, reliable, and disciplined. The less conscientious person is spontaneous, has no clear goals, and is more driven by desire than duty.

The "five factor" model was primarily developed as a test/tool for professional psychological purposes and has attained widespread use in connection with recruiting and research. Many other tests/tools have been adapted to this model (Kaufmann & Kaufmann 2003: 106). But the "five factor" model has also been criticised (Block 1995). Among other things, it has been proposed that the model is not based on a theoretical model of the personality but, instead, is based on a statistical analysis of a great number of questionnaire answers. This is called a factor analysis and is described in more detail later. In addition, critics have raised doubt about the extent to which the number of factors is necessarily precisely five (Mortensen 2003).

Test of personality type

Within the category of trait theories are the so-called personality profiles or type tests, such as the Myers Briggs Type Indicator (MBTI), the DISC model, the Adizes PAEI, and Belbin's team roles. These are rarely used in clinical psychology but are often used in connection with recruiting, management development, and cooperation training in many firms.

Some of the most utilised tests are the MBTI and Jung's Type Indicator (JTI), both of which are based on the description of psychological types by Swiss psychiatrist and psychoanalyst Carl Gustav Jung (Myers & Myers 1995; Ringstad & Ødegård 2003). The two type indicator tests, however, were not created by Jung but by, respectively, Isabel Myers and Katherine Briggs (MBTI) and Hallvard Ringstad and Thor Ødegård (JTI).[1] The difference between MBTI and JTI is small. The MBTI test consists of 88 questions in which the answer is a forced choice between two statements or two words. The JTI test consists of 56 questions. The answer is a forced choice between two statements. In addition, scoring is weighted slightly differently; the greatest difference is found in the assessment of the thinking/feeling function.

In his work on personality types, Jung described eight distinct types (Jung 1921). These eight types emerged when Jung first divided people into extraverted and

Personality and management **225**

introverted personality types (along the lines of the "five factor" model). Jung viewed this as the direction of the person's "interest". Then, Jung divided cognition into four functions:

Thinking has to do with the establishment of a logical order between the various conditions of reality. Jung called this function rational.

Feeling deals with the establishment of an emotional and value-laden order between the various conditions of reality.

Sensation is the internal, concrete experience of events, both by the person him/herself and in the external world. Jung called this function irrational because it is dominated by the strength of the sensation and is not controlled by rationally established orders.

Intuition is the unconscious establishment of connections between persons or situations in reality. This function, too, Jung called irrational because it is not based on a self-created order (Jung 1921: chap. 10; von Franz & Hillman 1971; Alsted 2005).

Each of these functions may dominate the personality and, thus, in combination with the direction of the person's interest gives eight types (see Table 13.1).

If we take the extravert thinking type as an example, this, according to Jung, is a person with a strong propensity to establish intellectual "formulas" for understanding the world. These formulas are based on objective, measurable criteria, and the extravert thinking type will, thus, be dismissive of emotion-based arguments and feeling generally. Such people view themselves as rational. To describe the introverted sensation type, Jung uses the artist as an example in several places. This person is focused on his/her own inner experience of events in the external world and not on the external world in itself. This person may be said to "ensoul" the world with his/her experience of it – as, for example, the Impressionist painters did. The introverted sensation type is often unreceptive to objective descriptions of the world (Jung 1921: chap. 10).

The MBTI/JTI tests work with Jung's concepts but add two new ones: judgement and perception. Judgement provides the ability and desire to plan and organise. Perception indicates a spontaneous and desire-driven approach to life. Moreover,

TABLE 13.1 The eight types

Extravert	*Introvert*
Thinking	Thinking
Feeling	Feeling
Sensation	Sensation
Intuition	Intuition

226 The manager's personality

the hierarchy between the concepts is changed so that they can be ordered into four pairs:

- Extravert-introvert
- Thinking-feeling
- Sensation-intuition
- Judgment-perception.

Thus, according to the MBTI/JTI tests, there are four elements to personality, which can be oriented in two directions. This means that the tests work with 16 different personality types.

An important element in most personality type tests is that they do not operate with a difference in abilities or assess any personality traits as being better than others. In a non-value-laden way, personality type tests describe differences in preferences and approaches to life, while they do not describe differences in performance – as intelligence tests do, for example. This is an important difference to keep in mind if personality type tests are used in the workplace.

The use of personality type tests

If you compare the categories that are used in trait theories with categories that are presented in the section on motivation in Chapter 2, a certain coincidence can be seen. This is because personality theory and motivation theory have a common subject field. It can be described in the way that personality theory shows what strategies the individual uses to satisfy his/her motivation.

The assessment of the aforementioned tests and the personality theories on which they are based will vary according to what view of personality one has. If one believes that personality is decisive for the choices one makes in a given situation, the result of a personality test will have the status of "truth" about one's own or others' personality. It is typically expressed as an observation that a person *is* a certain type. If, by contrast, one believes that there is no such thing as "personality" or that it has relatively little significance, a personality test will be viewed as a construct that has no relation to what is actually going on between people (Haslebo 2004: 32–33). If, on the other hand, one considers personality as a combination of intrapsychological and relational factors, the assessment of the personality models becomes a little more complex. In the following, therefore, there is a description of various qualities and problems about type tests and the assumptions about personality that are behind them.

It is an advantage that type tests make the complicated question of what personality is and contains simple and understandable. With the division into four elements and the 16 personality types that follow therefrom, type tests provide the ability to understand and describe differences between people in a structured and clear way. It could be claimed that, if one retains a conception that people have different innate or anchored personality traits, one must also be able to describe them.

Trait theories and type tests make this description possible, and the type tests, if they have an appropriate quality, will be able to say something important about the person who is tested. Different personalities will have different and, for them, typical reactions to the same situation. Correspondingly, different personalities will answer the test's questions differently. The tests can, thus, be used to reveal differences in a descriptive, non-judgmental way and illuminate real, existing differences between people's psychological constitution and characteristics.

In addition, type tests may be good levers to use in discussions that would otherwise be difficult to have in a group or between a manager and an employee. It can be difficult to say to a colleague that it is irritating that he is always so impatient about the completion of assignments. But with the type test in hand, one may in a less conflict-laden (and more "objective" or objectifying) way state that the colleague is a certain type. Thus, it becomes possible to speak about differences in a descriptive way instead of a judgmental way. Type tests present an opportunity for more open discussions about personal characteristics and differences and about how they affect cooperation.

But there are a number of objections to type tests. First, they often underestimate the plasticity and versatility in the respondent's personality. Can the responses to a greater or lesser number of questions to a questionnaire really reveal all the important sides of a person's complicated and complex preferences and patterns of behaviour? Personality is complex and contradictory. This implies that personality is more supple and plastic than trait theories suggest. It can be said that trait theories and type tests are based on more unequivocal assumptions about human personality than psychodynamic theories are. According to psychodynamic theory, the importance of relational conditions for the conduct of individuals is so decisive – and the inherent contradictions in the individual so complex – that one must be careful about placing unequivocal labels on the individual's personality. It can change under changed conditions, and personality is not unequivocal but ambiguous and filled with inconsistency and internal contradictions.

The other objection to type tests is that it is unclear how the various elements or characteristics of which personality consists are to be viewed. Two primary elements enter into the model of the individual's psychology that was provided in Chapter 2: conflicting motivational factors and psychological defences. The conflicting motivational factors are the most fundamental. Motivational factors are considered to be innate. The individual begins to construct psychological defences immediately after birth in order to handle his/her motivational needs, but the types of defences the individual uses can change throughout life and will typically do so as the individual matures.

There is no clear answer as to where the personality elements on which trait theories and type tests are based should be placed in relation to motivational factors and psychological defences. On one hand, it is a premise for trait theories and type tests that the personality elements are enduring components of the individual's psychology. This places them on a fundamental level in the psyche along the lines of motivational needs. On the other hand, many personality characteristics may also be described as identical to psychological defences. This is true, for example, with "conscientiousness" from the "five factor" model. Exaggerated as well as understated conscientiousness may be considered a repressive defence against feelings of anger, anxiety, or inferiority.

What the trait theories and type tests call personality elements or personality characteristics may, thus, be interpreted as psychological defences. This opens up another understanding of the concept of personality – namely, that parts of the personality are developed as a strategy for dealing with particular relationships or situations. This does not necessarily involve inborn traits but strategies that are developed by the person as a response to the challenges of life. This places personality elements somewhere else in the conceptual hierarchy – in the proximity of or identical to the psychological defences.

The theoretical justification for the concept of personality elements is, thus, unclear. This claim is strengthened if one investigates how trait theories and type tests establish the personality elements. In many instances, the so-called factor analysis is used. This is true, for example, for the "five factor" model and the MBTI. In a factor analysis, one looks for patterns in the test answers. If 1,000 persons each have answered 20 questions, one will look for which people have answered the 20 questions in the same way. Factor analysis can show which answers resemble each other and, therefore, try to explain which factors trigger this similarity. These factors as a rule will be fewer than the number of questions. In the example with 20 questions, for example, there may be two factors.

With the factor method as a starting point, many type tests claim that they have deduced personality elements from comprehensive studies of individual personality. But the factors can only be substantiated if one has a theory that explains them. The identification of factors builds on assumptions about why there is a coincidence of answers to the test's questions. This means that, if the theory that is the basis for the factor analysis is not thoroughly substantiated, then neither is the factor analysis itself. Furthermore, it is the researchers who decide how many underlying variables they are looking for. The same data may, thus, result in many, fewer, or very few underlying variables depending on the preferences of the researcher in question – see the disagreement about the number of factors in the "five factor" model (Østergaard 1975: 57–62; Mortensen 2003: 386).

In addition, factor analysis is dependent on the quality of the data: are people actually the way they say they are and do the respondents actually believe what they say they believe? In type tests, as a rule, people are supposed to answer hypothetical questions ("how would you react if . . ." or "what do you think others will believe about you if . . .") or hypothetical choices, such as "which of the following three words are most important to you: loyalty, competition, originality?" These imagined situations or hypothetical questions cannot embrace the various nuances of reality and its many contradictions. The answers, therefore, do not necessarily provide an accurate picture of how the test subjects would react in the relevant situation. The same phenomenon can be observed in opinion polls in which subsequent elections often show that the voters do not vote as they said they would. Another problem with the quality of the data is that it is possible to get respondents to express

Personality and management   **229**

contradictory opinions on the same question if one changes the formulation of the question (Olsen 1998).

The third objection to type tests is that they may have unfortunate effects on those tested. If one assumes that most people have a hard time finding out who they are and what they feel, then type tests are a welcome tool. By taking a type test, one can get an answer to the confusing feelings and questions with which everyone is confronted. The type test tells what sort of person one is and can function in a way as a repressive defence against insecurity and a lack of self-esteem. A type test, thus, contains a risk that the participants will pigeonhole themselves and others and thereby overlook or repress other aspects than the ones that appear in the test. In this way, type tests can give the participants a fixed, undynamic view of their personality.

In other words, type tests may be a target for projections and can function as an individual or collective defence in organisations. Test subjects project their desire for clarity and order onto the test and accept its "true" answer to the way their personality is put together. Type tests attain an exaggerated authority in this context for which there is no scientific basis.

The concept of personality and management

In conclusion, one may say that the concept of personality can be difficult to work with since it is often defined unclearly. This book considers personality as a combination of innate preferences and early established psychological defences. The early established defences are easily confused with innate preferences since they can be rather stable over time and are not changed simply by the force of will. The introduction of psychological defences into the concept of personality, however, means that one must view personality as more mutable than many trait theories and type tests indicate. Yet, it is possible to work consciously with the development of individual and collective defences if only one is prepared that the work will be long and complicated and implies intellectual as well as emotional realisations. On the other hand, this adds a dynamic dimension to the concept of personality that type tests lack.

After our discussion of the concept of personality, it is now possible to look more closely at some of these theories that deal with the importance of the manager's personality. Is a manager's personality something special? Do managers display common traits? And, if they do, are these traits, then, innate or learned? These questions are central to research into management but cannot be answered unequivocally. Some researchers claim that it is not possible to demonstrate special traits about the manager's personality. Other researchers claim the opposite. The following sections review the arguments for and against and try to create a synthesis.

The personality of a manager is nothing special

Paradoxically, this branch of theories about the manager's personality begins with the idea that managers are "great personalities". The manager is viewed as a person

230 The manager's personality

who is stronger and more intelligent than the rest of the group, and it is imagined that the manager must possess qualities of a special character that are called "leadership qualities". This view originates presumably in the class-divided society of the past in which the aristocracy viewed itself as "natural leaders". Examples of this view of management may be found in somewhat older, historical analyses. For example, *Grimbergs Verdenshistorie* [*Grimberg's World History*] consistently focuses on great persons in history – typically, kings and generals – and attributes to them the honour and responsibility for the events that created history (Grimberg 1958). But there are also examples of more recent historical analyses that operate with this understanding (Simonton 1994).

In the ordinary view of management, managers are frequently discussed as incredibly talented and charismatic. Beneath this also lies the notion that managers are superior to other people, professionally as well as personally.

When an executive manager is employed, it is often the manager's personality that is hired because what is wanted is for the manager's personal qualities to influence the firm. You hire a "problem-solver" when times are hard, you hire a "visionary motivator" for a firm that needs a lift, you hire a "tough administrator" for a firm that has gone a bit too far into creative chaos, and so forth. With the designation of an executive manager, media typically discuss the change in leadership with reference to such dominant personality traits in the new manager:

> Mats Jansson has the necessary robustness and energy for a job that, in Nordic conditions, has extreme exposure both internally and externally.
> (Berlingske Business, *17 October 2006; our translation*)

Egil Myklebust said this about the naming of the new head of the SAS concern, and the newspaper added that Mats Jansson was known as "Axfood's attack dog".

Many researchers have tried without luck to find the special qualities that "natural leaders" are presumed to possess (Brown 2000: 92; Bolman & Deal 2017: 338–339; Bakka & Fivelsdal 2014: 217; Yukl 2013: 166). It has proved difficult to identify particular, common characteristics of leaders even though leaders generally seem to be a bit more intelligent, self-assured, dominant, social, and results-oriented than those they lead. But these research results are subject to some uncertainty (Brown 2000: 92). When one tries to isolate special qualities in acknowledged "great" leaders, one ends up with so many different qualities that it is not possible to deduce anything about leadership qualities in general.

In a well-known study from 2002, however, respondents' assessment of a manager's quality was compared with the manager's score on the five major personality traits described earlier. Here, it was found that there was a certain positive correlation between good management and the following personality traits: emotional stability, extraversion, openness, and conscientiousness. Overall, these personality traits could explain 23% of the variation in the effectiveness of managers (Judge et al. 2002).

This result recurs in a number of studies of the connection between personality and management, which shows that there is a tendency for good managers more often to be emotionally calm, extraverted and assertive, open to new experiences, and conscientious and diligent. But it is important to note that these personality traits only have a limited explanatory power and that the variation in the personalities of successful managers is, in practice, quite large (Pendleton & Furnham 2016: chaps. 5, 8).

As a consequence of the problems in identifying a special manager personality, many have abandoned the idea of leadership abilities consisting of fixed personality traits and, instead, have begun to interest themselves more in the relationship between manager and employee (Brown 2000: 93–98; Bolman & Deal 2017: 335–338). These researchers focus on the interplay between the manager and other people in the organisation when they are to explain differences in management results and believe that one must not overemphasise the significance of the manager's personal qualities (Elmholdt et al. 2013: 14).

As early as 1939, Lewin, Lippitt, and White showed in a classic study that what is important for a manager's success is not *who* he is but *how* he acts (Lewin et al. 1939). In this study, they tried to eliminate the importance of the manager's personality by letting the same managers use different management styles – respectively, an autocratic, a democratic, and a laissez-faire management style. The conclusion was that it was the management style and not the manager's personality that was decisive for productivity and cooperation in the group.

Theories that consider the relationship between the manager and the employees to be the most important thing, therefore, focus on management skills that support this relationship, including communication, conflict resolution, and coaching. According to these theories, such skills, in principle, can be learned by anyone – regardless of personality.

But if management is only a question of learning some particular skills, then, does this mean that anyone can be a good manager? An answer to this question is sought in the following section.

The personality of the manager is something special

On one hand, research cannot document special leadership qualities. On the other hand, we experience that some leaders are better at promoting productivity and good cooperation than others. Is this simply because talented managers have acquired certain relational skills or is that too simple an explanation?

One can approach this question by examining Anton Obholzer's idea of authority "from within" (see Chapter 11 and Obholzer 2003). Obholzer believes that it is important for managers to have an internal source of authority. This source can be described as a fundamental faith in one's own judgment and ability to act and one's own ability to make decisions. Without this internal authority, managers can have a hard time exercising authority over employees and colleagues; and, as

232 The manager's personality

demonstrated in Chapter 11, authority is a vital part of the function of a manager. Internal authority is different from person to person and varies with the manager's personality.

Obholzer believes that the decisive thing for a manager's internal authority is the relationships a manager has had with authority (typically, parents) early in his/her life (see also Visholm 2004a: 93). The manager's idea of his/her own authority, therefore, may be healthy, exaggerated, or weak, depending on the manager's childhood experiences (Obholzer 2003: 71–72). Exaggerated as well as weak internal authority is the result of reduced self-esteem. Exaggerated authority may have developed as a result of a division of roles between parents and child in which the child (the future manager) was attributed responsibility for parents or siblings beyond what the child could handle cognitively and emotionally. In this situation, the child will develop internal authority early and may thereby get an exaggerated conception of the validity and necessity of this authority over other people.

Weak authority may be developed as a result of the division of roles between parents and child in which the child's own judgment and ability to act is constantly criticised and limited. This results in a reduced conception of one's own internal authority.

However, actual managers often hold complex views of their own internal authority, such as in the following case.

A young, charismatic woman is headhunted to be director of a knowledge-intensive firm in the private sector. In a short time, the firm blossoms; the employees find that it has become much more fun and inspiring to go to work; and, since the manager is also a talented salesperson, incoming orders are increasing rapidly.

As a consequence of the many new orders, however, the requirements for employee productivity and skill also increase, and the employees need more support from the manager. The manager cannot support everyone and, therefore, focuses on the employees she finds to be the most professionally challenging to talk to or who have the most important projects.

After some time, the employees are divided into two groups: (a) those who find they are receiving the manager's attention and support and, therefore, are flourishing and (b) those who feel overlooked and that the manager is not interested in them and, therefore, feel insecure (and, for some, actually unhappy) and complain to an increasing degree about stress due to the many new work assignments.

Admiration for the manager and the desire to live up to her requirements and expectations are equally great with everyone regardless of which group they belong to. This desire has the effect that employees hesitate to make independent decisions but want the manager's approval for even minor decisions. "When it comes down to it, the director decides" is the ordinary presumption among the employees.

The case shows how the manager's personality is a composite of elements of both exaggerated and weak authority. Both prove to be a result of her reduced self-esteem, which was established when she was a child. The manager had a domineering and successful father who was often absent from the home; and, during these periods, his daughter had to be her mother's support. She always tried to live up to her father's expectations, but she never felt his approval as opposed to her big brother, who was the father's favourite. The father is now dead, but his daughter is still struggling with this feeling of a lack of approval even though she has achieved great business success.

Exaggerated authority appears when the manager through his/her conduct reduces the employees' ability to make independent decisions. This happens, inter alia, when she overemphasises her own estimability and when her acknowledgement is distributed unequally pursuant to impenetrable criteria. The manager is felt to be unjust and unpredictable by the insecure employees, but her exaggerated authority has the effect that employees still admire her and do not question her skills and authority.

Weak authority appears when the manager has a hard time giving support to insecure employees. The insecure employees activate the manager's weak internal authority because she unconsciously identifies with their feelings. But it is connected with great unease for her, and she therefore splits off her own weak authority on the concrete plane to distance herself from the insecure employees. The self-assured employees with the interesting, prestigious project, by contrast, strengthen her weak authority; and, therefore, she prefers to be with them and finds it easy to show them approval.

In the case, it is clearly seen how the manager's blend of exaggerated and weak authority – and her lack of healthy authority – leads to unease and splitting among the employees, which in the long run may have negative effects on the firm's productivity.

Obholzer believes that good managers are characterised by having a healthy internal authority, but not all managers arrive on the job with a healthy authority in their duffel bag. The question is whether managers over time can develop healthy authority.

If one believes that there are special psychological qualities that a manager must possess in order to be a good manager and that they can be developed if one does not have them from the beginning, then the search for good leadership qualities becomes a matter of constant personal development, which happens in an interplay with others and in parallel self-reflection. It is not just a question of a set of skills or methods that can be acquired at a course.

Therefore, the conclusion is that managers neither possess innate, biological leadership qualities nor special personality types. Rather, managers are people who are willing to work with their personal psychological maturity because they understand the important role that this plays for the productivity of the enterprise and the flourishing of the employees.

The next chapter examines the importance of the manager's maturity in more detail and describes how the manager can work on it.

14

THE MATURITY OF THE MANAGER

A manager's personality has an important influence on that part of the organisation the person in question manages. The higher up in the hierarchy a manager is, the greater the potential influence on the overall organisation. An executive manager's personality thus leaves its mark many places in the organisation.

For example, a firm's business strategy may be an expression of dominant features in the manager's personality, and the firm's structure may be constructed so that it is in accord with or reflects conscious or unconscious traits in the manager's personality.

But most significant is the influence the manager's personality has on the emotional climate of the firm and on the nature of its relationships. Not only direct relationships between the manager and the employees, but relationships between all members of the firm – even the relationships in which the manager is not directly involved.

Organisational consultant Ulla C. Beck makes a similar point:

> Regardless of how an organisation is structured, it is central and determinative who the manager is: professionally, humanly, psychologically, and ethically. This does not mean that the way the organisation is ordered is a matter of indifference. Far from it. Of course, there are ways of ordering a firm that supports the primary task more and better than others. But it is still decisive what kind of people managers are.
>
> *(Beck 2004: 276–277; our translation)*

Perhaps, it would be more dynamic to say what kind of people managers *can become*; for, if one considers the concept of personality as a partially fluctuating thing that can change over time and in different social spaces (cf. Chapter 13), it does not make sense only to look at who the manager *is*. It is just as important into whom the manager can develop. This means that it is relevant to look at the relatively stable emotional, intellectual, and behavioural patterns (the "core" of the personality) the manager brings into the organisation and to investigate what effect these patterns have on the organisation. But it is just as important to look at the degree to which the manager is inclined and capable of changing those patterns that may have inexpedient or destructive effects.

This chapter examines three main subjects in this connection: first, the projective pressure *on* the manager from the employees; then, the projective pressure *from* the manager on the employees; and finally, what needs the manager must have fulfilled if he is to keep these projective processes from overpowering him.

Projective pressure on the manager – the manager's justified anxiety about employees

An important reason a manager must be self-reflective and work with his own maturity is the projective pressure placed on him by the organisation – and, for top management, also the surrounding world. Projective pressure is an important factor that affects the manager's maturity.

The manager may have anxiety about losing the respect of the employees and, as a consequence thereof, have anxiety about losing his own self-respect. There is a real risk that a manager may be "fired by the employees", which does not necessarily imply that the manager actually loses his/her job but that he or she is de facto incapable of managing employees because they have no confidence in or respect for the manager. One often hears managers speak relatively openly about their difficulties in achieving results and their fear or worry about what will happen if the goals are not achieved. By contrast, it is rarer that managers talk openly about their anxiety with respect to employees.

A potential loss of confidence or respect can be said to be present in any meaningful relationship (as in all love relationships), but the threat is repressed to a higher degree in the manager–employee relationship because it is unclear how emotionally meaningful this relationship is as opposed to a love relationship in which both parties agree that the relationship is emotionally important.

Kernberg expresses himself strongly with respect to the projective pressure on the manager. According to him, "paranoid and narcissistic" forces in the group place an "enormous pressure on the leader to become either paranoid, autocratic, and aggressive or self-indulgent, self-idealizing, and soothingly narcissistic" (Kernberg 1998: 110).

The projective pressure on the manager may be the most important reason people talk about "leadership traits". The conception of special leadership traits may be seen as a projection from the group. The group (or the organisation or the surrounding world) places a projective pressure on the manager by attributing to her special qualities that the group desires or fears or does not believe they possess themselves. It is said that the group chooses and creates certain leadership personalities depending on what needs the group has (Kaufmann & Kaufmann 2003: 101).

236 The manager's personality

The group's projection on the manager can become a projective identification (cf. Chapter 3) if the manager identifies with what is projected. For example, a group that has been a long time without a manager may receive a new manager with an intense projective pressure that the manager must be able to take care of all the group's problems. If the manager takes on this omnipotent role, he or she identifies with the projection.

Taking his starting point in Bion's three basic assumptions (cf. Chapter 7), Kernberg lists various projective identifications to which the manager may be subject by the group:

- *Dependence*: The group has greater freedom to "leave the responsibility" to the manager than the reverse. This tempts the manager to become a "dependency leader" (Bion's dependency basic assumption) (Kernberg 1998: 109–110).
- *Aggression*: The group defends itself against its own aggression by projecting it onto the manager. This tempts the manager to behave in a way that is too dominating or too submissive (Bion's fight/flight basic assumption).
- *Sex*: The group's mutual struggle for influence may be expressed as an "intimisation" or sexualisation of the relationship to the boss (see more about this in Alsted & Haslund 2016: chap. 2). This tempts the manager to let him/herself be seduced either literally or metaphorically (Bion's pairing basic assumption).

The extent of the group's projective pressure depends on the group's maturity. On the other hand, the manager's maturity is crucial for the extent to which he/she (a) identifies with what is projected, (b) establishes a counter-pressure to the group, or (c) is able to contain and return the projection to the group, which provides the opportunity for common development (cf. Chapter 3). Maturity, in the manager as well as the group, describes the ability to see oneself in a nuanced way and to have the capacity to recognise one's own projections – "to bring them home" – and to be capable of containing and returning the projections of others.

When the exchange between management and group functions at its best, both the group's and the manager's maturity are gradually increased through the common ability to discover and work with projections. But because of the manager's special function, the maturity of the manager plays a decisive role in how this procedure works out.

The relationship between manager and employees is an asymmetric power relationship. Therefore, it rests upon the manager to initiate a maturation process of communication and, through this, to instigate the use of more mature defences. The responsibility for this is with the manager for ethical reasons and because the manager, thanks to his/her placement in the asymmetry, is in the best position to affect and change communicative processes. By working on his/her own maturity – that is, his/her own ability to endure and handle unpleasant feelings and ambivalence, the manager also provides employees the opportunity to develop their maturity as individuals and as a collective. The manager's maturity, thus, sets the framework for how he or she handles projective pressure from employees. The manager must be able to "contain" (i.e., accept and return) employee projections, and that requires a certain maturity. But the manager also needs personal maturity to avoid placing too much projective pressure on the employees.

On one hand, if the manager does not possess or develop this maturity, she/he is in danger of burning out because the manager is overwhelmed by the projective conceptions of employees and unrealistic consequences deriving therefrom (Kernberg 1998: 110; Gabriel 1999: chap. 6). A lack of maturity in the manager, on the other hand, may also have the effect of developing an instrumental attitude toward employees in which they are viewed merely as "resources" for the fulfilment of the manager's projective need.

By contrast, in order to be able to contain the projections of employees, a manager is required to have, first of all, the knowledge and understanding of how projective defence mechanisms work. Second, the manager must be able to feel and tolerate to a certain degree his/her own anxiety-arousing feelings, so that he/she does not need to withdraw from communication as soon as unpleasant feelings arise. Regardless of whether there is a physical withdrawal or a mental withdrawal, the consequence is that no maturation of the participants' relationships takes place. It happens every so often that employees on their own – so to speak, despite an immature manager – are capable of maturing the cooperation; but, in our experience, this is relative rare. The manager's ability to feel and contain his/her own feelings, therefore, is discussed as the chapter's second main theme.

Projective pressure from the manager

Employees read the manager's behaviour incredibly precisely. This reading takes place mainly unconsciously and, as a result, even employees who may be called mature as individuals wind up acting immaturely in an unconscious imitation of the manager's behaviour (Kets de Vries & Miller 1986). For example, the way the manager talks about other departments infects employee language use, and employees generally avoid bringing up what the manager avoids talking about – except, maybe, as whispers in corners.

If the manager is not sufficiently conscious of his/her own emotional themes and problems, he or she may unconsciously transfer these feelings through projective pressure on employees. For example, it may concern the manager's own professional insecurity, which is conveyed as an exaggerated, critical attitude toward employees or the manager's lack of self-esteem, which is conveyed either in the form of suspicion or being compliant and conflict-averse. Since the relationship is asymmetric, a projective pressure from the manager often has comprehensive concrete and psychological consequences for employees. It can be said that employees are forced or seduced unconsciously to act out the manager's internal drama, as the following case illustrates.

238 The manager's personality

A younger man is named manager of a group in which he had previously been a colleague. Externally, the manager has a humorous and relaxed management style, but inwardly he is rather insecure about his management position and why he has been chosen before his other colleagues. He compensates for this by overemphasising that he is nothing special in relation to the others and that he has no fine airs about his new title. He also avoids making unpopular decisions since he is afraid that it will create conflicts and further distance between him and the other employees.

The group, which had functioned rather well under the previous manager, reacts to this by becoming less and less serious about their work, which appears, inter alia, in that they do not carry out the assignments they are given. Meetings are chaotic; everyone has an opinion on everything, and no one holds back from expressing it. At least two of the employees openly challenge the manager's authority and take over the de facto management of the meetings on several occasions. In this same period, the group becomes less productive, and complaints begin to come in about its work and behaviour from the rest of the organisation.

After about six months, a job satisfaction survey shows that employees are not doing well and that many are thinking about changing jobs.

As it appears from the preceding, managers have a decisive influence on how cooperative relationships develop and, thus, have a comprehensive influence on how productive the firm is as a task resolution unit. The less emotionally disturbed the communication between the participants is, the better the participants are able to focus on the execution of their assignments. But with the manager's consciousness of his/her own significance – for the individual and for the employees as a whole – the anxiety of making a mistake, wronging someone, overlooking opportunities, breaking promises, being unjust, hurting someone, and disappointing and letting people down also follows.

Managers repress their own significance

In our experience, managers often repress the significance they have as persons for their employees' well-being, self-confidence, flourishing on the job, and general happiness in life – and thus their productivity. This does not mean that managers consider themselves to be without influence, but it does mean that, in practice, they attribute too much weight to certain types of activities at the expense of other activities. Activities such as meetings, analyses, budgets, case management, plans, and representation are experienced as the most important thing about the job; and, even though this view is not expressed directly (they may explicitly say the opposite), it appears implicitly from the manager's concrete behaviour. The manager is inaccessible because his calendar is packed with meetings from morning to night, so he is often physically absent from the office. Personnel meetings are cancelled because of visiting foreign guests. Employee appointments are put off for a last-minute meeting with a government official. The manager never participates in coffee breaks because of pressing administrative tasks, and so forth. The consequence of this management behaviour is that spontaneous, direct, and more informal contact with employees is deprioritised and, in some cases, does not take place at all. Contact is ritualised in the form of fixed personnel meetings, performance appraisal meetings, and the like, but it is the rule rather than the exception for this type of manager that these meetings are regularly postponed or cancelled or that they are performed as a sham ritual.

This sort of behaviour and implicit prioritisation may be interpreted as a defence to anxiety aroused by being significant, as mentioned earlier. The manager is not conscious of his/her basic function as a supervisor, motivator, and protector of people who – within the framework of a formal structure – are dependent on the manager. It is not that a manager is not supposed to deal with meetings, planning, and budgets because that is an important part of the job. But the manager must regularly ask him/herself whether the countless chores are simply acting as a bulwark against contact with employees. The manager is the only one who can answer this.

The consequences of the manager's repression

Because of the manager's position and right to make decisions in relation to work, his/her communicative behaviour has a central meaning for the employees, who generally attribute it greater weight than other communications in the firm. This is partially due to the manager's authority but also to the fact that the relationship to the manager activates vital, emotionally charged experiences with previous authority figures or caretakers of whom parents are the most important (Winnicott 1986).

With the entirety of their verbal and non-verbal behaviour, managers communicate with employees about their relationship to life and fundamental view of people. This communication takes place consciously as well as unconsciously from both the manager and the employees, and it constitutes the fundament for and core of the manager's opportunity to exercise true leadership. It is not possible for a manager *not* to communicate – not even in cases in which there is little or no contact with employees. No contact is also communication and will be attributed some form of significance by the employees.

When managers repress the prominent importance their relationship with employees and their own relationship to fundamental human themes has, a defensive displacement of attention from what is more important and more difficult about the job (their relationship to employees) to what is less important and less difficult (for example, concrete planning tasks) easily occurs. This sort of displacement arises when something that arouses unease or anxiety is unconsciously pushed into the background, and focus is instead directed toward something more controllable and less anxiety-arousing, such as planning and case management (for a discussion of organisational structure as displacement, see Haslund & Alsted 2014).

240 The manager's personality

A manager's repression is problematic for ethical reasons. Our experience is that managers are generally very conscious of the power relationship it implies to be a manager. It is a rarity for a manager to dismiss an employee without thorough ethical consideration (cf. Chapter 5). But, as a manager, it is also necessary to include another type of ethical consideration that has to do with one's personal view of life and relationship to other people. If one is not conscious of how important one is as a manager, it is not possible to relate consciously to the ethical obligation that lies in taking this position in other people's lives. Repression makes it difficult to work with these themes, on a deeper plane, and it hampers persistent reflection on and integration of these things, which is entirely necessary to develop and vitalise one's leadership.

To be conscious of one's own significance as a manager inevitably brings one in contact with life's "great" questions such as the purpose or meaning of life (including one's own), the value and dignity of the individual, the overall purpose of the organisation, the connection between this purpose and one's own values, the organisation's place and significance in society, one's own view of the social order, and − as an undercurrent to this − what one believes oneself to be the purpose or meaning of human existence.

A manager is not required to have the right answers to these questions (for they do not exist, of course). But it is a great limitation of one's leadership if one is not capable of asking oneself these fundamental questions and if one is not with a certain degree of self-insight capable of thinking about the extent to which one's own conduct reflects one's convictions and ideals. This is not possible if one does not possess a certain maturity and if one cannot understand and accept the fact that one's personality and ability to relate to employees is the core of leadership.

To be a good (enough) manager, therefore, does not consist of being able to live up to somewhat diffuse and fatuous ideals of always being understanding, open, and appreciative (even though, of course, they are in themselves fine qualities to display). Rather, being a good (enough) manager means that one is conscious of oneself, one's relationship to others, and one's deeper view of life and humankind and that one realises how this and one's behaviour affect and are affected by this constant dance between oneself and others. This makes it both easier and more difficult to be a manager. One does not need to be the perfect person; one can have different convictions and character flaws and problematic habits without being a bad leader for that reason. But the good manager understands that everything about him or her is important for the employees, and a good manager is able to communicate about his/her own and the employees' behaviour, feelings, and intentions in such a way that the employees feel they are in safe hands. It is that simple and that hard (see Alsted & Haslund 2016: chap. 1 for a more detailed discussion of this topic).

The manager is both important and not important

With this, we have reached a paradox. On one hand, as described in the foregoing, the manager must be able to carry great personal importance for the organisation's

The maturity of the manager **241**

success. On the other hand, the manager must understand that this importance is structurally based and that the role of manager is a composite of authority and learning relationships that plays out in a sea of unconscious, projective processes. This is how it is no matter who assumes the role at any given point (see Drath et al. 2008 for a model of management as a product instead of a position). In other words, the manager must also be able to endure his own *lack* of importance and avoid developing an exaggerated conception of the importance of himself.

The manager's lack of importance as a person appears in two ways. First, the manager loses (almost) all significance in the moment he or she is no longer manager. This may occasion an abrupt awakening for a manager and is presumably the reason that it is relatively rare for a former manager to continue working with his/her previous employees. The former manager, the new manager, and the employees typically find this model difficult, conflict-laden, and, perhaps, embarrassing. Some firms even implement a principle that a manager who has ceased to be a manager must change departments, at a minimum, and often also employer even though it is difficult to argue rationally for this principle.

Psychologically, it is no small span in consciousness that is demanded of a manager with this paradox. On one hand, one must think: "My person is decisive for how my employees view me and for how well I can administer my job as manager". On the other hand, one must think: "I am only important by virtue of my position as manager and not because I am a special and fantastic person". By contrast, it is just as essential for the manager to understand that, even though she or he invests enormous personal resources in the job, there are many factors that lie outside the manager's control and will influence his/her relationship to the employees – for example, an external restructuring or financial cuts. It is a part of the recognition of one's lack of importance that one realises this and can convey this to employees in a way that one does not take responsibility for something over which one has had no influence but, at the same time, help employees to relate to it as best they can. Here, the manager's calm, overview, and integrity have great significance. So, even when it comes to factors over which the manager has no influence, the person is nevertheless important.

It seems obvious that it requires maturity in the manager to be able to orient himself in this paradox. Maturity is to protect the manager against internal grandiosity (or the opposite), which otherwise would sooner or later hollow out and burden the manager and, thus, increase the level of anxiety. Correspondingly, it burdens the manager if he/she is unable to contain the projective pressure of employees but identifies with it. Thus, the manager's maturity protects the employees from being stuck in splitting projections (whether they are of an idealised or a devalued sort).

The other way the manager's lack of importance is shown is by the fact that the better the manager is in working with the maturation of employee's primitive projections, the better employees will be able to take over parts of management. They become capable of arranging, distributing, and completing tasks and working with the conflicts and difficulties linked thereto. This actually constitutes a paradox in the paradox! By virtue of his/her maturity, the manager is able to surrender at

242 The manager's personality

an appropriate pace parts of management to employees and show thereby that, at least, in some areas, they are just as competent or more competent than the manager. In this way, the manager "reveals" his/her lack of specialness and replaceability but, by doing this, demonstrates at the same time – and this is the paradox – that his/her personality is colossally important because only a mature manager, who is comfortable with him/herself, is capable of surrendering competence and influence in such a way that employees feel safe and challenged at the same time. When employees encounter a manager who enjoys being "overtaken" by more and more competent employees and who does not feel threatened by this, a workplace is created in which the manager helps individuals find themselves and their place in the community and, at the same time, helps employees work together as a productive community.

But it is important for the manager to be aware that maturity is not a linear process, but a process that is constantly subject to regression because of external and internal changes. Therefore, the manager does not become superfluous but has an important role even in a generally mature organisation as the person who has a special focus on regression and encourages a reestablishment of maturity when it is temporarily under pressure.

The manager's motives and emotional dividend

An important factor in the maturity of managers is the individual manager's motive for being a manager. Therefore, one must ask: why do some people choose to become managers? Some of the answers one gets when managers are asked about this gives an impression that their management position dropped out of the sky as a result of external circumstances: "I was encouraged to apply for the job", "They needed a manager", "I happened on an advertisement", "It was a natural step in my career", and so forth. Correspondingly, managers may have a hard time justifying why they exactly – out of many applicants – got the job. It is hard to describe what qualifications the job requires, and it can be even harder to formulate which of these qualifications one possesses.

When managers are to describe their personal motivation to seek a management job, the word "challenge" is probably the most frequently used word, whereas there are not so many who say that their choice was based on their ambitions, their wish for power, or their desire for more money (see, e.g., "Lederne" ["Managers"] 2014: 9).

The fact that people place the responsibility for their management position outside themselves and that they speak in a less nuanced way about their personal reasons for wanting to be a manager may be a result of inappropriately splitting off aspects of their motives that touch on the personal desire to be prominent, to get recognition, admiration, and reward, and to attain control and power.

This development, which has been visible in management – "Fra håndværk til holdning" ["From Profession to Conviction"] as Fogh Kirkeby expresses it (Kirkeby 2004: 35) – has resulted in the fact that certain aspects of the motivation to be a manager have become less "acceptable". Therefore, people talk about them less openly. However, it is still a fact that a management job in most cases provides more prestige, more pay, more influence, and more power than a non-management job.

The manager should investigate with self-reflection the various – perhaps, mutually contradictory – motives he or she has for being a manager. If the manager is unconscious of (aspects of) his own motives, he risks problems with his internal authority. If the manager splits off his desire for prestige, power, and influence, there is a risk of projecting it onto employees or fellow managers, which in both cases leads to the manager becoming a "weak" or nebulous manager.

If one looks at what the research says about the emotional dividend of being a manager, there is a lot to indicate that the dividend is positive. In an overview of various research contributions in the area, the Danish sociologist Poul Poder has stressed a number of emotional advantages to being a manager.

First, it seems that one's placement in the hierarchy has influence on what one feels. The higher one is in the hierarchy, the more motivated one is for the job. Thus, managers find greater satisfaction and involvement in the job than people farther down the ladder. Second, managers have greater freedom to express their feelings than employees do. This is true for both positive feelings such as joy and engagement and negative feelings such as anger and fear. In managers, therefore, there is a greater connection between what is felt and what is expressed, which has the effect that the manager is less emotionally burdened than many employees. It is considered psychologically demanding and burdensome to have a job that encourages one to express the opposite of what one actually feels (a phenomenon that is especially widespread in the service industries but may occur within all branches). This pressure, according to Poder, is less on managers, and it may be explained by two factors: managers are subject to a lesser degree to normative demands for a certain type of conduct, and the feelings of managers are considered in many cases to be more important than those of employees (Poder 2004: 52–60).

Even though managers have greater freedom to express their feelings in their job, however, they cannot express their feelings completely freely and unhindered. To the contrary, many managers find that they must be careful about expressing themselves too categorically and that, in many situations, they must keep their emotions in check. This apparent contradiction may be explained in that, although managers may allow themselves to use their emotions more expressively on the job, they must, therefore, also have more control over them.

A third emotional advantage of being a manager is connected to the so-called status shield (Hochschild 1983, quoted in Poder 2004). This term indicates that the placement of managers in the hierarchy provides them with a sort of protection against employee feelings. If one has a powerful status shield, one is not so easily subject to others' aggression and frustration. That is, the higher one is placed in the hierarchy, the fewer signals one gets of negative feelings from people lower in the hierarchy.

This does not mean that it is impossible for a manager to get information about his/her employees' feelings, but the manager must invite it and, perhaps, actively

244 The manager's personality

seek it out. Whether the manager does this or consciously or unconsciously uses his/her status shield depends on the manager's psychological maturity. Especially for a top manager, maturity becomes important because the top manager, due to his/her placement in the hierarchy, is better protected than middle managers against the emotional feedback from the organisation. Employees can have powerful emotional reactions to events or conditions in the organisation without the executive manager being aware of it. If the personal maturity of the executive manager does not spur him/her to invite employees to talk about their feelings, there is a risk that management will get things wrong because it lacks important information about the feelings of the employees. A CEO who introduces comprehensive structural changes because he deduces from the smiling faces of employees that they think it is a fine idea may not understand the widespread resistance to the change that did not appear until its actual implementation.

Generally speaking, research indicates that the emotional dividend of being a manager is greater than not being a manager. But it is important to be aware that this is not simple or easy to see through. The relationship between manager and employees, as described in a number of places, can be viewed as a trade-off. Earlier in this book, it was indicated that the benefits to employees of having a manager can be great and that the projective pressure on the manager can also be great. Thus, 72% of the managers in the study "Det Danske Ledelsesbarometer" ["The Barometer of Danish Management"] from 2011 states that it is somewhat or to a high degree "psychologically burdensome to be a manager" (Jensen et al. 2011). Similarly, Kets de Vries et al. describe a number of costs associated with being a manager (Rook 2016).

Being a manager, thus, has both psychological costs that make demands on his/her maturity and, at the same time, provides the manager an opportunity for a significant emotional dividend. But the manager cannot get all his/her needs met by employees. As this chapter's third primary topic, therefore, we deal later with how the manager can work with himself.

What needs must a manager have met – the manager as employee

The great importance of a manager and the responsibility and opportunities that are linked to the function of manager have been stressed throughout this book. But one must not forget that the manager is also an employee who has the same needs as any other employee: security, challenge, self-realisation, and recognition from the community. Another important factor that affects the maturity of the manager, therefore, is what management the manager him/herself receives.

Managers who have a well-functioning relationship with the employees have some of their motivational needs met by employees. But it is important that the employees are not the manager's primary (or only) source of need fulfilment because it can affect the dynamic between manager and employee in an unsuitable way. The manager may feel emotionally dependent on his/her employees, which weakens the manager's ability to keep an overview and to make decisions that go against the employees. The manager can develop an appreciative management style in which employees' praise and recognition become the most important goals, which can make the employees feel "used". At the same time, the appealing manager has a hard time providing the security and clarity that employees seek from a manager. Too strong an emotional alliance or dependence between manager and employees weakens the manager's ability to preserve an overall perspective.

Therefore, the manager must have his/her needs met primarily where he/she is an employee or colleague – that is, from his/her immediate superior, through cooperation with the management group, and through internal or external management networks.

Many middle managers get no or only a little personal management from their immediate superior, which leads to problems throughout the organisation because, then, middle managers are not able to manage their own employees and may compensate for their lack with the help of the employees. Therefore, it is essential that all managers have close contact with their immediate superior. Managers, who for some reason or other (for example, because of their physical location or because they are executive managers) do not have any immediate, close manager, should use external sparring and coaching.

No manager should act in a managerial vacuum – neither for the sake of the manager him/herself nor for that person's employees.

Tools and coaching: no easy shortcut

Not everyone is an equally good manager (something most people have experienced) because some managers, by virtue of their personality and experience and the maturity they bring to the job, are better than others. But, for all managers, good as well as less good, it is true that they can become better if they have the will to investigate their inner, partially unconscious conceptions of themselves and the world in which they live and if they have the will to accept the world's – often emotional – response to their conduct. This cannot be done by giving a manager a handful of "tools". The widespread use of this metaphor at management courses and in coaching sessions is interesting and thought-provoking due to its associations to machines that need repairing. The metaphor labels employees as resources or raw materials that, with the help of these tools, can be made to meet the manager's (projective) needs. With this, an instrumentalisation of employees and an objectivisation of difficult-to-handle psychological processes occur. The tool metaphor has the character of a repressive defence whose goal is to simplify what is complex in these processes and make them less anxiety-arousing for the manager (and for teachers and consultants). But this defence can do more harm than good. If the manager does not also deal with what the causes may be when tools and methods do not work as imagined, it becomes a hollow mimicry of human forms of communication. The employees can feel the difference between the genuine article and mimicry even though they may not express it precisely this way.

246 The manager's personality

> A manager had been through a course called Appreciative Management. When he had been back a few weeks, one of his staff was heard to say in the canteen: "If he comes into my office one more time to say something appreciative, I'll scream and throw something heavy at him!"

In itself, it is positive that managers to a higher degree than before go to courses and coaching. This indicates a growing consciousness that management is a profession one is not necessarily born able to do but which can be learned along the way. But teaching managers to become better is a job that demands personal involvement for the manager as well as the teacher or coach – if the teaching is supposed to lead to a genuine maturation of the manager. The coach or the teacher must actually give the manager something of the same thing that the manager is to give his/her employees: an insight into the unconscious, projective mechanisms that may be at play in connection with management, and some suggestion for what significance and impact the manager's emotional response has for them. This requires a certain maturity from the teacher or coach to help the manager with these insights. If this is not the case, the same thing can happen as happens between employees and an immature manager – namely, that the relationship is not developed, and insight and learning do not take place on a level that leads to true change.

One often sees long-term education programmes or coaching sessions for managers that include a personality test, an identification of learning points, and an action plan but which do not lead to deep, lasting changes in the manager. This is, first and foremost, because it is difficult to change and become more mature. Change only takes place in the person in question if he/she is motivated and capable of it. Other people can only offer a safe framework and give-and-take in the process. If management development sessions do not always lead to development, it is because the coach (or teacher) and the manager often unconsciously establish a common psychological defence, so certain topics may not be touched on or only touched upon superficially and so that certain conflicts are never put into words.

The conclusion is that, unfortunately, there are no easy shortcuts, with or without tools, to maturity and, thus, to better management. The good manager must be prepared to enter into a permanent – at times joyful, at times painful – development process (see Majgaard 2017 for a description of the connection between self-development and management, seen through the careers of four managers). For this, the managers need backing and sparring from many sides. From their own manager, from their fellow managers, and from their employees, all of whom must be willing to enter into an honest and direct dialogue about the challenges of management. Because personal maturity is so important, we call the manager's development a self-therapy project. For periods, the manager may need help and sparring outside the organisation. But if the manager's development is a self-therapy project, is the consequence, then, that all managers should go to psychotherapy?

Should managers go to psychotherapy?

In a therapy session, the client may freely talk about his insecurity, his anxiety, his painful experiences, and those aspects of himself he most despises but also about his hopes, his victories, and his successes without having to hide behind false modesty. This provides a great relief and can in the long term provide deeper self-acceptance and more intricate self-knowledge, which makes for a necessary starting point for any changes the client may wish to carry out in his life. A therapy session on a psychodynamic foundation is based on the fact that a person can never know himself completely. Over the course of therapy, however, the client may attain much self-insight by becoming conscious of feelings that have previously been banished to the unconscious because they were so hard to deal with. The therapist listens to and reflects upon what the client relates and, in this way, may give the client some open suggestions for what unconscious mechanisms might be at play that hamper or hinder the client's joy in life and ability to exploit his opportunities. Some of these suggestions the client can use, others not. It is the client's decision whether a suggestion feels relevant and whether it hits a nerve. Simultaneously, the client tells about his current, concrete life and discusses various events and what feelings this unleashes. Here, work life takes up a quite a bit of many therapy sessions just as it often does for people generally.

Maturity is the goal for psychodynamic therapy. The therapist tries through the session to increase the client's ability to feel and endure difficult feelings and not to react to them with splitting or repressive defences. Through this, the therapist tries to help the client to achieve a greater psychological maturity with a view toward a more satisfactory life.

Psychotherapy and management have in common the goal of achieving maturity; and, therefore, it may very well help the manager to go to therapy or a form of sufficiently "personal" coaching, because a grey zone is developing in which certain forms of coaching approach therapy. This is true, for example of those forms that have to do with the manager's entire life – such as Halina Brunning's six domains of coaching (Brunning 2006). It is also true of coaching that is focused on the significance of unconscious factors – for example, Ulla C. Beck's psychodynamic coaching (Beck 2009). The decisive thing here is not what it is called but that the manager and the coach/therapist do not avoid, as if in accord with a common agreement, problematic and deep-lying personal themes. This requires the manager to know what she is getting into and to want to do that. Likewise, the coach/therapist should be a professional and personally equipped to enter into this challenging work.

Through his own therapy, the manager may attain a good sense of where the limit is between conscious, emotionally aware management and therapy and, thus, avoid committing psychological assaults on employees (see more on this in Chapter 15).

Not all managers need therapy. Some managers already possess sufficient psychological ballast in the job to be good managers. Nevertheless, they may still benefit from being periodically challenged by an outside, competent sparring partner.

248 The manager's personality

Other managers have a clear need to develop personally but are not prepared to do so, and one must respect this. It is not possible to force someone to develop. But somewhere or other in the organisation, there is someone who has responsibility for whether the relevant manager continues as manager, and the person in question should take this responsibility seriously because somewhere else in the organisation is a group of employees who are very probably paying a high price for having an immature manager who does not want or have the ability to develop. However, many managers desire self-development and can feel where they do not come up to snuff. One must understand the great search for shorter and longer management development courses as an expression of this and assume that, gradually as this trend becomes more rooted, managers will not allow themselves to accept stones for bread. Managers will require more of themselves and the dividends they derive from courses, and therefore one must expect that development courses will become more therapy-like and encourage more commitment in all parties.

The next chapter will explore more concretely how the manager's level of maturity affects the organisation and how the manager and employees can work on this together.

15

THE MANAGER'S INFLUENCE ON THE ORGANISATION

As described several places, the manager influences cooperation in an organisation directly with his/her own personality. In this chapter, examples are given of how managers affect their employees with each of the three levels of maturity: splitting, repression, and integration.

In the following, we shall look more closely at how mature and immature managers, respectively, can be described more generally.

The mature manager

> A manager must be able to reconcile himself with power in order to seem credible. But he can only do that if this power is grounded in something other than himself.
>
> *(Kirkeby 2004: 17)*

Fogh Kirkeby believes that the manager must have a humanist education – that is, that managers must be able to connect their knowledge with their convictions because modern management has shifted from "profession to conviction". Every day, the manager must make decisions in which short-term choices are balanced with long-term goals. Being able to live and act in these dilemmas requires the manager to have convictions and be guided by "the criteria for what is good", which in this connection means that the manager is just to employees and grants them recognition (Kirkeby 2004: chap. 3).

Fogh Kirkeby formulates here a sort of management ethics. It is not enough for the manager to be a self-reflecting, mature human being (or become so), the manager must also be guided by "the criteria for what is good". Here, it may be added that, in practice – in the many everyday dilemmas and decisions, it can

250 The manager's personality

be difficult to decide what "the good" is. Therefore, the manager's convictions about other people and the manager's self-esteem are fundamental. The convictions about other people and a healthy self-esteem are two phenomena that are closely connected. If the manager is comfortable with him/herself and has a respectful and interested approach to other people, things will not go entirely wrong even if the manager inevitably winds up making mistakes and inadvertently hurting other people's feelings.

In the psychodynamic tradition, Kernberg has investigated the relationship between the manager's personality and its effect on the organisation. He describes the psychologically healthy manager personality as being in possession of the following characteristics (Kernberg 1998: 47):

- Healthy narcissism
- Mild paranoia
- High intelligence
- Honesty and integrity
- Ability to create and maintain deep relationships.

An appropriate amount of narcissism ensures that the manager does not become self-effacing. Paranoia to a mild degree protects the manager against naive credulity, which might otherwise make it difficult to survive power struggles and conflicts of interest in the organisation. These narcissistic and paranoid traits in a healthy manager personality must be balanced and hold each other in check. High intelligence is necessary for the manager to carry out the strategic conceptualisation that must exist to preserve an overview. High intelligence also makes it easier to understand organisational phenomena at a higher level of abstraction than immediate appearance and, thus, be able to propose actions that have a more long-term or general perspective. Honesty and integrity are personality traits on which the manager must base him/herself and by which he/she orients him/herself in the political process surrounding power in the organisation. If the manager does not possess these character traits, his/her management will have a tendency to manipulation and power abuse. So, here, too, Kernberg is focused on the ethics of management (cf. Fogh Kirkeby's "the criteria of what is good").

Finally, the manager's ability (and desire) to create deep relationships with others, his/her interest, understanding, and respect for other people, and his/her ability to understand the nuances in the personalities of others is crucial.

Kernberg's key to the healthy manager may seem overwhelming and difficult to live up to; but, if one studies it closely, one will discover that all the points describe what in this book is called the mature personality. It may be debated what "high intelligence" has to do with psychological maturity. It does not necessarily have anything to do with it; but as Kernberg uses the concept here, it becomes an aspect of maturity. Being capable of shaping a successful strategy on the basis of abstract thinking requires a person with a nuanced, approach to him/herself, the firm, and the world, which is anchored in reality. If the manager does not have this approach, other aspects, such as vilification, an unrealistic conception of the future, or a compulsion toward self-assertion will dominate and distort his/her thinking.

Ulla C. Beck is not so focused on particular leadership qualities but believes that the manager's personal relationship to the role of manager is decisive for how management is carried out. She believes one must inquire into the manager's:

- Fundamental view of people
- Internal picture of the organisation
- Understanding of his/her own role and tasks
- Ability to stand alone
- Ability to self-reflect
- Administration of authority
- Integration and psychological maturity.

in order to assess the person in question's suitability as manager and where the person in question needs to develop (Beck 2004: 280). As a supplement to Ulla Beck's emphasis on the manager's ability to self-reflect, psychologist Jan Molin has argued that self-irony is an important management skill (Molin 2006).

The immature manager

All managers are not necessarily mature just as there is no guarantee that "great managers" are more mature. This is because managers are often appointed through unconscious processes and that groups (for example, hiring committees or boards of directors), therefore, may choose immature people to be managers without being conscious of it.

The opposite of the "healthy manager" may be said to be the "dysfunctional manager", which, according to Kernberg, can be divided into four different personality types (Kernberg 1998: chap. 5):

1 *The obsessive manager*, who focuses on order, precision, and clarity and needs to control everything. This person may be pedantic and perfectionist and is inclined to make decisions from rules and routines rather than intuition. This type of manager creates passive employees.
2 *The narcissistic manager*, who has an exaggerated need for praise and admiration. This person may seem charismatic and engaging but does not tolerate criticism or contradiction very well (becomes angry and offended). This type of manager has only a superficial interest in and understanding of his employees and is inclined to compete with his best employees or is envious of them.
3 *The paranoid manager*, who has a highly simplified view of reality and sees his own organisation as the best and everyone else as an evil-minded enemy. Therefore, this type sets up strict boundaries for self-criticism in the organisation and may be very controlling as manager – to the point of totalitarianism.

252 The manager's personality

4   *The schizoid manager*, who is unstable and fluctuating. Therefore, he makes vague decisions that are typically not communicated clearly to the organisation. This type of manager may also be emotionally withdrawn, which, for example, may lead to the person being physically absent or "invisible" in the organisation.

With a similar conceptual apparatus, Manfred Kets de Vries and Danny Miller claim that the manager's dysfunctions are mirrored directly in the culture of the firm. Where the manager suffers from fantasies of persecution, one will find a paranoid culture. Where the manager is helpless and hopeless, the culture is depressive. The grandiose and narcissistic manager is the source of a dramatic culture, while the compulsive, control-fixated manager leads to a bureaucratic culture. If the manager is socially isolated with weak personal relations with others, the culture becomes politicised and full of intrigue (Kets de Vries & Miller 1986).

Thus, there seems to be agreement among the aforementioned researchers that there is a connection between the manager's psychological maturity and the organisation's mode of functioning (Jørgensen 2004: 168).

As it was stressed earlier, managers and employees have a common responsibility for the development of maturity in the organisation. If the manager is designated as the person who influences the organisation's mode of functioning to a special degree, it must not be understood to mean that the manager alone has responsibility for the organisation's maturity. Because of his placement in the system, the manager has decisive influence on it, but the work on maturity is a common responsibility for manager and employee (for a similar point, see Kernberg 1998: 126).

Managers have the employees they deserve, but it also works the other way around: employees have the manager they deserve. Managers need help from employees to become better and vice versa. Through reciprocity, both parties have an incredible number of opportunities to influence and change their organisation for the better.

When the manager's personality leads to splitting

It can be illustrated how inner conflicts in the manager's personality can lead to splitting by continuing the case from Chapter 13 about the younger female director whose employees were divided into the happy ones who were thriving and the unhappy ones who were not,

> The manager herself does not think that she favours some employees and rejects others. She believes that those with whom she speaks most are determined exclusively on professional grounds. She also thinks that the employees place too much weight on her attention, and she gradually feels enervated by this apparently inexhaustible need for attention from the employees.
>
> When the manager is confronted with the feelings of a group of "bad" employees, she recognises them spontaneously as resembling her own

relationship to her father. She is desolated to discover that some of her employees feel this way and is uncomprehending about how it happened – completely against her conscious wishes for the firm. She wanted a flat structure and an appreciative, trusting culture for everyone. So, how could it go so wrong?

The organisation is caught in an apparent contradiction: the manager and the employees are in favour of a flat, self-governing organisation; but, in practice, the firm functions hierarchically in a struggle for the manager's attention and appreciation.

The manager's own problems with her father's lack of recognition have been projected onto one group of employees (the more insecure) at the same time she has allied herself with the other group of employees (the more self-assured) and has favoured them. This has taken place unconsciously for the manager as well as the employees, but the effects of it were noticed throughout the organisation. The manager's unspoken but unmistaken signs of lack of recognition were experienced by the employees who were subject to them as confusing and diffuse precisely because no explanations followed. The unclear signals inclined the employees to direct their anxiety inward and blame themselves.

It was experienced as an individual phenomenon by each individual employee in which the "good ones" felt that each had a special and unique relationship with the manager (which was often expressed as "I'm not afraid of her!") and the "bad ones" believed that there was something wrong with them personally ("I'm probably not good enough to work here"). Both groups talked about anxiety in connection with the manager; but, in the first group, it was expressed as an absence of anxiety about the manager; and, in the second group, it was expressed as anxiety about not being good enough. In reality, this was a projective identification with the manager's anxiety split into a (self-)idealising and a (self-)demonising version.

The manager clearly and verbally gave recognition to the "good" group in the form of attention, meetings, positive feedback, and new, interesting assignments. The lack of recognition for the "bad" group was expressed indirectly and non-verbally since the manager was not conscious of it. For example, it happened in the form of absent glances, drumming fingers on the table, sighs, and other signs of impatience, lack of feedback, lack of new assignments, absence of smiles at meetings in the hallway, and forgetting people's names. The manager also frequently sent regrets with little prior notice to meetings with "bad" employees, or she forgot to show up at all. But, first and foremost, she showed a lack of recognition in the withholding of the energy and charisma she displayed so willingly to the others.

In Chapter 9, Bolman & Deal's four frames for management functions were presented. As a part of their analysis, they also described how poor management looks. With inspiration from Bolman and Deal's descriptions of poor management,

254 The manager's personality

TABLE 15.1 Overview of forms of management that can activate splitting defence mechanisms in the organisation

Motivational model in chap. 2	Bolman and Deal's frames	Management form in splitting	Metaphor
Individuality	Political frame	Manipulation, use of power (zero–sum negotiation) and fraud	Sly fox, bully
Community	Structural frame	Unsystematic and arbitrary control of details and issuance of decrees	Petty tyrant
Stability	Humanistic frame	Give in, yield, too nice	Weakling, wimp
Change	Symbolic frame	Excessive romanticisation of reality: delusion, lays smokescreens	Fanatic, fool

placed within the four frames, one can construct the following overview of what forms of management can activate splitting defence mechanisms in the organisation (Bolman & Deal 2017: 346). The forms of management are combined in Table 15.1 with the four motivational needs from Chapter 2: individuality/community and stability/change.

Conduct such as what is outlined in the table will often be triggered by the manager's own inner anxiety, which she splits off in order to cope with it. Through projective identification (see Chapter 3), the anxiety is transferred to the manager's immediate surroundings – the employees and the rest of the organisation. Because of the manager's importance as a symbol of the organisation, the employees will have a hard time resisting this projective pressure from the manager. After a period, the entire organisation, therefore, will be affected by the manager's splitting or binary defence mechanisms. Thus, it can be said – simplifying somewhat – that the manager's own splitting defence "infects" the organisation. This will typically be seen in managers Kernberg characterises as paranoid and narcissistic (Kernberg 1998: 110).

An important symbol of community is the organisation's structure. The connection between an organisation's structure and the manager's personality is not exactly conspicuous, but it exists nevertheless. An organisational structure is justified most often with rational arguments such as outside circumstances and requirements or an internal need for a suitable division of labour and an efficient exploitation of resources. These arguments may very well be valid at the same time that there can be other – often unconscious – reasons that the structure looks the way it does, reasons that have to do with traits in the manager's personality.

> A firm has a director who is inclined to paranoid thinking and is fiercely controlling of his managers.
>
> When the firm moves to new premises, the director announces a new management structure at the same time. The deputy manager position is eliminated (the justification being a desire to make the structure flatter), and middle managers now refer directly to the director.
>
> The previous meeting forum, where all middle managers met once a month with the deputy manager, is done away with and replaced by individual reporting conferences between the director and the individual middle managers (the justification being the need for more support for middle managers).
>
> A special status schema is worked out that the middle managers must fill out for every reporting conference (the justification being the firm's quality control system).
>
> The director gets the office highest in the building, while middle managers are placed at the bottom (the justification being their need to be close to the employees).

A hierarchical structure such as the one mentioned earlier can have both historical and functional justifications but, at the same time, may reflect the manager's personal, psychological needs – in this case, for control and status. The manager increases control over middle managers by changing their reporting procedures, getting rid of their common meeting forum, and introducing a structural control mechanism in the form of a reporting schema. In addition, he stresses, with the help of the physical structure, his (symbolic and literal) supremacy.

The changes are justified rationally with other reasons that are not necessarily "wrong", because the middle managers, for example, did need to be close to the employees. But the justifications are not sufficient because they omit the manager's personal motives for the changes that the manager himself is not conscious of.

In this case, the director's measures left the middle managers confused and insecure about the changes but without any capacity to argue rationally against them. They had no other choice but to accept the changes and identify psychologically with the projection. Because the deputy manager position was eliminated, the middle managers were now more directly dependent on the director, and a struggle for the director's favour now commenced. The result was a regression of the entire management group to an immature splitting level. This regression gradually spread to the employees in the form of poor cooperation between the departments and more conflicts of a splitting character.

When the manager's personality leads to repression

As mentioned earlier, repression is presumably the most ordinary defence in organisations.

256 The manager's personality

As in the previous section on splitting, Table 15.2 shows various forms of management behaviour that can promote repression, placed within Bolman and Deal's four frames.

Management behaviour such as that outlined earlier will be characterised by a desire to avoid personal conflicts. The manager will try to solve problems in the least emotionally burdensome way. This is often called being "conflict-averse". The manager tries to avoid confrontation with areas of him/herself that are difficult to handle. With repression, this avoidance does not happen by splitting off but by internal and external control. Thus the manager sets up a number of systems and rules to keep control of his/her internal unease. This inclination to set up systems and rules is used both on the manager's internal plane and with respect to the group or the organisation, which in this way also becomes characterised by repression.

A central character trait of the repressive manager is personal distance. The repressive manager has an interest in avoiding more binding contact to his/her employees and colleagues since this can threaten repression. The repressive manager has countless, sophisticated ways to avoid contact. For example, the manager may be extraverted but, at the same time, distancing by avoiding contact on a deeper emotional plane.

Employees react to the manager's signals for distance and unconsciously fashion their own behaviour accordingly. As mentioned many times, employees read their manager in countless ways. There is a myriad of opportunities for interpretation and symbolisation of the manager's non-verbal behaviour, such as facial expressions, body language, voice volume, eye contact, and much else. All this together provides employees with an internal picture of the manager and an understanding of what can and cannot be done, and the "rules" for how it is to be done.

TABLE 15.2 Overview of management behaviour that can promote repression

Motivational model in chap. 2	Bolman and Deal's frames	Management form	Metaphor
Individuality	Political frame	Postponing difficult decisions, preservation of the status quo	Conservator
Community	Structural frame	Systematic (or rigid) use of micromanagement and control	Judge
Stability	Humanistic frame	Indirect care: Christmas parties, pay, perks	Benefactor
Change	Symbolic frame	Focus on tradition, harmony, and solidarity	Patriarch/matriarch

The manager's influence **257**

In their immediate contact with others, people do not distinguish between a person's behaviour and the intention they attribute to the person's behaviour. The traditional linear understanding claims that it is possible to separate observation from interpretation and evaluation, but most often one cannot in direct contact between people (Haslebo 2004: chap. 12.5). It requires practice and reflection. In other words, if employees interpret the manager's behaviour as repressive, the preferred defence level in the organisation will, most often, also be repressive. The following case illustrates how this can take place.

> A manager has a habit of walking down the hallway every morning, lost in his own thoughts without saying good morning to employees. According to the manager himself, it is because he is already deep into his considerations on the coming day and, therefore, forgets to say good morning.
>
> But the employees do not know that. Therefore, they come up with various interpretations of the manager's behaviour.
>
> Some believe that the manager looks worried because there must be problems in the firm. Some think he looks preoccupied and take this to be a sign that he is not interested in the firm and is considering changing jobs. Some believe he is unhappy in his marriage. But most take the manager's behaviour personally and believe that he will not say good morning because there is something special about them – he does not like them or he is dissatisfied with their efforts.
>
> However, no one asks the manager directly why he does not say good morning, and no one insists on saying good morning to him themselves.

It is not possible to control employee interpretations of the manager's behaviour, as the case here shows. In the interpretative climate that dominates this firm, there was a prior history with a former manager who was authoritarian and subject to mood swings, where silence was an ominous sign of unpleasantness. Therefore, employees were inclined to interpret how silent or talkative the manager was and attribute meaning to it from their personal understanding of the situation. The new manager had no way of knowing this; but, if he had been more attentive in his contact with employees, that is, less repressive, he would have discovered their unease. If the manager had also been more conscious of how great a meaning greeting rituals have (as a symbolic expression of familiarity and interest), he could have spared his employees much unnecessary discomfort and disturbing fantasies. At the same time, it is characteristic that employees synchronise their behaviour with the manager's and, therefore, do not believe they can take the question up with him.

The employees do not just interpret the non-verbal behaviour but also what the manager says. Words are not just words but pass through a layer of interpretive filters, which consist, in part, of unique filters for each employee and, in part, of the collective interpretive climate in the firm culture or in the culture generally.

258 The manager's personality

A countless number of managers have pulled their hair in despair, saying: "But I *have* told them a hundred times, and now they say they never heard me!" Told, perhaps, it was, but it was apparently not understood or it was interpreted to mean something else. A manager must take this phenomenon into account in his communication.

For the repressive manager, however, it can be difficult because the reaction of employees to what is said may primarily be read in their emotional reactions, and they can be difficult for the manager to relate to. If the previous formulation is maintained that emotions are information about internal states, it can be said that the repressive manager misses important information about what is going on with employees. Thus, it becomes more difficult for the manager to understand employee behaviour. The manager in the following case thinks that she has a clear agreement with her employees but is subsequently disappointed.

At an information meeting, a manager relates that all employees are to provide a personal action plan to her before the next meeting.

Her irritation and disappointment are great, when she subsequently does not receive a single plan!

Upon closer investigation, it turns out that some employees had not heard what she said because: "Nothing important is ever said at those meetings".

Others heard her but took it as an expression of the manager's desire to control employees. Therefore, they intended to put off drawing up a plan as long as possible.

Others heard her but did not believe that the action plan would have any effect at all: "It will be just like all the other plans management comes up with, all of which come to nothing". Therefore, they did not want to draw up an action plan and did not expect there to be any consequences for failing to do so.

In other words, it is not enough that the manager *says* something – in fact, that is only the smallest part of it. She must be conscious of how and when she says it and how it is understood by the employees. If she cannot sense how the employees understand what is said, she must ask them. And, again, this is not straightforward because the way one asks defines the answer one gets. The answer depends on how and under what circumstances the manager asks; but, first and foremost, it depends on the relationship between manager and employee.

If the relationship is fragile, it is not probable that the manager would even ask a question of the type: "What do you think about this?", "Do you have any desire to do an action plan?" If the relationship is distant and formal (i.e., repressive), the manager may ask the question but will only get a polite answer back: "It is an excellent idea, we should do that", whereupon the employees walk out and do as they like.

The manager's influence **259**

If the manager wants a realistic view of what employees really think and feel, she has to demonstrate it with her own conduct, including the way she asks the question. If the manager wants an answer she can use, it requires a relationship with employees that is direct and without too many evasions and, at the same time, in which there is a good emotional atmosphere and a feeling of mutual respect.

Employees take a reading of whether they think the manager wants an emotionally honest answer – with the conflicts that can follow from that – or whether they think the manager wants a repressive answer. If they think the latter, they will often adapt themselves to this to avoid emotional conflicts; and manager and employees have, thus, established a common repressive defence.

One of the great costs and limitations about this is that genuine energy and optimism are negatively affected because life in the organisation is experienced as less authentic and less relevant in relation to the individual's emotional life. Manager and employees mutually affect each other in a downward spiral in which there is a particular focus on the manager's personal communication of hope or the opposite. Employees observe the manager's behaviour to decode whether the manager seems genuine and convincing in his/her belief in the activities of the organisation. If the manager does not do that, employees will be less inclined to invest themselves in the firm. This is seen very clearly in the following case.

A manager comes late to a department meeting. He sits down at a corner of the table, where many of the participants cannot see him, and looks for his agenda, which he cannot find. Therefore, he has to borrow one from his neighbour.

HIs body then crumples; he sighs, looks at an indeterminate point on the back wall, and says in a low voice: "It's good you're all here. I think we'll have an interesting meeting".

The meeting was anything but interesting! A despondent mood and lack of focus quickly spread. The manager's late arrival, his location at the table, his lack of preparation, his body posture, lack of eye contact, and low voice signalled something other than what he said. The participants interpreted the manager's behaviour as a sign of despair and reacted with vague confusion and lack of energy. Some of them found various reasons to leave the meeting early. Since the manager's repressive behaviour did not confront either his own inner conflicts or the employees' reactions, the employees imitated his repressive behaviour themselves. No one asked the manager what was wrong or called his attention to the negative effect his conduct was having. They quickly gave up getting anything constructive out of the meeting and, instead, looked for individual solutions, such as leaving early.

Finally, in this section about repressive management behaviour, the importance of structure must be mentioned. Structure cannot be avoided when many people are to work on a common product, but there is a connection between the

260 The manager's personality

manager's personality and the organisation's structure as mentioned in connection with the splitting manager. Often, structure functions as a part of a repressive defence. Structure defines hierarchy, division of labour, and work procedures, so that the participants do not need to negotiate about these things. The roles and rules are described in advance, so the participants do not have to discuss them. Thus, structure comes to function as a sort of storage room for the conflicts that would otherwise have taken place. In this way, structure can be part of a repressive defence.

At the same time, structure can have both a rational and an irrational justification. A flat organisation structure, for example, may be justified rationally in that it frees up more employee resources, but it can at the same time be an unconscious expression of the fact that the manager has an unresolved and conflict-ridden relationship to his/her own authority and power. In the same way, an organisation in which people establish many committees can be rationally justified by a desire to engage the employees, but it can at the same time be an expression of the manager's unconscious desire to avoid conflicts by sending matters to a committee. Seen from the unconscious perspective, structure functions in this context as repressive (see Haslund & Alsted 2014 for a more detailed discussion of this).

When the manager's personality brings about integration

Again with inspiration from Bolman and Deal, one can establish the following overview of the forms of management that can activate integrating defence mechanisms in an organisation (Bolman & Deal 2017: 346).

The management behaviour described in the table presumes a manager with a good knowledge of him/herself and an ability to draw on many different qualities.

TABLE 15.3 Overview of management forms that can activate integrative defence mechanisms in an organisation

Motivational model in chap. 2	Bolman and Deal's frames	Management form	Metaphor
Individuality	Political frame	Open coalition building, spokesperson, principled action	Negotiator, advocate
Community	Structural frame	Realistic analysis and planning	Analyst, architect
Stability	Humanistic frame	Support, empowerment, personal engagement	Coach, catalyst
Change	Symbolic frame	Inspiration, interpretation of experience	Prophet, poet

The manager's influence **261**

In short, the behaviour describes a psychologically mature manager who is able to behave in an integrating way. Correspondingly, the goals for increased self-reflection in managers (and employees) may also be described in this way:

- To be conscious of the effect of one's own actions
- To be able to apply many perspectives to the stories told
- To have a number of ways of positioning oneself in relation to others
- To be better at seeing one's own part in patterns of interaction (Haslebo 2004: chap. 13.1.6).

In the following, two cases are examined that show the significance of the manager's ability for self-reflection and use of mature defences for an organisation.

As mentioned, everything connected with a manager may be an object for symbolic processing by employees. The following case shows a manager who, through her integrative behaviour, is able to change employee interpretations of her person.

> A woman of small stature and with a delicate voice is named manager.
>
> The employees, who have been waiting for a long time and have great expectations for a new manager, are very disappointed when they meet her. They have never before had a female manager (almost all the employees are men), but their formulated scepticism and disappointment is not about her gender or stature but that she does not have any technical expertise in the area.
>
> Individual conversations with employees, however, show that they view the slender woman as fragile and insecure and that they view her appointment as a mockery of them and a lack of respect for their area of expertise.
>
> The manager notes the employee scepticism and reticence but is not cowed by that. She actively seeks out employees and, whenever there is an occasion, she has individual conversations with people about professional issues, and she participates in all the different group meetings and professional events.
>
> After an extended period in which the manager works eagerly to become acquainted with the professional field, the scepticism of the employees begins to die down. It is replaced by a certain pride in having a female manager because they think it shows that the firm is forward-looking and progressive.

In this case, the manager was up against tough odds from the beginning because her gender, her stature and voice, and her lack of technical expertise were against her. This could have led to an inflexible situation in which the employees would never have accepted the manager's authority but without being conscious of the real reason: that the manager's appointment was subjectively experienced as a lack of respect for the employees.

The manager does not realise that the employees have this interpretation of her hiring and actually never finds out, but she is able to read the employees' emotional

262 The manager's personality

reaction to her. She feels their scepticism and reserve but is not (too) afraid of it. She can deal with their feelings because she partially understands them and because her own anxiety about failing in the new job is not too dominant.

With good empathy, she senses that the culture of that particular place is not to talk a lot about feelings but that the way to good contact with employees goes through becoming familiar with their professional field. Therefore, she spends significant more time on that than she originally imagined because she understands the symbolic value it has for the employees. The time she invests in understanding their field becomes a symbol for the employees of respect from the manager.

The manager's perspective, however, is something else: she invests the time because she knows that confidence in her is a precondition for good relations between her and her employees and because she understands that trust in this culture is closely connected to professional competence and respect. The time she uses to become familiar with the field, she also uses to construct positive relations. She could also have chosen to sit in her office with a handful of technical manuals or to take some courses but, because her perspective is to get to know her employees, she does this by going out among them. She understands that her most important future task is to develop her relationship with her employees.

The result is a particularly successful integration and a transformation of the manager's symbolic value from being a negatively charged symbol of a lack of respect to a positively charged symbol, which represents the entire firm for the individual employee.

Whitener et al. has provided the following list of what makes employees have confidence in their managers (Whitener et al. 1998):

1   *Consistency of behaviour*: The manager is predictable.
2   *Integrity in behaviour*: The manager does what she says she will do.
3   *Delegation of control and influence*: The manager involves the employees.
4   *Clear communication*: The manager is precise and open.
5   *Demonstration of care*: The manager is interested in the employees.

The next case shows a good example of a manager who is able to resolve an inflexible situation by revising his own behaviour and beginning to ask those involved about their underlying feelings and motives.

A legal department in a major firm has grown over the years from one employee to five. The original lawyer – a man in his mid-fifties – is still in the department and has a great deal of experience and competence in the area.

The formal leader of the department is a department manager who is also in charge of other departments, but he has never interfered in the work of the legal department – in part, because it is professionally outside his expertise and, in part, because the original lawyer acted as informal manager in this area.

> There have been ongoing problems with integrating new employees into the legal department. The new employees complain about a lack of knowledge-sharing and documentation, and they find that the original employee monopolises the interesting assignments.
>
> In the last three years, four employees have left the department for these reasons; and, when the department manager receives a fifth resignation, it leads to considerations of firing the original lawyer. The manager has many times called the employee's attention to the problems without any apparent effect, and now the manager is losing patience.

Instead of firing the "old" lawyer, however, the department manager decides to ask him how he sees the situation and begins at the same time to reflect more deeply on his own practices. This provides the department manager with a different understanding of the repeated dynamic that has led to the many resignations. He realises that the lawyer has interpreted the department manager's lack of intervention as a lack of respect and interest in the area and not as the declaration of confidence it was intended to be.

The lawyer felt compelled to take on responsibility for all the important assignments by doing them himself. He felt pressured and stressed by this, and it had made him worse at sharing and documenting his knowledge. At the same time, he felt seriously let down by the manager because of his lack of support. The department manager, for his part, had noted that the lawyer had been reserved in his contact with him and had taken it as a sign that the lawyer did not want his interference, which is why he had stayed even more out of the picture. The primary contact between them had been consistently negative – namely, when the manager was to convey complaints about the lawyer from new employees.

Gradually, the manager realised his own part in this destructive pattern of interaction, and he made a break by stepping more actively into his management function in relation to the legal department. He clarified the structure, so that it was apparent that he was the manager of the employees and that all the employees in the department were equal. He became better at explaining when he expected the department to solve problems itself and when he would like to be involved. He helped employees to achieve a better distribution of assignments and areas of responsibility and helped systematise documentation.

The new employees chose the lawyer as their contact person with the department manager, and they now met weekly, which served as a personal support for the lawyer and his feeling of responsibility for the area and which also made it possible for the manager to draw on the lawyer's tremendous competence. The vicious circle was broken thanks to the department manager's integrative interaction.

264 The manager's personality

The manager as therapist?

As demonstrated in the foregoing sections, the requirements for the integrative manager's psychological insight are quite comprehensive. This raises the question of whether a manager should straight out function as a therapist for his/her employees. The answer to this question is not entirely simple. By way of introduction, why the question is even raised is discussed.

The acquisition of new skills or new knowledge often entails that the view of oneself and one's identity is challenged. It may be experienced either as a possibility or as a threat; but, in many cases, it is experienced as both and, thus, gives rise to a significant ambivalence in relation to developing and changing. Therefore, many managers find that "developing competence" in employees can be quite tough. Learning is connected with both desire and aversion, and this ambiguity means that learning and development can be met with resistance (Illeris 2000: chap. 9).

Knowledge about the importance of psychological defences makes this toughness easier to understand and work with. Having to acquire new knowledge and new skills gives rise to internal conflicts, and psychological defences protect the individual against these conflicts. The defence may consist of splitting off what is conflict-ridden by, for example, putting the blame for one's lack of skills on a poor teacher or manager or by declaring oneself in advance a world champion in the new skills. What is conflict-ridden in learning may also be repressed by claiming that one never has the time for learning or one may deny any need at all for learning.

Since the manager's job is to create a framework in which learning can take place, this means that the manager must be capable of helping employees to process these inner conflicts to which learning and change give rise. For example, an employee must learn to sell and is happy to get this opportunity but, at the same time, is reluctant to see himself as a salesman. The reasons for this reluctance may be many and complicated. The sales situation may confront the employee with an internal doubt about his authority and competence and give him problems with his identity.

The organisation can try to control the distaste by placing sales work in a system — for example, in the form of sales manuscripts and reward systems. The systematisation may provide the employee a sort of sham authority and sham competence but will not necessarily help the employee with his deeper doubts and distaste. These can only be processed through reflection and experience, placed into new interpretive frames. This is what normally goes on in the therapeutic process described in Chapter 14.

Every single moment of human interaction in organisations is filled with relational phenomena which it is not possible to map completely since they have to do with people's internal, subjective experiences of reality. These experiences, by definition, are diffuse, contradictory, fleeting, and partially unconscious. It can be difficult to "put words to feelings" for which, in some cases, there may hardly be

The manager's influence **265**

words or for which the feelings may be charged with guilt or shame (e.g., envy, anger, and inferiority). For the same reason, the manager may be hesitant to open up a conversation on these topics. It can be unpleasant to ask an employee whether he feels inferior with respect to an assignment or a new skill – in part because it can be personally burdensome for the manager him/herself to get that close to an employee, and in part because it can seem like an intrusion into the employee's private sphere. The manager may be afraid to open up something uncontrollable and destructive (for him or for the employee) with which he is not trained to deal. What does the manager do if the employee breaks down and relates that he has suffered from a severe inferiority complex throughout his entire life?

It is not appropriate for the manager to be a therapist for his/her employees, and there are many reasons for this. First, there is a power relationship between manager and employee, making power neutrality, which is fundamental in a therapeutic relationship, impossible. Second, there is no therapeutic contract between the manager and the employee in which the employee voluntarily chooses to speak to the manager about his/her innermost thoughts and experiences with respect to personal development. Third, the manager cannot ensure a therapeutic framework for the relationship (the therapist's duty of confidentiality, the client's self-determination, consistency over time) but may get into a situation in which, for one reason or another, he or she must breach confidentiality, give the employee an order, dismiss the employee, or perhaps stop being manager.

Isabel Menzies Lyth, who was an organisational psychologist based in psychodynamic theory, has dealt explicitly with this problem in connection with her consultant work (Lyth 1989). Her considerations, however, are not only relevant for consultants but also for managers, who face similar problems in relation to helping employees learn and develop. Lyth compares ethical rules for individual therapeutic work with the work conditions of an organisational consultant. In individual therapeutic work, it is a central concern to be able to identify and control projective identifications (see Chapter 3) between client and therapist. Therefore, certain particular rules hold for classical psychodynamic therapy: there must not be contact between therapist and client outside of therapy, the therapist must not talk about him/herself, and the therapist must not have contact with the client's colleagues, friends, or family (see, e.g., Langs 1998: Part 2). These conditions, of course, cannot be observed in the relationship between manager and employee. Therefore, there are compelling ethical grounds for the manager to avoid imitating the therapeutic process and to avoid conversations with employees that develop into true therapy.

On the other hand, as mentioned in Chapter 14, many people have found that they cannot work on a maturation of relations and psychological defences in a superficial way. Everyday cooperation is not sufficiently changed by going on a team-building weekend or taking a three-day course in communication or agreeing to the rules for how to socialise ideally. This is because changes in the way people feel, think, and act – changes in the way they experience themselves and the world – do not solely happen through an intellectual achievement. To have lasting

266 The manager's personality

substance, changes must also be solidly founded in an emotional realisation. And since feelings are not directly under the control of thought, new realisations and changes take time.

Intellectually, for example, it is not hard to understand that trust is necessary for good cooperation; but, emotionally, trust is a complicated thing to establish and maintain. This is particularly true for people who are only tied to each other through the relatively fragile community a firm constitutes. Intellectually, one may gain great insights from learning about communication and different methods of communication, such as the appreciative approach. But the intellectual understanding does not in itself change anyone's mode of relating to others because this understanding is shaped just as much by one's internal, emotional convictions about the world and its nature.

Internal convictions and the emotions linked to them are only changed slowly. This happens by becoming conscious of one's feelings, which provides an opportunity to reflect on them. Thus, new and previous experiences will gradually be able to be put into a different framework of interpretation and understanding and, thus, may begin to be felt and experienced differently. This changed emotional experience, thus, provides an opportunity to act differently than one has done before and, depending on how deep the changes are, one can speak in certain cases about a change of personality. But personality is long under construction. Therefore, it takes time to change it (Illeris 2000: 173).

There may be great opportunities for managers to take inspiration from a more psychological approach to management. But to avoid the aforementioned ethical and human problems that can arise when a manager gets emotionally closer to his/her employees, Lyth recommends that the manager try to:

- Keep a certain distance – employees are not friends
- Divide his/her time as equally as possible among different employee groups
- Avoid working alone on interpretations of employee behaviour (Lyth 1989: 38–39).

The process is further complicated when it has to do with a whole group of people who must synchronically work on their individual self-images and their common pictures of reality. Organisations and groups consist of an intense complexity of information and relations. There are great demands placed on the manager who wants to work with this. The manager must be able to sustain insecurity and doubt for periods at a time and not cling to a preconceived conception. To maintain this openness can be difficult and painful:

> I am frequently the only person present who does not think I know what is going on.
>
> *(Lyth 1989: 4)*

Thus says Lyth about her work as a consultant, and the same can be said in many cases about the manager's work with psychodynamic processes.

The manager's influence **267**

Lyth recommends the following work method with respect to group relations:

- Interpretation of group processes to expand the self-insight of group members;
- Interpretations focused on what is going on here and now, and not on previous history or external situations;
- Focus on transference (projection and projective identification) between group members;
- Registration via counter-transference: the manager's own feelings are a measure for the events in the group.

Employees attain greater insight into unconscious conflicts if the manager invites them to speak as openly and freely about relationships at the workplace as possible. The manager and the employees together can test various interpretations. This process must be repeated again and again. But with these means, the manager helps the employees to bear the anxiety, insecurity, frustration, and anger to which life in an organisation can give rise. The manager helps by analysing problems and feelings together with employees in order thereby to change unsuitable patterns of thought and action (see also Wilke 2014: chaps. 1 and 8 for a discussion of this type of process). The following case gives an example of this.

Two employees in a group have a strained relationship with each other that has roots in many years of conflict around their area of expertise. They are both ambitious and proud. But they feel that they have their relationship under control and do not believe that their colleagues on the team have noticed anything: "We only fight behind closed doors!"

However, the manager observes that meetings in the group become more and more stiff and formal. The two employees and the manager are talking, while the others sit passively or do not turn up at the meeting at all.

After some time, the manager confronts the group with his impression: "I think our meetings have become rather boring!?" Everyone agrees spontaneously; and, for a period, they experiment with different structural measures (new meeting locale, alternating meeting leaders, new agenda) but without any special effect.

Only when the manager begins to inquire into their mutual relations does something happen. It turns out that the rest of the group suffers from the strained relationship between the two employees. Their colleagues have experienced the conflict much more clearly than the two realised through the way the two have talked about and not talked to each other, their body language, and so forth. This has made the others think that the meetings were unpleasant, and the atmosphere has felt strained and cramped. The other employees have reacted to this by withdrawing from the conversation or by staying away from the meeting.

268 The manager's personality

The conflict, which the two believed was invisible, in reality had a decisive influence on the well-being of the entire group. Everyone registered unconsciously that something "dangerous" was going on that was hard to put one's finger on because it was never formulated. The only ones who were not affected were the two employees because they knew very well what was going on and were, in many ways, fine with it. They knew each other well enough and also had a certain sympathy and respect for each other – but their mutual competition was more dominant. But the rest of the group had to fill in their lack of knowledge with fantasies, the danger of which was much greater than the reality. Therefore, it was a relief to get help formulating and understanding what was going on. The effect on the group – which was otherwise well on its way into a basic assumption in the form of a negative pairing condition (see Chapter 7) – was that productive energy was liberated, so the group became a work group. The relationship between the two employees changed noticeably for the better simply because they had the opportunity to speak openly to each other about it and, at the same time, they became aware of what influence their relationship had on the overall group.

If the manager in the case had stopped the process after they had experimented without effect with structural measures, it would have left the employees with a feeling of powerlessness and hopelessness because the meetings were still tense and unpleasant. It could have made the employees become cynical and lose engagement. But cynicism is actually a protection against losing hope that something can be better.

Some managers have a fear that, if they move into the psychological field, they will not be able to do anything but sit in a circle with their employees and talk about how they feel. But this fear turns things upside down. It is only when problems that disrupt mutual relationships are *not* talked about that they are inclined to swell up and swallow all the resources, as this case illustrates.

16
CONCLUSION

The purpose of this book has been to provide managers and others who work in organisations with greater knowledge about what psychological processes are at play when people work together. There is a need for this knowledge because the requirements for modern organisations are rising steadily with respect to productivity, skills, efficiency, and quality.

Therefore, our desire has been to present a number of basic theoretical concepts that help the reader to understand some of the at times chaotic and difficult-to-grasp phenomena that appear in organisations. The goal is twofold: on the one hand, to make it more satisfying and pleasurable for an individual to work in an organisation; on the other hand, to support the ability of the overall organisation to live up to the increasing demands.

The book has treated an organisation as a system consisting of subsystems of increasing complexity: the employee, the community, management, and the manager's personality as a special subsystem.

Each subsystem has been dealt with separately and described in the book's four parts. This form of structure is necessary in order to investigate a many-sided phenomenon such as an organisation, but the division into subsystems also constitutes a simplification that borders on abstraction. In practice, the subsystems constitute an inseparable whole, and the phenomena that are described in the book as separate are closely connected. That is what is meant when system theory talks about systems referring to and constituting each other. But this also means that it can be difficult to orient oneself in the concrete situation in the actual organisation, because what is what? In addition, these general psychological, theoretical concepts are in themselves somewhat "airy" in that they cannot be proved in a scientific sense. Life in organisations can never wholly be captured or understood in its entirety, and being in an organisation will always be connected with a certain uncertainty and non-knowledge.

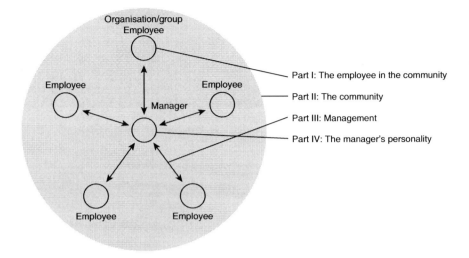

FIGURE 16.1 Subsystems dealt with in the book

Psychological processes are not phenomena that appear occasionally or "alongside" the rational organisation with its strategies, budgets, job descriptions, and so forth. People are feeling and thinking creatures regardless of the context in which they find themselves; and, therefore, a workplace consists of a whirl of processes that can have rational and psychological causes and effects at one and the same time. When one develops an eye for this and acquires the concepts with which to describe and analyse the less visible psychological processes, organisational life becomes easier to move in and influence in a constructive direction – also on a rational plane.

The manager's maturity and authenticity, and view of humankind

As the book shows, ambivalence is a fundamental psychological concept in the organisational context because the recognition of ambivalence is a precondition for understanding the dual relationship people have to working with others. People need each other and want to cooperate; but at the same time, people also need to be themselves and to be different from others. As described many places in this text, this dilemma gives rise to many problems and conflicts in organisations and entails, together with the dilemma between stability and change, that the psyche protect itself from the anxiety the dilemmas cause with the help of psychological defences. In order not to be locked into immature defences that limit the view of reality too much, individuals and groups need management.

The manager's task from this perspective is to help the individual as well as the group bring their psychological defences to an appropriate level. The defences must protect effectively but must not be too rigid in relation to the individual's or the

Conclusion **271**

group's needs at a given point in time or in a given situation. It is the manager's job to work with the individual's or the group's tolerance for ambivalence in order to increase psychological maturity and, thereby, the ability to act expediently in relation to the possibilities that exist or can be created.

Here, it is necessary for the manager him/herself to possess a certain maturity and to be willing to go through a process of reflection and development. A manager must be driven by genuine curiosity to understand other people and their motives and have an open attitude, that there are many ways to deal with life and all have equal validity. Many people will, perhaps, concur with this sort of attitude in principle, but the work of integrating it so that it permeates all contact with other people is a continuing process.

Since a great deal of the manager's work consists of communicating with others and since the quality of this communication is decisive for the organisation's productivity and the flourishing of its employees, it is important that the manager is conscious of – and constantly investigates and challenges – his/her personal view of life and human beings. As with everything that touches on the relationship between people, it is a matter of – as mentioned earlier – not confusing methods with techniques. Communication methods are not "techniques" or "tools" that can be used with a guarantee for a particular result because people and organisations are not machines. If methods are used pure and simply as techniques, they will seem artificial and inauthentic, and those who are subject to them will get an unpleasant feeling of being manipulated and being the object of some other goal rather than being a goal in themselves.

The decisive thing, then, is for the use of different methods to be borne by an attitude that values all people by virtue of their existence and their demand for respect. In addition, the attitude must be based on a conviction that people – seen from their own point of view – have well-founded intentions with their behaviour. This means that the individual's intention can be understood if one puts oneself into that person's shoes. And in doing this, one will often discover that the other person's motives are strangely recognisable because they almost always have to do with an inner struggle for self-esteem – and human beings have this struggle in common with each other.

At the same time, it is important to make it clear that a firm is a special form of human activity because it has a particular goal. A firm is a task-oriented unit that, in accordance with its purpose, is to produce certain products or services. This means that there is a corresponding purpose with every person's functional affiliation with the firm and with the relationships that are built up between the participants. The purpose is for the participants to complete the firm's assignments to the best of their ability. It is a precondition for the manager to be conscious of this relationship; and it is an advantage if the employees are as well because this makes them better at accepting or rejecting the firm's assignments from the viewpoint of their own needs and wishes.

It is precisely in this connection that the basic freedom and equality in the relationship between firm and employee becomes decisive. Both parties are ultimately free to dissolve the relationship if there is no accord between the needs, desires, ethics, or morals of the firm and the employees.

BIBLIOGRAPHY

Abrahamowitz, F. (2001). *Psykologileksikon*. København: Høst & Søn.

Adizes, I. (1979). *Lederens faldgruber*. København: Børsens Forlag.

Alderfer, C.P. (1987). An intergroup perspective on group dynamics. In J.W. Lorsch (ed.). *Handbook of Organizational Behavior*. Englewood Cliffs: Prentice Hall.

Alsted, J. (2001). *De menneskelige samfunds udvikling – en kritisk introduktion til historisk sociologi*. Frederiksberg: Roskilde Universitetsforlag.

Alsted, J. (2005). *A Model of Human Motivation for Sociology*. Frankfurt: Peter Lang.

Alsted, J. (2007). Terrorisme som mangel på kollektiv modenhed. In M. Thorup and M. Brænder (eds.). *Antiterrorismens idehistorie – stater og vold i 500 år*. Århus: Århus Universitetsforlag.

Alsted, J. and D. Haslund (2016). *Sex, sladder og stress i organisationer*. Frederiksberg: Samfundslitteratur.

Andersen, K.L. (2006). Ledelse og autoritet. In P. Helth (ed.). *Lederskabelse*. Frederiksberg: Samfundslitteratur: 143–154.

Andersen, L.P. and H.B. Riis (2016). *Fra studie til arbejdsliv*. København: Frydenlund.

Andersen, V., B. Clematide et al. (2004). *Arbejdspladsen som læringsmiljø*. Frederiksberg: Roskilde Universitetsforlag.

Armstrong, D. and M. Rustin (eds.) (2014). *Social Defences Against Anxiety: Explorations in a Paradigm*. London: Karnac.

Ashbach, C. and V.L. Schermer (1987). *Object Relations, the Self, and the Group*. London: Routledge.

Ashforth, B. and R. Humphrey (1995). Emotion in the Workplace: A Reappraisal. *Human Relations*, vol. 48, no. 2: 97–126.

Ashforth, B. and G. Kreiner (2002). Normalizing Emotion in Organizations: Making the Extraordinary Seem Ordinary. *Human Resource Management Review*, vol. 12: 215–235.

Bakka, J.F. and E. Fivelsdal (red.) (2002). *Organisationsteoriens klassikere*. København: Handelshøjskolens Forlag.

Bakka, J.F. and E. Fivelsdal (2014). *Organisationsteori*. 6th. ed. København: Handelshøjskolens Forlag.

Bales, R.F. (1950). *Interaction Process Analysis: A Method for the Study of Small Groups*. Chicago: University of Chicago Press.

Bibliography   **273**

Bay, P. and L. Blicher-Hansen (eds.) (2006). *Mødebogen*. København: Kursuslex.

Beck, U.C. (2004). Organisationspsykologiske kommentarer til tidens sygehusvæsen. In T. Heinskou and S. Visholm (eds.). *Psykodynamisk organisationspsykologi*. København: Hans Reitzels Forlag: 265–286.

Beck, U.C. (2009). *Psykodynamisk coaching*. København: Hans Reitzels Forlag.

Berger, P. and T. Luckmann (1966). *Den samfundsskabte virkelighed*. København: Lindhart og Ringhof.

Bion, W.R. (2006 [1961]). *Experiences in Groups*. Hove: Routledge.

Blake, R. and J.S. Mouton (1985). *Managerial Grid III*. Houston: Gulf.

Blanchard, K.H., P. Zigarmi et al. (1985). *Leadership and the One Minute Manager: Increasing Effectiveness Through Situational Leadership*. New York: William Morrow & Co.

Block, J. (1995). A Contrarian View of the Five-factor Approach to Personality Description. *Psychological Bulletin*, vol. 117, no. 2: 187–215.

Bolman, L.G. and T.E. Deal (1984). *Modern Approaches to Understanding and Managing Organizations*. San Francisco: Jossey-Bass.

Bolman, L.G. and T.E. Deal (2017). *Reframing Organizations*. 6th. ed. San Francisco: Jossey-Bass.

Borum, F. (1995). *Strategier for organisationsændring*. København: Handelshøjskolens Forlag.

Bottrup, P. and P. Hagedorn-Rasmussen (2011). Når ledere skaber organisatorisk forandring og transformation. In P. Helth (ed.). *Ledelse og læring i praksis*. Frederiksberg: Samfundslitteratur: 33–64.

Brenner, C. (1982). *The Mind in Conflict*. New York: International Universities Press.

Brown, R. (2000). *Group Processes*. Oxford: Blackwell Publishers.

Brunning, H. (2006). The six domains of executive coaching. In H. Brunning (red.). *Executive Coaching – Systems-Psychodynamic Perspective*. London: Karnac Books: 131–151.

Brunsson, N. and J.P. Olsen (1993). *The Reforming Organisation*. London: Routledge.

Canetti, E. (1996). *Masse og magt*. København: Politisk Revy.

Christensen, A. (ed.) (1997). *Den lærende organisations begreber og praksis*. Aalborg: Aalborg Universitetsforlag.

Christensen, P.H. (2007). *Motivation i videnarbejde*. København: Hans Reitzels Forlag.

Christensen, S. and P.-E.D. Jensen (2001). *Kontrol i det stille*. Frederiksberg: Samfundslitteratur.

Cini, M., R.L. Moreland et al. (1993). Group Staffing Levels and Responses to Prospective and New Members. *Journal of Personality and Social Psychology*, vol. 65: 723–734.

Clematide, B. (2006). Ledelse af læring. In P. Helth (ed.). *Lederskabelse*. Frederiksberg: Samfundslitteratur: 171–183.

Coleman, J.S. (1990). *Foundations of Social Theory*. Cambridge: Cambridge University Press.

Collins, R. (1990). Stratification, emotional energy, and the transient emotions. In T.D. Kemper (ed.). *Research Agendas in the Sociology of Emotions*. Albany: State University of New York Press.

Cooperrider, D.L. and S. Srivastva (1987). Appreciative inquiry in organizational life. In R. Woodman and W. Pasmore (eds.). *Research on Organizational Change and Development*. Greenwich: JAI Press.

Cox, S.A. and M.W. Kramer (1995). Communication During Employee Dismissals: Social Exchange Principles and Group Influences on Employee Exit. *Management Communication Quarterly*, vol. 9, no. 2: 156–190.

Dahl, R.A. (1957). The Concept of Power. *Behavioural Science*, årg. 2, nr. 3: 201–214.

Dall, M.O. and S. Hansen (eds.) (2001). *Slip anerkendelsen løs! – Appreciative Inquiry i organisationsudvikling*. København: Frydenlund.

DiMaggio, P.J. and W.W. Powell (1991). Institutional isomorphism and collective Rationality. In W.W. Powell and P.J. Dimaggio (eds.). *The New Institutionalism in Organizational Analysis*. Chicago: The University of Chicago Press.

274 Bibliography

Drath, W.H., C.D. McCauley et al. (2008). Direction, Alignment, Commitment: Toward a More Integrative Ontology of Leadership. *The Leadership Quarterly*, vol. 19: 635–653.

Elias, N. (2000). *The Civilizing Process*. Oxford: Blackwell Publishers.

Elmholdt, C. (2006).Værdsættende anerkendende udforskning. *Erhvervspsykologi*, vol. 4, no. 3: 22–35.

Elmholdt, C., H.D. Keller and L. Tanggaard (2013). *Ledelsespsykologi*. Frederiksberg: Samfundslitteratur.

Engelsted, N. (1989). *Personlighedens almene grundlag*. 1. Århus: Aarhus Universitetsforlag.

Engquist, A. (2000). *Kommunikation på arbetsplatsen*. Stockholm: Prisma.

Flyvbjerg, B. (1993). *Rationalitet og magt*. København: Akademisk Forlag.

Fonagy, P. and P. Luyten (2012). The multidimensional construct of mentalization and its relevance to understanding borderline personality disorder. In A. Fotopoulou, D. Pfaff and M.A. Conway (eds.). *From the Couch to the Lab – Trends in Psychodynamic Neuroscience*. Oxford: Oxford University Press: 405–426.

Ford, M.E. (1992). *Motivating Humans*. Newbury Park: Sage Publications.

Foucault, M. (1976). *The History of Sexuality – An Introduction*. Harmondsworth: Penguin.

Foulkes, S.H. (1964). *Therapeutic Group Analysis*. London: George Allen & Unwin.

Gabriel, Y. (1999). *Organizations in Depth*. London: Sage.

Gergely, G. (2007).The social construction of the subjective self: The role of affect-mirroring, markedness, and ostensive communication in self-development. In P. Fonagy, L. Mayes and M. Target (eds.). *Developmental Science and Psychoanalysis: Integration and Innovation*. London: Karnac: 87–144.

Gergen, K. (1990). Social understanding and the inscription of self. In J.W. Stigler, R.A. Schweder and G. Herdt (eds.). *Cultural Psychology*. Cambridge: Cambridge University Press

Gergen, K. (1997). *Virkelighed og relationer*. København: Dansk psykologisk Forlag.

Gergen, K. (1999). *An Invitation to Social Construction*. London: Sage.

Gergen, M.M. and K.J. Gergen (1998).The relational rebirthing of wisdom and courage. In S. Srivastva and D.L. Cooperrider (eds.). *Organizational Wisdom and Executive Courage*. San Francisco: New Lexington Press: 134–153.

Geus, A.D. (1997). *Den levende virksomhed*. *Viby*: Centrum.

Ghais, S. (2005). *Extreme Facilitation*. San Francisco: CDR Associates.

Giddens, A. (1984). *The Constitution of Society*. Cambridge: Polity Press.

Gjerde, S. (2006). *Coaching – hvad, hvorfor, hvordan*. Frederiksberg: Samfundslitteratur.

Goleman, D. (2006). *Social Intelligence*. London: Hutchinson.

Gould, L. (2001). Introduction. In L. Could, L.F. Stapley and M. Stein (eds.). *The Systems Psychodynamics of Organizations*. London: Karnac: 1–15.

Grimberg, C. (1958). *Verdenshistorien*. København: Politikens Forlag.

Guldager, J. (2007). *Coaching*. København: Nyt Nordisk Forlag Arnold Busck.

Halton, W. (2003). Ubevidste aspekter af organisationslivet. In A. Obholzer and V.Z. Roberts (eds.). *Det ubevidste på arbejde*. København: Dansk psykologisk Forlag: 31–40.

Hammond, S.A. (1998). *The Thin Book of Appreciative Inquiry*. Plano: The Thin Book Publishing Co.

Handest, P., L. Jansson et al. (2003). *Skizotypi og borderline*. København: PsykiatriFondens Forlag.

Hareli, S. and S.S. Tzafrir (2006). The Role of Causal Attributions in Survivors' Emotional Reactions to Downsizing. *Human Resource Development Review*, vol. 5, no. 4: 400–421.

Harré, R. and W.G. Parrott (eds.) (1996). *The Emotions: Social, Cultural and Biological*. London: Sage.

Haslebo, G. (2004). *Relationer i organisationer*. København: Dansk psykologisk Forlag.

Haslund, D. and J. Alsted (2004). Organisationers modenhed. *Erhvervspsykologi*, vol. 2, no. 4: 50–73.

Bibliography **275**

Haslund, D. and J. Alsted (2014). Organisationsstruktur – psykologiske behov og forsvar. In M. Elting and S. Hammer (eds.). *Ledelse og organisation – forandringer og udfordringer*. Frederiksberg: Samfundslitteratur: 99–128.

Hasselager, A. (2006). Ledelse og gruppens psykologi. In P. Helth (ed.). *Lederskabelse*. Frederiksberg: Samfundslitteratur: 155–170.

Hatch, M.J. (1993). The Dynamics of Organizational Culture. *Academy of Management Review*, vol. 18, no. 4: 657–663.

Hatch, M.J. (1997). *Organization Theory*. Oxford: Oxford University Press.

Heinskou, T. (2004). Den lille gruppe på arbejde. In T. Heinskou and S. Visholm (eds.). *Psykodynamisk Organisationspsykologi*. København: Hans Reitzels Forlag: 49–68.

Heinskou, T. and S. Visholm (eds.) (2004). *Psykodynamisk Organisationspsykologi*. København: Hans Reitzels Forlag.

Helth, P. (2006). Ledelse i den relationsskabte organisation. In P. Helth (ed.). *Lederskabelse*. Frederiksberg: Samfundslitteratur: 35–56.

Helth, P. (2011a). Indledning. In P. Helth (ed.). *Ledelse og læring i praksis*. Frederiksberg: Samfundslitteratur: 9–31.

Helth, P. (ed.) (2011b). *Ledelse og læring i praksis*. Frederiksberg: Samfundslitteratur.

Hersey, P. and K.H. Blanchard (1969). *Management of Organizational Behaviour: Utilizing Human Resources*. Englewood cliffs: Prentice Hall.

Hirschhorn, L. (1988). *The Workplace Within*. Cambridge: The MIT Press.

Hochschild, A. (1979). Emotion Work, Feeling Rules and social Structure. *American Journal of Sociology*, vol. 85, no. 3: 551–575.

Hochschild, A. (1983). *The Managed Heart: Commercialisation of Human Feeling*. Berkeley: University of California Press.

Hogg, M. (1992). *The Social Psychology of Group Cohesiveness*. London: Harvester Wheatsheaf.

Hogg, M. (2014). From Uncertainty to Extremism: Social Categorization and Identity Processes. *Current Directions in Psychological Science*, vol. 23, no. 5: 338–342.

Holm, I.S. (2010). *Anerkendelse i ledelse*. København: Hans Reitzels Forlag.

Holm, I.S. (2012). *Ledergruppen – dynamiske læreprocesser*. København: Hans Reitzels Forlag.

Høeg, B. and A.L. Thybring (2014). Teamledelse på et systemisk grundlag. In T. Molly-Søholm, N. Stegeager and S. Willert (eds.). *Systemisk ledelse*. Frederiksberg: Samfundslitteratur: 237–267.

Illeris, K. (2000). *Læring*. Frederiksberg: Roskilde Universitetsforlag.

Illeris, K. (red.) (2012a). *49 tekster om læring*. Frederiksberg: Samfundslitteratur.

Illeris, K. (2012b). Læringsteoriens elementer – hvordan hænger det hele sammen? In K. Illeris (ed.). *49 tekster om læring*. Frederiksberg: Samfundslitteratur: 17–38.

Jacobsen, D.I. and J. Thorsvik (2002). *Hvordan organisationer fungerer*. København: Hans Reitzels Forlag.

Jaques, E. (1976). *A General Theory of Bureaucracy*. New York: Halstead.

Jensen, S.A., K.M. Laursen et al. (2011). *Det Danske Ledelsesbarometer – Dokumentationsrapport*. Århus: Aarhus Universitet & Lederne.

Johansen, J. and N. Toft (2001). *Sig hvad du mener*. København: Aschehoug.

Judge, T.A., J. Bono et al. (2002). Personality and Leadership. *Journal of Applied Psychology*, vol. 87: 765–780.

Jung, C.G. (1921). *Psychological Types*. London: Routledge & Kegan Paul.

Jørgensen, B. (2004). Psykodynamiske perspektiver på ledelse. In T. Heinskou and S. Visholm (eds.). *Psykodynamisk organisationspsykologi*. København: Hans Reitzels Forlag: 159–174.

Jørgensen, C.R. (2006). *Personlighedsforstyrrelser*. København: Akademisk Forlag.

Katzenelson, B. (1993). Angstteoriernes landskab. *Psyke & Logos*, vol. 14, no. 1: 6–45.

Kaufmann, G. and A. Kaufmann (2003). *Psykologi i organisasjon og ledelse*. Bergen: Fagbokforlaget.

Kegan, R. (1982). *The Evolving Self*. Cambridge: Harvard University Press.

276 Bibliography

Kernberg, O.F. (1976). *Object Relations Theory and Clinical Psychoanalysis*. New York: Jason Aronson.

Kernberg, O.F. (1980). *Internal World and External Reality*. New York: Jason Aronson.

Kernberg, O.F. (1998). *Ideology, Conflict and Leadership in Groups and Organizations*. New Haven: Yale University Press.

Kets de Vries, M. and D. Miller (1986). Personality, Culture, and Organization. *Academy of Management Review*, vol. 11, no. 2: 266–279.

Kirkeby, O.F. (2002). *Loyalitet – udfordringen til ledere og medarbejdere*. Frederiksberg: Samfundslitteratur.

Kirkeby, O.F. (2004). *Det nye lederskab*. København: Børsens Forlag.

Klausen, K.K. (2004). *Strategisk ledelse – de mange arenaer*. Odense: Syddansk Universitetsforlag.

Klein, M. (1977). *Envy and Gratitude and Other Works: 1946–1963*. New York: Delta.

Langs, R. (1998). *Ground Rules in Psychotherapy and Counselling*. London: Karnac Books.

Laustsen, C.B. and J. Myrup (eds.) (2006). *Magtens tænkere – politisk teori fra Machiavelli til Honneth*. Frederiksberg: Roskilde Universitetsforlag.

Lave, J. and E. Wenger (2003). *Situeret læring – og andre tekster*. København: Hans Reitzels Forlag.

Leary, M.R. and J.P. Tangney (2012). The self as an organizing construct in the behavioral and social sciences. In M.R. Leary and J.P. Tangney (eds.). *Handbook of Self and Identity*. London: Guilford Publications: 1–20.

Lederne (2014). *Køn, uddannelse og karriere*. København: Lederne.

Lee, D. and H. Newby (1983). *The Problem of Sociology*. London: Unwin Hyman.

Levine, J.M. and R.L. Moreland (1994). Group Socialization: Theory and Research. *European Review of Social Psychology*, vol. 5, no. 1: 305–336.

Lewin, K., R. Lippit et al. (1939). Patterns of Aggressive Behaviour in Experimentally Created "Social Climates". *Journal of Social Psychology*, vol. 10: 271–299.

Lichtenberg, J.D., F.M. Lachmann et al. (1992). *Self and Motivational Systems*. Hillsdale: The Analytic Press.

Lieberman, M.A., I.D. Yalom et al. (1973). *Encounter Groups: First facts*. New York: Basic Books.

Lorentzen, B. (2007). Autoritetsrelationer og kollektive forsvar. *Erhvervspsykologi*, vol. 5, no. 4: 38–52.

Lyth, I.M. (1988). *Containing Anxiety in Institutions*. Selected essays vol. 1. London: Free Association Books.

Lyth, I.M. (1989). *The Dynamics of the Social*. Selected essays vol. 2. London: Free Association Books.

Mackenzie, R., M. Stuart et al. (2006). "All that is solid?": Class, Identity and the Maintenance of a Collective Orientation amongst Redundant Steelworkers. *Sociology*, vol. 40, no. 5: 833–852.

Madsen, K.B. (1968). *Motivation*. København: Munksgaard.

Majgaard, K. (2017). *Handlekraft i velfærdsledelse*. København: Hans Reitzels Forlag.

March, J.G. and J.P. Olsen (1989). *Rediscovering Institutions*. New York: Free Press.

Maslow, A. (1970). *På vej mod en eksistenspsykologi*. København: Nyt Nordisk Forlag – Arnold Busck.

Maslow, A.H. (1987 [1954]). *Motivation and Personality*. New York: Harper and Row.

McAdams, D.P. (1996). Personality, Modernity, and the Storied Self: A Contemporary Framework for Studying Persons. *Psychological Inquiry*, vol. 7: 295–321.

McCrae, R.R. and P.T. Costa (2016). *Neo-PI-3 vejledning – Erhverv*. København: Hogrefe.

McIntosh, D. (1979). The Empirical Bearing of Psychoanalytic Theory. *International Journal of Psychoanalysis*, vol. 60: 405–431.

Bibliography **277**

McNamee, S. (1998). Reinscribing organizational wisdom and courage: The relationally engaged organization. In S. Srivastva and D.L. Cooperrider (eds.). *Organizational Wisdom and Executive Courage*. San Francisco: New Lexington Press: 101–117.

Molin, J. (2006). Selvironi som ledelseskompetence. *Erhvervspsykologi*, vol. 4, no. 1: 26–45.

Mortensen, K.V. (2003). *Fra neuroser til relationsforstyrrelser*. København: Gyldendal.

Myers, I.B. and P.B. Myers (1995). *Gifts Differing: Understanding Personality Type*. Mountain View: Davies-Black Publishing.

Obholzer, A. (2003). Autoritet, magt og lederskab – bidrag fra grupperelationstræning. In A. Obholzer and V.Z. Roberts (eds.). *Det ubevidste på arbejde*. København: Dansk Psykologisk Forlag: 69–80.

Obholzer, A. and V.Z. Roberts (2003). Den besværlige person og den bekymrede organisation. In A. Obholzer and V.Z. Roberts (eds.). *Det ubevidste på arbejde*. København: Dansk Psykologisk Forlag: 189–201.

Olsen, H. (1998). *Tallenes talende tavshed – måleproblemer i surveyundersøgelser*. København: Akademisk Forlag.

Olsen, O.A. and S. Køppe (1985). *Freuds psykoanalyse*. København: Gyldendal.

Østergaard, L. (1975). *Testmetoden: Intelligens – Personlighed – Diagnose*. København: Munksgaard.

Pearce, W.B. (1993). *Interpersonal Communication*. New York: Harper Collins College Publishers.

Pendleton, D. and A.F. Furnham (2016). *Leadership: All You Need to Know*. London: Palgrave Macmillan.

Poder, P. (2004). *Feelings of Power and the Power of Feeling*. Københavns Universitet: Ph.d.-dissertation.

Qvortrup, L. (2001). *Det lærende samfund*. København: Gyldendal.

Rasmussen, J.G. (1997). Ledelse år 2000: Læringsbetingelser i organisationer med dynamiske strategier. In A. Christensen (ed.). *Den lærende organisations begreber og praksis*. Aalborg: Aalborg Universitetsforlag.

Riemann, F. (1961). *Angstens grundformer*. København: Klitrose.

Ringstad, H.E. and T. Ødegård (2003). *Typeforståelse – Jungs typepsykologi*. Bergen: Optimas.

Roberts, V.Z. (2003). Organisering af arbejde. In A. Obholzer and V.Z. Roberts (eds.). *Det ubevidste på arbejde*. København: Dansk Psykologisk Forlag: 53–67.

Rook, C. (2016). Introduction: A psychodynamic approach to leadership development. In M. Kets de Vries, K. Korotov, E. Florent-Treacy and C. Rook (eds.). *Coach and Couch: The Psychology of Making Better Leaders*. Basingstoke: Palgrave Macmillan.

Schein, E.H. (1990). *Organisationspsykologi*. Århus: Systime.

Scheuer, J. (1998). *Den umulige samtale*: København: Akademisk Forlag.

Scheuer, S. (1999). *Motivation – aktørmotiver i arbejdslivet*. København: Handelshøjskolens Forlag.

Schwarz, R. (2002). *The Skilled Facilitator*. San Francisco: Jossey-Bass.

Senge, P. (1990). *The Fifth Discipline*. London: Random House.

Simonton, D.K. (1994). *Greatness*. New York: The Guilford Press.

Srivastva, S. and D.L. Cooperrider (eds.) (1998). *Organizational Wisdom and Executive Courage*. San Francisco: The New Lexington Press.

Stern, D.N. (2000). *Spædbarnets interpersonelle verden*. København: Hans Reitzels Forlag.

Stone, W.N. and G. Spielberg (2009). A Self Psychological Perspective of Group Development. *Group*, vol. 33, no. 1: 27–44.

Sørensen, E.E. (ed.) (2008). *Ledelse og læring i organisationer*. København: Hans Reitzels Forlag.

Tomkins, S.S. (1992). *Affect, Imagery, Consciousness*. Vol. 4. New York: Springer.

278 Bibliography

Trillingsgaard, A. (2015). *Ledelsesteamet gentænkt.* København: Dansk Psykologisk Forlag.

Trillingsgaard, A. and K. Albæk (2011). Det møgbeskidte ledelsesteam. In C. Elmholdt and L. Tanggaard (eds.). *Følelser i ledelse.* Århus: Klim: 89–109.

Tuckman, B.W. (1965). Developmental Sequence in Small Groups. *Psychological Bulletin,* vol. 63, no. 6: 384–399.

Turner, J.C. (1982). Towards a cognitive redefinition of the social group. In H. Tajfel (ed.). *Social Identity and Intergroup Relations.* Cambridge: Cambridge University Press.

Uzzi, B. and S. Dunlop (2005). How to build your network. *Harvard Business Review,* december.

Visholm, S. (2004a). Autoritetsrelationen. In T. Heinskou and S. Visholm (eds.). *Psykodynamisk organisationspsykologi.* København: Hans Reitzels Forlag: 84–108.

Visholm, S. (2004b). Intergruppedynamik. In T. Heinskou and S. Visholm (eds.). *Psykodynamisk organisationspsykologi.* København: Hans Reitzels Forlag: 127–158.

Visholm, S. (2004c). Modstand mod forandring – psykodynamiske perspektiver. In T. Heinskou and S. Visholm (eds.). *Psykodynamisk organisationspsykologi.* København: Hans Reitzels Forlag: 174–201.

Visholm, S. (2004d). Organisationspsykologi og psykodynamisk systemteori. In T. Heinskou and S. Visholm (eds.). *Psykodynamisk organisationspsykologi.* København: Hans Reitzels Forlag: 23–48.

Visholm, S. (2005). Uklare roller i postmoderne organisationer – om ledelse og selvstyrende grupper. *Tidsskrift for Arbejdsliv,* vol. 7, no. 1: 27–42.

Von Franz, M. and J. Hillman (1971). *Jungs Typology.* Irving: Spring Publications.

Wahba, M.A. and L.G. Bridwell (1976). Maslow Reconsidered: A Review of Research on the Need Hierarchy Theory. *Organizational Behavior and Human Performance,* vol. 15: 212–240.

Weber, M. (1947). *Wirtschaft und Gesellschaft.* Tübingen: P. Siebeck.

Weidner, M. (2005). *Møder med mening og mål.* København: Jyllands-Postens Forlag.

Whitener, E.M., S.E. Brodt et al. (1998). Managers as Initiators of Trust: An Exchange Relationship Framework for Understanding Managerial Trustworthy Behaviour. *Academy of Management Review,* vol. 23, no. 3: 513–530.

Whitmore, J. (1996). *Coaching på jobbet.* København: Peter Asschenfeldts nye Forlag.

Wilke, G. (2014). *The Art of Group Analysis in Organisations: The Use of Intuitive and Experiential Knowledge.* London: Karnac.

Winnicott, D.W. (1986). *Home is Where We Start from.* Harmondsworth: Penguin.

Yalom, I.D. (1999). *Eksistentiel psykoterapi.* København: Hans Reitzels Forlag.

Yukl, G. (2013). *Leadership in Organizations.* Harlow: Pearson Education. 8. udgave.

INDEX

Figures are indicated by page numbers in *italic* type; tables are indicated by page numbers in **bold** type.

Abrahamowitz, F. 7, 42
abstract thinking 250–251
acceptance of new employees 48–69; background 48–49; by community 64–65; culture malleability 65–67; encounters 49–50; the initial period 61–64, 67–68; integration 68–69; job interviews 52–54, 57–60; mutual trust 51–52; the parallel company 54–55; projective pressure and wishful thinking 55–57; the symbolic contract 60–61; voluntariness 50–51
active listening 169–175
adaptation 1, 25, 62, 92, 101, 132, 177, 187, 190, 259
Adizes PAEI 224
agendas 139
aggression 36, 58, 78, 81, 121, 145, 236
agreeableness 224
AI (appreciative inquiry) 110, 163–168
Albæk, K. 204
alcohol abuse 72–74
Alderfer, C.P. 92
Alexandra, Countess 115
alliances 204, 206
Alsted, J. 94, 111, 116–117
ambiguous/conflicting drives 24–25
ambitions 32
ambivalence 21, 25, 32, 34, 38, 40, 44, 73, 99, 207–208, 270–271

amelioration of feelings 101
analysis of meeting 132, 139–146
Andersen, L.P. 48
Andersen, V. 158
Anerkendelse i ledelse [Appreciation in Management] (Holm) 167–168
anger 78–79, 114
anxiety: of change 26–27; of choosing wrongly 34–35, 51; in the community 26; denial and 38; existential 168–169; of failing 217; firing 85; job interviews 54; of manager 235–237; performance 48; projective identification and 254–255; repression of 41–43, 56–57, 121
Appreciation in Management [Anerkendelse i ledelse] (Holm) 167–168
appreciative inquiry (AI) 110, 163–168
"Appreciative Inquiry in Organizational Life" (Cooperrider and Srivastva) 163
appreciative management style 245
Armstrong, D. 111
artefacts 65–66
Ashbach, C. 95, 99
Ashforth, B. 101
assessments, managerial 86–87
assumptions 65, 111–114, 116
asymmetrical power relationships 50, 187–188
attention: emotional 52; lack of 62–65, 75–76; managerial 49, 81

280 Index

authorisation 161, 193, 195, 197, 201–202, 207–208, 218
authority, managers as 184–199; from above 188–190; background 184–185; from below 191–199; models of 185–188; personalities of 231–232
authority systems *186*
autocratic manager 150
autonomous "I" 26
avoidance 43, 60, 63, 87, 121, 256

Bakka, J.F. 6, 23
Bales, R.E. 150
bargains 155–157, 161
"Barometer of Danish Management, The" ["Det Danske Ledelsesbarometer"] 177, 244
basic assumptions state 111–114, 116, 236
basic drives 22–24
basic emotions 29
Bay, P. 130
beautiful, the 152
Beck, U.C 234, 247, 251
behaviours 16–17, 30–31, 74–76, 78–81, 120, 175–177, 239, 256–257
Belbin's team roles 224
Berger, P. 20
binary defence mechanisms *see* splitting
biological/instinctive fundament of the brain 28
biological needs 22–23, 27
biological theory of emotions 28–29
Bion, W. 111–116, 141, 156, 236
black and white thinking 40, 80, 116–117, 165
Blake, R. 150
Blanchard, K. 150
Blicher-Hansen, L. 130
Block, J. 224
body language 101, 173–176
Bolman, L. 152, 253–254, 256, 260
bonding 114
Bono, J.E. 275
boredom 121
Borum, F. 92
Bottrup, P. 159
boundaries 9, 29–30, 81, 191, 219, 251
brain, the 28
breathing 174
Brenner, C. 35
Bridwell, L.G. 24
Briggs, K. 224
Brodt, S.E. 278
Brown, R. 150

Brunning, H. 247
Brunsson, N. 15
brutalisation 84
bureaucracies 76, 96, 121–122, 158–159, 185, 252
Business Psychology [Erhvervspsykologi] (Elmholdt) 167

Canetti, E. 98
caring 137, 151–152
cases: accessibility of manager 179–180; appreciative inquiry (AI) in an immature organisation 166–167; biological/psychological behaviour 30–31; confidence in management 262–263; dramatic employee 79–82; exercising authority 194–195; existing cultures 66–67; feedback 210–211; firing 72–74, 85–88; information 133; internal authority 232–233; interviews 57–60; management of managers 209; meeting analysis 139–146; motivational structures 96–98; non-verbal behaviour 175–176; organisational structure 254–255; pairings 115–116; parallel company 54–55; political arena 205–206; projections 55–57, 238–239; relational problems 192–194; repressive defences 62–64, 257–260; Rockwool layer 211–212; self-reflection 261–263; service trap 181; splitting 35–37, 252–255; symbols 137–138, 203–204; trust and loyalty 46–47; unconscious conflicts 267–268; unconscious process 103–105
causes of behaviours 75–76, 79–80
centralisation/decentralisation 15–16
CEOs 180
change 26–27, 31–32, 94, 163–165, 246, 266
chaos 35, 54, 80–81, 190, 230
charisma 151, 230, 253
Charles, Prince 115
cheerfulness 121
chinks in management groups *214*
Christensen, P.H. 156
Cini, M. 55
circular dialogue 108–110
clarification 171
Clematide, B. 158
Clinton, B. 115
Clinton, H. 115
coaching 245–247
cognition 101, 225
Coleman, J.S. 18

Index **281**

collaboration 7, 15–17, 64, 89, 97, 116, 126–127, 129, 191–192
collective defences 102–105
Collins, R. 98
common psychological defences 99–100
communication 57–60, 64, 72, 85–86, 100–102, 122, 125, 132–135, 203–204
communities 62, 64–65, 187
community of interests 185–186
compartmentalisation 101
competency 94–95, 264
competition 97, 117, 120, 204–205, 268
complexity 150–153, 203–204, 210
compliance 76, 99
compromises 35, 94–95, 97–98
conclusions 173
concurrence 83
conduct, demands on 243
confidence 58, 60, 98, 194, 214–215, 235, 262–263
confidentiality 265
conflict-averse behaviour 256
conflicts 44, 57–59, 64, 74, 79, 121–127, 162, 167–168, 191–192
conscientiousness 224, 228
consciousness 28, 110
consensus method 163
content in management 149–157
content of meetings 130–132
contracts 28, 60–61, 80
cooperation 31–32, 34–47, 71, 80, 94, 96, 161, 163, 168, 187, 194–195
Cooperrider, D.L. 20, 110, 167; "Appreciative Inquiry in Organizational Life" 163
coordination, organisational 15–16, 93, 101, 129
core self 222–223
Costa, P.T. 223
counter-projection 216
Cox, S.A. 85
creativity 122
criticism 75–76, 119, 122, 125, 135
cross-pressure on managers 177–182
crying 168
culture 65–67, 73
curiosity 26–27, 59, 164, 171, 224, 271
cynicism 268

Dahl, R.A. 184
Dall, M.O. 164
data 180, 228–229, 252
deadlines 123
Deal, T.E. 152, 253–254, 256, 260

decision-making 204, 213
defence mechanisms: collective 102–105; defined 38–40; immature 38, 49, 51, 58, 62–63, 80, 102–105; integration 44–46; motivational 227; projective 237; repression 35–36, 42–44, 54–55, 57–58, 62–64; splitting 40–42, 55–56, 83–85, 115–122, 165, 252–255, **254**; subconscious 116; in young organisations 189
defensive levels, reservations against 127–128
delegation 126, 160
democratic manager 150
demonisation 42, 63, 84–85, 114–115, 119
denial 37–38, 165
dependence/independence 18–19, 114, 141, 165, 236
depression 111, 252
design 164
destiny 164
"Det Danske Ledelsesbarometer" ["The Barometer of Danish Management"] 177, 244
Det lærende samfund [The Learning Society] (Qvortrup) 203–204
Det nye lederskab [The New Leadership] (Kirkeby) 152
developing competence 264
development theories 40, 106–108, 111
diagrams, organisational 93
dialogue 108, 133–135
Diana, Lady 115
dilemmas 25–28, 31–32, 34–36, 39, 94, 98, 162
DiMaggio, P.J. 93
disagreements 125, 135, 170, 215
DISC model 224
discovery 164
dismissal see expulsion from the community
displacement 238
distancing/avoidance 43, 60, 63, 87, 121, 256
diversity 118
division of labour 92–93
divorce 115
dominance 119
dramatic employees 78–82
Drath, W.H. 241
dreams 164
drive theories 22–25
Dunlop, S. 91
dynamic processes 65
dysfunction 189–190, 252

282 Index

economy of the group 94, 97
education 94–95, 246, 249
ego, the 95
Elias, N. 29–30
Elmholdt, C., *Business Psychology* [*Erhvervspsykologi*] 167
emotional energy 65
emotional stimulation 151–152
emotions 139–146; conflicting 59, 102; controlling 101; group 114–116; internal conviction 255; isolation from 44; in manager-employee relationship 235, 243–244; of meeting participants 131–132; motives and 242–244; relating to 39–40; repression of 121–122; subtext of 52; theories 27–32
empathy 36, 62, 80–81, 262
employees 13–87; acceptance of 48–69; background 13–14; cooperation and psychological defences of 34–47; expulsion of 70–87; feelings of 243–244; and group relationships 15–33; instrumentalisation of 237, 245–246; management group importance to 212–215; managers as 244–248
employees, difficult 74–82; background 74; behaviour 74–75, 78–79; causes 75–76, 79–80; handling 76–78, 80–82
employment contracts 60–61
encouragement 75
Engelsted, N. 25
Engquist, A. 133
envy 114
equality 50
Erhvervspsykologi [*Business Psychology*] (Elmholdt) 167
estimation of group 119
ethics 1, 87, 236, 240, 249–250, 265–266
evaluations 126
exaggerated authority 232–233
exclusion 65
executive function 152
existential dilemmas 25–28, 31–32, 34–36, *39*, 49, 94, 98, 103, 154, 223
expectations 49, 51, 55–58, 60–61, 76, 217
expressive technique 101
expulsion from the community 68, 70–87; background 70; of difficult employees 74–82; good dismissals 85–89; pain of 70–74; scapegoats and 82–83; as solution 83–85
extroversion/introversion 223–225
eye contact 174

facial expression 174
factor analysis 224, 228
fantasies 59, 63, 117, 252, 268
fear 81
feelings 29, 32–33, 78–79, 81, 83, 100–102, 163, 225, 243–244
fellowship 18
fight/flight 114
firing 70–74, 83–88, 137
five factor model 223–224, 228
Fivelsdal, E. 158
flourishing 48, 72, 89, 216, 233, 271
Flyvbjerg, B. 184
follow-up 77, 122–123
Fonagy, P. 33
Ford, M.E. 24
forgetting 42
forming stage 107
formulation 171
Foucault, M. 29
Foulkes, S.H. 99
fragmented psyche 21
"Fra håndværk til holdning" ["From Profession to Conviction"] (Kirkeby) 242–243
framework of meetings 130, 140
Frederik, Crown Prince 115
freedom 76, 124, 153, 271
free will 19
Freud, S. 22–23, 27–28, 30, 95
"From Profession to Conviction" ["Fra håndværk til holdning"] (Kirkeby) 242–243
functionalism 19, 155
functions, management 8, 149–152, **152**, 154
Furnham, A. 231

Gabriel, Y. 237
genealogical understanding 184
Gergely, G. 33
Gergen, K. 20, 149
Geus, A.D. 49
Giddens, A. 20
Gjerde, S. 162
Goleman, D. 223
good, the 152, 249–250
good dismissals 85–89
gossip 73, 124
Gould, L. 7
Greek square and management tasks, the 153, **153**
Grimberg's World History [*Grimbergs Verdenshistorie*] 230

group processes 89–146; background 89–90; independent units and 91–105; meetings for 129–146; productivity and 106–128

group psychology 91–92, 98–100, 111–112

groups 15–33; background 15–16; coherent 142–143; culture of 65–67; demands made by 55; described 8–9; and emotion management theories 27–32; functioning of 151–152; hierarchy of systems within 37; identity threat within 16–18; influence on individuals 18–21; integrating 124–128; maturity of 102–105, 111–114; motivation of individuals in 22–27; and the self 32–33; self-managing 207–209; self-view of 119; splitting 115–122; *see also* independent groups

guilt 30, 265

Hammond, S.A., *The Thin Book of AI* 164

handling of difficult employees 76–78, 80–82

Haslebo, G. 20, 149, 222

Hatch, M.J. 65–66

Heinskou, T. 20

Helleland, A. 221–222

helplessness 180–181

Helth, P. 108

herd experience 17–19

Hersey, P. 150

hierarchy: in bureaucracies 121–122, 158, 185; and goals achievement 93; management 208, 255; of needs theory 23–24, 27; position in 243–244; of systems 36–37

hiring 51–55

Hirschhorn, L. 193

Hochschild, A. 101

Høeg, B. 82

Hogg, M. 187

Holm, I.S., *Appreciation in Management* [*Anerkendelse i ledelse*] 167–168

homogenisation 98–99

honesty 77, 250

hopes 55

humanist education 249–250

human resources frames 152

Humphrey, R. 101

id, the 95

idealisation 42, 84, 114–115, 165, 217

identity: appreciative inquiry (AI) and 167–168; firing affect on 70–71; of

managers 207; pressure on group 102–103; threats of group to 16–18, 115–120

ideology 94, 96–97, 206

idolisation 84, 114–115, 119

Illeris, K. 264

imitation 177

immature defence mechanisms 38, 49, 51, 58, 62–63, 80, 102–103

immaturity: in managers 251–252; in organisations 62–65; in persons 38–39; psychological 80, 192–195; structural 16–17, 190

implicit management model 149–150

importance of manager 240–242

inclusion 60–61, 64–65

independent groups 91–105; background 91–92; collective defences of 102–105; membership uniformity of 98–102; structure of 92–98

indifference 65

individuality *versus* community 26–27, 31–32, 118

individuals: autonomous 26; and community 48–50; development of 23–24; employees as *13*; group influence on 16–21; internal systems of 37; motivations of 35, 94, 154; psychology of 13, 21

infantilisation 207

influence 16–21, 66, 204–205, 234, 238, 249–268; background 249; of the immature manager 251–252; and integration 260–263; of manager as therapist 264–267; of the mature manager 249–251; and repression 255–260; and splitting 252–255

information, providing 132–133, 144

inherited employees 75

initiative 122

inner core 222

innovation 122, 163

insecurity 48, 58–59, 78

inspiration 163

instincts 22

institutionalists 93

instruction and support 127, 150

integrated organisations 165–166

integration 44–45, 68–69, 84–85, 102, 117, 124–128, 260–263

integrative defence mechanisms **260**

integrity 250

intelligence 250

interest, showing 75–77

284 Index

internal authority 232–233
internal convictions 266
interpretation 57–60, 257
interpretive frames and management
 tasks **152**
introductions 61–64, 81
intuition 52, 54, 225
isolation 44

Jansson, M. 230
Jaques, E. 111, 189
Joachim, Prince 115
job interviews 52–54, 57–60
job protection 50
Jørgensen, C.R. 222
judgment 225
Jung, C.G. 28, 224–225
Jung's Type Indicator (JTI) 28, 224
just, the 152

Kaufmann, G. 155
Kegan, R. 33
Kernberg, O. 16–17, 111, 147, 156, 235,
 236, 250–251, 254
Kets de Vries, M. 244, 252
Kirkeby, O.F. 249–250; "From Profession
 to Conviction" ["Fra håndværk til
 holdning"] 242–243; *The New Leadership*
 [*Det nye lederskab*] 152
Klausen, K.K., *Strategic Management – The
 Many Arenas* [*Strategisk ledelse – De mange
 arenaer*] 204
Klein, M. 111
Kreiner, G. 101
Køppe, S. 22

Langs, R. 265
language 83, 164
leadership 140, 221, 230–231, 235–236
learning, social 30, 32
learning and development process 158–183;
 background 158–159; cross-pressure
 on managers in 177–182; managers as
 teachers in 162–177; organisational role
 in 182–183; personnel management
 159–162
Learning Society, The [*Det lærende samfund*]
 (Qvortrup) 203–204
Levine, J.M. 61
Lewin, K. 230
libido 22
Lichtenberg, J.D. 33
Lieberman, M.A. 151
life cycles 107–108
linear dialogue 108, *109*
Lippit, R. 230

listening 168–175
logic of appropriateness 93, 99
loneliness 26, 108, 120, 161
Lorentzen, B. 186
loyalty 46–47, 60–61, 73, 97, 118, 124–126,
 211, 215
Luckmann, T. 20
Lyth, I.M. 111, 265–267

Majgaard, K. 246
management group, the 200–218; attention
 focus of 217–218; background 200–201;
 importance of 212–215; management
 of 207–208; motivational structure of
 206–207; as political arena 204–206;
 reaction to projective pressure 216–217;
 strategic and tactical relationship of
 209–212; as a system 201–204
management/managers 147–219; authority
 of 184–199; background 147–148;
 content of 149–157; described 2–6; and
 dismissals 71–74, 83–85; duties of 64;
 functions of 8, 149–152, *151*, **152**, 154;
 insights into 9f; at job interview 52–53;
 of rigid employees 76–78; in splitting
 groups 119–121; as teachers 158–183; *see
 also* personality and management
management system *202*
managers, personality of 219–268;
 background 219–220; influence on
 organisation 249–268; and management
 221–233; maturity and 234–248
manipulation 119, 271
manners 29
March, J.G. 19
Mary, Princess 115
Maslow, A. 23, 27
matrix 99
maturity: appreciative approach and
 164–168; differences in individual
 36–39; group 102–105, 111–114,
 127–128; levels of 39–46, 83–85; of
 managers 234–248; of new employee
 and management 50; psychological 27,
 32, 111–114, 196–199, 247, 250, 252
MBTI (Myers Briggs Type Indicator) 28,
 224, 228
McCrae, R.R. 223
McIntosh, D. 28
McNamee, S. 27
meaning attribution 151–152
meetings 16–17, 123, 126, 129–146;
 analysis of 139–146; background
 129–130; dimensions of 130–131;
 process 131–138
mentalise, ability to 33

Index **285**

mentor programmes 63, 65–66
meritocracy 158–159
middle managers 160, 178, 180, 203, 245
Miles, M. 151
Miller, D. 252
misinterpretations 215
mistrust 58, 168
misunderstandings 57–60
model, 4-D 164
Molin, J. 251
monitoring 187
moods 121, 140–141, 143–145
Moreland, R.L. 61
Mortensen, K.V. 223
motivation 13, 22–27, 93–98, 155–157,
206–207, 227, 242–244
Mouton, J.S. 150
mutual recognition 60
Myers, I. 224
Myers Briggs Type Indicator (MBTI) 28,
224, 228
Myklebust, E. 230

narcissism 250–252, 254
natural leaders 230
needs 22–24, 27, 120, 155–157, 162, 206,
244–248
negotiation 100
networks 91, 99
neuroticism 223
neutralisation 101
new institutionalist perspective 93, 98–99
New Leadership, The [Det nye lederskab]
(Kirkeby) 152
non-verbal behaviour 175–177, 257–258
normalisation 101
normative consensus 19
norming stage 107
norms 5–7, 20, 29, 45, 99, 142

Obholzer, A. 186, 231–233
objects 65
observation 137–138, **138**
obsessive manager 251
Ødegård, T. 224
Olsen 229
openness 85–86, 224
organisational adjustments see expulsion
from the community
organisation/group connection 10
organisations: described 6–7; learning
182–183; structured of 254; theory
65–66, 92–93, 98, 152

pain 40
pairing theory 114–116

paradox, importance of manager 241–243
parallel companies 54–55
parallel monologues 134
paranoia 63, 111, 235, 250–252, 254
participation 142
passivity 132, 144–145, 169
Pearce, W.B. 20
Pendleton, D. 231
perceptions 132, 136, 141, 225
performing stage 107
personal development 233
personality and management 221–233;
background 221–233; concept of
management and 229–233; recreation of
35; traits 223–229
personality tests 28, 53, 223–229
person-based authority 185
personnel management 2, 132, 157, 159–162
perspectives 82
pessimism 168
phenomena, organisational 65
planning 123, 127, 189
pleasure 27, 40
plenum democratic discussions 16–17
pluralist understanding 184
Poder, P. 243
political arena concept 204–206
political frames 152
politics 252
positive learning 159, 162, 182–183
positive thinking 165
postponement 101
posture 174
Powell, W.W. 93
power: distribution of 148; from knowledge
75, 119; relationships 50, 53, 59, 71, 167,
236–237, 265; representation of 155;
struggle for 204–205
praise 76, 119, 122, 125, 135
predictability of reactions 28
preparedness 140
prescription 101
prestige 204–205
prioritisation 97, 161, 178, 180–181, 239
private lives 120, 265
problem-oriented approach 164–166
problem-solvers 230
process of meetings 130–138
production/productivity 64, 66–67, 72, 94,
98, 102–105
productivity of groups 106–128; Alsted's
theories 116–117; background
106; Bion's theories 112–116, 236;
psychodynamic theories of 111–112;
relational theories of 108–110; splitting
117–128; stage theory of 106–108

286 Index

professionalism 159–161
programmes, introduction 61
projection 43–45, 55–59, 80, 82–83, 101, 147, 156, 168, 229
projective identification 40–42, 44, 63–64, 100, 156, 236, 254–255
projective pressure 204–205, 216–218, 235–238
projects, personal 48–49
protection 75
pseudo-dialogue 134–135
psyche, the 21–22, 25, 28–29, 32–35, 38, 40, 270
psychodynamics: coaching 247; described 7; in employee introductions 61; organisational theories 8, 20–21, 28, 31–32, 50, 111–112; personality theory 227; of scapegoating 82–83; therapy conditions 265; and understanding 184
psychological costs 244–245
psychological defences 34–47; in authority relations 191; background 34–36; group 70–71, 99; immature 80, 194; integration 44–46; knowledge about 264; manipulation as 216; mature 36–40, 191, 207–208; personality traits 227–228; relationships 46–47; repression 42–44; splitting mechanism 40–42; in young organisations 189
psychological maturity 27, 32, 111–114, 196–199, 241, 250, 252
psychology: group 91–92, 98–100, 111–112; individual 13, 20–21; tests/tools 224
psychotherapy 246–248
putting out fires 178
pyramid of needs 23–24

questions 51, 164, 228, 240
Qvortrup, L., *The Learning Society* [*Det lærende samfund*] 203–204

rapport 100–102
rationalism 18, *18*, 28, 42–43, 101
reactions 83–85
reality 37–38, 80, 99–100, 164
reciprocity 2, 5–6, 155–156
recognition 4, 60, 75–76, 166–168
redundant, made *see* expulsion from the community
reformulation 172
regression 16, 63, 156, 208, 242, 255
relational theories 29–31, 108–110, 149–150

relationships: asymmetric 1, 50, 59, 155, 187–188, 236–237; described 1–2, 8; employment 28, 50, 60–61; group 20, 67–68, 91–92; hierarchy of systems in mutual 37; and loyalty 46–47; management and employee 162–163, 231; with other people 27; personality and 35, 234; power 50, 53, 59, 71, 167
re-organisation 122
repetition 171
representations, psychic 22, 24–25
repression 35–36, 42–44, 54–55, 57–58, 60, 73, 84–85, 98, 116–117, 238–240, 254–260, **256**
repressive organisations 62–64, 121–125, 165
resources, use of 82
respect 62, 75, 235
responsibilities 109, 148
restructuring 93
retirement 35–36
Riemann, F. 25
rigid employees 74–78
Ringstad, H. 224
rituals 101, 118, 121
Roberts, V.Z. 95
Rockwool layer 210–211
role-based authority 185–186
role models 162, 183
royal weddings 115
rules 43–46, 53, 61, 79, 94–95, 206, 256
Rustin, M. 111

scapegoats 42, 82–83, 120, 156, 165, 194, 253–254
Schein, E.H. 93
Schermer, V.L 95
Scheuer. S. 18
schizoid manager 251
secrecy 215, 217
self, the 21, 32–33, 40, 45, 118, 222–223
self-acceptance 247
self-actualisation 23–24
self-categorisation 187
self-determination 61–62, 79, 207, 214
self-development 245–246, 248
self-esteem 205, 235, 250
self-in-firm symbol 66
self-protection 36
self-reflection 251, 261–263
self-therapy 245–246
self-understanding 207–208, 218, 247
sensation 225
service trap 181

sex 236
shame 29–30
sick leave 123–124
signals, interpreting 192–194
significance, repression of 238–240
Situational Leadership II (SLII) 150,
151
situational management 150
skills, problem-solving 159
social constructivism/constructivists 3,
19–20, 35–36, 49–50, 71, 155–157
social intelligence 223
socialisation 23–24, 27, 48, 67
soft skills 76
solidarity among workers 73
Sørensen, V. 221–222
space, positive learning 159, 162, 182–183
speakers 122, 144, 170–174
speculation 59, 84, 190
splitting 40–42, 55–56, 73–74, 83–85,
115–122, 165, 252–255, **254**
spontaneous exclamation 174
Srivastva, S. 20, 110, 167; "Appreciative
Inquiry in Organizational Life"
163
stability 26–27, 31–32, 94
stage theory 106–108
stagnation 66
stars 42
states, basic assumption **113**
status shield 210, 243
stereotypes 98, 216
Stern, D.N. 222
stories 55–56, 83, 164, 216
storming stage 107
strategic management 209–215
Strategic Management – The Many Arenas
[*Strategisk ledelse – De mange arenaer*]
(Klausen) 204
stress 123
structures 92–98, 152, 188–189, 201–204,
254, 259–260
subconscious 110, 116
subsystems *270*
success of managers 230
summation 172
superego 95
support: defined 150; for the group 118;
instruction and 127; for new employees
66–67; plan 127; for rigid employees 75,
77, 79
suspicion 108, 118, 237
swallowed up, being 26, 132, 168–169,
212, *213*
symbolic frames 152

symbols/symbolism 60–61, 65–66, 69, 133,
136–137, 139–146, 177, 203, 262
systems 8–9, 52, 108, *186*, 201–204, 264

tact 62
tactical management 209–215
talent 230
task resolution 96–98, 209
teachers, managers as 162–177
team development 106–108
teamwork 147
techniques 101, 271
tension 22
terminology **112**
testing period 68
"The Barometer of Danish Management"
["Det Danske Ledelsesbarometer"] 177
theories: Alsted's 116–117; Bion's 112–116;
of bureaucracy 158–159; development
40, 106–108; drive 22–25; economic
18; emotions management 27–32;
functionalist 19, 155; hierarchy of
needs 23–24, 27; management function
151–154; maturity of groups 112–117;
motivational 94, **154**; organisational
65–66, 92–93, 98, 152; pairing 114–116;
productivity 106–108; psychodynamic *8,*
20–21, 28, 31–32, 34–36, 50, 111–112,
227; rational 28; relational 29–31,
108–110; social constructivist 3, 19–20,
35–36, 49–50, 71, 155–157; splitting
117–128; stage 106–108; systemic 52,
108; traits 223–229
therapeutic contract 265
therapy 107, 247–248, 264–268
Thin Book of AI, The (Hammond) 164
thinking 225
Thorsvik, J. 23
threats 16–17, 61, 103, 115–120
Thybring, A.L. 82
time 61, 63, 180
tone, the 59
tools 245–246, 271
totalitarianism 118
traits, personality 223–229
transference 100
transparency 180, 215
true, the 152
trust 51–52, 75, 77, 117, 120–121, 129–130
Tuckman, B. 106–108
type indicator tests 28, **225**
types, personality 28, 224–229, **225**

unambiguous drives 22–24
uncertainty 27, 120, 141, 192

288 Index

unconscious: anxiety and 41–42; biological needs and the 23; conflicts 255; defences 55; in group development 95–96; insights into the 267; relations 99; repression 100; scapegoating 82–83; therapy and the 247
understanding 75–76, 184, 215, 258
unemployment 26
uniformity 98–102, 118

values 65, 271
verbalisation 176
verbal tools 170–173
victims 73, 85
Visholm, S. 20, 40–42, 185
visible management 178
visionary 163–164, 230

voluntariness 50–51
vulnerability 169

wages 94
weak authority 232–233
Weber, M. 158–159
White, R.K. 230
Whitener, E.M. 262
Wilke, G. 267
Winnicott, D.W. 239
wishful thinking 55–57
withdrawal 108, 156, 161, 191, 193, 195, 237
work group state 111–112
workplace behaviours 30–31, 73–74

Yalom, I.D. 151